Workplace Health and Safety
SOURCEBOOK

Health Reference Series

First Edition

Workplace Health and Safety SOURCEBOOK

Basic Consumer Health Information about Workplace Health and Safety, Including the Effect of Workplace Hazards on the Lungs, Skin, Heart, Ears, Eyes, Brain, Reproductive Organs, Musculo-skeletal System, and Other Organs and Body Parts:

Along with Information about Occupational Cancer, Personal Protective Equipment, Toxic and Hazardous Chemicals, Child Labor, Stress, and Workplace Violence

Edited by
Chad T. Kimball

Omnigraphics

615 Griswold Street • Detroit, MI 48226

Bibliographic Note

Because this page cannot legibly accommodate all the copyright notices, the Bibliographic Note portion of the Preface constitutes an extension of the copyright notice.

Each new volume of the *Health Reference Series* is individually titled and called a "First Edition." Subsequent updates will carry sequential edition numbers. To help avoid confusion and to provide maximum flexibility in our ability to respond to informational needs, the practice of consecutively numbering each volume will be discontinued.

Edited by Chad T. Kimball

Health Reference Series

Karen Bellenir, *Series Editor*
Peter D. Dresser, *Managing Editor*
Joan Margeson, *Research Associate*
Dawn Matthews, *Verification Assistant*
Jenifer Swanson, *Research Associate*

EdIndex, Services for Publishers, *Indexers*

Omnigraphics, Inc.

Matthew P. Barbour, *Vice President, Operations*
Laurie Lanzen Harris, *Vice President, Editorial Director*
Kevin Hayes, *Production Coordinator*
Thomas J. Murphy, *Vice President, Finance and Comptroller*
Peter E. Ruffner, *Senior Vice President*
Jane J. Steele, *Marketing Consultant*

Frederick G. Ruffner, Jr., *Publisher*

© 2000, Omnigraphics, Inc.

Library of Congress Cataloging-in-Publication Data

Workplace health and safety sourcebook : basic consumer health information about workplace health and safety, including the effect of workplace hazards on the lungs, skin, heart, ears, eyes, brain, reproductive organs, musculoskeletal system, and other organs and body parts, along with information about occupational cancer, personal protective equipment, toxic and hazardous chemicals, child labor, stress, and workplace violence / edited by Chad T. Kimball.-- 1st ed.
    p. cm. -- (Health reference series)
    Includes bibliographical references and index.
    ISBN 0-7808-0231-4 (alk. paper)
    1. Industrial hygiene--Popular works. 2. Industrial safety--Popular works. I. Kimball, Chad T. II. Series

RC967 .W668 2000
616.9'803--dc21

00-058477

∞

This book is printed on acid-free paper meeting the ANSI Z39.48 Standard. The infinity symbol that appears above indicates that the paper in this book meets that standard.

Printed in the United States

Table of Contents

Part III: Skin and Eye Issues

Part IV: Noise and Hearing Issues

Part V: Preventing Work-Related Musculoskeletal Disorders

Part VI: Infectious Disease Issues

Part VII: Toxins, Hazardous Chemicals, Electromagnetic Fields, and Cancer in the Workplace

Part VIII: Reproductive and Pregnancy Issues

Part IX: Personal Protective Equipment Issues

Part X: Child Labor, Workplace Violence, and Job Stress Issues

Part XI: Additional Help and Information

Preface

About This Book

Workplace health and safety is a subject which concerns almost everyone. Workplace hazards can range from the risk of tendonitis for a computer programmer to the hazards of working with heavy machinery for a construction worker. Nearly all jobs have the potential of presenting a risk to the worker's health. If proper procedures are followed, however, most workplace hazards can be avoided or eliminated. With proper medical care, many health disorders resulting from these hazards can be successfully treated.

This *Sourcebook* will help readers to identify the hazards associated with their workplace, the ways these hazards can be avoided, and steps toward recovery for those who have been diagnosed with a workplace-related disorder. Issues concerning personal protective equipment, toxic and hazardous chemicals, child labor, stress, workplace violence, and the effects of workplace hazards on the body are also discussed. This *Sourcebook* also offers a glossary and a lists of resources and references for further help and information.

How to Use This Book

This book is divided into parts and chapters. Parts focus on broad areas of interest. Chapters are devoted to single topics within a part.

Part I: Workplace Health and Safety Basics introduces basic workplace hazards and describes general employee responsibilities and rights in the workplace. Different safety training methods are discussed, along with the advantages and disadvantages of each method.

Part II: Lung Issues focuses on various occupational lung hazards including asbestos, silica dust, decayed grain dust, hay, silage, and cotton dust. It also includes information about the relationship between workplace hazards and asthma, chronic obstructive pulmonary disease, and lung cancer. The section ends with a guide to workplace respiratory protection.

Part III: Skin and Eye Issues presents information about how to protect the skin and eyes from burns, allergens, and other injuries at work. It also provides tips on reducing computer-related eyestrain and avoiding occupational dermatitis, or eczema.

Part IV: Noise and Hearing Issues describes the causes of work related-hearing loss, as well as the Occupational Safety and Health Administration's efforts to protect workers from hearing loss. Chapters on noise in office environments and protective hearing equipment are also included.

Part V: Preventing Work-Related Musculoskeletal Disorders gives information about the causes and prevention of work-related back injuries, carpal tunnel syndrome (CTS), and occupational neck and arm disorders. Techniques for designing ergonomically sound workstations, offices, and tools are also presented.

Part VI: Infectious Disease Issues includes information about tuberculosis, human immunodeficiency virus (HIV), and other occupational infections.

Part VII: Toxins, Hazardous Chemicals, Electromagnetic Fields, and Cancer in the Workplace discusses hazardous workplace chemicals including lead, pesticides, formaldehyde, carbon monoxide, chloroform, and waste anesthetic gasses. It also answers common questions about electric and magnetic fields, flammable liquids, and cancer in the workplace.

Part VIII: Reproductive and Pregnancy Issues explains how exposure to workplace hazards affect male and female reproductive health, sexual performance, and pregnancy.

Part IX: Personal Protective Equipment Issues gives guidelines for various kinds of personal protective equipment including chemical protective equipment and heat and cold protection. Construction site safety is also presented.

Part X: Child Labor, Workplace Violence, and Job Stress Issues focuses on the effects of stress, fatigue, violence, grief, and trauma on the health and performance of workers. Child labor and shiftwork are also discussed.

Part XI: Additional Help and Information includes a glossary of workplace health and safety-related terms, a bibliography of reliable occupational health-focused publications and articles, and a list of resources for people seeking further information about workplace hazards.

Bibliographic Note

This volume contains documents and excerpts from publications issued by the following U.S. government agencies: Agency for Toxic Substances and Disease Registry (ATSDR), Centers for Disease Control and Prevention (CDC), Environmental Protection Agency (EPA), National Institute for Occupational Safety and Health (NIOSH), National Institutes of Health (NIH), Occupational Safety and Health Administration (OSHA), U.S. Department of Energy, Office of Training and Human Resource Development, U.S. Department of Health and Human Services, U.S. Department of Labor (DOL), U.S. Office of Personnel Management, and the Office of Workforce Relations (OWR).

This volume also contains documents issued by the following state government agencies: California Occupational Safety and Health Administration (CalOSHA), New York Committee for Occupational Safety and Health (NYCOSH), Washington Industrial Safety and Health Act (WISHA), Washington State Department of Labor and Industries.

In addition, this volume contains copyrighted documents from the following organizations: Advanstar Communications, Inc.; American Academy of Family Physicians; American Medical Association; The Asbestos Institute; Asthma Foundation of Western Australia; British Medical Association; Information Today, Inc.; American Cancer Society; Lippincott, Williams & Wilkins; Penton Media Inc.; Medical Economics Publishing; G.S. Sharpe Communications, Inc.; Trustees of Columbia University in the City of New York; and Crown Publishers, a division of Random House, Inc. Copyrighted articles from *The Journal of Family Practice* and *PC Magazine* are also included.

Full citation information is provided on the first page of each chapter. Every effort has been made to secure all necessary rights to reprint the copyrighted material. If any omissions have been made, please contact Omnigraphics to make corrections for future editions.

Acknowledgements

In addition to the organizations listed above, special thanks are due to document engineer Bruce Bellenir, researchers Jenifer Swanson and Joan Margeson, verification assistant Dawn Matthews, and permissions specialist Maria Franklin.

Note from the Editor

This book is part of Omnigraphics' *Health Reference Series*. The series provides basic information about a broad range of medical concerns. It is not intended to serve as a tool for diagnosing illness, in prescribing treatments, or as a substitute for the physician/patient relationship. All persons concerned about medical symptoms or the possibility of disease are encouraged to seek professional care from an appropriate health-care provider.

Our Advisory Board

The *Health Reference Series* is reviewed by an Advisory Board comprised of librarians from public, academic, and medical libraries. We would like to thank the following board members for providing guidance to the development of this series:

Dr. Lynda Baker,
Associate Professor of Library and Information Science,
Wayne State University, Detroit, MI

Nancy Bulgarelli,
William Beaumont Hospital Library, Royal Oak, MI

Karen Imarasio,
Bloomfield Township Public Library, Bloomfield Township, MI

Karen Morgan,
Mardigian Library, University of Michigan-Dearborn,
Dearborn, MI

Rosemary Orlando,
St. Clair Shores Public Library, St. Clair Shores, MI

Health Reference Series *Update Policy*

The inaugural book in the *Health Reference Series* was the first edition of *Cancer Sourcebook* published in 1992. Since then, the *Series* has been enthusiastically received by librarians and in the medical community. In order to maintain the standard of providing high-quality health information for the lay person, the editorial staff at Omnigraphics felt it was necessary to implement a policy of updating volumes when warranted.

Medical researchers have been making tremendous strides, and it is the purpose of the *Health Reference Series* to stay current with the most recent advances. Each decision to update a volume will be made on an individual basis. Some of the considerations will include how much new information is available and the feedback we receive from people who use the books. If there is a topic you would like to see added to the update list, or an area of medical concern you feel has not been adequately addressed, please write to:

Editor
Health Reference Series
Omnigraphics, Inc.
615 Griswold Street
Detroit, MI 48226

The commitment to providing on-going coverage of important medical developments has also led to some format changes in the *Health Reference Series*. Each new volume on a topic is individually titled and called a "First Edition." Subsequent updates will carry sequential edition numbers. To help avoid confusion and to provide maximum flexibility in our ability to respond to informational needs, the practice of consecutively numbering each volume has been discontinued.

Part One

Workplace Health and Safety Basics

Chapter 1

Caution: Work Can Be Hazardous to Your Health

Health hazards in the workplace are pervasive and serious—but too often unrecognized by physicians. No job is 100% risk-free, and no history and physical exam are complete without touching this base.

When you hear the words "occupational hazard," what images come to mind? Most likely the hard hat or painter perched high atop scaffolding; the jackhammer operator in the trenches blasting his ears away; the plant worker mixing vats of toxic chemicals; and, closer to home, the nurse, physician, phlebotomist, or hospital housekeeper whose day could be ruined by an inadvertent needlestick.

But what about these people:

- The truck driver whose sleep apnea causes daytime drowsiness and turns him into an accident waiting to happen. A recent study found that nearly half the drivers for a major commercial hauler had some type of irregular breathing during sleep.[1] Truckers with sleep apnea or hypopnea have twice the rate of accidents as drivers without those conditions.

- The self-employed artist who, as she mixes her paint pigments, is mixing organic solvents and heavy metals. Many artists work

Excerpted from "Caution: Work Can Be Hazardous to Your Health," Thomas J. Chester; M. Joseph Fedoruk; Ricky L. Langley; Carol Wilkinson, *Patient Care*, February 15, 1996, Vol. 30, N. 3, pp. 70-84, copyright 1996 by Medical Economics Publishing. Reprinted with permission.

long hours in close quarters with potentially dangerous agents but without proper gear to protect their eyes, lungs, and skin.[2]

- The teenager driving a forklift in a warehouse or flipping burgers at a fast-food restaurant. Teens are an especially high-risk group, often because they are not trained in the safety aspects of their jobs.

- The farm laborer whose risks include being around all sorts of machinery, animals, chemicals, and plants, not to mention the sun.[3] Down on the farm, occupational ill health may mean anything from hearing loss to zoonotic diseases and from contact dermatoses to contact with herbicides that are known to cause soft-tissue sarcoma and lymphoma.

Too Much to Ask?

Occupational morbidity affects people in every setting imaginable. It is the stiff neck or eye strain of the computer jockey; the respiratory infection the day-care worker or schoolteacher picks up from her young charges; the performance anxiety of the professional musician; the Lyme disease of the forest ranger; the potentially disabling back or knee injury that results from poor lifting techniques; and the outright risk of bodily harm that comes with some occupations (not just police and prison guards but also convenience store clerks and gas station attendants).

Job hazards affect people of all ages: In a recent survey of work-related fatalities in New Mexico, the youngest victim was 13 and the oldest was 87.[4]) In the United States, the leading cause of work-related death is not the fall or the explosion or the electrocution but the all-too-familiar motor vehicle accident.

Does the vast reach of occupational medicine seem overwhelming? To be sure, entire textbooks are written on the topic. Your own exposure was probably limited. You don't have to be an occupational medicine specialist to weave this perspective into your daily practice. Just knowing the basics will go a long way.

Getting Started: Four Questions

The cardinal principle is to maintain a high index of suspicion that a symptom or cluster of symptoms may have a connection to the patient's job. That 52-year-old man with elevated liver enzymes may have an alcohol problem, but he also may be exposed to hepatotoxic substances every day he punches his time card.

You're used to asking questions routinely about lifestyle and the home environment; it's just as worthwhile to be knowledgeable about work style and the work environment. The following four questions won't take the place of a full-fledged occupational history, but they can generate much useful information:

- How's work been lately? Consider keeping brief job descriptions in your files, including an outline of a typical workday.
- What materials do you work with?
- Do you wear any protective equipment?
- Do you have any safety or health concerns about your job?

Remember that the home is often a work site and may be overlooked as a source of occupational conditions. Cottage industries and small businesses are more likely than big corporations to escape the watchful eye of federal health and safety agencies. It's also helpful to ask about previous jobs in patients with chronic disorders, such as respiratory diseases, musculoskeletal problems, and cancers.

Occupational medicine plays directly to two of the basic strengths of primary care: identifying risk factors and recognizing the importance of prevention. In the construction industry, which has a disproportionate number of workdays lost and job-related deaths, virtually all morbidity and mortality is considered preventable.[5] In a genuine way, you practice occupational medicine when you do something as basic as keeping a patient's tetanus immunizations up-to-date. Detecting and treating any problem that interferes with work offers a double benefit by improving job performance while reducing the risk of harm employees pose to themselves and others.

Risk factors go beyond specific job tasks and equipment to the work conditions: long hours, high volume, deadline pressure, isolation, rotating shifts, boredom. Think about how work might be contributing to or even causing a patient's depression or anxiety; consider whether alcohol or substance abuse is a problem on the job as well as at home; and keep in mind the possibility of posttraumatic stress disorder in those whose calling—emergency services, for example—exposes them to the rawest edges of life.

Knowing about a patient's job is important not only to develop a better understanding of illnesses and injuries that arise in the workplace, but also to recommend modifications that will help speed the return to work. Instead of dwelling on a person's limitations, this approach enables you to emphasize individual capabilities.

5

Carving Out a Role

It is the employer's responsibility, under federal law, to provide a hazard-free, safe, and healthy working environment. What then is the physician's role? You can provide valuable checks and balances by

- exploring the work connection when taking histories, performing examinations, and evaluating symptoms

- educating patients about basic injury and illness prevention. Anything is possible in a world in which workers at an electroplating plant were found cooling watermelons in a cyanide bath

- following up on information about specific workplace hazards by speaking to company safety officers or by alerting local, state, or federal authorities. You can also request an inspection of the work site by the state health department or Occupational Safety and Health Administration (OSHA); in some states, these inspections are automatically triggered by reports of work-related illnesses and injuries.

In North Carolina, a 1994 law requires physicians to report four occupational health conditions: asbestosis, silicosis, elevated blood lead levels in adults, and preventable farm injuries.[6] A physician's report may prompt a visit from a state-employed industrial hygienist or occupational nurse to assess the hazard and provide advice on prevention.

The North Carolina program is one of 10 model projects funded by the National Institute for Occupational Safety and Health (NIOSH); the program is known as the Sentinel Event Notification Systems for Occupational Risk (SENSOR). Conditions monitored in other states include cadmium overexposure, carpal tunnel syndrome, dermatitis, noise-induced hearing loss, pesticide health effects, spinal cord injuries, tuberculosis, occupational asthma, and work-related burns.

For these and countless other workplace hazards, take advantage of the vast educational resources available to you and your patients. When evaluating a potential work-related illness, you can turn to state health departments, the American College of Occupational and Environmental Medicine (ACOEM), occupational medicine experts at universities, a number of excellent textbooks, and sophisticated electronic databases.

Reams of information are cranked out by government agencies such as NIOSH and private groups like the National Safety Council (NSC).

Pamphlets cover everything from the general ("Workplace exposure to asbestos") to the highly specific ("Preventing knee injuries and disorders in carpet layers"). These publications do an excellent job of outlining perilous situations and suggesting preventive remedies.

Major Workplace Hazards

Here's a quick review of the major workplace hazards.

Toxic Exposures

You don't have to become an expert on every toxic substance known to the human race. In fact, not even 1 in 5 industrial chemicals used in this country have been tested sufficiently for their toxicity to humans.[7]

What you can do is ask patients about the materials they work with and the manufacturing processes used. Find out if they are wearing proper gear (protective clothing, eye shields, shoes or boots, gloves). Working with or near a substance does not have to mean being directly exposed to it.

Substances often associated with occupational illness include dyes, solvents, dusts, powders, fumes, acids, alkalis, gases, and metals. A recent report on chronic renal failure links it to a wide range of occupational exposures, including heavy metals (lead, cadmium, mercury), silicon-containing compounds (sand, cement, coal, grain dust), and solvents found in glues and paints.[8]

The neurotoxic effects of lead and organic solvents are well-documented. Researchers are now beginning to investigate whether exposure to organic solvents increases the risk or alters the course of such neurologic insults as Alzheimer's disease.[9]

Remember that exposures to toxic substances occur in occupations other than the obvious. Apart from lead mining and smelting, for example, workers at risk for lead toxicity include plumbers and pipe fitters, auto mechanics, construction crews, firing range instructors, police officers, steel welders, printers, shipbuilders, and people involved in manufacturing glass, rubber, plastics, and batteries.

Employers are required by law to maintain Material Safety Data Sheets (MSDS) describing toxic substances, their proper handling, and the symptoms that may arise from contact with them. The quality of information varies, however, and the sheets may provide a laundry list of symptoms that does not show how they manifest at different levels and durations of exposure.

In addition to protecting themselves on the job, people who work in and around toxic substances should change out of their work clothes and shower before they go home. Otherwise they may pose a risk to family members.

Reproductive Hazards

Women aren't the only ones who need to be concerned about reproductive hazards at work. Exposure to certain substances (such as lead) or environmental factors (such as heat) may reduce a man's sperm count. Other agents considered to be spermatotoxic include ionizing radiation, the nematocide dibromochloropropane (DBCP), now banned in this country, and ethylene glycol ethers, which are solvents used to make jet fuel deicers, inks, dyes, and printed circuit boards. Early studies, which require verification, have even suggested that a father's occupational exposure to lead and organic solvents may increase the infant's risk of pre-term birth or perinatal death.[10]

Daily or high exposure to organic solvents has been associated with reduced fertility in women.[11] Most of what is known about occupational hazards, however, focuses not on female fertility but on adverse pregnancy outcomes. Substances clearly known to harm the fetus include lead (spontaneous abortion, prematurity, neurologic dysfunction); ionizing radiation (central nervous system defects, skeletal and eye anomalies, mental retardation); and organic mercury (central nervous system malformation, cerebral palsy).

Pregnant women who are exposed to ionizing radiation where they work should ask for monthly readings of their exposure. National standards suggest that exposure should not exceed 0.05 rads in any month of pregnancy or 0.5 rads for the entire pregnancy. For all other workers, the suggested limit is 1.25 rads per quarter or 5 rads per year.

Keep in mind that millions of women are fully capable of working late into their pregnancy with no problem. However, physical stress that exceeds the demands of normal daily living may increase the risk of premature birth. A recent study of physical workload and pregnancy outcome suggests that women should

- avoid "extremely heavy" physical exertion (close to maximal capacity) early in pregnancy

- cut back on the workload and be afforded rest periods in the second and third trimesters

- avoid continuous standing or walking, at least during late pregnancy and preferably at other stages.[12] Job tasks involving heavy lifting, carrying, and climbing may need to be modified.

What about psychological stress? A recent study found that stressful work—high psychological demands with low control over those demands—did not significantly increase the overall risk of spontaneous abortion.[13] However, the risk was increased in women who had job stress and were older (over 32), were smokers, and in their first pregnancy.

Aches and Pains, Sprains and Strains

Many injuries that occur in the workplace are similar to injuries that occur in athletics: They relate to body mechanics and overall conditioning. Think of the worker as an industrial athlete, and encourage your patients to be in good general physical condition and to get regular exercise.

Back and knee injuries often result from jobs that involve lifting, turning, and loading. Many employees don't know that the "twisted lift"—turning the body without moving the feet—is harmful. Other bad practices include lifting while bending forward or reaching.

The National Institute for Occupational Safety and Health (NIOSH) recommends that employers implement ergonomically sound programs to reduce the risk of back injuries. In jobs that require frequent lifting, preventive steps include keeping the lifted load close to the body, keeping the load between shoulder and knuckle height, eliminating twisted lifts, allowing gravity to move the load when possible, and using other devices such as hand trucks, chutes, hoists, and slides. For information on a lifting ergonomics program, call (800) 35-NIOSH.

It's become almost fashionable in some job settings for workers to wear back belts for support. NIOSH, however, has concluded that the existing scientific evidence does not show that wearing a back belt reduces the risk of injury. In fact, it may create a hazard if workers take on harder tasks thinking that the belt will be protective.[14]

Overall, half of the working population reports some type of back problem each year, and back symptoms are the most common cause of disability for people under age 45.[1*] The approach to low-back complaints now favored by experts is to keep the patient as active as possible; more than 2–3 days of bed rest will likely lead to deconditioning. The most helpful step may be to arrange a modified duty program to allow less strenuous work temporarily with a gradual return to normal duties.

Carpal tunnel syndrome is often invoked as an explanation for repetitive-motion disorders. Most occupational medicine specialists now feel it is overdiagnosed and often mistaken for other conditions such as tendinitis that can be treated conservatively with rest, nonsteroidal anti-inflammatory drugs, or other measures well short of surgery.

Investigators have found that psychosocial factors play a role in the development of upper-extremity disorders. These factors may include job pressures (deadlines, quotas, etc.), surges in the workload, fear of being replaced by computers, the boring nature of work, lack of control over the job, and absence of support from supervisors and coworkers. Regular exercise, relaxation techniques, and changes in job design may be helpful.

Computer Woes

Upper back and neck stiffness is common in people who maintain a static posture for a long period of time—primarily people with desk jobs, although plumbers and others who must work in awkward positions are also at risk. Two diagnoses to keep in mind are tension neck syndrome and occipital cephalgia.[2*] Regular stretching breaks every hour or so and easy range-of-motion exercises for the neck and shoulder are usually helpful.

Neck and shoulder complaints are also common in people who spend a lot of time on the telephone. A headset is a simple, effective remedy for this problem.

Much attention has been paid to the proper ergonomics of setting up a computer workstation. Employers, however, may vary in their diligence in following through. The Center for Office Technology publishes helpful brochures on ergonomics, with special emphasis on working with video display terminals—write to 301 North Fairfax, Suite 102, Alexandria, VA 22314; (703) 684-7760.

In many cases, the employee can determine what's most comfortable through a process of trial and error. Eye strain, for example, can be minimized if the worker keeps the screen clean, adjusts the brightness, and controls glare (special filters are available). The employee who wears bifocals may need a separate pair of glasses to work efficiently at a computer.

Almost inevitably, anecdotal reports of shoulder and wrist pain have accompanied the addition of the computer mouse to the desktop. The mouse is often positioned too high and too far away. It should be at the same typing height as the keyboard and within easy reach. If the mouse is uncomfortable to use, the worker should look for another—the varieties are endless.

There's no evidence from ongoing studies that non-ionizing radiation from video display terminals, microwave ovens, and other sources poses a health hazard. A recent review indicates that exposure to magnetic fields from video terminals is less than that from photocopying machines, printers, and other items found in the office.[15]

The evidence for some workplace hazards is simply more compelling and more established than it is for others. Some occupational cancers—like the incidence of urothelial cancer in workers exposed to certain dyes[16]—have been known for more than a century, while the work on electromagnetic fields is just evolving. By keeping this in perspective, you can help patients avoid getting alarmed every time a study is reported on the evening news.

Skin Problems

Dermatologic problems account for about one third of all work-related illness. Most often, the trouble is an irritant or allergic contact dermatitis, with irritant cases outnumbering the allergic ones by about 4 to 1.

Solvents and metals are to blame, of course, but so are soaps, detergents, and other cleaning agents. Not surprisingly, health-care workers have one of the highest rates of job-related hand dermatitis, along with beauticians and dishwashers. Cutting oils used in machine shops are another common source of skin eruptions.

Ask patients who develop a rash about the materials they work with on the job. Do the symptoms improve over the weekend or on vacation? This is generally a good clue to ruling out many types of work-related illness, not just skin disorders.

Ask if the company has recently begun making new products with new ingredients. The epidemiology is forever changing; consider that "environmentally friendly" paper has now been cited as a cause of dermatitis in rosin-sensitive people.[17]

Many substances that cause skin problems can also cause respiratory difficulty such as rhinitis and asthma. A prominent example is latex allergy. Another such double agent is [alpha]-amylase, a flour additive used in baking.[18]

The logical starting point of prevention, of course, is proper use of gloves, although the latex experience indicates that not just any gloves will do. Different exposures may call for different types of gloves—neoprene, butyl rubber, or polyvinyl acetate—and for regular changes of gloves.

Even if proper gloves are worn, the arms, face, and other parts of the body may be exposed, creating a risk of systemic absorption. NIOSH recently issued an alert for "green tobacco sickness"—dermal absorption of nicotine from tobacco leaves that produces nausea, vomiting, dizziness, severe weakness, abdominal cramping, headache, and difficulty breathing—all of which mimic the symptoms of organophosphate poisoning.

To evaluate a possible occupational dermatitis, consider a skin scraping and potassium hydroxide (KOH) preparation to rule out fungal infection; culture or biopsy to rule out other infectious etiologies; and patch testing if a contact allergen is suspected. Skin prick testing can help identify allergies to materials used at work or to environmental factors such as pollens, molds, and dust mites.

Treatment of irritant dermatoses may include antibiotics for secondary infection, debridement of crusts, and the use of topical emollients. Corticosteroid ointments may help when an irritant produces a marked inflammatory response. Avoidance of the irritant can be achieved by wearing protective equipment or modifying the job. The patient should also avoid harsh detergents, abrasives, and solvents when cleaning the skin. Allergic contact dermatitis may respond to systemic antihistamines and short courses of oral corticosteroids. However, only 25% of cases of occupational contact dermatitis are fully resolved; 25% persist and 50% lead to periodic flare-ups.

Noise

Noise-induced hearing loss is a readily preventable problem; you can help by encouraging patients to wear protective equipment if they work in a noisy environment. Noise-related hearing loss is often overlooked because the patient may not notice the impairment until it is severe. The process is insidious; high-frequency hearing loss occurs first and does not affect speech frequencies. The patient is oblivious to the loss, but it is detectable by an audiogram. Think about hearing loss when a patient begins to complain about losing the directionality of sound or not being able to tell one noise from another, such as difficulty picking out the sound one wants to hear from background noise.

At a noise level of 85 dBA (a time-weighted average over eight hours), employers are required to have a hearing conservation program. This may include measures to suppress and monitor noise as well as regularly scheduled audiograms. At 85 dBA, employees also must be provided with ear plugs or other protection. After 10 years of exposure to 90 dBA for eight hours a day five days a week, 15% of workers have a risk of developing significant hearing loss.

The Occupational Safety and Health Administration (OSHA) establishes only minimum levels of protection from exposure to noise. People who work with older machinery without sound controls are at risk for hearing loss. In a recent study of tractors, noise levels in excess of the federal safety threshold were detected in 75% of tractors without cabs.[19] The authors recommended the use of hearing protection when time on a tractor without a cab approaches 1 1/2–2 hours (3–4 hours if the tractor has a cab).

You need to distinguish age-related hearing loss from noise-related loss.[3*] A dip in hearing at 4,000 hertz (Hz) on the audiogram is a quick clue to noise-induced hearing loss. Formal standards are available for distinguishing age-related from noise-related hearing loss and for determining the relative contributions of each. The International Organization for Standardization, ISO-1999, can be used if the level and duration of noise exposure are known or can be estimated.[20]

You can't always assume that noise-related loss is job-related. Ask about military experience and hobbies such as hunting. Hearing loss can develop in members of weekend rock bands or even in people who listen to music at high volumes. And don't forget the person who has a regular weekend date with his leaf blower.

Violence

Violence in the workplace is now recognized as a major threat that requires concerted preventive efforts.[21] The statistics are sobering: In the 1980s, 7,600 people in this country were victims of homicide while at work. Murder accounted for 12% of all work-related deaths and was the leading cause of work deaths among women. High-risk occupations include taxicab drivers, chauffeurs, law enforcement officers, hotel clerks, gas station workers, security guards, stock handlers and baggers, store owners and managers, and bartenders.

While homicides make the headlines, other types of violence, like interpersonal threats, physical assaults on coworkers, and rape, pose more of a day-to-day problem.[22] Employers are busy developing protocols to deal with such incidents; some will dismiss an employee for any threat that is made. You can help by identifying patients who make specific threats in your presence or by recognizing and treating people who appear to resolve conflict in violent ways.

Stress

Work-related stress is ubiquitous but, from an occupational medicine standpoint, quite elusive. One recent study indicated that job stress was not associated with an increased prevalence of cardiovascular disease.[23] Another study, however, suggested that six or more years of rotating shift work may increase the risk of coronary heart disease among nurses.[24]

The Japanese have coined the term "karoshi" for sudden death from work stress, but this phenomenon is not well-studied in the United States. Some have suggested that stress, by stimulating the sympathetic nervous system, may precipitate arrhythmias.

Stress is a palpable problem even if it is generally not a compensable work-related condition. When asking about stresses in your patient's personal and family life, it also makes sense to ask about stresses at work, such as long hours, tedious tasks, general dissatisfaction, conflict with coworkers or superiors, perceptions of unfair treatment, or sexual harassment. Although data are hard to come by, as many as 10% of women are reported to change jobs because of sexual harassment.

As with any stress in life, the question is how to modify if not eliminate the source. Be aware of Employee Assistance Programs, which many companies provide in addition to regular health insurance. Typically, the program covers the cost of short courses of counseling for a wide range of personal problems, from the stress of juggling family and career responsibilities to domestic violence, depression, divorce, grief, concerns about work performance, financial worries, and care for elderly parents.

Be alert for alcohol and other substance abuse.[4*] These conditions are unrecognized in practice, and by the time they affect work performance the person's home life is often a shambles. In addition to screening, you can provide appropriate support after a patient is placed in a treatment program.

The Workplace Is No Place to Die

The most visible occupational fatalities in history, according to NIOSH, were the deaths of the Space Shuttle Challenger astronauts in 1986. But NIOSH officials point out that at least 16 other Americans died on the job that day... among them a retail manager and a special investigator shot to death... two plasterers who plummeted from a scaffold... a lineman electrocuted... the president of a drilling

14

Table 1.1. Leading Causes of Job-Related Death[1]

Motor vehicle crashes	23%
Machine-related incidents	14%
Homicides	12%
Falls	10%
Electrocution	7%
Falling objects	7%

company killed in an explosion... a lumberman pinned by a log against his truck... two truckers, a farm laborer, and a schoolteacher killed in separate traffic accidents.

Even without the Challenger tragedy, January 28, 1986, was close to an average day in this country, in which 17 people die on the job.[1,2] The leading cause of occupational death is prosaic—the motor vehicle crash—followed by machine-related incidents and, perhaps a surprising third, homicides. Other leading causes include falls, electrocutions, and falling objects (see the accompanying graph).

Dying on the job is a particularly male hazard: Men accounted for 94% of fatal occupational injuries in the United States from 1980 to 1989, even though they made up just 56% of the workforce. For women, however, homicide was the number one threat, accounting for 41% of all work-related deaths. Suicide is included in the statistics and accounts for 3% of male deaths and 4% of female deaths at work; concurrent alcohol use is a known risk factor for on-the-job suicide.

Public health officials stress the preventable nature of virtually all of these fatalities. A national objective for the year 2000 is to reduce the death rate from work-related injuries to no more than 4 per 100,000 workers. We have a long way to go: The average annual rate during the 1980s was 7 per 100,000, with the highest fatality rates in mining (31.9/100,000) and construction (25.6/100,000).

The challenge is one that beckons all industries, government regulatory agencies, and public health officials—and all health-care providers with a commitment to prevention.

Carcinogens at Work

Occupational and environmental exposures are responsible for an estimated 5–10% of cancers. To help determine if a patient's cancer is work-related, it is important to assess several key aspects of the work history. Although carcinogenic chemicals may be present at the work site, the patient may or may not be exposed to them.

Ricky L. Langley, MD, MPH, an occupational medicine specialist at Duke University Medical Center and a consultant for this chapter, suggests asking the following questions:

- What are the physical characteristics of the compound? Is it volatile, fibrous, or in a solid or liquid state?

- Are the materials handled inside a fume hood? Is respiratory protective equipment used if the chemical is handled on the bench?

- What is or was the duration of exposure?

- Is the exposure associated with cancer in the literature, and, if so, with any particular type?

- Has the latency from exposure to the onset of cancer been of sufficient duration to support biologic plausibility?

- Has there been a cluster of cancer cases at the work site?

- Does the patient smoke?

- Have radon levels been evaluated at the patient's home?

- Does the patient live close to a hazardous waste site?

After collecting this information and reviewing the literature, it may be beneficial to refer the case to an occupational medicine physician for a risk assessment.

Bringing the Job Home

When a physician discovered an elevated blood lead level in an infant, the family home was tested extensively for possible sources of contamination. Nothing turned up, even though the house was old and in an urban area.

No clues surfaced until the inquiry turned to the family's occupational history. The father worked in a foundry, polishing brass parts. Brass, an astute observer noted, contains about 5–6% lead.

The father would come home from the overnight shift while his wife was getting out of bed, taking care of the three older children, and preparing to leave for her job. Before changing out of his work clothes, Dad would gently rock and feed the baby. The infant's nose lay right next to his uniform... sporting a thin film of lead dust.

In another case, an infant's high blood lead level was equally mysterious until attention turned to the grandparents' home. A sporting shop based in the house included an indoor, unventilated rifle range. Seven family members who visited the house regularly were tested, and all underwent chelation therapy to reduce high blood lead levels.[1]

These cases illustrate a phenomenon known as para-occupational disease: workers who unknowingly carry toxic substances home to other family members on their clothes, shoes, or in the car.[2]

Lead is a common culprit in these reports, but it's not the only one. Mercury poisoning has been traced to contamination of work clothes worn in a thermometer manufacturing plant. And in one eerie instance, cotton cloth sacs used for asbestos insulation were taken home by a worker and used for diapers. The spouse, who laundered the sacs and her husband's work clothes, died of mesothelioma at age 49, and the child who'd been diapered eventually developed mesothelioma and died at age 33.

The remedy is simple: Workers who are exposed to hazardous agents should change clothes and shower before heading home. But life is not so simple: Many workplaces do not have changing facilities and do not pay close attention to other aspects of basic industrial hygiene.

Article Consultants

Thomas J. Chester, MD, MPH, is Associate Professor and Acting Chairman, Department of Public Health and Preventive Medicine, University of North Texas Health Science Center at Fort Worth. He is chairman of the Epidemiology Committee for the American College of Occupational and Environmental Medicine.

M. Joseph Fedoruk, MD, is Assistant Clinical Professor, Center for Occupational and Environmental Medicine, University of California, Irvine, College of Medicine. His firm, M. Joseph Fedoruk, MD, Inc., and Associates advises corporations, government agencies, and others on the avoidance of occupational hazards.

Ricky L. Langley, MD, MPH, is Assistant Clinical Professor, Department of Family and Community Medicine, Division of Occupational and Environmental Medicine, Duke University Medical Center, Durham, N.C. In 1995, he was guest editor of a special issue of the North Carolina Medical Journal titled "Staying Well at Work: Occupational Medicine in North Carolina."

Carol Wilkinson, MD, MPH, is Regional Medical Director, IBM Corp., Armonk, N.Y. She speaks to health-care professionals and corporate executives on the topic of violence in the workplace and is active in professional organizations developing office ergonomic guidelines.

References

Caution: Work Can Be Hazardous to Your Health

Patient Care References

1*. "The New Thinking on Low-Back Pain," *Patient Care* July 15, 1995, page 140.

2*. "Stiff Neck: An Occupational Hazard," *Patient Care* July 15, 1995, page 172.

3*. "Adult Hearing Loss: Some Tips and Pearls," *Patient Care* September 15,1995, page 77.

4*. "Quick, Effective Screening for Alcohol Abuse," *Patient Care* July 15, 1995, page 56.

Other References

1. Stoohs RA, Bingham L, Itoi A, et al: "Sleep and Sleep-Disordered Breathing in Commercial Long-Haul Truck Drivers," *Chest* 1995;107:1275–1282.

2. Lesser SH, Weiss SJ: "Art hazards," *Am J Emerg Med* 1995;13:451–458.

3. Bernhardt J, Langley RL: "Agricultural hazards in North Carolina," *N C Med J* 1993;54:512–515.

4. Fullerton L, Olson L, Crandall C, et al: "Occupational Injury Mortality in New Mexico," *Ann Emerg Med* 1995;26:447–454.

5. Ringen K, Seegal J, Englund A: "Safety and Health in the Construction Industry," *Annu Rev Public Health* 1995;16:165–168.

6. Frazier LM, Jones B, Darcey D, et al: "Mandatory Reporting of Occupational Health Problems: A New Surveillance Program in North Carolina," *NC Med J* 1994;55:526–531.

7. Newman IS: "Occupational Illness," *N Engl J Med* 1995;333:1128–1134.

8. Nuyts GD, Van Vlem E, Thys J, et al: "New Occupational Risk Factors for Chronic Renal Failure," *Lancet* 1995;346:7–11.

9. Kukull WA, Larson EB, Bowen JD, et al: "Solvent Exposure as a Risk Factor for Alzeimer's Disease: A Case-Control Study," *Am J Epidemiol* 1995;141: 1059–1071.

10. Kristensen P, Irgens LM, Daltveit AK, et al: "Perinatal Outcome among Children of Men Exposed to Lead and Organic Solvents in the Printing Industry," *Am J Epidemiol* 1993;137:134–144.

11. Sallmen M, Lindbohm M-L, Kyyronen P, et al: "Reduced Fertility among Women Exposed to Organic Solvents," *Am J Ind Med* 1995;27:699–713.

12. Ahlborg G Jr: "Physical Work and Pregnancy Outcome," *J Occup Environ Med* 1995;37:941–944.

13. Fenster L, Schaefer C, Mathur A, et al: "Psychological Stress in the Workplace and Spontaneous Abortion," *Am J Epidemiol* 1995;142:11761183.

14. National Institute for Occupational Safety and Health: "Back Belts: Do They Prevent Injury?" DHHS (NIOSH) Publication No. 94-127, September 1994.

15. Lindbohm M-L, Hietanen M: "Magnetic Fields of Video Display Terminals and Pregnancy Outcome," *Occup Environ Med* 1995;37:952–956.

16. Naito S, Tanaka K, Koga H, et al: "Cancer Occurrence among Dyestuff Workers Exposed to Aromatic Amines: A Long-Term Follow-Up Study," *Cancer* 1995;76:1445–1452.

17. Karlberg A-T, Gafvert E, Liden C: "Environmentally Friendly Paper May Increase Risk of hand Eczema in Rosin-Sensitive Persons," *J Am Acad Dermatol* 1995;33:427–432.

18. Morren MA, Janssens V, Dooms-Gossens A, et al: "[alpha]-Amylase, a Flour Additive: An Important Cause of Protein Contact Dermatitis in Bakers," *J Am Acad Dermatol* 1993;29:723–728.

19. Holt JJ, Broste SK, Hansen DA: "Noise Exposure in the Rural Setting," *Laryngoscope* 1993;103:258–262.

20. Dobie RA: "Separating Noise-Induced from Age-Related Hearing Loss," letter, *West J Meal* 1994;160:564–565.

21. "NIOSH Alert: Request for Assistance in Preventing Homicide in the Workplace," DHHS (NIOSH) Publication No. 93-109, September 1993.

22. Alexander BH, Franklin GM, Wolf ME: "The Sexual Assualt of Women at Work in Washington State, 1980 to 1989," *Am J Public Health* 1994;84: 640–642.

23. Hlatky MA, Lam LC, Lee KL, et al: "Job Strain and the Prevalence and Outcome of Coronary Artery Disease," *Circulation* 1995;92:327333.

24. Kawachi I, Colditz GA, Stampfer MJ, et al: "Prospective Study of Shift Work and Risk of Coronary Heart Disease in Women," *Circulation* 1995;92:3178–3182.

The Workplace Is No Place to Die

1. "Fatal Injuries to Workers in the United States, 1980–1989: A Decade of Surveillance." US Dept of Health and Human Services, Public Health Service, Centers for Disease Control and Prevention, National Institute for Occupational Safety and Health, DHHS (NIOSH) Publication No. 93-108S, August 1993.

2. "Occupational Injury Deaths—United States, 1980–1989." *MMWR* 1994;43:262–264.

Bringing the Job Home

1. Moore RS, Ducatman AM, Jozwiak JA: "Home On the Range: Childhood Lead Exposure Due to Family Occupation," *Arch Pediatr Adolesc Med* 1995; 149: 1276–1277.

2. McDiarmid MA, Weaver V: "Fouling One's Own Nest Revisited," *Am J Ind Med* 1993; 24:1–9.

Chapter 2

Occupational Safety and Health Administration (OSHA): Employee Workplace Rights and Responsibilities

The Occupational Safety and Health Act of 1970 (hereafter called the Act) created the Occupational Safety and Health Administration (OSHA) within the Department of Labor and encouraged employers and employees to reduce workplace hazards and to implement safety and health programs.

An employee is anyone who works for an employer whose business affects commerce. Thus, OSHA covers virtually all private sector workers except the self-employed.

The OSH Act gives employees many rights and responsibilities. They have the right to:

- review copies of appropriate standards, rules, regulations, and requirements that the employer should have available at the workplace.

- request information from the employer on safety and health hazards in the workplace, precautions that may be taken, and procedures to be followed if an employee is involved in an accident or is exposed to toxic substances.

- have access to relevant employee exposure and medical records.

- request the OSHA area director to conduct an inspection if they believe hazardous conditions or violations of standards exist in the workplace.

Occupational Safety and Health Administration, Fact Sheet 95-35, January 1995.

- have an authorized employee representative accompany the OSHA compliance officer during the inspection tour.

- respond to questions from the OSHA compliance officer, particularly if there is no authorized employee representative accompanying the compliance officer on the inspection "walkaround."

- observe any monitoring or measuring of hazardous materials and see the resulting records, as specified under the Act, and as required by OSHA standards.

- have an authorized representative, or themselves, review the Log and Summary of Occupational Injuries (OSHA No. 200) at a reasonable time and in a reasonable manner.

- be informed by posting of any citation issued by OSHA as part of an inspection.

- object to the abatement period set by OSHA for correcting any violation in the citation issued to the employer by writing to the OSHA area director within 15 working days from the date the employer receives the citation.

- submit a written request to the National Institute for Occupational Safety and Health (NIOSH) for information on whether any substance in the workplace has potentially toxic effects in the concentration being used, and have names withheld from the employer, if that is requested.

- be notified by the employer if the employer applies for a variance from an OSHA standard, and testify at a variance hearing, and appeal the final decision.

- have names withheld from employer, upon request to OSHA, if a written and signed complaint is filed.

- be advised of OSHA actions regarding a complaint and request an informal review of any decision not to inspect or to issue a citation.

- file a discrimination complaint under Section 11(c) of the Act if punished for exercising the above rights or for refusing to work when faced with an imminent danger of death or serious injury and there is insufficient time for OSHA to inspect; or file a Section 405 reprisal complaint (under the Surface Transportation Assistance Act [STAA]); or file a complaint within 90 days under Section 211 of the Asbestos Hazard Emergency Response Act, which protects employees of primary and secondary schools who complain of exposure to asbestos in their work area; or file a complaint within 60 days under Section 7 of the International Safe Container Act, which protects employees who report safety hazards associated with cargo containers transported on sea and land carriers.

Before OSHA issues, amends or deletes regulations, the agency publishes them in the *Federal Register* so that interested persons or groups may comment.

The employer has a legal obligation to inform employees of OSHA safety and health standards which may apply to their workplace. Upon request, the employer must make available copies of those standards and the OSHA law itself. If more information is needed about workplace hazards than the employer can supply, it can be obtained from the nearest OSHA area office.

Under the Act, employers have a general duty to provide work and a workplace free from recognized hazards. Citations may be issued by OSHA when violations of standards are found, and for violations of the general duty clause, even if no OSHA standard applies to the particular hazard. The employer also must display in a prominent place the official OSHA poster which describes rights and responsibilities under OSHA's law.

Employee Responsibilities

Although OSHA does not cite employees for violations of their responsibilities, employees "shall comply with all occupational safety and health standards and all rules, regulations, and orders issued under the Act" that apply to them. Employee responsibilities and rights in states with their own occupational safety and health programs are generally the same as for workers in Federal OSHA states:

An employee should:

- read the OSHA poster at the jobsite.

- comply with all applicable OSHA standards.

- follow all employer safety and health regulations, and wear or use prescribed protective equipment while working.

- report hazardous conditions to the supervisor.

- report any job-related injury or illness to the employer, and seek treatment promptly.

- cooperate with the OSHA compliance officer conducting an inspection if he or she inquires about safety and health conditions in the workplace.

- exercise rights under the Act in a responsible manner.

Right to Know

Employers in manufacturing industries must establish a written, comprehensive hazard communication program that includes provisions for container labeling, material safety data sheets, and an employee training program. The program must include a list of the hazardous chemicals in each work area, the means the employer uses to inform employees of the hazards of non-routine tasks (for example, the cleaning of reactor vessels), hazards associated with chemicals in unlabeled pipes, and the way the employer will inform contractors in manufacturing facilities of the hazards to which their employees may be exposed.

Access to Exposure and Medical Records

The existence, location, and availability of medical records and records of employees' exposure to toxic substances and harmful physical agents must be provided by the employer to affected employees upon their first entering into employment and at least annually thereafter. Whenever an employer plans to stop doing business and there is no successor employer to receive and maintain these records, the employer must notify employees of their right of access to records at least three months before the employer ceases to do business.

When OSHA standards require the employer to measure exposure to harmful substances, the employee (or representative) has the right to observe the testing and to examine the records of the results. If the exposure levels are above the limit set by the standard, the employer must tell employees what will be done to bring the exposure down.

OSHA Inspections

OSHA encourages employers and employees to work together to remove hazards. Employees should discuss safety and health problems with the employer, other workers, and union representatives (if there is a union). As a last resort, if a hazard cannot be corrected, an employee should contact the nearest OSHA area office. If necessary, the OSHA area director can order an inspection if the employee is willing to submit a formal complaint.

Discrimination for Using Rights

Although there is nothing in the OSHA law that gives an employee the right to refuse to perform an unsafe or unhealthful job assignment, OSHA's regulations, which have been upheld by the U.S. Supreme Court, provide that an employee may refuse to work when faced with an imminent danger of death or serious injury.

The conditions necessary to justify a work refusal are very stringent, however, and a work refusal should be an action taken only as a last resort. If time permits, the unhealthful or unsafe condition should be reported to OSHA or other appropriate regulatory agency.

Thus, employees have a right to seek safety and health on the job without fear of punishment. That right is spelled out in Section 11(c) of the Act. The law says the employer cannot punish or discriminate against employees for exercising such rights as complaining to the employer, union, OSHA, or any other government agency about job safety and health hazards; or for participating in OSHA inspections, conferences, hearings, or other OSHA-related activities.

Workers believing they have been punished for exercising safety and health rights must contact the nearest OSHA office within 30 days of the time they learn of the alleged discrimination. A representative of the employee's choosing can file the 11(c) complaint for the worker. Following a complaint, OSHA will contact the complainant and conduct an in-depth interview to determine whether an investigation is necessary.

Chapter 3

Safety Training

Chapter Contents

Section 3.1

What Is the Best Safety Training Method?

From "What Is the Best Safety Training Method?" by Mike Coleman;
Chuck Sims; David Threlfall, in *Occupational Hazards*, Vol. 60, N. 10, Oct.
1998, pp. 159–165. Copyright 1999 by Penton Media Inc.
Reprinted with permission.

A Critical Look at the Four Most Common Training Methods Used in the Workplace

An infrequent but recurring challenge to any safety trainer is the promulgation of a new OSHA regulation. Do you remember a time when...? Although you may have been able to keep your professional distance for years while the "new" standard was maturing, today's *Federal Register* lying on your desk forces you to face reality. You move through the lengthy preface, stopping now and then to scan an interesting provision. Then you see it, right there in paragraph (h). The words fill you with both anticipation and anxiety, all at the same time: "Employee Information and Training."

Anticipation? Well, sort of. It is, after all, something "new." In most cases, however, the anticipation pales in comparison with the anxiety. In the past five years, you've been down-sized, right-sized and made to do so much more with so much less to the point that you're not looking for anything more to do.

As you carefully read the new training requirements, you realize the magnitude of this performance standard. Some bottom-line questions begin to crowd your mind: "How am I going to get extra time for training?" "Can we make the training deadline?" "How should I schedule the training?" "What training technique will work best for communicating this information...?"

This last question might seem puzzling. After all, who has the time to worry about the best training technique to use? We're often glad to just get all the training done. Like an agile hurdler, we sometimes leap over important questions that we should actually spend time thinking about, and the best way to do safety training is one of those questions.

There are many methods used in safety training. Let's look at four of them. For each method, we'll examine the advantages and disadvantages and suggest a few tips to ensure that you're using the technique effectively.

Instructor-Led Training

Virtually all of us have spent time in a classroom. Although the experience probably varied greatly from class to class and teacher to teacher, most of us have managed to learn something in the classroom. For most of us, despite new technologies in the school classroom, the traditional, instructor-led learning environment is the touchstone of our formal learning experience.

Advantages to Instructor-Led Training

If classroom space and an instructor are already available, the start-up cost and time-to-delivery of an instructor-led course is relatively low, compared with media-intensive training options. Nothing is "free," of course, and costs can rise dramatically if the training is held off site or if an outside consultant is brought in to do the training.

Unless you canned it yourself, no off-the-shelf generic videotape offers the custom content and pacing of an instructor-led session. An agile instructor can even adjust the presentation in real time, depending on the feedback received from the session participants.

People are often most easily motivated to take action by other people, not by bare facts or whiz-bang special effects. Think back to your own school experience. Think of that teacher who made the subject so interesting that the class was over before it hardly had begun. Think of that teacher who believed in you and encouraged you to excel so that his/her high expectations became yours. Or the teacher who made the subject so relevant that you couldn't help discussing the class with your friends later in the day. There's no reason why an instructor-led safety training session can't have the same effect.

In an energized classroom experience, participants motivate and challenge one another. As participants pose questions and sometimes provide unconventional solutions, a synergistic effect is created. If team learning is a goal of your safety training, it would be difficult to achieve in any other way.

Disadvantages to Instructor-Led Training

Besides adjusting the head count downward, many companies have also downsized facility space, such that suitable classrooms may be difficult to reserve or may not exist at all.

As each person's job in the organization has become more critical, the option of assembling even small groups of employees at one time and in one place has almost become nonexistent. As workers become increasingly unavailable for training, formal instructor-led sessions become increasingly expensive.

Unsuitable instructors can provide a learning experience that is worse than no learning at all. This unsuitability may result from lack of competence as a trainer, lack of knowledge about the subject being taught or lack of credibility with the work force. When employees leave the training session with a worse attitude toward the subject than when they entered, everyone loses.

Tips to Ensure Success of Instructor-Led Sessions

Make sure you understand the topic you are teaching and how it specifically applies to the employees you are training. If you don't know the answer to an employee's question, don't fake it. Tell them you don't know, but will find out and get back to them. Then do it.

Never merely lecture. Spice up the session with other training methods such as demonstrations, questions and answers, discussions, case studies, role-plays, and re-creations.

Learn the principle of training adults. Although we might complain that our employees are "acting like children," it would be counterproductive to employ training methods that are ineffective with adults.

Engage the minds of the audience through interactivity. The more the participants actively participate in the training session, the more they will learn today so that they can apply it tomorrow.

Using Videotape

Since the mid-1980s, when the videotape recorder became affordable for consumers, live-action video programs have been the media of choice for many safety trainers. Almost overnight, trainers retired their 80-slide trays and audiocassettes with those annoying beeps for a new technology. Although crude by today's production standards, they represented a giant leap for safety training. Now audiences could actually see the significance of a moving pinch point, experience the drama of an accident recreation or observe the explosive results of a chemical reaction. No longer would a spokesperson be frozen in time or movement merely represented by a blur.

Advantages to Videotape Training

Most companies do not have the resources to hire outside consultants to do their safety training. Instead, they turn to their own in-house people to do it. Using a videotape helps in-house trainers fill in the gaps and ensures that all the relevant information is covered. It also breaks up the training into manageable segments and focuses or refocuses the attention of the audience.

Sometimes it is very difficult to get all the "stuff" you really need into the average training classroom. Using a videotape can eliminate having to haul a lot of things around. 3-D animation can show how a pump works or what happens to feedstock when it enters a processing tower.

Many videotapes use a creative or entertaining approach when they deal with a training topic. Most audiences find viewing a videotape with a fresh approach to a subject a welcome relief, particularly when the alternative is a 3-hour lecture.

Using a videotape helps to validate the information the trainer is presenting. It's no longer just the safety guy who says that the information is important. A videotape is like an outside expert who enhances the credibility of the presenter.

Disadvantages to Videotape Training

There is nothing that will put an audience to sleep faster than a videotape that is poorly produced or lacks some entertainment value. People are used to the high production values they see on network and cable TV. If the video is not well done, employees may discount what it says. The more employees enjoy watching a tape, the more of its content they retain.

Producers take great care to ensure they have covered a topic in sufficient depth for the intended audience. They agonize over the order of presentation, choosing the right words and metaphors, and visualizing the topic to enhance communication. When the video is really good, trainers are sometimes tempted to put the video in the player and walk away; however, the videotape is always a training tool. It is the means, never the end.

Some people criticize videotape because it is linear, not interactive. It is linear, but don't VCRs have a STOP button, as well as a START button? Can't that STOP button be pressed anytime during the presentation, rather than only at the end? Can't the presenter ask relevant questions at the appropriate time to generate interactivity? Interactivity is not something inherent in new computer-based technology; it's a tool that effective presenters have always used.

Some trainers refuse to use a videotape if it shows a different method of doing something or it shows people using a technique that they feel is incorrect. This apparently formidable objection is really no objection at all for an effective presenter. If the safety trainer properly sets up the principle, the audience should be able to apply that principle. For example, the presenter might say, "The video you'll see next shows a procedure different from the one we've talked about in class. I want you to think about any disadvantages of doing it the way the video shows."

Tips for Successful Videotape Training

Be careful about safety sessions that last for hours. The result is usually information overload (Dave Robbins, Division of Safety and Hygiene, Ohio Bureau of Workers' Compensation).

A video should never be the training program. It is always a tool. Always choose a video that is technically correct and up-to-date. Pick it carefully. A video has to be both informational and entertaining to prevent audience boredom (Ron Divan, GenCo safety program leader, Lower Colorado River Authority).

A video with a little humor is great for boring or routine topics. The more the audience knows about a subject, the shorter the video ought to be. Use a 4- to 6-minute video to drive home a specific point. Be sure to set the videotape up properly. Emphasize the key points before you show it, and always leave time for questions (Michael Coates, Industrial Hygiene, Division of Safety and Hygiene, Ohio Bureau of Workers' Compensation).

Have the audience look for specific things while they watch the video. Emphasize application issues right from the start. Make sure you use the vocabulary of the video throughout the rest of the class (Jim Fograsher, training center manager, Division of Safety and Hygiene, Ohio Bureau of Workers' Compensation).

CD-ROM Training

When CD-ROM started in the late 1970s, it came on a 12-inch platter, required special cards that had to be installed in a computer, a special player that cost around $2,000 and lots of spaghetti cable to hook it all together. Individualized interactive training has come a long way since then. Today, it's almost impossible to find a computer that is not multimedia-ready right out of the box. The size of the platter is not the only thing that has shrunk. Equipment cost has plummeted to less than $1,000, rendering the traditional objection against interactive training moot.

The term "CD-ROM training" really refers to an instructional design that features individualized interactive training. You might have heard the terms "CBT" or "multi-media instruction" used for the same idea. This year it's stored on a silver platter about five inches in diameter called a CD-ROM. Next year, it could be DVD or an acronym that hasn't even been invented yet.

Advantages to CD-ROM Training

Today's safety trainer faces many problems, but none more taxing than how to do safety training when multiple shifts are involved, or how to make up training when employees are absent, or how to schedule training in 12 remote sites at the same time. Individualized CD-ROM based safety training is the answer and is available on demand at your local multimedia-ready PC.

During an average presentation, only 20 percent of the audience are on pace with the instructor. The rest are either bored silly or still trying to understand what the instructor said 5 minutes ago. But with CD-ROM based interactive safety training, employees can progress at an individual pace. This saves both time and money.

Look around an average instructor-led training session. You can see the employees who are in gear and the ones who merely coasting. Compare that with employees sitting at computers taking CD-ROM courses. They are actively involved in the training session, asking for more information, answering a question, making a choice or asking a question. Studies have shown that the more involved a participant is in the training process, the higher the retention rate.

Managing the mass of paperwork used to document training is a difficult task. Add to that scheduling employees for training and communicating to employees the courses they need to take, and the task becomes almost impossible. But administering the training and documentation is what CD-ROM-based training does best.

Disadvantages to CD-ROM Training

"It won't work on the six different platforms found at my site." That could be true. Many reasonably priced systems limit themselves to a few common platforms such as Windows '95 or NT. You'll pay more for the development of course materials designed to run on lots of different platforms.

"There's no instructor to answer questions." That's true, but given the extremely limited time allotted to safety training in many companies, this objection may not be an exclusive problem. Many CD-ROM training systems have built-in e-mail capability so that employees can ask questions about things they do not understand. This feature may actually free an instructor to focus on individual needs.

"It's just like a videotape: You either can't customize the content easily or it will cost you an arm and a leg." The question that separates CD-ROM training courses today is not "Can you customize?", but "How easily can you customize?" Most systems will allow you to add multimedia content about site-specific issues, then test employees on that specific content.

"It's going to put me out of a job." Hardly! It will simply give you more time to do the things that you were trained to do, and help you focus on the real training needs. After all, don't you have safety audits to do, workstations to analyze, "what if" scenarios to consider and near misses to analyze?

Tips for Using CD-ROMs

There seems to be a built-in resistance to change with most people. This is especially true when the change concerns a newer technology. If your people have never used CD-ROM training before, make sure the first program you introduce is light, easy to do and fun. Once they succeed at this, they will be hooked (Jim Chandler, former Senior Training Development Specialist, AT&T).

When you buy a CD-ROM course you are not buying an individual program, but a system. Make sure it works on your PCs and that there is an adequate support mechanism with an 800 number in case you need help. Make sure it is user-friendly for both employees and the administrator. Make sure you understand the functionality of the system and that it will meet your current and future needs (Don Leonard, president, The MARCOM Group, Ltd.).

If you plan to develop your own CD-ROM training materials, choose your developer with care. The more experience a developer has with the subject area, the better. You'll save your sanity, as well as time and money (Jim Chandler, former senior training development specialist, AT&T).

Do your planning up front before you implement the course. Will you have open enrollment? Will you schedule employees by job class or department? What options will you allow employees to access? How will employees know how to use the options available to them? Would a "test-out" option be appropriate? Who will orient employees before they use the software (Don Leonard, president, The MARCOM Group, Ltd.)?

If you have looked at CD-ROM training in the past and didn't like what you saw, you might want to take a second look. Certain sections of the country that experience wide variations in weather conditions have this saying: "If you don't like the weather, just wait until this afternoon." The same can be said of CD-ROM materials.

Distance Learning

Distance learning sounds like a new concept, but it isn't. The first document ever written, whatever it was, was an example of "distance learning" because it allowed communication to flow from one person in one place to another person in another place.

In modern usage, "distance learning" is a broad term, referring to a combination of media, methods and materials delivered by satellite, the Internet, videoconferencing, teleconferencing or other means. It might include lectures, panel discussions, demonstrations, case studies, exercises, video images, still photographs, text, and graphics.

Advantages to Distance Learning

Distance learning strategies can provide a cost-effective solution to bridge the distance between trainer and trainee. Other options for communicating in person with a widely scattered group of employees present a challenge. You could fly each employee in to attend your training session or take your training session on the road. When you consider airfare, hotel and living expenses, these options may not be reasonable.

Distance learning, unlike videotape or CD-ROM training, also allows real time interaction between trainer and trainee. The interaction may be synchronous or asynchronous. Synchronous interaction (e.g., a question from a remote site during a live, satellite-delivered seminar) affords trainees an immediate answer to their questions. Asynchronous interaction (e.g., e-mail) allows the trainer to assemble questions from various locations and answer them at one time.

Distance learning provides a consistent message with all participants hearing the same message in the same way. This eliminates miscommunication and misinformation because the message is standardized.

35

Distance learning can reach almost anywhere. Many organizations have television monitors throughout the facility: in the lunchroom, over the soft drink machine and in the break area. Often, the monitors serve as billboards. They say such things as "Happy Birthday, Joe!" or "Flu Shots Tomorrow!" These monitors could serve as a pipeline to deliver a continuous stream of education and information.

Disadvantages to Distance Learning

The traditional complaint about distance learning is that it does not allow for hands-on training. To overcome this, be prepared to supplement distance learning with supervised, hands-on practice, especially if you are trying to teach skills.

Distance learning requires planning and resources to create the videos, graphics and training modules. These materials must often be given to an external provider for placement on a distance learning platform.

Tips for Successful Distance Learning

Obtain buy-in from all levels of management.

Ensure that participants know how the training is relevant to the job, what the training will cover and what the outcomes will be.

Consider application-based exercises (e.g., brainstorming or other breakout sessions) to enhance the learning experience.

Assign a mentor to each trainee to help him or her through the training process. A mentor can ensure that all the trainee's questions have been answered and encourage him or her to take full advantage of the training.

Conclusions

What's the best method to use for safety training? It depends on two key factors: instructor implementation and audience acceptance. All the methods that we've covered are good methods, but even a good method can turn bad if poorly implemented. Poor implementation shines a spotlight on all the disadvantages of a method. Effective implementation hides all the disadvantages.

The training method you choose should not become a barrier to communication. When the method you choose is not acceptable to the audience, is perceived by them as difficult to use or understand, or is something less than they expect, it can become a barrier to communication, and may not be effective.

In safety training there is no single solution. There are, however, a number of valuable alternatives that should be implemented properly and selected with audience in mind.

— by Mike Coleman

Mike Coleman is Director of Education for Tel-A.Train (www.tela train.com), Chuck Sims is Director of Education for WTN, the Workplace Training Network (www.workplacetraining.com) and David Threlfall is Director of Education for ITS Corporation (www.its.pwpl. com). Each company is a division of PRIMEDIA Workplace Learning (www.pwpl.com).

Section 3.2

Safety Training That Sticks

From "Safety Training That Sticks" by Stephen G. Minter, in *Occupational Hazards*, Vol. 58, N. 7, July 1996, pp. 33–36. Copyright 1999 by Penton Media Inc. Reprinted with permission.

Safety training stands little chance of success unless you create the right conditions for it. John Cheeseman, education specialist with the Ontario Natural Resources Safety Association, tells how to make "learning pay off in performance."

Every day in businesses across North America, thousands of employees are trained on a wide range of safety and health topics. That training ought to be paying off in greatly improved safety performance, but there is evidence that much of that effort is being wasted.

According to *Training* magazine, U.S. corporations with 100 or more employees spend $52 billion annually on training. But as John Cheeseman, education specialist with the Ontario Natural Resources Safety Association, points out, researchers contend that anywhere from 20 percent to 80 percent of what people learn in a classroom fails to transfer into the workplace. Take 50 percent as a middle-ground estimate and the waste is dramatic.

"Is that a direct dollar loss or are you only realizing 50 percent of the potential gain that you could possibly get from investing in training?"

Cheeseman asked. "We're all looking for ways to be more competitive. Why not take a look at training?"

The tendency in many companies is to blame employees when training occurs and no change happens in the workplace. While employees certainly play a role in the eventual success or failure of training, there are a variety of factors that contribute to what learning psychologist Edward Thorndike called the "transfer of training."

Transfer of training means the use of the information provided in training on the job. "[Thorndike] said that the closer you approximate the conditions in the classroom to real life, the higher the probability that that learning will be generalizable or transferable to real life," noted Cheeseman.

Essential to successful training, said Cheeseman, a former underground miner and mine supervisor, is the idea that not just employees and trainers, but also front-line supervisors and top managers be involved in and support training efforts.

"The front-line supervisors need to show up to the training courses themselves to find out what is going on. They have to be kept informed about why the training is necessary, what it's all about and how it is supposed to be used," Cheeseman explained. "The managers have to be involved in explaining and communicating how important this is and how they expect employees to use what they've learned. They need to show visible commitment and change the whole organizational culture to one that places a very high value on training. If that ever happens, we will see more and more learning applied on the job and a higher return."

Before Training

How do you weed out the obstacles to successful training? Cheeseman recommends you start with the following steps:

Determine Training Needs. Training needs are defined as "the skills and knowledge required by employees to perform job tasks safely and efficiently." Cheeseman recommends a team approach involving managers, trainers, supervisors and employees to identify where performance problems exist and what sort of training will be needed. By having these employees all participate, he said, they are more likely to take ownership in the training program and support it on the plant floor.

Conduct a Workplace Environmental Assessment. Take a hard look at your worksite and try to identify any barriers to training that might exist among trainees, supervisors, and managers, or that have to do with the training program itself or the organization. For example, a poor labor-management climate, lack of success with past training programs, or indications from top management that they are only going through the motions with safety could all interfere with training. Cheeseman recommends surveys, interviews, job observations and document searches to identify these concerns.

"Interviews, where you pick up anecdotal information, may not be all that scientific, but they can be very revealing," he noted.

Review Potential Training Programs. Audit, on a regular basis, the content of your training programs to make sure they are current, relevant, and cost-effective, advised Cheeseman. Assess whether there are sound instructional design principles guiding the learning activities. For example, are your training materials and presentation drab or colorful and varied? "The more vivid the stimuli in your program, the more interesting it is and the easier it is to keep people's attention. The more you hold people's attention, the more they are going to learn," he said. Another important principle is to make conditions in training as similar to what will be encountered on the job as possible.

Cheeseman warns against simply showing workers a video and then asking for questions afterward. "Video is most effective when it creates a strong emotional impact in your audience and that is followed up by a very good interactive discussion," he said, adding: "Our favorite videos are those in which we stage accidents. That sets up the discussion: What were the hazards? What were the contributing factors that led up to this thing happening? What could we do to prevent this from happening again?"

Develop Effective Instructors. "Experience is not enough to make a good instructor," warns Cheeseman. Trainers, he noted, must organize or develop materials, facilitate the learning process and conduct evaluations. He recommends that managers help trainers to build their course development and presentation skills by sending them to train-the-trainer courses.

Carefully Select Who Will Attend Training. Cheeseman recommends selecting employees on a "need to know" rather than a "nice to know" basis. That means choosing employees who are going to apply the training in your firm.

Win Support from Supervisors. If supervisors don't support a training program, said Cheeseman, "you're dead in the water." It is the supervisor who has immediate contact with the employees, and who provides them with "encouragement, support, feedback and guidance." He recommends including supervisors in the team that identifies training needs, and having managers hold an orientation meeting with them to explain the content and purpose of the training. Adds Cheeseman: "Why not have the supervisor help the trainer out somehow during the training course?"

Prepare Trainees in Advance. Pre-training meetings are an important way for managers to "set the stage" for training by describing what the course will cover and why it is important to the company and to them. "If you can tell everybody what to expect before they get there and you can convince them that it is important and valuable and relates directly to their own needs, you are creating a state of readiness in your learner," said Cheeseman, adding: "You want them to be open-minded, receptive and anxious to learn."

Distribute Pre-Course Material. Participants in training should receive pre-course materials so that they have some familiarity with the subject matter and can start to develop questions and concerns.

During Training

Here are some steps to take during training to make sure it is as effective as possible:

Demonstrate management commitment to training. Managers who show up at the kickoff of a training session and offer a few inspirational words send "a clear signal of commitment and support the process of building positive expectations and productive working relationships." Cheeseman tells managers: "Never underestimate the importance of your presence at training sessions."

Provide adequate training facilities. Proper facilities help demonstrate management commitment and provide the comfort and privacy that helps the learning process. Cheeseman says companies should consider room size, lighting, indoor air quality, temperature control, seating, and isolation from outside noises. If training is held on-site, he added, make sure that distractions and interruptions do not occur.

Provide adequate resources for the trainer. Trainers need the right tools to be effective, notes Cheeseman. That means access to flip charts, slide projectors, VCRs, "current videos," photocopy machines, up-to-date statistics and other training materials.

Insist on documentation. Managers should feel free to insist on "documented evidence that people have learned something," Cheeseman said. "Certainly, people have to be held responsible as adults for learning, but the trainer also has to be held accountable for delivering the training according to standard. That means some prearranged format and standard that is acceptable in communicating the information that was identified in a front-end analysis, evaluating those activities and determining whether or not these people are confident" to perform the duties for which they have been trained.

Offer recognition. Show that the company values the employees' participation in training by providing them with a certificate of achievement. Provide well-designed certificates that employees will be "proud to hang on the office wall or work area," Cheeseman urged.

Return to Work

Training classes and activities are important, but they are not the end of the training process. It's critical that your company take the steps to ensure that training takes root in the workplace. Otherwise, it's time and money down the drain.

Meet with trainees. As soon as employees return to the workplace, the first thing managers should do is meet with them, says Cheeseman. Use this opportunity to reinforce how important the training is and to clarify any misunderstandings about how the training is to be applied.

Provide opportunities to apply training. Practice makes perfect—that's one cliché that is absolutely true with respect to training. "I took a computer training course recently and I hardly ever get an opportunity to use the program, so I can't remember what I learned anymore," said Cheeseman. "You have to make sure there is plenty of time for employees to apply that learning as soon as, and as often as, possible."

Provide feedback and support. "The number one obstacle to the transfer of training is lack of feedback and support," warns Cheeseman. Front-line supervisors play the crucial role here because of their immediate contact with employees. "Feedback, whether it is used to support desired behaviors or correct ineffective ones, should be immediate, specific, task-oriented and non-threatening," he explained.

Provide expert coaching. Encourage trained or expert employees to provide help and guidance on the subject matter covered in the training. "Coaching can be a powerful, cost-effective 'safety net' to help reinforce learning and bridge any possible gaps left by training," said Cheeseman.

Provide resource material. Reinforce your training sessions with a variety of reference materials. Cheeseman suggests providing an on-site library for staff, circulating magazine articles or industry reports, and including safety information in the company newsletter.

Provide job aids. Booklets, checklists, flowcharts, even posters or software can help employees remember or retrieve information covered in training. Said Cheeseman: "A well-developed, functional job aid will communicate critical job procedures, alert workers to health and safety hazards, or remind employees of certain guidelines to remember."

Evaluate performance. Has the training you've conducted resulted in changes on the shop floor? To find out, Cheeseman recommends conducting follow-up surveys to identify "how many employees are using the training, how often it is applied, if it is being performed to standard, and if any barriers are interfering with employee development."

Beyond that, Cheeseman believes that employers should consider auditing the transfer of training, looking for "evidence that there is a behavioral change happening and that longer-term results are starting to materialize."

Provide periodic refresher training. After employees have had "ample" time to practice the skills they have learned in training, conduct refresher training to review the material learned and correct any misconceptions or bad habits. "Refresher training is especially important when there are infrequent opportunities to apply newly learned skills and knowledge," said Cheeseman. Accident investigation and emergency rescue are two examples of this, he noted.

These steps may represent a more resource-intensive approach to safety training, but the result should be training that sticks, not simply slips away.

Section 3.3

Roles for Involvement at All Levels

From " Roles for Involvement at All Levels," in *Occupational Hazards*, Vol. 59, N. 8, Aug. 1997, p50–51. Copyright 1999 by Penton Media Inc. Reprinted with permission.

In an effective safety change-effort, personnel at all levels are participating and involved in ways that contribute to continuous improvement. The following are examples of the roles that are often appropriate for the different levels of an organization:

Wage-Roll Personnel

- The reason to involve employees in data collection and analysis of this kind is that they are the ones closest to the actual working conditions. They need to have ownership for the data collection and analysis so that they can see the challenges, identify the remedies, and keep track of the improvements.

- A work group involved in safety in this way generates safety data that are the objective foundation for problem solving and action planning.

Vice Presidents (VPs) or Directors of Operations (DOs)

- Set and communicate expectations for safety performance, and include outcomes in annual performance reviews of their direct reports. Provide coaching to direct reports on managing safety efforts.

- Monitor and give regular feedback on both upstream and downstream indicators. Upstream indicators include: quality and level of employee involvement in incident investigations; speed of completion of safety-related maintenance work orders; and number of work group action plans addressing performance issues. Downstream indicators include: injury rates and workers' compensation costs.

- Review and approve appropriate safety budget levels for departments and facilities.

- Express support for safety as a high value for the organization, for example:
  - attending employee involvement training
  - participating in kickoff meetings for the change-effort
  - meeting regularly with personnel in safety, including employee steering committees

- Elicit feedback from subordinates concerning the VP's or DOs support of safety.

Plant Managers

- Where relevant, "model" the procedures and identified behaviors of the safety change-effort. Example: During plant tours, use all required personal protective equipment.

- Discuss the change-effort using positive terms, and set positive expectations.

- Review change-effort data and problem-solving activities monthly.

- Discuss current and potential barriers to safety performance.

- Include support activities in the annual performance reviews of direct subordinates and provide feedback at least semiannually.

- Ensure that change-effort roles and responsibilities for a successful outcome are established, understood and followed.

- Include in annual budgeting process consideration of personnel, training and equipment needs for safety.

- Ensure that specified employee involvement does not lead to disciplinary action.

- Don't let frictions in labor-management relations stop continuous improvement in safety performance.

- Implement system to reward participation versus punishment for nonparticipation.

- Provide necessary information about the change-effort upward as well as downward in organization.

Department Managers/Superintendents

- Wherever relevant, "model" the procedures and identified behaviors of the safety change effort.

- Allow time so personnel can fulfill designated roles and responsibilities.

- Provide necessary information about the change-effort upward as well as downward in organization.

- Help identify and remove barriers and roadblocks to continuous improvement in safety.

- Provide recognition and reinforcement for employee steering committee members and other employees who are actively supporting change.

- Interact regularly with the steering committee to receive reports and to provide guidance and coaching as appropriate.

- Support continuing education for the change-effort and problem-solving effectiveness in meetings.

Supervisors

- Review and use change-effort data at crew meetings.

- Preserve confidentiality of change-effort data.

- Work with employee steering committees to resolve action plans.

- Serve as a technical resource.

- Help identify, remove, minimize barriers to continuous improvement.

- Serve on steering committee if appropriate for the site's culture.

- Ensure that change-effort audits and findings get back to the database.

- "Model" identified safe behaviors on the shop floor.

Part Two

Lung Issues

Chapter 4

Sick Building Syndrome

Introduction

The term "sick building syndrome" (SBS) is used to describe situations in which building occupants experience acute health and comfort effects that appear to be linked to time spent in a building, but no specific illness or cause can be identified. The complaints may be localized in a particular room or zone, or may be widespread throughout the building. In contrast, the term "building-related illness" (BRI) is used when symptoms of diagnosable illness are identified and can be attributed directly to airborne building contaminants.

A 1984 World Health Organization Committee report suggested that up to 30 percent of new and remodeled buildings worldwide may be the subject of excessive complaints related to indoor air quality (IAQ). Often this condition is temporary, but some buildings have long-term problems. Frequently, problems result when a building is operated or maintained in a manner that is inconsistent with its original design or prescribed operating procedures. Sometimes indoor air problems are a result of poor building design or occupant activities.

Indicators of SBS Include

- Building occupants complain of symptoms associated with acute discomfort, e.g., headache; eye, nose, or throat irritation; dry

United States Environmental Protection Agency, Indoor Facts No. 4 (revised), April 1991. Despite the age of this document, readers seeking an understanding of sick building syndrome will still find the information useful.

49

cough; dry or itchy skin; dizziness and nausea; difficulty in concentrating; fatigue; and sensitivity to odors.

- The cause of the symptoms is not known.
- Most of the complainants report relief soon after leaving the building.

Indicators of BRI Include

- Building occupants complain of symptoms such as cough; chest tightness; fever, chills; and muscle aches.
- The symptoms can be clinically defined and have clearly identifiable causes.
- Complainants may require prolonged recovery times after leaving the building.

It is important to note that complaints may result from other causes. These may include an illness contracted outside the building, acute sensitivity (e.g., allergies), job related stress or dissatisfaction, and other psychosocial factors. Nevertheless, studies show that symptoms may be caused or exacerbated by indoor air quality problems.

Causes of Sick Building Syndrome

The following have been cited causes of or contributing factors to sick building syndrome:

Inadequate Ventilation

In the early and mid 1900s, building ventilation standards called for approximately 15 cubic feet per minute (cfm) of outside air for each building occupant, primarily to dilute and remove body odors. As a result of the 1973 oil embargo, however, national energy conservation measures called for a reduction in the amount of outdoor air provided for ventilation to 5 cfm per occupant. In many cases these reduced outdoor air ventilation rates were found to be inadequate to maintain the health and comfort of building occupants. Inadequate ventilation, which may also occur if heating, ventilating, and air conditioning (HVAC) systems do not effectively distribute air to people in the building, is thought to be an important factor in SBS. In an effort to achieve acceptable IAQ while minimizing energy consumption, the American Society of Heating, Refrigerating and

Air-Conditioning Engineers (ASHRAE) recently revised its ventilation standard to provide a minimum of 15 cfm of outdoor air per person (20 cfm/person in office spaces). Up to 60 cfm/person may be required in some spaces (such as smoking lounges) depending on the activities that normally occur in that space (see ASHRAE Standard 62-1989).

Chemical Contaminants from Indoor Sources

Most indoor air pollution comes from sources inside the building. For example, adhesives, carpeting, upholstery, manufactured wood products, copy machines, pesticides, and cleaning agents may emit volatile organic compounds (VOCs), including formaldehyde. Environmental tobacco smoke contributes high levels of VOCs, other toxic compounds, and respirable particulate matter. Research shows that some VOCs can cause chronic and acute health effects at high concentrations, and some are known carcinogens. Low to moderate levels of multiple VOCs may also produce acute reactions. Combustion products such as carbon monoxide, nitrogen dioxide, as well as respirable particles, can come from unvented kerosene and gas space heaters, woodstoves, fireplaces and gas stoves.

Chemical Contaminants from Outdoor Sources

The outdoor air that enters a building can be a source of indoor air pollution. For example, pollutants from motor vehicle exhausts; plumbing vents, and building exhausts (e.g., bathrooms and kitchens) can enter the building through poorly located air intake vents, windows, and other openings. In addition, combustion products can enter a building from a nearby garage.

Biological Contaminants

Bacteria, molds, pollen, and viruses are types of biological contaminants. These contaminants may breed in stagnant water that has accumulated in ducts, humidifiers and drain pans, or where water has collected on ceiling tiles, carpeting, or insulation. Sometimes insects or bird droppings can be a source of biological contaminants. Physical symptoms related to biological contamination include cough, chest tightness, fever, chills, muscle aches, and allergic responses such as mucous membrane irritation and upper respiratory congestion. One indoor bacterium, Legionella, has caused both Legionnaires' Disease and Pontiac Fever.

These elements may act in combination, and may supplement other complaints such as inadequate temperature, humidity, or lighting. Even after a building investigation, however, the specific causes of the complaints may remain unknown.

A Word about Radon and Asbestos

SBS and BRI are associated with acute or immediate health problems; radon and asbestos cause long-term diseases which occur years after exposure, and are therefore not considered to be among the causes of sick buildings. This is not to say that the latter are not serious health risks; both should be included in any comprehensive evaluation of a building's IAQ.

Building Investigation Procedures

The goal of a building investigation is to identify and solve indoor air quality complaints in a way that prevents them from recurring and which avoids the creation of other problems. To achieve this goal, it is necessary for the investigator(s) to discover whether a complaint is actually related to indoor air quality, identify the cause of the complaint, and determine the most appropriate corrective actions.

An indoor air quality investigation procedure is best characterized as a cycle of information gathering, hypothesis formation, and hypothesis testing. It generally begins with a walkthrough inspection of the problem area to provide information about the four basic factors that influence indoor air quality:

- the occupants
- the HVAC system
- possible pollutant pathways
- possible contaminant sources

Preparation for a walkthrough should include documenting easily obtainable information about the history of the building and of the complaints; identifying known HVAC zones and complaint areas; notifying occupants of the upcoming investigation; and, identifying key individuals needed for information and access. The walkthrough itself entails visual inspection of critical building areas and consultation with occupants and staff.

The initial walkthrough should allow the investigator to develop some possible explanations for the complaint. At this point, the investigator may have sufficient information to formulate a hypothesis, test the hypothesis, and see if the problem is solved. If it is, steps should be taken to ensure that it does not recur. However, if insufficient information is obtained from the walkthrough to construct a hypothesis, or if initial tests fail to reveal the problem, the investigator should move on to collect additional information to allow formulation of additional hypotheses. The process of formulating hypotheses, testing them, and evaluating them continues until the problem is solved.

Although air sampling for contaminants might seem to be the logical response to occupant complaints, it seldom provides information about possible causes. While certain basic measurements, e.g., temperature, relative humidity, CO_2, and air movement, can provide a useful "snapshot" of current building conditions, sampling for specific pollutant concentrations is often not required to solve the problem and can even be misleading. Contaminant concentration levels rarely exceed existing standards and guidelines even when occupants continue to report health complaints. Air sampling should not be undertaken until considerable information on the factors listed above has been collected, and any sampling strategy should be based on a comprehensive understanding of how the building operates and the nature of the complaints.

Solutions to Sick Building Syndrome

Solutions to sick building syndrome usually include combinations of the following:

Pollutant source removal or modification is an effective approach to resolving an IAQ problem when sources are known and control is feasible. Examples include routine maintenance of HVAC systems, e.g., periodic cleaning or replacement of filters; replacement of water-stained ceiling tile and carpeting; institution of smoking restrictions; venting contaminant source emissions to the outdoors; storage and use of paints, adhesives, solvents, and pesticides in well ventilated areas, and use of these pollutant sources during periods of non-occupancy; and allowing time for building materials in new or remodeled areas to off-gas pollutants before occupancy. Several of these options may be exercised at one time.

Increasing ventilation rates and air distribution often can be a cost effective means of reducing indoor pollutant levels. HVAC systems should be designed, at a minimum, to meet ventilation standards in local building codes; however, many systems are not operated or maintained to ensure that these design ventilation rates are provided. In many buildings, IAQ can be improved by operating the HVAC system to at least its design standard, and to ASHRAE Standard 62-1989 if possible. When there are strong pollutant sources, local exhaust ventilation may be appropriate to exhaust contaminated air directly from the building. Local exhaust ventilation is particularly recommended to remove pollutants that accumulate in specific areas such as rest rooms, copy rooms, and printing facilities.

Air cleaning can be a useful adjunct to source control and ventilation but has certain limitations. Particle control devices such as the typical furnace filter are inexpensive but do not effectively capture small particles; high performance air filters capture the smaller, respirable particles but are relatively expensive to install and operate. Mechanical filters do not remove gaseous pollutants. Some specific gaseous pollutants may be removed by adsorbent beds, but these devices can be expensive and require frequent replacement of the adsorbent material. In sum, air cleaners can be useful, but have limited application.

Education and communication are important elements in both remedial and preventive indoor air quality management programs. When building occupants, management, and maintenance personnel fully communicate and understand the causes and consequences of IAQ problems, they can work more effectively together to prevent problems from occurring, or to solve them if they do.

Additional Information

For more information on topics discussed in this chapter, contact your state or local health department, or a non-profit agency such as your local American Lung Association. Contact information for the Indoor Air Quality Information Clearinghouse [IAQ INFO] (sponsored by the U.S. EPA), the National Institute for Occupational Safety and Health, and the American Society of Heating, Refrigerating and Air-Conditioning Engineers (ASHRAE) is available in the Resources section of this sourcebook. This article can be found at http://www.epa.gov/iaq/pubs/sbs.html.

Chapter 5

Asbestos

Asbestos-Related Lung Disease

Definition and Cause

Lung damage from asbestos-related lung diseases results from inhalation of the dust of asbestos, a widely used building material prized for its fire resistance and insulation characteristics.

Asbestos may cause lung cancer and fibrosis in anyone exposed to it. According to the National Cancer Institute, among some groups of workers who are heavily exposed to asbestos, as much as 20 to 25 percent of all deaths are due to lung cancer. (In the general population, lung cancer causes only about 5 percent of all deaths.)

But asbestos exposure is not limited to workers. Asbestos, a virtually indestructible fiber, has been used broadly in construction, insulation, and other building materials for many years. Its much prized durability may make it a hazard for those who live, work, or go to school in buildings that were built with asbestos products. Demolition

This chapter includes text from Robert B. Mellins, "Asbestos-Related Lung Disease," from *The Columbia University College of Physicians and Surgeons Complete Home Medical Guide.* Copyright © 1985, 1987, 1995 by G.S. Sharpe Communications, Inc. and the Trustees of Columbia University in the City of New York. Reprinted by permission of Crown Publishers, a division of Random House, Inc., and "Safe Use of Chrysotile Asbestos: A Manual on Preventive and Control Measures," an undated manual published by The Asbestos Institute, Canada, chapter 1 and 4, http://www.asbestos-institute.ca/safemanual/content.html. Reprinted by permission of The Asbestos Institute.

workers and do-it-yourselfers who renovate older buildings run the risk of extensive asbestos exposure. Public buildings—including schools in Wyoming, New York, and New Jersey, as well as university buildings in Connecticut and California—were temporarily closed because asbestos was flaking from the walls or ceilings.

Asbestos occurs in several different forms. The medically significant ones are crocidolite and amosite.

Types of Asbestos-Related Lung Diseases

Asbestosis. This is fibrosis caused by asbestos and begins when asbestos fibers accumulate around the lungs' terminal bronchioles. The body surrounds these fibers with tissues called fibroids. When these fibroids increase and begin to merge, the results may include cough, sputum, weight loss, and increasing breathlessness. Asbestosis patients usually die about 15 years from the onset of the disease.

Lung cancer. The asbestos worker who smokes is estimated to be 90 times as likely to get lung cancer as the smoker who has never worked with asbestos.

Mesothelioma. Mesothelioma (cancer of the pleura or chest lining surrounding the lungs) accounts for 7 to 10 percent of the deaths among asbestos workers. It is inoperable and invariably fatal. Most cases of mesothelioma occur when workers are exposed to crocidolite fibers, which are fine and straight. The disease has also been reported in those with very little exposure to crocidolite fibers, such as spouses of asbestos workers and people living near asbestos plants.

Other cancers. Asbestos workers have a higher than average rate of other cancers, particularly of the esophagus, stomach, and intestines. Asbestos-contaminated mucus, cleared from the lungs and swallowed, is thought to be to blame. In recent years, the number of asbestos-related diseases has been increasing. Much tighter controls on all uses of asbestos are clearly needed as well as the use of substitute materials wherever possible.

Diagnosis

Chest x-rays and tests of pulmonary function are used to diagnose asbestos-related lung disease.

Treatment

There is no treatment for these diseases. They are invariably

Other Dust-Related Conditions

Many other dusts may accumulate in workers' lungs. At this p
most are not regarded as being disease-producing. But a number,
as aluminum, beryllium, carbon black, fiberglass, fuller's earth,
olin, mica, talc, and tungsten carbide, have recognized adverse eff
on lung health.

Some workers may be exposed to a variety of dusts; their works
may include several different types of dust-producing materials. Ot
workers change industries and inhale first one kind of dust, t
another. Pneumoconiosis caused by a mixture of dusts can be d
cult to diagnose. As a general rule, the amount of fibrosis presen
dependent on how much silica has been inhaled.

Safe Use of Chrysotile Asbestos

The Asbestos Family Fibers

Asbestos is a commercial term given to 6 naturally occurring m
erals that are incombustible and separable into filaments: chrysoti
amosite, crocidolite, anthophyllite, tremolite and actinolite. Only t
first three have wide-spread commercial use. Chrysotile is a memb
of the serpentine group of minerals; crocidolite, amosite and the ot
ers belong to the amphibole group.

Chrysotile, or white asbestos, currently accounts for more than 98
of world asbestos consumption. Its fibers are characterized by high te
sile strength, resistance to alkalis, high flexibility and good spinnab
ity.

In some countries, and for some special applications, the amphi
oles continue to be used. Crocidolite or blue asbestos is the stronge
of the asbestos fibers. It has high tensile strength and acid resistanc
Amosite or brown asbestos, is highly resistant to heat and quite flexibl
but may be susceptible to strong acids and alkalis. It has less tensi
strength than chrysotile or crocidolite and has only fair spinnabilit

Other Natural and Man-Made Fibers

Chrysotile asbestos is but one of many natural and man-made f
bers. Other naturally occurring mineral fibers include wollastonit

and attapulgite. Man-made mineral fibers include glass, rock and slag wool, refractory ceramic fibers, whiskers made of silicon carbide. Important organic fibers of interest are the para-aramids and poly-acrylicnitrate fibers.

Use of Fibers and Products

Chrysotile asbestos is found in a wide range of practical applications, including:

- as a reinforcing agent in the asbestos-cement industry, whose products include pipe, shingles and sheets
- as a fire retardant in textiles and paper products
- as a friction product in brakes and clutch linings
- as an agent to improve wear in vinyl floor tiles
- as a cohesive agent in asphalt surfaced roadways
- as a filler in resins, plastics, caulking and sealants
- as a resisting agent to acids and alkalis and battery boxes, packings, acid pumps, valves and gaskets
- as a filtering material in the chemical, drug and food industries

Chrysotile asbestos was also used as an insulation material in various fire resistant, thermal and acoustic insulation applications, including pipe and boiler lagging. These applications of chrysotile asbestos are no longer allowed in most countries of the world today, because of the risk to workers during installation and removal.

Man-made fibers are widely used in insulation applications, which represent over 80% of current day uses. However, they also have a wide variety of applications in friction products, textiles, acoustic, ceiling tiles, high efficiency filtration, etc.

Asbestos-Related Diseases

For many years, dust concentrations of up to 200 f/cc could be found in certain asbestos industry sectors, particularly those involving the use of friable (spray-on) applications. In many workplace environments, dust clouds were so thick that it was difficult for workers to see each other even at short distances. Construction and maintenance workers were subject to high intermittent exposure on work sites. This resulted in a number of asbestos-related diseases among workers.

Evidence regarding the association of asbestos exposure to other various diseases is unclear, particularly in the case of laryngeal cancer and ovarian cancer. In the case of gastrointestinal cancer, laboratory experiments have failed to produce gastrointestinal tumors in animals exposed to asbestos. In addition, epidemiological studies conducted to date provide little convincing evidence of an association between asbestos in public water supplies and cancer. Therefore there is broad scientific consensus that asbestos does not present a significant risk of cancer by the route of ingestion.

Smoking and Asbestos

The greatest cause of lung cancer is undoubtedly smoking tobacco. However, lung cancer also occurs among asbestos workers exposed to high levels of dust. This risk is significantly increased if the asbestos worker also smokes.

Many studies have shown a synergism of action between asbestos exposure and smoking. Therefore, all asbestos workers should refrain from smoking on the work site and be encouraged to stop smoking altogether. While there is still some controversy, it is believed by many scientists that asbestosis is a necessary precondition for the development of lung cancer associated with asbestos.

The Three Ds of Fiber-Related Diseases

The 1990s have seen significant advances in the understanding of mechanisms of fiber-induced disease. Today it is known that the risk of fiber related disease is determined by essentially 3 factors:

- dose—the quantity of dust inhaled over time

- dimension—whether a material generates respirable dust; that is dust that contains fibers which are longer than 5 microns in length and less than 3 microns in diameter with an aspect ratio greater than 3 to 1

- durability—or biopersistence of such dust in the human lung

In general, long, thin, durable fibers are the most hazardous to health. Fibers shorter than 5 microns in length are not considered to present a health risk because of the ability of the body's natural defense mechanisms to deal effectively with contaminants of this size and nature.

Based on both animal and human studies, all forms of asbestos have been classified as Class I "known human carcinogens" by the

International Agency for Research on Cancer. However, there is also a clear international scientific consensus that chrysotile is less hazardous than the amphibole varieties of asbestos. Not only is chrysotile a less dusty material because of its physical properties, it also has a tendency to break down and dissolve in body fluid and thus is more easily cleared from the lungs by natural defense mechanisms.

Amphibole forms, on the other hand, are more dusty materials as well as more durable and persist in the lung once inhaled. The increased potency of amphibole forms of asbestos to chrysotile is corroborated by both animal and human studies.

Chrysotile Asbestos and Mesothelioma

Mesothelioma is a rare cancer of the membrane lining of the chest or abdominal cavities. The tumor typically develops 30 to 45 years after first exposure, and most often to blue or brown asbestos. For many years it was thought that exposure to asbestos was the sole cause of mesothelioma in man. However, extensive scientific reviews of this disease have concluded that 35 % of the known cases have nothing to do with asbestos exposure. Human and animal studies show that causes or suspected causes of mesothelioma also include exposure to erionite, ionizing radiation, and various chemical substances. It is also strongly suspected that the presence of tremolite fibers in some of the chrysotile asbestos deposits mined in the 50s and 60s may have been the cause of the few cases of mesothelioma among asbestos miners.

Based on a review of the scientific literature and close scrutiny of mesothelioma cases, there is broad consensus that mesothelioma is most likely to result from crocidolite exposure; it has a strong association with amosite exposure; and, a very weak, if any, association with chrysotile exposure.

Is There a Threshold Level for Chrysotile Asbestos?

There is ample human and animal evidence that at high and prolonged levels of exposure, chrysotile asbestos can cause disease. The question that remains to be answered is whether or not there exists a threshold level of exposure below which there is no risk of disease.

In the case of asbestosis, there is broad consensus that a threshold level of exposure exists for chrysotile. Indeed, the Ontario Royal Commission on Asbestos (ORCA) reached the following conclusion "In our judgment, asbestosis will not occur in workers exposed to the regulated levels of occupational exposure now in force in Ontario (e.g. 1.0 f/cc on an 8-hour time-weighted average)."

In the case of lung cancer, such broad consensus has not yet been reached, although there is now mounting human evidence pointing to the existence of a threshold. For example, a small number of epidemiological studies of workers exposed only to low levels of chrysotile have concluded that there was no statistically significant excess mortality resulting from chrysotile asbestos exposure.

Because of the small number of studies involving exposure to chrysotile only, it is difficult to draw firm conclusions. However, in reviewing this and other data, a group of experts convened by the World Health Organization (WHO) in April 1989, reached the conclusion that a level of control for chrysotile asbestos can be achieved, at which the lifetime risks of lung cancer and mesothelioma are very small. Subsequently, the Oxford meeting recommended an exposure limit of 1.0 f/cc or below for chrysotile. It was also recommended that the use of crocidolite and amosite be banned as soon as possible.

Therefore, despite mounting evidence, there is not as yet broad scientific consensus of a threshold level of exposure for chrysotile asbestos. What is clear is that, at present levels of occupational exposure, if there are risks, they are exceedingly small.

Occupational Risks

The risks to workers at recommended exposure levels of 1.0 f/cc have been estimated by a number of scientific bodies. For example, the ORCA Commission estimated that there would be a 1 in 4 chance of 1 premature death amongst the 1200 workers engaged in chrysotile asbestos product manufacturing (excluding textiles)—a risk level equivalent to that faced by workers in general manufacturing in Ontario.

Similar conclusions were reached by a group of experts convened by the WHO at Oxford, England, in April 1989. In short, WHO predicted lifetime risks under a 1.0 f/cc chrysotile standard for non-smokers for both mesothelioma and lung cancer would be approximately 2 in 40,000 or 0.05 in 1,000.

The risk estimates contained in both the ORCA and WHO Oxford reports were based on a linear dose-response curve. However, a recent paper by Liddell concludes that at low levels of exposure for chrysotile asbestos, the dose-response curve is more likely to be sublinear thus rendering risk estimates based on a linear dose-response curve to be seriously overstated.

The risk to workers exposed to chrysotile asbestos at present occupational exposure levels is therefore extremely low, if indeed one exists at all. Very few industrial sectors can offer such a safe working environment. This underscores the point that a well controlled chrysotile asbestos product industry can be a model for most other industrial sectors.

Dust Control Measures: A General Overview

Introduction

The general principles of dust control apply to the manufacture of asbestos-cement pipes and sheets, friction products (such as car brake linings), sealants, gaskets, coatings, textiles and to the installation and repair of these products. The methods of dust control described in this chapter are simple, effective and are readily available or can be made locally.

The reason it is necessary to control asbestos dust is because long term exposure to high concentrations can cause occupational diseases amongst workers. The inhalable dust of concern is not visible to the human eye. There are many locations in asbestos using factories where asbestos dust could be generated and released into the air. Controls are needed to prevent this from happening. This section is intended to provide guidance as to when controls are needed and what controls are available. Work practices and ventilation installations are described, along with methods for using them efficiently. Information concerning low level airborne concentrations which can result from an effective dust control program is also provided.

Good control measures should include:

- control at the source
- engineering controls
- work practices
- housekeeping
- personal protective equipment

Control at the Source

Control of dust should be achieved as near the source as possible. This increases the efficiency of the control process, minimizes costs and prevents the spread of dust into adjacent areas. The process of control must prevent emissions to the environment in order that a localized hazard in the factory is not converted into an environmental hazard. Therefore, if enclosure of the source is possible, this would be the first step to be taken.

Engineering Controls

Good engineering controls should include the following equipment:

- dust hoods
- ductwork

- dust collector and fan
- make up air

Proper engineering of each one of these components is essential. Among the different operations where industrial ventilation will be used are debagging, mixing, weighing, cutting, grinding, etc.

A source of make up air or air to replace that exhausted through the hood must always be provided. The hood encloses the operation to the extent possible and provides a face velocity of air into the hood. As an example, for manual debagging, bags must be cut, emptied and disposed of inside a hood fitted with an exhaust connection. Cutting bags in half and handling empty bags outside the hood should be avoided.

Enclosure is practical when the operator does not need to have contact with the operation. In asbestos-cement plants a number of machine operations, such as the interior machining of couplings, can be enclosed. Enclosure is more common for the processing of smaller pieces but it is also used on larger equipment like belt conveyors and carding machines.

It is important that all parts of the enclosure should be at a lower pressure than the associated worker's area. This may be achieved with a small amount of suction air. This air, after passing through the entrance to the hood, is exhausted through a series of proper size ducts to an air cleaner which is usually an industrial cloth filter or "bag house". The ducting may be joined with any number of other hoods and cleaning systems and may have pre-cleaning cyclones or settling chambers along the ducting. Good practice requires that the ducting have no blast gates or dampers, that the velocity be sufficiently high everywhere that the dust not fall out and plug the ducting and that the corners and bends of the ducting be designed so as to minimize wear and erosion. The bag house must be sized to handle the quantity of air flow being exhausted through the hoods. The clean air passes through the suction fan and is exhausted to the outside. If consideration is to be given to environmental concerns, a dust monitor can be placed at this point. However, this dust monitor is not considered an accurate measurement of asbestos dust but rather of the relative changes in total dust concentrations over time. (Permissible concentration of respirable dust in recirculated air is 0.1 mg/m3). In modern practice the bag filter is the universally approved method of removing asbestos dust from air. Cotton is the most efficient filter fabric for asbestos dust collection.

The environment can be well controlled at all work places provided good preventive maintenance on all dust control equipment is performed and that inspections are made on a regular basis.

Preventive Maintenance

Assuming that care has been taken to ensure that the selected equipment has been designed to allow easy maintenance, a proper preventive maintenance schedule should be introduced to keep the equipment in good order. Air moving and cleaning devices are hardworking and need good preventive maintenance. There are many examples of systems that have been satisfactorily installed, only to become inefficient soon afterwards due to lack of care.

To ensure a safe working environment, maintenance work of dust control equipment should be given priority over maintenance of the manufacturing machinery, equipment and process itself. Preventive maintenance should include the following:

Ductwork System

- proper adjustment or replacement of flexible connections between hoods and ductwork or between ductwork and fans

- removal of any accumulation which could create blockages and dusty conditions at different operations

- taking a static pressure reading at each dust hood and comparing it with the original reading. It indicates immediately if air flow-rate is what it should be at each hood.

- stop any water vapor leaking into the negative or suction side of the exhaust system before it causes accumulations of dust to solidify and to create blockages

Dust Collector

If not initiated automatically, cleaning of filter bags must be made on a regular basis. This is necessary in order to maintain the resistance of the bags within the range for which they have been designed. In so doing, proper air flow within the dust collection system as a whole will be maintained.

The resistance of the bags must be taken and recorded on a regular basis. In the short term, it will indicate whether bag cleaning is necessary. On the long term, it will show whether bags are blinding or if other problems occur. Bag life will vary widely from one application to another. However, bags should be replaced before they blind too much or before they start breaking on a regular basis. This is why it is important to record the date and the location of the bags being replaced.

Any accumulation of dust in the hopper of the dust collector should be cleaned. If cyclone collectors and fabric-type dust collectors are equipped with rotary air-locks, the wiper seals of these air-locks must be replaced before they start leaking abnormally. If this is not done, there would be re-entrainment of dust inside the collector and blinding of the bags.

Special care should also be given to mechanical parts that require lubrication, such as bearings. Water should be flushed from compressed air supply dryers on a regular basis in order to prevent the introduction of water into the filter bags.

Fans

If the system is designed to permit the dust to pass through the fan prior to reaching the dust collector, the fan wheel or lining must be replaced before the wheel breaks or before wear holes begin to show on fan casings. Bearings must be lubricated according to manufacturer's specifications. If the fan is belt driven, belt tension must be checked and adjusted regularly. The belt must be replaced before breakage.

Inspections

A procedure should be laid down for the regular inspection and testing of the complete installation. Of course, this is over and above the daily inspection which should be conducted by the operator and by the supervisor in order to detect leaks, breakages, holes in ductwork, etc. Several relatively simple techniques can be used.

Since the small particles produced by industrial processes cannot be seen by the naked eye, inspection can be difficult without the help of special lighting techniques to make the dust cloud visible. The Tyndall Beam backlighting technique highlights dust released into the atmosphere which can then be recorded by normal photographs if desired.

Smoke Capsules or Puffer Tube is another technique. When used, they produce a white or yellow smoke that can be used to observe flow patterns around an exhaust aperture. They may also be used to detect leaks in sealed hoods, ducting or filter units.

As mentioned previously, hood static pressure readings can give a very good estimate of the amount of air flowing at each hood. However, if more precise results are required, many instruments can be used, i.e. pilot tube and manometer, rotating vane anemometer, velometer, hot wire anemometer, etc. The monitoring of workplace ambient concentrations and measurements of personal exposure to fibers, which is also a part of environmental control, is explained in detail in the chapter named "Monitoring of Fibers."

Wet Methods and Processes

There are very few viable alternatives to exhaust ventilation, except the use of water in specific instances. Generally, this consists of the application of a fine spray directed at the source of dust, such as a cutting tool or saw, drilling, material deposited on the floor, etc. The spray must be gentle or asbestos is likely to be distributed together with very small water droplets. Also, care must be taken to collect and properly dispose of the wetted material and/or water containing the material. Since this is usually to be carried out by a worker rather than through the use of a piece of equipment, it is essential that the workers have the know-how and tools to perform these tasks. If not, training should be provided.

Wet processing is extremely effective in reducing the possibility of dust generation. Processes which may be wetted typically have much lower dust levels than processes that must be run entirely dry.

Dust in an asbestos-cement plant, from the asbestos-cement vat to the curing tanks, can be controlled by keeping the product, equipment and floor area wet at all times. If proper tools and wet spraying are used in conjunction with immediate clean-up of debris, the finishing section of an asbestos-cement plant can also be kept clean.

Of course, the wetting procedure requires some attention to electrical safety and other operational problems associated with water in the presence of lathes, drills, saws, etc. Many plants spray water over machining processes such as drilling and lathe cutting. This process usually produces significant reductions in fiber levels.

Due to the water droplets which frequently remain in the air during spraying, wetting in the presence of local exhaust ventilation systems is not recommended. The water spray will enter the exhaust ventilation system and produce a slurry with the asbestos, cement and other additives. When hardened, this slurry can contaminate the ventilation ducting and destroy the effectiveness of the bags in the baghouse (an industrial filter which cleans the dust from the air).

A possible problem with floor spraying is that over time, asbestos and water paste can collect in floor cracks, forming a hard, cement-like substance. If allowed to dry out, this material can be a minor source of dust when walked on. The solution is to perform complete sluicing operations during floor cleaning. The water used for wetting purposes may be incorporated into the process if it is appropriate for asbestos-cement application. Otherwise, it may be directed to settling tanks where the solids can settle before the slurry is removed.

For the disposal of bag house waste or other operations where large quantities of asbestos chips and powder are present, wetting can be made significantly more effective by the use of wetting agents. The two most common agents are ordinary liquid detergents or ethylene glycol added to water in the proportion of approximately 1 to 1,000. These agents considerably increase the dust suppression capacity of the water and prevent emissions from the surface of disposal sites. However, wetting is not applicable everywhere.

Work Practices

The best industrial ventilation system or any other type of well engineered system designed to improve the working environment and reduce the amount of dust generated can be easily defeated by bad work practices of the operators or employees. Each person is different by nature, experience, intelligence, attitude, etc. The result of personal dust samples carried out on two employees working side-by-side, handling the same product on the same type of machine can be extremely different because of the way they work. It is very important when a dust control program is initiated in a factory that, at the same time, work practices of each employee be analyzed. There is no easy method by which the work habits of all employees can be quickly changed. Each one has to be dealt with so that within a reasonable time he begins to show improvement. The key to making employees "dust conscious" is information and training.

The work practices necessary in all parts of the plant are straightforward. These work practices include wetting where such a process is applicable, clean-up of any waste generated during manufacturing, vacuuming or wet removal of all chips and small pieces throughout the plant and enforcement of straightforward regulations such as forbidding dry sweeping and the use of compressed air for cleaning purposes. Needless to say, good work practices are as important as all other efforts made in order to provide a dust-free working environment.

Housekeeping

Housekeeping is unquestionably the most important of all dust control methods. Simply cleaning-up all possible emission sources as quickly as possible is the most effective dust suppression technique. Such practices as vacuuming and wet floor cleaning not only prevent high dust levels, they also improve already clean, efficiently controlled asbestos-using environments. By introducing these simple housekeeping techniques, a factory can reduce dust levels by half or even three-quarters. Good housekeeping and work practices require workers' time. Because they are labor intensive rather than capital intensive, they can be used in plants working at any level of technology.

As in all other issues of health and safety at work, good housekeeping will only be achieved if both management and workers are committed to it. It is important that workers' representatives be involved in the discussions about housekeeping problems and possible solutions.

Storage, Transportation, Handling of Bags

Asbestos is usually delivered in 50-kilogram, or less, pressure-packed plastic or paper bags, which are combined into 1-ton lots of 20 bags and placed on wooden pallets. The bags are covered by shrink or stretch-wrapped plastic for extra protection during shipping and warehousing. Pallets are shipped to the asbestos-using plants in containers, by truck, rail or ship. They are then unloaded (and removed from the containers) by forklift truck, hoist, crane, hand, etc., and stored in a warehouse which is either part of the plant or located immediately adjacent to it.

Problems with respect to dust control arise immediately upon arrival of the asbestos fiber shipment because there are bags that may be damaged in some way. This results in fiber being spilled on the floor of the truck, railroad car, vessel or inside the container. The spill should be removed by vacuuming using a HEPA (High Efficiency Particulate Air) vacuum cleaner. After taping the broken or cut bags, the pallets can be unloaded and transported to the warehouse.

It should be kept in mind that the outside of unbroken bags in the vicinity of the spill are often contaminated with fibers that must also be removed by vacuuming before the pallets are moved to the warehouse. This is most conveniently done by moving the contaminated bags to a special clean-up building adjacent to the unloading site. If contaminated bags are moved into the main storage building or into the plant, contamination is usually the result.

If the spill is a major one, the unloading crew must wear protective clothing as well as respiratory protection. Special HEPA vacuum equipment may be needed if the normal vacuum system associated with the plant cannot be used. The purpose of the special equipment is to transfer the spilled fiber into bags to be properly disposed of. In case of any spill, the truck, container, etc., used to ship the asbestos, should be cleaned prior to leaving the plant site.

If bags are damaged while stored in the warehouse, severe contamination will occur. Corrective measures are difficult because many areas in the warehouse cannot be reached. Even under the best circumstances, a well managed warehouse should be cleaned regularly using appropriate HEPA vacuum equipment.

Prevention of Spillage / Spread of Contamination

Too often housekeeping problems are tackled from the wrong end. The response to a process which causes asbestos to spread over the floor, workbench, etc., is normally to simply introduce regular cleaning to remove the spillage. Although this is necessary, the real effort should be put into finding and resolving the cause of the problem. Additional protection for the worker may be necessary during this period.

Think about the process. It may be possible to prevent the spillage by a change in work method, a redesign of the plant or even a change of process. It will be difficult to change long established work practices. Involvement and cooperation of the workforce is essential and retraining of operators will be needed. This provides a strategy for tackling housekeeping problems. When spillage or spread of asbestos is found, act along the following lines:

Investigate. Examine the process in detail to find the cause of the spillage/spread. Remember that the problem may be at an earlier operation. The operator should be involved as he or she may be aware of the cause. Additional cleaning should be introduced to cope with the problem in the meantime.

Eliminate or reduce spillage. Once the cause or causes are known every effort should be made to eliminate, or if this is not possible, reduce the spillage. This can be done by:

- changing the process;

- changing the working method; or

- providing improved containment around the process. If possible the waste collected should be automatically removed.

Make cleaning easier. If it is not possible to prevent spillage, steps should be taken to make cleaning easier. This could range from providing trays or bins to collect the spillage to making the floor below the process smooth and eliminating ledges, etc.

Successful prevention usually needs a combination of both improved plant design and working method. However, designers should make the plant suit the way people work and move rather than expect them to adapt their working methods to cope with a poorly designed machine. Even when a process is partly automated, careless or unsatisfactory work practices will often result in spillage or spread of contamination. It will help employees and supervisors if correct methods of working are laid down in written job procedures or systems of work.

Cleaning Techniques and Procedures

There are two vital points if cleaning is to be done well and as safely as possible. They are:

- The cleaning method should be dustless (in other words no asbestos dust should escape into the air either from the cleaning action or from the cleaning equipment).

- The cleaning should be done often enough and at the appropriate time.

In order to achieve this, a combination of suitable and sufficient equipment, good procedure, adequate supervision and monitoring is needed.

The traditional method of cleaning was with a brush or broom. But this creates a dust cloud even if the brush is damp, or oiled, or water is sprinkled on the material to be swept up. This happens because dust rapidly builds up on the brush and it becomes effectively dry again. Brushing or sweeping is NOT a dustless cleaning method and should not be used.

Equipment and Techniques

There are different types of equipment which can achieve dustless cleaning if they are used correctly and properly maintained. They are

70

listed below in order of preference, with an indication of the advantages and disadvantages of each one.

Fixed vacuum installations. Such an installation consists of a central source of suction and dust collection connected to a network of fixed pipes which have connection points for cleaning hoses and attachments in all parts of the building served. Proper design and installation is essential and should only be tackled by qualified contractors.

As with all other cleaning systems, it is important that it is readily available for use in every area which it serves. At the time of planning a system, it is necessary to balance the convenience of having numerous connection points against the additional cost of each extra point. However, the problems which will arise from an under-designed system suggest that it is better to have too many connection points rather than too few.

Cleaning should be organized to prevent too many points being used at the same time. If too many are used together they will not work effectively because the suction will be too low.

The advantages and disadvantages of fixed vacuum cleaning installations can be summarized as follows:

Advantages

- relatively little maintenance
- centralized collection of waste
- reasonable running costs
- easy operation

Disadvantages

- high initial costs
- failure can cause relatively serious problems (all connections out of action)
- still need back-up by portable systems

Portable vacuum cleaning equipment. This type of equipment is self-contained having its own suction fan, filter unit and dust collection bag. There must be enough of them so that they are readily available in all areas that require service. They also need to be sufficiently portable to allow cleaning of difficult and restricted spaces.

The number will depend to some extent on the way cleaning is organized.

Advantages

- lower capital cost
- more versatile and flexible

Disadvantages

- continual maintenance
- potential hygiene problems during dust bag changing
- trailing electric cables

Mobile floor cleaners. This type of equipment usually includes a powerful suction and filtration unit connected to a floor cleaning attachment. Some types also have a rotary brush. Not all types of floor cleaners will be capable of dustless cleaning or will have an adequate standard of filtration. Therefore careful assessment is needed when selecting such equipment for use in asbestos contaminated areas.

Despite these reservations, such equipment may be the only practical way of cleaning large floor areas and gangways in a reasonable time. They should NOT, however, be used as an alternative to portable vacuum cleaners, for other types of cleaning.

Advantages

- clean large areas quickly

Disadvantages

- some types may not be dustless
- doubtful filtration standard
- emptying waste collection bins/trays is dusty and will require the use of protective equipment

Other techniques. Wet cleaning techniques can be dustless, providing that they are genuinely "wet" and not just "damp." The waste to be cleaned up must be thoroughly wetted and kept wet until it is in a sealed container. The wet waste should be scraped into a collection tray or bin. Alternatively, wet waste can be washed or sucked into a collection sump and disposed of as liquid waste by a specialist contractor.

Asbestos Waste

Waste collected during cleaning should be put into a suitable container such as a heavy duty plastic sack. The container should be closed and sealed and should be labeled "Asbestos Waste." The label should also indicate the type of asbestos. The local waste disposal authority should be consulted for advice on correct methods of disposal.

Procedure

Having ensured that the right equipment and techniques are available for dustless cleaning, it is essential that they are properly used and maintained. For this to happen employees must know what they have to do and how to do it. Supervisors/managers must monitor how well it is done. It will usually help if the procedures are laid down as a written system of work. This should deal with responsibilities for cleaning, maintenance of equipment and monitoring in general terms. The detail of how and when to clean particular areas can be given in separate cleaning schedules.

Responsibility for Cleaning

The responsibility can be placed on individual employees, a specialist employee (or team) or a combination of these. One system cannot be said to be better than the others; rather, the allocation of employees to cleaning duties needs to be matched to the equipment and techniques provided. The most important point is that the responsibility should be clearly laid down in written procedures and schedules.

Cleaning Schedules

Cleaning schedules should be prepared for all areas, machines, etc. Therefore, every effort should be made when planning cleaning procedures to stagger the cleaning times throughout the premises. There are advantages for both cleaners and supervisors if cleaning schedules are displayed at the machine in the area to which they relate.

Personal Protective Devices

In many situations, particularly those dealing with maintenance, repair, and equipment failures, it is not possible to ensure low dust levels at all times in the plant environment. As a result, respirators and special clothing may occasionally be required. Use of respirators should be regarded as a temporary or emergency measure only and not as an alternative to other control procedures. The more common types of respirators can be uncomfortable for extended periods. In fact, workers frequently refuse to wear them except for short periods.

For emissions which are above the recommended permissible exposure limit value, appropriate respirators fitted with replaceable filters are necessary. Workers should be informed of when and why a respirator must be used, and the importance of using it continuously and properly. The correct procedures for the use and verification of protective equipment should be demonstrated.

Chapter 6

Occupational Asthma and Chronic Obstructive Pulmonary Disease

Chapter Contents

Section 6.1

Occupational Asthma: Key Information

From "Occupational Asthma: A Guide," an undated website produced
by The Asthma Foundation of Western Australia (WA) and WorkSafe WA,
www.asthmawa.asn.au/occasthma
Reprinted with permission.

What Is Occupational Asthma (OA)?

Damage may occur to your lungs if you breathe in dusts, vapors, mists or particulates when at work. Breathing in irritants at work may lead to a lung disease known as "occupational asthma."

When a person suffers from occupational asthma they may:

- feel tightness in their chest;
- wheeze;
- cough; and/or
- have difficulty in breathing.

Someone who has occupational asthma may develop to a stage that there is a high risk of serious problems, even death.

Could I Get Occupational Asthma?

You may be at risk if:

- you work in an area where you are exposed to irritants;
- you have members of your family with asthma;
- you have had asthma or allergies in the past; or
- you smoke.

Have I Got Occupational Asthma?

Detecting occupational asthma can be difficult as the symptoms can occur 4–24 hours after exposure to the irritant (so symptoms can occur either at work or after work). In some cases this has led people to believe that their asthma is caused by other triggers. If a worker's asthma symptoms improve while away from work, especially when on holidays or weekends, then possible work-related causes of the asthma need to be considered.

If you think you have occupational asthma you should first tell your doctor. Your doctor will be able to check your lungs and will ask you some questions about your work.

Could My Workplace Harm My Lungs?

There are a number of workplace hazards that may harm your lungs. These may be man-made (e.g. chemicals) or natural (e.g. flour, dust etc.). If there are chemicals used in your workplace, find out what chemicals are being used. Your employer should be able to supply [information about] every chemical used in the workplace. The Asthma Foundation has a list of many chemicals that may cause occupational asthma—find out if the chemicals used in your workplace are on this list. Know about the chemicals used at your workplace and reduce your exposure.

When trying to identify breathing hazards (irritants) there are some simple methods you can use.

Tips for Recognizing Breathing Hazards

Eye irritation. If your eyes are itchy or stinging there is a good chance that there is something in the air causing it.

Odors. Caution—you can't always smell what is making your lungs react, but smelling chemicals, dusts, fumes or particulates is a good indication that there may be something harmful in the air.

Visible dust clouds or fumes. This often means your workplace is poorly ventilated.

Chemical spills can often cause injuries and illness. Chemicals should be stored safely and your employer should have a Material Safety Data Sheet (MSDS) for each chemical used in the workplace. The MSDS includes first aid information for use in case of an emergency. It may be necessary to wear protective clothing (possibly including a face mask), when cleaning up a workplace chemical spill.

What Should I Do If I Think I Am at Risk?

If there is a problem with you and your fellow workers breathing irritants, your safety and health representative or employer should be told. In many cases there are easy methods to reduce any problems with air quality at work.

You can also seek advice from your union or the government department in your state that is responsible for occupational safety and health.

Can I Prevent Occupational Asthma?

To reduce the likelihood of damaging your lungs you can do the following:

- avoid long exposure
- follow safety rules
- practice good personal habits, i.e. washing up
- keep your workplace clean
- ensure good ventilation
- use respiratory protection—e.g. masks
- don't smoke
- report symptoms and signs of danger

For further information on occupational asthma contact your doctor, safety and health representative or the Asthma Foundation in your state.

Summary

- Despite vastly improved treatments over the past 10 to 15 years, asthma has increased seriously in both incidence and severity. Mortality rates have almost doubled in Western Australia.

- Many and varied air pollutants—a phenomena of modern industrialized societies—have been identified as airway irritants and allergens capable of causing asthma.

- A recent survey has indicated that 40% of American physicians believe that air pollutants are the leading cause of an increasing asthma problem.

- Workplace or occupation-related causes arising from regular contact with air pollutants might induce asthma little by little over time, unrecognized and unsuspected.

- "Late onset" asthma is increasing. With no obvious changes in the patient's circumstances it is often unexplained and the workplace not considered.

- Modern highly effective asthma treatments, particularly symptom relieving medications, may mask a slowly progressing deterioration in asthma.

- Not all workers exposed to workplace irritants and allergens will develop asthma. Factors such as smoking, past history of asthma, asthma in the family, low physical fitness and the accumulative effects of other allergens or respiratory infections may make an individual more susceptible to asthma when exposed to workplace allergens or irritants.

- Responsibility for the recognition and diagnosis of workplace-induced asthma initially must rest heavily with the individual.

- Patients and doctors need a high index of suspicion of possible occupational causes, particularly when symptoms tend to ease and the condition improve over weekends and holidays.

Section 6.2

What Is Occupational Asthma?

From "Occupational Asthma: A Guide," an undated website produced
by The Asthma Foundation of Western Australia (WA) and WorkSafe WA,
www.asthmawa.asn.au/occasthma
Reprinted with permission.

Asthma is described as a disease that causes narrowing of the airways and constricted breathing. The asthma sufferer has a bronchial system that is abnormally sensitive and which reacts to certain stimuli causing serious breathing difficulty.

The usual symptoms of asthma include wheezing, shortness of breath, tightness in the chest etc., ranging in severity to a life threatening condition.

Occupational asthma is asthma caused by employees being exposed to substances in the workplace (chemicals, vapors, dust etc.) which are, or become, progressively offensive to his or her airways system.

Who May Develop Occupational Asthma?

Obviously enough, long-term asthma sufferers (those who have asthma which is induced by infection, allergy or exertion) are prime targets for work-related asthma.

Workers who have a history of asthma, perhaps from childhood, and those who have minimized asthma attacks through successful treatment and lifestyle management, are most susceptible to a reoccurrence of asthma through an offensive working environment.

Occupational asthma, however, given heavy or long term exposure to an offending agent can develop in people who have no previous personal or family history of asthma or allergy.

Prevention and Control

Recognition

Typically, occupational lung disease is slow to appear, sometimes taking years of regular contact with the responsible allergen or irritant before concerning symptoms appear.

The progress of work-related asthma is rarely obvious to the patient or to the doctor. To some extent, this is because it is only in recent years that work environments have been suspected, let alone identified and confirmed, as being potential sources of irritants that can cause asthma.

Diagnosis is made also difficult because "workplace-induced" asthma symptoms may occur between 4 and 24 hours after exposure, often obscuring obvious cause-and-effect associations.

Symptoms may be mistakenly accepted as resulting from other common allergens e.g. pollens, house dust, certain foodstuffs etc. In some allergic patients, isolating provoking factors can be difficult, especially if the work environment has not been previously suspected.

It is important that the patient's occupation is fully considered as a possible source of either causing lung disease or exacerbating an existent airway sensitivity. It is possible that a newly acquired allergy to animals or pollens or a greater susceptibility to chest infections for example may have its origin in the patient's exposure to a chemical at his workplace.

If the patient's condition tends to improve over weekends, or when the patient is away on holidays, then a possible occupational cause for the asthma should be seriously considered.

Prevalence of Occupational Asthma

Estimates of the prevalence of occupational lung disease are extremely difficult. It has been suggested that up to 15% of all asthma cases are at least partly work-related. In different communities the incidence of occupational asthma will depend primarily on the nature of industries in the area. In some industries up to 50% of all long-term workers have been found to suffer from work-related asthma.

With the great diversification of industry, ever changing technology and the multiple uses of chemicals and materials in many different processes, it is nearly impossible to tabulate at any time all those working environments which may present a particular hazard to workers.

Many, however, have been identified in recent years. We have listed some of the substances known to cause occupational asthma elsewhere and we have identified some of the possible industries and occupations where these substances are found.

Section 6.3

Risk Factors

From "Occupational Asthma: A Guide," an undated website produced
by The Asthma Foundation of Western Australia (WA) and WorkSafe WA,
www.asthmawa.asn.au/occasthma
Reprinted with permission.

Workplace Dangers and Asthma

Something in the Air?

Over 400 airborne pollutants, mostly man-made, have been identified as asthmagenic (i.e. capable of inducing asthma). There are lit-
erally hundreds of processes, products and wastes which can produce
potentially dangerous air contaminants that have been introduced
into the relatively closed spaces and surrounding environments of
modern industries, factories, workshops, warehouses, shops, and offices as a result of new technologies.

These substances are present as powders, pastes, gases, liquids, foams
or in solid form and may seem totally innocent. Many however, "give off"
air pollutants that can be airborne asthma causing agents.

In the course of a day at work, we typically breathe in perhaps 6 or 8
cubic meters of air from our workspace. This air will carry into our bronchial system the fumes, smokes, odors, vapors, and dusts of the environment. Sometimes these pollutants will "catch" in the airways, "smart"
the eyes, or taste unpleasant. Others will sting or otherwise irritate tissue in eyes, nose and mouth giving some warning of danger. Yet others
will be received into the lungs relatively unnoticed and unsuspected.

Our airways are, by nature, well-equipped to handle the normal
types and levels of foreign matter in the air we breathe. In abnormal
circumstances they simply cannot cope with concentrated or long-term
exposure to irritating substances which can overcome the body's natural cleaning process.

Substance categories from which numerous asthma allergies and
irritants are recognized:

- acid anhydrides
- adhesives

- amines
- arthropods
- birds
- chemicals
- crustaceans
- disinfectants
- drugs
- dyes
- enzymes
- fish, corals and sponges
- fuels and explosives
- jointing agents
- land animals
- metals
- micro-organisms
- plants
- plastics
- solvents
- spices
- storage mites
- timbers and wood products

Some Occupations in Which Asthmagenic Substances May Be Encountered

- acid workers
- bakers
- beekeepers
- blast furnace operators
- boiler cleaners
- brewery workers
- cabinet makers
- carpenters
- cement manufacturers
- chemical plant workers
- chicken pluckers
- chromium platers
- concrete workers
- cork workers
- cotton workers
- cutting machine operators
- demolition workers
- drug manufacturers
- dyers
- edible oil workers
- electricians
- entomologists
- farm hands
- farriers
- fertilizer workers
- fish shop workers
- fishermen
- fitters and turners
- food handlers
- food process workers
- french polishers
- furniture makers
- furriers
- grain farmers
- grain handlers
- grinder operators
- hairdressers
- hard metals manufacturers
- honey processors
- insulation installers
- insulation manufacturers
- jewellers
- laboratory technician
- latex workers
- librarian
- market gardeners
- meat wrappers
- museum workers
- mushroom growers
- nickel platers
- nurserymen
- orchardists
- panel beaters
- pastry cooks

- pearl shell workers
- pesticide operators
- pet shop workers
- pig farmers
- plastic molders
- polyurethane foam workers
- pool cleaners
- poultry farmers
- printers
- rabbiters
- refinery workers
  (oil and metals)
- refrigeration workers
- research workers
- sander operators
- sawmillers

- scaffolders
- service station attendants
- shearers
- solderers
- spray painters
- stainless steel welders
- stockmen
- strappers
- textile workers
- timber workers
- veterinarians
- vineyard workers
- violinists
- welders
- wool store workers
- zoo workers

Section 6.4

Chronic Obstructive Pulmonary Disease

This section contains text from "Asthma and Chronic Obstructive Pulmonary Disease," National Institute of Occupational Safety and Health (NIOSH), National Occupational Research Agenda (NORA), http://www.cdc.gov/niosh/nrpulm.html, June 11, 1999, and "Chronic Obstructive Pulmonary Disease," National Institutes of Health (NIH) pamphlet, November 1993. Copyright 1993 by National Institutes of Health.

Asthma and Chronic Obstructive Pulmonary Disease— Introduction

Occupationally-related airway diseases, including asthma and chronic obstructive pulmonary disease (COPD), have emerged as having substantial public health importance. Nearly 30% of COPD and adult asthma may be attributable to occupational exposure. Occupational asthma is now the most frequent occupational respiratory disease diagnosis. More than 20 million U.S. workers are exposed to substances that can cause airway diseases. Research is needed to clarify the prevalence, risk factors, and exposure-disease relationships, to refine techniques for monitoring worker health and the job environment, and to develop effective and practical means for preventing work-related airway diseases in at-risk workers.

Importance

Asthma and chronic obstructive pulmonary disease (COPD—primarily chronic bronchitis and emphysema) are diseases of the lung airways. More than 20 million workers are potentially exposed to occupational agents capable of causing these diseases—including nearly 9 million workers occupationally exposed to known sensitizers and irritants associated with asthma. Occupational asthma is now the most frequent occupational respiratory disease diagnosis among patients visiting occupational medicine clinics.

Asthma and COPD accounted for nearly 18 million physician visits in 1985 and an estimated 800,000 hospital admissions in 1987. In 1992, asthma and COPD caused nearly 92,000 deaths in the United States, making airway diseases the fourth leading cause of death overall. Mortality from asthma and COPD is increasing annually. Estimated yearly costs for occupational asthma are approximately $400 million.

The relationship of COPD to workplace exposures is well documented in studies of several occupational agents (e.g., coal dust, grain dust, and cotton dust). Investigations of the health consequences of particulate exposure in the general environment—where exposures are at a far lower level than in the workplace—also suggest that COPD resulting from generally dusty conditions may be an important cause of preventable disease and death. Those with lung disease from other causes are especially vulnerable to occupational respiratory hazards. Although cigarettes remain the primary cause of pulmonary diseases in the United States, many occupational and environmental exposures (both by themselves or in combination with smoking) are known to cause COPD. One estimate of the proportion of COPD attributable to occupational exposure in the general population is 14%.

Research Opportunities

Disabling effects of asthma and COPD may in many cases drive a person out of a line of work or out of work completely. The machinist who becomes asthmatic from breathing droplets of cutting fluids and the nurse allergic to latex may have to relinquish their skilled professions. An agricultural worker with an obstructive lung disease may

85

become unemployable. These personal effects have serious business consequences beyond issues of medical costs and workers' compensation. Employee turnover in highly skilled professions is especially costly. Scientists associating dust exposures in specific work operations with high levels of COPD can test alternative approaches to dust suppression, evaluate the impact of providing workers with respirators, and determine the benefit of medical screening in reducing disease effects. There has been little research to evaluate the potential impact of occupational risk information on smoking among workers at risk. Research that investigates how workers become sensitized to substances causing asthma, (e.g., such as latex) may enable employers to screen for biomarkers or other early indications of risk before workers become disabled; such studies may also enable researchers to develop methods to replace or control exposures to the sensitizing agent. Development of tests to identify substances and processes that may cause asthma would have enormous benefits, enabling health scientists to work with product designers to assure the safety of new materials before they are introduced to the workplace, preventing disease before any cases occur, and avoiding the need for employers to implement additional prevention programs.

Chronic Obstructive Pulmonary Disease

What Is Chronic Obstructive Pulmonary Disease?

Chronic obstructive pulmonary disease (COPD), also called chronic obstructive lung disease, is a term that is used for two closely related diseases of the respiratory system: chronic bronchitis and emphysema. In many patients these diseases occur together, although there may be more symptoms of one than the other. Most patients with these diseases have a long history of heavy cigarette smoking.

COPD gets gradually worse over time. At first there may be only a mild shortness of breath and occasional coughing. Then a chronic cough develops with clear, colorless sputum. As the disease progresses, the cough becomes more frequent and more and more effort is needed to get air into and out of the lungs. In later stages of the disease, the heart may be affected. Eventually death occurs when the function of the lungs and heart is no longer adequate to deliver oxygen to the body's organs and tissues.

Cigarette smoking is the most important risk factor for COPD; it would probably be a minor health problem if people did not smoke. Other risk factors include age, heredity, exposure to air pollution at work and in the environment, and a history of childhood respiratory infections. Living in low socioeconomic conditions also seems to be a contributing factor.

More than 13.5 million Americans are thought to have COPD. It is the fifth leading cause of death in the United States. Between 1980 and 1990, the total death rate from COPD increased by 22 percent. In 1990, it was estimated that there were 84,000 deaths due to COPD, approximately 34 per 100,000 people. Although COPD is still much more common in men than women, the greatest increase in the COPD death rate between 1979 and 1989 occurred in females, particularly in black females (117.6 percent for black females vs. 93 percent for white females). These increases reflect the increased number of women who smoke cigarettes.

COPD attacks people at the height of their productive years, disabling them with constant shortness of breath. It destroys their ability to earn a living, causes frequent use of the health care system, and disrupts the lives of the victims' family members for as long as 20 years before death occurs.

In 1990, COPD was the cause of approximately 16.2 million office visits to doctors and 1.9 million hospital days. The economic costs of this disease are enormous. In 1989, an estimated $7 billion was spent for care of persons with COPD and another $8 billion was lost to the economy by lost productivity due to morbidity and mortality from COPD.

What Goes Wrong with the Lungs and Other Organs in Chronic Obstructive Pulmonary Disease?

The most important job that the lungs perform is to provide the body with oxygen and to remove carbon dioxide. This process is called gas exchange, and the normal anatomy of the lungs serves this purpose well. The lungs contain 300 million alveoli whose ultra-thin walls form the gas exchange surface. Enmeshed in the wall of each of these air sacs is a network of tiny blood vessels, the capillaries, which bring blood to the gas exchange surface. When a person inhales, air flows from the nose and mouth through large and small airways into the alveoli. Oxygen from this air then passes through the thin walls of the inflated alveoli and is taken up by the red blood cells for delivery to the rest of the body. At the same time, carbon dioxide leaves the blood and passes through the alveolar walls into the alveoli. During exhalation, the lung pushes the used air out of the alveoli and through the air passages until it escapes from the nose or mouth. When COPD develops, the walls of the small airways and alveoli lose their elasticity. The airway walls thicken, closing off some of the smaller air passages and narrowing larger ones. The passageways also become plugged with mucus. Air continues to get into alveoli when the lung expands during inhalation, but it is often unable to escape during exhalation because the air passages tend to collapse during exhalation, trapping the "stale" air in the lungs. These abnormalities create two serious problems which affect gas exchange:

- Blood flow and air flow to the walls of the alveoli where gas exchange takes place are uneven or mismatched. In some alveoli there is adequate blood flow but little air, while in others there is a good supply of fresh air but not enough blood flow. When this occurs, fresh air cannot reach areas where there is good blood flow and oxygen cannot enter the bloodstream in normal quantities.

- Pushing the air through narrowed obstructed airways becomes harder and harder. This tires the respiratory muscles so that they are unable to get enough air to the alveoli. The critical step for removing carbon dioxide from the blood is adequate alveolar airflow. If airflow to the alveoli is insufficient, carbon dioxide builds up in the blood and blood oxygen diminishes. Inadequate supply of fresh air to the alveoli is called hypoventilation. Breathing oxygen can often correct the blood oxygen levels, but this does not help remove carbon dioxide. When carbon dioxide accumulation becomes a severe problem, mechanical breathing machines called respirators, or ventilators, must be used.

Pulmonary function studies of large groups of people show that lung function—the ability to move air into and out of the lungs—declines slowly with age even in healthy nonsmokers. Because healthy nonsmokers have excess lung capacity, this gradual loss of function does not lead to any symptoms. In smokers, however, lung function tends to worsen much more rapidly. If a smoker stops smoking before serious COPD develops, the rate at which lung function declines returns to almost normal. Unfortunately, because some lung damage cannot be reversed, pulmonary function is unlikely to return completely to normal.

COPD also makes the heart work much harder, especially the main chamber on the right side (right ventricle) which is responsible for pumping blood into the lungs. As COPD progresses, the amount of oxygen in the blood decreases which causes blood vessels in the lung to constrict. At the same time many of the small blood vessels in the lung have been damaged or destroyed as a result of the disease process. More and more work is required from the right ventricle to force blood through the remaining narrowed vessels. To perform this task, the right ventricle enlarges and thickens. When this occurs the normal rhythm of the heart may be disturbed by abnormal beats. This condition, in which the heart is enlarged because of lung problems, is called cor pulmonale. Patients with cor pulmonale tire easily and have chest pains and palpitations. If an additional strain is placed on the lungs and heart by a normally minor illness such as a cold, the heart may be unable to pump enough blood to meet the needs of other organs. This results in the inability of the liver and kidneys to carry out their normal functions which leads to swelling of the abdomen, legs, and ankles.

Another adjustment the body makes to inadequate blood oxygen is called secondary polycythemia, an increased production of oxygen-carrying red blood cells. The larger than normal number of red blood cells is helpful up to a point; however, a large overpopulation of red cells thickens the blood so much that it clogs small blood vessels causing a new set of problems. People who have poor supply of oxygen usually have a bluish tinge to their skin, lips, and nailbeds, a condition called cyanosis.

Too little oxygen and too much carbon dioxide in the blood also affect the nervous system, especially the brain, and can cause a variety of problems including headache, inability to sleep, impaired mental ability, and irritability.

What Is the Course of Chronic Obstructive Pulmonary Disease?

Daily morning cough with clear sputum is the earliest symptom of COPD. During a cold or other acute respiratory tract infection, the coughing may be much more noticeable and the sputum often turns yellow or greenish. Periods of wheezing are likely to occur especially during or after colds or other respiratory tract infections. Shortness of breath on exertion develops later and progressively becomes more pronounced with severe episodes of breathlessness (dyspnea) occurring after even modest activity.

A typical course of COPD might proceed as follows. For a period of about 10 years after cigarette smoking begins, symptoms are usually not very noticeable. After this, the patient generally starts developing a chronic cough with the production of a small amount of sputum. It is unusual to develop shortness of breath during exertion below the age of 40, after which it becomes more common and may be well developed by the age of 50. However, although all COPD patients have these symptoms, not all cigarette smokers develop a notable cough and sputum production, or shortness of breath.

Most patients with COPD have some degree of reversible airways obstruction. It is therefore likely that, at first, treatment will lead to some improvement or stability in lung function. But as COPD progresses, almost all signs and symptoms except cough and sputum production tend to show a gradual worsening. This trend can show fluctuations, but over the course of 4 or 5 years, a slow deterioration becomes evident.

Repeated bouts of increased cough and sputum production disable most patients and recovery from coughing attacks may take a long time. Patients with severe lung damage sleep in a semi-sitting position because they are unable to breathe when they lie down. They often complain that they awaken during the night feeling "choked-up," and they need to sit up to cough.

Survival of patients with COPD is closely related to the level of their lung function when they are diagnosed and the rate at which they lose this function. Overall, the median survival is about 10 years for patients with COPD who have lost approximately two-thirds of their normally expected lung function at diagnosis.

How Is Chronic Obstructive Pulmonary Disease Detected?

Researchers are still looking for accurate methods to predict a person's chances of developing airway obstruction. None of the current ways used to diagnose COPD detects the disease before irreversible lung damage occurs. While many measures of lung function have been developed, those most commonly used determine: 1) air-containing volume of the lung (lung volume), 2) the ability to move air into and out of the lung, 3) the rate at which gases diffuse between the lung and blood, and 4) blood levels of oxygen and carbon dioxide.

In most cases, it is necessary to compare the results of several different tests in order to make the correct diagnosis, and to repeat some tests at intervals to determine the rate of disease progression or improvement. It is hoped that current research will result in more accurate and earlier measures for detecting lung destruction and diminished function.

How Is Chronic Obstructive Pulmonary Disease Treated?

Although there is no cure for COPD, the disease can be prevented in many cases. In almost all cases the disabling symptoms can be reduced. Because cigarette smoking is the most important cause of COPD, not smoking almost always prevents COPD from developing, and quitting smoking slows the disease process.

If the patient and medical team develop and adhere to a program of complete respiratory care, disability can be minimized, acute episodes prevented, hospitalizations reduced, and some early deaths avoided. On the other hand, none of the therapies have been shown to slow the progression of the disease, and only oxygen therapy has been shown to increase the survival rate.

Home Oxygen Therapy Can Improve Survival of COPD Patients

Home oxygen therapy can improve survival in patients with advanced COPD who have hypoxemia, low blood oxygen levels. This treatment can improve a patient's exercise tolerance and ability to perform on psychological tests which reflect different aspects of brain function and muscle coordination. Increasing the concentration of oxygen in blood also improves the function of the heart and prevents the development of cor pulmonale. Oxygen can also lessen sleeplessness, irritability, headaches, and the overproduction of red blood cells. Continuous oxygen therapy is recommended for patients with low oxygen levels at rest, during exercise, or while sleeping. Many oxygen sources are available for home use; these include tanks of compressed gaseous oxygen or liquid oxygen and devices that concentrate oxygen from room air. However, oxygen is expensive with the cost per patient running into several hundred dollars per month, depending on the type of system and on the locale.

Medications Frequently Prescribed for COPD Patients

- Bronchodilators help open narrowed airways. There are three main categories: sympathomimetics (isoproterenol, metaproterenol, terbutaline, albuterol) which can be inhaled, injected, or taken by mouth; parasympathomimetics (atropine, ipratropium bromide); and methylxanthines (theophylline and its derivatives) which can be given intravenously, orally, or rectally.

- Corticosteroids or steroids (beclomethasone, dexamethasone, triamcinolone, flunisolide) lessen inflammation of the airway

91

walls. They are sometimes used if airway obstruction cannot be kept under control with bronchodilators, and lung function is shown to improve on this therapy. Inhaled steroids given regularly may be of benefit in some patients and have few side effects.

- Antibiotics (tetracycline, ampicillin, erythromycin, and trimethoprim-sulfamethoxazole combinations) fight infection. They are frequently given at the first sign of a respiratory infection such as increased sputum production with a change in color of sputum from clear to yellow or green.

- Expectorants help loosen and expel mucus secretions from the airways.

- Diuretics help the body excrete excess fluid. They are given as therapy to avoid excess water retention associated with right-heart failure. Patients taking diuretics are monitored carefully because dehydration must be avoided. These drugs also may cause potassium imbalances which can lead to abnormal heart rhythms.

- Digitalis (usually in the form of digoxin) strengthens the force of the heartbeat. It is used very cautiously in patients who have COPD, especially if their blood oxygen tensions are low, because they are vulnerable to abnormal heart rhythms when taking this drug.

- Other drugs sometimes taken by patients with COPD are tranquilizers, pain killers (meperidine, morphine, propoxyphene, etc.), cough suppressants (codeine, etc.), and sleeping pills (barbiturates, etc.). All these drugs depress breathing to some extent; they are avoided whenever possible and used only with great caution.

A number of combination drugs containing various assortments of sympathomimetics, methylxanthines, expectorants, and sedatives are marketed and widely advertised. These drugs are undesirable for COPD patients for several reasons. It is difficult to adjust the dose of methylxanthines without getting interfering side effects from the other ingredients. The sympathomimetic drug used in these preparations is ephedrine, a drug with many side effects and less bronchodilating effect than other drugs now available. The combination drugs often contain sedatives to combat the unpleasant side effects of ephedrine. They also contain expectorants which have not been proven to be effective for all patients and may have some side effects.

Other Treatments

Bullectomy, or surgical removal of large air spaces called bullae that are filled with stagnant air, may be beneficial in selected patients. Recently, use of lasers to remove bullae has been suggested.

Lung transplantation has been successfully employed in some patients with end-stage COPD. In the hands of an experienced team, the 1-year survival in patients with transplanted lungs is over 70 percent.

Pulmonary rehabilitation programs, along with medical treatment, are useful in certain patients with COPD. The goals are to improve overall physical endurance and generally help to overcome the conditions which cause dyspnea and limit capacity for physical exercise and activities of daily living. General exercise training increases performance, maximum oxygen consumption, and overall sense of well-being. Administration of oxygen and nutritional supplements when necessary can improve respiratory muscle strength. Intermittent mechanical ventilatory support relieves dyspnea and rests respiratory muscles in selected patients. Continuous positive airway pressure (CPAP) is used as an adjunct to weaning from mechanical ventilation to minimize dyspnea during exercise. Relaxation techniques may also reduce the perception of ventilatory effort and dyspnea. Breathing exercises and breathing techniques, such as pursed lips breathing and relaxation, improve functional status.

Keeping air passages reasonably clear of secretions is difficult for patients with advanced COPD. Some commonly used methods for mobilizing and removing secretions are the following:

- Postural bronchial drainage helps to remove secretions from the airways. The patient lies in prescribed positions that allow gravity to drain different parts of the lung. This is usually done after inhaling an aerosol. In the basic position, the patient lies on a bed with his chest and head over the side and his forearms resting on the floor.

- Chest percussion or lightly clapping the chest and back, may help dislodge tenacious or copious secretions.

- Controlled coughing techniques are taught to help the patient bring up secretions.

- Bland aerosols, often made from solutions of salt or bicarbonate of soda, are inhaled. These aerosols thin and loosen secretions. Treatments usually last 10 to 15 minutes and are taken three or four times a day. Bronchodilators are sometimes added to the aerosols.

How Can Patients with Chronic Obstructive Pulmonary Disease Cope with Their Illness?

In most instances of COPD, some irreversible damage has already occurred by the time the doctor diagnoses the disease. At this point, the patient and the family should learn as much as possible about the disease and how to live with it. The goals, limitations, and techniques of treatment must be understood by the patient so that symptoms can be kept under control, and daily living can proceed as normally as possible. The doctor and other health care providers are good sources of information about COPD education programs. Patients and family members can usually take part in educational programs offered at a hospital or by a local branch of the American Lung Association. Patients with COPD can help themselves in many ways. They can:

- Stop smoking. Many programs are available to help smokers quit smoking and to stay off tobacco. Some programs are based on behavior modification techniques; others combine these methods with nicotine gum or nicotine patches as aids to help smokers gradually overcome their dependence on nicotine.

- Avoid work-related exposures to dusts and fumes.

- Avoid air pollution, including cigarette smoke, and curtail physical activities during air pollution alerts. Refrain from intimate contact with people who have respiratory infections such as colds or the flu and get a one-time pneumonia vaccination (polyvalent pneumococcal vaccination) and yearly influenza shots.

- Avoid excessive heat, cold, and very high altitudes. (Note: Commercial aircraft cruise at high altitudes and maintain a cabin pressure equal to that of an elevation of 5,000 to 10,000 feet. This can result in hypoxemia for some COPD patients. However, with supplemental oxygen, most COPD patients can travel on commercial airlines.)

- Drink a lot of fluids. This is a good way to keep sputum loose so that it can be brought up by coughing.

- Maintain good nutrition. Usually a high protein diet, taken as many small feedings, is recommended.

- Consider "allergy shots." COPD patients often also have allergies or asthma which complicate COPD.

Of all the avoidable risk factors for COPD, smoking is by far the most significant. Cessation of smoking is the best way to decrease one's risk of developing COPD.

Chapter 7

Occupational Lung Cancer

Introduction—Occupational Lung Cancer

Cigarette smoking is acknowledged to be the single most important cause of lung cancer. But considerable evidence now suggests that workplace air pollutants are significant causes as well. Many cancers, including lung cancer, occur more frequently in industrialized areas than in rural areas. And lung cancer occurs more frequently among workers handling a variety of substances, including arsenic, bis-chloromethyl ether, coal tar and pitch volatiles, petroleum, mustard gas, coal carbonization products, chromates, asbestos, x-rays, radium uranium, nickel, and isopropyl oil. Chemists, painters, and printers also seem to have an increased risk of lung cancer.

Cigarette smoking, added to the effects of industrial cancer-inducing agents, greatly increases the incidence of lung cancer in workers. Lung cancer, although very seldom curable, is largely preventable. Cigarettes are the single most important factor in lung cancer, but occupational substances that produce cancer can be controlled or replaced.

Exposure to Environmental Tobacco Smoke— Identifying and Protecting Those at Risk

More effort is needed to ban smoking in indoor areas. Passive smoking has been linked to lung cancer, heart disease, and other illnesses. Anyone who lives or works with smokers is at risk of passive smoking. People who work in airplanes, casinos, restaurants, bars, bingo halls, and bowling alleys are most at risk. Studies have shown that educating people is not enough. The Occupational Safety and Health Administration (OSHA) has proposed a total ban on smoking in worksites except in separately ventilated areas. Until this regulation is finalized, individual lawsuits may be the best way to stop smoking in workplaces.

Environmental Tobacco Smoke

The dangers of exposure to environmental tobacco smoke (ETS) are now well established. Reports from the U.S. Environmental Protection Agency[1] and the California Environmental Protection Agency[2] and meta-analyses published last year have shown convincingly that exposure to ETS causes lung cancer, heart disease, and other serious illnesses.

The California Environmental Protection Agency report estimated that each year in the United States, ETS exposure causes 3,000 deaths due to lung cancer, 35,000 to 62,000 deaths due to ischemic heart disease, and 1,900 to 2,700 deaths due to sudden infant death syndrome. Exposure to ETS is also responsible for 9,700 to 18,600 cases of low-birth-weight infants annually, 8,000 to 26,000 new cases of asthma in children, exacerbation of asthma in 400,000 to 1 million children, and 150,000 to 300,000 cases of bronchitis or pneumonia in children aged 18 months and younger (of which 7,500 to 15,000 require hospitalization[2]).

Who Is at Risk?

Virtually everyone in the United States is at some risk of harm from exposure to secondhand smoke. The reasons are that nearly everyone is exposed to tobacco smoke,[5] and there is no evidence of a threshold level of exposure below which exposure is safe.[1] Neverthe-less, it is useful to address the question: who is at greatest risk from passive smoking?

Most people spend about 90% of their time in 2 "microenviron-ments": home and work.[6] Thus, populations at greater risk of harm from ETS are those who live with smokers and those who work where smoking is allowed. Data from the Third National Health and Nutri-tion Examination Survey (NHANES III) showed that the number of smokers in the household and the hours exposed to ETS at work were significantly associated with levels of serum cotinine (a metabolite of nicotine[5]).

Some people are more susceptible to harm from a given level of exposure to ETS because of their age or health status. Infants and children exposed to ETS are more likely to develop pneumonia, bron-chitis, asthma, and middle ear disease.[1,2,7] One reason infants and children may be more susceptible to harm from ETS is that their lungs and other respiratory tissue are still developing. The infant lung has immature immunologic function, very small airways that are vulner-able to obstruction, and fewer alveoli in relation to the number of air-ways.[8] Children are also more prone to illness from ETS because they have a higher respiratory rate than adults and because some ETS-associated conditions (e.g., middle ear disease) occur primarily at young ages.

Persons with certain chronic conditions are more likely than healthy people to suffer when exposed to ETS. Passive smoking ex-acerbates symptoms of asthma in adults.[2] In addition, persons with allergies, chronic obstructive pulmonary disease, chronic heart dis-ease, and peripheral vascular disease may be more susceptible to the ill effects of ETS and its constituents (e.g., carbon monoxide[9-11]).

For a given microenvironment, the harm from passive smoking depends on time spent in that environment and the concentration of ETS in that air space. The concentration of ETS, in turn, is affected by the size of the space, the number of people smoking there, and the ventilation rate. Those factors create a substantial risk of harm from ETS in certain occupational settings.

Workers at Great Risk

Before smoking on commercial aircraft was banned in the United States, flight attendants were at high risk of illness from secondhand smoke. Many passengers smoked, the air space was small, and the air filtration and outside air flow rates were inadequate in removing

ETS.[12] Moreover, separation of smokers and nonsmokers in the aircraft cabin did not protect passengers in nonsmoking areas or flight attendants assigned to work in those areas from exposure to ETS.[13] Flight attendants who work for foreign airlines that still allow smoking on their flights continue to be exposed to dangerous levels of ETS.

Casino workers represent another occupational group at high risk of disease from ETS. Very few casinos restrict smoking on their premises, and smokers are likely to be over-represented among patrons of these establishments. Moreover, the risk-taking ambiance and the free flow of alcohol at casinos probably encourage a high level of smoking among gamblers. A health hazard evaluation of a large casino in Atlantic City, NJ, conducted by the National Institute for Occupational Safety and Health, showed that employees working in the gaming areas of the casino were exposed to ETS at levels greater than those observed among participants in the NHANES III who had reported exposure to ETS at both home and work.[14,15] Employees working at nonsmoking tables had similar serum and urine cotinine levels as employees working at tables where smoking was permitted.

Howard et. al.[16] studied 74 nonsmokers, 38 of whom were exposed to ETS at work and 36 of whom were not (none of the 74 had exposure to ETS at home). Those exposed to ETS at work (the majority[31,38] of whom were casino workers [written communication from Dr. Chris A. Pritsos to James Repace, June 8,1998]) had higher serum cotinine levels and increased levels of oxidative DNA mutagens when compared with those not exposed at work.[16] Kado et. al.[17] measured mutagenic activity in air sampled from a casino and a bingo parlor using a Salmonella microsuspension assay and found that mutagenic activity correlated with airborne nicotine and total suspended particulate matter.

Restaurant and bar workers comprise yet another group who are affected disproportionately by ETS. In a meta-analysis, Siegel[18] found that levels of ETS are 1.6 to 2.0 times higher in restaurants and 3.9 to 6.1 times higher in bars than in office workplaces of other businesses. Levels of ETS in restaurants and bars were 1.5 times higher and 4.4 to 4.5 times higher, respectively, than in residences with at least 1 smoker. Based on published studies of lung cancer risk among food service employees that controlled for active smoking, Siegel[18] concluded that "there may be a 50% increase in lung cancer risk among food-service workers that is in part attributable to tobacco smoke exposure in the workplace." The Massachusetts Department of Public Health also found a 50% excess risk of lung cancer among food service workers, most likely related to their exposure to secondhand smoke.[19]

Based on measurements from published studies, Siegel[18] calculated the ratio of mean nicotine concentration in several usually smoky worksites to the concentration in typical offices. Bingo parlors were the smokiest (ratio = 13.0), followed by bars (4.8), billiard halls (4.7), betting establishments (3.7), bowling alleys (2.6), and restaurants (1.6).[21]

Eisner et. al.[21] provide another line of evidence concerning the hazards of passive smoking for workers in these establishments. They studied the respiratory health of a cohort of bartenders before and after passage of state legislation in California prohibiting smoking in bars and taverns. The study cohort was composed of 53 bartenders from a random sample of 25 bars and taverns in San Francisco. At baseline (in the month preceding imposition of the smoking ban), all of the bartenders reported ETS exposure at work and most reported heavy exposure. Self-reported ETS exposure at work declined from a median of 28 hours per week at baseline to 2 hours per week at follow-up (1-2 months after the smoking ban was in place). A marked decline in the prevalence of respiratory symptoms (wheezing, dyspnea, cough, and phlegm production) and sensory irritation symptoms (eye, nose, or throat irritation) occurred, and improvement in pulmonary function (FVC—forced vital capacity and FEV_1—forced expiratory volume in 1 second) was observed after controlling for personal smoking and upper respiratory tract infections. As Eisner and colleagues note, their study provides evidence that workplace smoking prohibitions have immediate beneficial effects on adult respiratory health, not to mention their likely effect in reducing the long-term risk of lung cancer and cardiovascular disease.

Eliminating Exposure

Because of the risks of passive smoking, nonsmokers' exposure to secondhand smoke needs to be eliminated. That goal can be accomplished through 2 different approaches: prohibiting smoking indoors or limiting smoking to rooms that have been specially designed to prevent smoke from escaping to other areas of the building.[22] The former approach is the preferred option, as it ensures maximum protection of nonsmokers, is easier and less expensive to implement, and avoids exposing smokers to the added risk of concentrated ETS in designated smoking areas.[23]

Strategies to protect nonsmokers can be divided into 4 categories: education, regulation, legislation, and litigation. Education about the dangers of passive smoking is important for 2 reasons. First, it lays the groundwork for good compliance with legislation and regulation. Public support for smoking restrictions and bans in the United States has grown through the years,[24] helping to ensure smooth implementation of those policies. In France, by contrast, public smoking restrictions were imposed by "top-down" action of the federal government, without meaningful grass-roots pressure;[25] as a result, compliance has been less than ideal. A second reason education is important is that some areas—such as private homes—are difficult to control through legislation, so education is the main intervention strategy that is available.[26]

Education alone is usually not effective in protecting nonsmokers. Even though most Americans believe that passive smoking is harmful to health and most nonsmokers are annoyed by exposure to ETS, many smokers light their cigarettes inside public places without asking if others mind, and few nonsmokers ask smokers to put out their cigarettes when they light them indoors.[27] Because children cannot protect themselves and because nonsmoking adults are prone to suffer in silence when exposed to ETS, public policies are needed to protect them.

Regulation by the Occupational Safety and Health Administration (OSHA) could protect workers throughout the United States from exposure to ETS. In 1994, OSHA proposed sweeping rules that would ban smoking in worksites except in separately ventilated areas.[28] Unfortunately, final rules have not been promulgated, and there is no indication that they will be anytime soon. President Clinton signed an executive order in August 1997 banning smoking in federal buildings,[29] and governors in at least 7 states (Colorado, Idaho, Michigan, Ohio, South Dakota, Washington, and Wyoming) have done the same for state government worksites.[30] Two states, Washington and Maryland, have promulgated strong clean indoor air regulations.[30]

Legislation at the federal level bans smoking on commercial aircraft for flights that are 6 hours or less in duration.[31] Federal legislation also requires that organizations and agencies have smoke-free indoor facilities if they receive federal funding for children's services.[32] At the state level, as of December 31,1997, 21 states banned smoking in day care centers or restricted it to designated areas with separate ventilation, but only 10 states had such a policy for government worksites, only 1 state (California) had such a policy for private worksites, and only 3 states (California, Utah, and Vermont) had such a policy for restaurants.[33] Clean indoor air legislation has also been passed by many local jurisdictions.[34]

Despite the abundant research that has established the harmfulness of passive smoking,[1-4] and despite the education, regulation, and legislation that have grown out of the nonsmokers' rights movement in the United States, a large number of Americans continue to be exposed involuntarily to ETS at worksites and other public places.[5,35] As a result, litigation is now being used increasingly to protect nonsmokers from exposure to ETS. Much of this litigation is aimed at protecting workers at highest risk of harm from ETS.

A class action lawsuit filed against the tobacco industry on behalf of flight attendants harmed by secondhand smoke was settled for $350 million.[36] Similar class action lawsuits have been filed in Nevada and New Jersey on behalf of casino workers harmed by ETS.[37] Many companies have been sued for not offering their employees smoke-free work space, workers' compensation claims have been filed based on workplace exposure to ETS, and parental smoking is being considered in child custody cases.[38,39] Some of these cases have been brought under the public accommodation provisions of the Americans With Disabilities Act.[40]

In June 1993, the U.S. Supreme Court ruled that the Nevada state prison may have subjected a convicted murderer to cruel and unusual punishment (in violation of the 8th Amendment to the U.S. Constitution) by forcing him to live with a smoking cellmate.[41] Millions of Americans outside prison are exposed involuntarily to secondhand smoke every day, and many of them will suffer the cruel fate of lung cancer, heart disease, or some other malady caused by that exposure. As a society, we need to intensify our efforts to convince parents, employers, building managers, legislators, and other decision makers to ban smoking in the indoor space under their control. In the absence of such action, slow and costly litigation will become the main strategy for addressing this problem. And passive smoking will continue to cause a great deal of premature death, disability, and suffering in the interim.

References

1. U.S. Environmental Protection Agency. "Respiratory Health Effects of Passive Smoking: Lung Cancer and Other Disorders." Washington, DC: Environmental Protection Agency, Office of Air and Radiation; 1992. Environmental Protection Agency publication EPA/600/6-90/006F.

2. California Environmental Protection Agency. "Health Effects of Exposure to Environmental Tobacco Smoke." Sacramento: California Environmental Protection Agency, Office of Environmental Health Hazard Assessment; 1997.

3. Hackshaw AK, Law MR, Wald NJ. "The accumulated evidence on lung cancer and environmental tobacco smoke." *BMJ*. 1997;315:980–988.

4. Law MR, Morris JK, Wald NJ. "Environmental tobacco smoke exposure and ischaemic heart disease: an evaluation of the evidence." *BMJ*. l997;315:973–980.

5. Pirkle JL, Fiegal KM Bernert JT, Brody DJ, Etzel RA, Maurer KR. "Exposure of the U.S. population to environmental tobacco smoke: the Third National Health and Nutrition Examination Survey, 1988 to 1991." *JAMA*. 1996;275:1233–1240.

6. Szalai A. *The Use of Time: Daily Activities of Urban and Suburban Populations in Twelve Countries*. The Hague, Netherlands: Mouton Publishers; 1972.

7. Mannino DM, Siege M, Husten C, Rose D, Etzel R. "Environmental tobacco smoke exposure and health effects in children: results from the 1991 National Health Interview Survey." *Tob Control*. 1996;5:13–18.

8. National Research Council. *Environmental Tobacco Smoke: Measuring Exposures and Assessing Health Effects*. Washington, DC: National Academy Press; 1986:209–211.

9. Aronow WS. "Effects of passive smoking on angina pectoris." *N Engl J Med*. 1978;299:21–24.

10. Aronow WS, Ferlinz J, Glauser F. "Effect of carbon monoxide on exercise performance in chronic obstructive pulmonary disease." *Am J Med*. 1977;63:904–908.

11. Aronow WS, Stemmer EA, Isbell MW. "Effect of carbon monoxide exposure on intermittent claudication." *Circulation*. 1974;49:415–417.

12. National Research Council. *The Airliner Cabin Environment: Air Quality and Safety*. Washington, DC: National Academy Press; 1986.

13. Mattson ME, Boyd G, Byar D, et al. "Passive smoking on commercial airline flights." *JAMA*. 1989;261:867–872.

14. Trout D, Decker J. "NIOSH Health Hazard Evaluation Report, HETA 95-0375-2590, Bally's Park Place Casino Hotel,

Atlantic City, New Jersey." Cincinnati, Ohio: NIOSH Publications Office; July 1996.

15. Trout D, Decker J, Mueller C, Bernert JT, Pirkle J. "Exposure of casino employees to environmental tobacco smoke." *J Occup Environ Med*. 1998;40:270–276.

16. Howard DJ, Ota RB, Briggs LA, Hampton M, Pritsos CA. "Environmental tobacco smoke in the workplace induces oxidative stress in employees, including increased production of 8-hydroxy-2-deoxyguanosine." *Cancer Epidemiol Biomarkers Prev*. 1998;7:141–146.

17. Kado NY, McCurdy SA, Tesluk SJ, et al. "Measuring personal exposure to airborne mutagens and nicotine in environmental tobacco smoke." *Mutat Res*. 1991;261:75–82.

18. Siegel M. "Involuntary smoking in the restaurant workplace: a review of employee exposure and health effects." *JAMA* 1993;270:490–493.

19. Brooks DR, Davis LK. "Employment as a Waiter or Waitress and Risk of Lung Cancer." Boston: Massachusetts Department of Public Health, Bureau of Health Statistics, Research and Evaluation, Occupational Health Surveillance Program; 1995.

20. Siegel M. "Smoking and Bars: A Guide for Policy Makers." Boston, Mass: Boston University School of Public Health; January 1998.

21. Eisner MD, Smith AK, Blanc PD. "Bartenders' respiratory health after establishment of smoke-free bars and taverns." *JAMA* 1998;280:1909–1914.

22. U.S. Environmental Protection Agency. "Secondhand Smoke: What You Can Do About Secondhand Smoke as Parents, Decisionmakers, and Building Occupants." Washington, DC: Environmental Protection Agency; July 1993. Environmental Protection Agency publication EPA-402-F-93-004.

23. Siegel M, Husten C, Merritt RK, Giovino GA, Eriksen MP. "Effects of separately ventilated smoking lounges on the health of smokers: is this an appropriate public health policy?" *Tob Control* 1995;4:22–29.

24. U.S. Department of Health and Human Services. "Reducing the Health Consequences of Smoking: 25 Years of Progress: A Report of the Surgeon General." Rockville, Md: U.S. Public Health Service, Centers for Disease Control, Office on Smoking and Health, 1989: chapter 4. U.S. Dept of Health and Human Services publication CDC 89-8411.

25. Vogel D, Kagan RA, Kessler T. "Political culture and tobacco control: an international comparison." *Tob Control.* 1993;2:317–326.

26. Ashley MJ, Ferrence R. "Reducing children's exposure to environmental tobacco smoke in homes: issues and strategies." *Tob Control.* 1998;7:61–65.

27. Davis RM, Boyd GM, Schoenborn CA. "Common courtesy and the elimination of passive smoking: results of the 1987 National Health Interview Survey [published correction appears in *JAMA.* 1990;263:3025]." *JAMA.* 1990;263:2208–2210.

28. Occupational Safety and Health Administration. "Notice of proposed rulemaking: notice of informal public hearing." 59 *Federal Register* 15968 (April 5,1994) (codified at 29 CFR §1910, 1915, 1926, 1928).

29. Associated Press. "Clinton bans smoking in U.S. buildings, not outside." *Washington Post.* August 10, 1997:A9.

30. Centers for Disease Control and Prevention. "State Tobacco Control Highlights—1996." Atlanta, GA: Centers for Disease Control and Prevention, Office on Smoking and Health, 1996. Centers for Disease Control and Prevention publication 099-4895.

31. 49 USC 41706.

32. 20 USC 6081–6084.

33. Centers for Disease Control and Prevention. "State and national tobacco control highlights." Available at: http://www.cdc.gov/tobacco/statehi/statehi.htm. Accessed November 10, 1998.

34. Rigotti NA, Pashos CL. "No-smoking laws in the United States: an analysis of state and city actions to limit smoking in public places and worksites." *JAMA* 1991;266:3162–3167.

35. Gerlach KK, Shopland DR, Hartman AM, Gibson JT, Pechacek TF. "Workplace smoking policies in the United States: results from a national survey of more than 100,000 workers." *Tob Control*. 1997;6:199–206.

36. Navarro M. "Cigarette makers reach settlement in nonsmoker suit." *New York Times*. October 11, 1997:A1.

37. Smothers R. "Workers challenge casinos' role as a haven for smokers." *New York Times*. May 25, 1998:B1.

38. Sweda EL. "Summary of Legal Cases Regarding Smoking in the Workplace and Other Places." Boston, Mass: Tobacco Control Resource Center; July 1997.

39. Sweda EL, Gottlieb MA, Porfiri RC. "Protecting children from exposure to environmental tobacco smoke." *Tob Control*. 1998;7:1–2.

40. Parmet WE, Daynard RA, Gottlieb MA. "The physician's role in helping smoke-sensitive patients to use the Americans With Disabilities Act to secure smoke-free workplaces and public spaces." *JAMA*. 1996;276:909–913.

41. Helling vs. McKinney, 113 S Ct 2475 (1993).

—by Ronald M. Davis, MD

Dr. Davis has served as an expert witness in class action lawsuits filed on behalf of flight attendants and casino workers harmed by second-hand smoke (Broin et al. vs. Philip Morris Companies et. al., Avallone et al.; vs. American Tobacco Company et al.; and Badillo et al. vs. American Tobacco Company et al.) and in several other tobacco lawsuits. He derives no personal income from this work, but his employer (Henry Ford Health System) charges a fee to secure compensation for his time lost from work due to his service as an expert witness. From the Center for Health Promotion and Disease Prevention, Henry Ford Health System, Detroit, Michigan.

Chapter 8

Silica Dust

Preventing Silicosis

What Is Silicosis?

Silicosis is a disabling, non-reversible and sometimes fatal lung disease caused by overexposure to respirable crystalline silica. Silica is the second most common mineral in the earth's crust and is a major component of sand, rock, and mineral ores. Overexposure to dust that contains microscopic particles of crystalline silica can cause scar tissue to form in the lungs, which reduces the lungs' ability to extract oxygen from the air we breathe. Typical sand found at the beach does not pose a silicosis threat.

More than 1 million U.S. workers are exposed to crystalline silica. Each year, more than 250 American workers die with silicosis. There is no cure for the disease, but it is 100 percent preventable if employers, workers, and health professionals work together to reduce exposures.

In addition to silicosis, inhalation of crystalline silica particles has been associated with other diseases, such as bronchitis and tuberculosis. Some studies also indicate an association with lung cancer.

This chapter includes text from "A Guide to Working Safely with Silica" and "Preventing Silicosis," U.S. Department of Labor, http://www.cdc.gov/niosh/silfact1.html, October1996, and "Silica Dust Exposures Can Cause Silicosis," Occupational Safety and Health Administration, Fact Sheet 96-54, http://www.osha-slc.gov/OshDoc/Fact_data/FSNO96-54.html, January 1996.

Who Is at Risk?

Working in any dusty environment where crystalline silica is present potentially can increase a person's chances of getting silicosis. If a number of workers are working in a dusty environment and one is diagnosed with the silicosis, the others should be examined to see if they might also be developing silicosis.

Some examples of the industries and activities that pose the greatest potential risk for worker exposure include:

- construction (sandblasting, rock drilling, masonry work, jack hammering, tunneling)

- mining (cutting or drilling through sandstone and granite)

- foundry work (grinding, moldings, shakeout, core room)

- ceramics, clay, and pottery

- railroad (setting and laying track)

- manufacturing of soaps and detergents

- stone cutting (sawing, abrasive blasting, chipping, grinding)

- glass manufacturing

- agriculture (dusty conditions from disturbing the soil, such as plowing or harvesting)

- shipbuilding (abrasive blasting)

- manufacturing and use of abrasives

More than 100,000 workers in the United States encounter high-risk silica exposures through sandblasting, rock drilling, and mining. Workers who remove paint and rust from buildings, bridges, tanks, and other surfaces; clean foundry castings; work with stone or clay; etch or frost glass; and work in construction are at risk of overexposure to crystalline silica

What Are the Types, Symptoms and Complications of Silicosis?

There are three types of silicosis, depending upon the airborne concentration of crystalline silica to which a worker has been exposed:

- Chronic silicosis usually occurs after 10 or more years of overexposure.

- Accelerated silicosis results from higher exposures and develops over 5–10 years.

- Acute silicosis occurs where exposures are the highest and can cause symptoms to develop within a few weeks or up to 5 years.

Chronic silicosis, the most common form of the disease, may go undetected for years in the early stages; in fact, a chest X-ray may not reveal an abnormality until after 15 or 20 years of exposure. The body's ability to fight infections may be overwhelmed by silica dust in the lungs, making workers more susceptible to certain illnesses, such as tuberculosis. As a result, workers may exhibit one or more of the following symptoms:

- shortness of breath following physical exertion
- severe cough
- fatigue
- loss of appetite
- chest pains
- fever

How Can Workers Determine If They Have Silicosis?

A medical examination that includes a complete work history and a chest X-ray and lung function test is the only sure way to determine if a person has silicosis. Workers who believe they are overexposed to silica dust should visit a doctor who knows about lung diseases. The National Institute for Occupational Safety and Health (NIOSH) recommends that medical examinations occur before job placement or upon entering a trade, and at least every 3 years thereafter.

What Can Employees Do to Limit Their Exposure to Crystalline Silica?

- Be aware of the health effects of crystalline silica and that smoking adds to the damage.

- Know the work operations where exposure to crystalline exposure may occur.

- Participate in any air monitoring or training programs offered by the employer.

- Use type CE positive pressure abrasive blasting respirators for sandblasting.

- For other operations where respirators may be required, use a respirator approved for protection against crystalline silica-containing dust. Do not alter the respirator in any way. Workers who use tight-fitting respirators cannot have beards or mustaches which interfere with the respirator seal to the face.

- If possible, change into disposable or washable work clothes at the worksite; shower (where available) and change into clean clothing before leaving the worksite.

- Do not eat, drink, use tobacco products, or apply cosmetics in areas where there is dust containing crystalline silica.

- Wash your hands and face before eating, drinking, smoking, or applying cosmetics outside of the exposure area.

What Can Employers Do to Prevent Silicosis?

- Make a commitment to prevent silicosis at your worksite.

- Comply with regulations on respirable crystalline silica. If your employees are overexposed, reduce exposure levels through the use of engineering controls. While these controls are being installed, or if they are being repaired, provide appropriate respiratory protection.

- Perform air monitoring of worksites as needed, and when required by law, and take corrective action when silica levels are excessive. Monitoring provides a basis for:
  - selecting and ensuring the effectiveness of engineering controls
  - selecting proper respiratory protection
  - seeing if work practices to reduce dust levels are effective
  - determining if a medical surveillance program is necessary

- Install and maintain engineering controls to eliminate or reduce the amount of silica in the air and the build-up of dust on equipment and surfaces. Examples of controls include: exhaust ventilation and dust collection systems, water sprays, wet drilling, enclosed cabs, and drill platform skirts. Practice preventive maintenance because the extreme abrasiveness of the silica dust can damage the systems you install.

- Substitute less hazardous materials than crystalline silica for abrasive blasting, when possible. Try to use automatic blast cleaning machines or cabinets that allow operating the machines from the outside using gloved armholes.

- Supply vacuums with high-efficiency particulate air (HEPA) filters, and advise employees to vacuum, hose down, or wet sweep work areas instead of dry sweeping.

- Train workers about health effects, engineering controls, and work practices that reduce dust; the importance of maintenance and good housekeeping; as well as on the proper type and fitting of respirators. Make sure they know what operations and materials present a silica hazard.

- Establish a written respiratory protection program. Outfit employees with appropriately selected, properly fitted, approved respirators when engineering controls alone are insufficient to keep exposures within safe levels. Be sure respirators are kept clean and properly maintained and that employees are trained in their use.

- Provide medical examinations for employees who may be exposed to respirable crystalline silica, as recommended by the National Institute of Occupational Health and Safety (NIOSH), and have X-rays read by a specialist in dust diseases. Develop a plan for reducing exposures of employees whose X-rays show changes consistent with silicosis.

- Report all cases of silicosis to state health departments and to the Mine Safety and Health Administration (MSHA), and record cases on Occupational Safety and Health Administration (OSHA) logs, as required.

- Post warning signs to identify work areas where respirable silica is present.

Chapter 9

Organic Dust Hazards

Chapter Contents

Section 9.1

Dusts from Decayed Grain, Hay, and Silage

National Agriculture Safety Database, http://www.cdc.gov/niosh/nasd/docs6/pa98001.html, June 1992. Despite the age of this document, readers seeking an understanding of organic dust hazards will still find this information useful.

Summary

A number of farm tasks involve potential exposure to spoiled hay, grain, and silage: breaking open bales of hay, removing the top layer of silage from a silo, shoveling grain or cleaning out grain storage structures. When these activities are performed in a barn, bin, silo, or other enclosure, farmers may inhale significant quantities of bacterial and fungal spores and byproducts. These can induce either of two respiratory reactions: hypersensitivity pneumonitis, referred to here as farmer's lung, and a toxic organic dust syndrome (TODS) similar to that caused by inhalation of grain dusts ("grain fever") and confinement house dusts.

Cases of TODS and acute cases of farmer's lung present themselves in a similar way: as delayed febrile illness of variable severity with cough, dyspnea, myalgia, and malaise, following exposure circumstances similar to those mentioned above, and typically resolving spontaneously within days. However, the two illnesses differ in several significant ways. Farmer's lung is an allergic alveolitis, while TODS is a non-allergic inflammatory response of the alveoli. TODS is relatively common and often occurs simultaneously in a cluster of exposed persons, while farmer's lung is a fairly rare response of sensitized individuals. Only farmer's lung can become chronic, with some cases resulting in progressive irreversible damage to lungs leading to permanent disability or death. Differentiation of acute farmer's lung and TODS may be difficult, and the latter may be misdiagnosed as farmer's lung. Tests helpful in separating the two illnesses include chest radiographs, blood gas measurements, immunoserology, and pulmonary function tests; lung biopsy, bronchoalveolar lavage, and bronchoprovocation may be useful in selected cases.

Farm management and engineering changes that reduce exposure to dusts from spoiled plant material are advisable for all farmers. For farmers suffering from chronic farmer's lung or from repeated attacks of acute illness, such changes are mandatory to prevent possible permanent impairment that may necessitate leaving the farm.

Decayed Grain, Hay, and Silage Dusts on the Farm

Animal feed (hay, silage, and grain) that is put into storage with a high moisture content favors the growth of bacteria and fungi. These microorganisms produce spores and byproducts (mycotoxins and endotoxins) of respirable size which, when released into the air, can be inhaled in large quantities and induce respiratory effects within the airways or alveoli.

More specifically, hay baled while it is moist heats spontaneously, and proceeds through a natural succession of fungal and bacterial populations. The last organisms to grow in the hay are a number of bacterial species termed "thermophilic actinomycetes", which include Micropolyspora faeni and several species of Thermoactinomyces. Silage, which includes chopped oats ("oatlage"), hay ("haylage"), or corn ("cornlage"), is purposefully stored wet in order to undergo the anaerobic ensilage process, which preserves plant material. The uppermost layer of silage remains aerobic and spoils. Grain, when stored before being adequately dried, likewise will spoil and harbor quantities of microorganisms. The species of fungi and bacteria that dominate will change with the type of plant material in storage, moisture and heat conditions, and storage conditions, but typically will include the thermophilic actinomycetes and a variety of fungi.

While feed-related microorganisms and their by-products pose a major threat to farm workers, these workers can suffer the same type of response (hypersensitivity pneumonitis) when they are exposed to other agents. These other agents range from fungi and bacteria growing in wood chips to proteins of bird droppings. Some of the many agents found on the farm that are capable of producing hypersensitivity pneumonitis are listed in the following table. Since these are associated with production or processing of agricultural products, they all could be considered agricultural occupational hazards.

Who Is Exposed to These Dusts, and When?

Almost any farmer, but especially a livestock or grain farmer, is likely to be exposed to dust consisting of bacterial and fungal spores

Table 9.1. Agriculturally-Related Hypersensitivity Pneumonitis

Agent	Exposure	Common Name of Disease
Thermophilic actinomycetes and fungi:		
Micropolyspora faeni, other thermophilic actinomycetes, and fungi	Spoiled hay and other fodder	Farmers Lung
Thermoactinomyces vulgaris	Moldy compost	Mushroom worker's lung
Thermoactinomyces viridis	Moldy compost	Mushroom worker's lung
Alternaria spp.	Moldy wood chips	Wood worker's lung
Pullularia pullulans	Moldy redwood dust	Sequoisis
Aspergillus clavatus	Moldy cheese	Cheese washer's lung
Aspergillus spp.	Moldy malt and barley dust	Malt worker's lung
Cryptostroma corticale	Moldy maple bark	Maple bark stripper's lung
Penicillium caseii	Cheese mold	Cheese worker's lung
Penicillium roqueforti	Cheese mold	Cheese worker's lung
Thermophilic actinomycetes	Vineyards	Vineyard sprayer's lung
Animal proteins:		
Chicken proteins	Chicken products	Feather plucker's lung
Duck proteins	Feathers	Duck fever
Hair proteins	Hairdust	Furrier's lung
Hair serum proteins	Hen droppings	Hen worker's lung
Pigeon serum proteins	Pigeon droppings	Pigeon breeder's lung
Turkey proteins	Turkey products	Turkey handler's lung
Arthropods:		
Sitophilus grainarius	Infested wheat	Wheat weevil lung
Unknown antigens:		
	Cereal grain	Grain measurer's lung
	Tobacco plants	Tobacco

and their by-products. This dust will be released any time a farmer is transporting or working with moldy animal feed, but exposures are not likely to be threatening unless the feed and farmer are enclosed in a barn, silo, or other structure.

The following section describes the two respiratory responses to spoiled fodder: the hypersensitivity pneumonitis farmer's lung, and the toxic organic dust syndrome (TODS). Either of these can occur from any exposure to moldy feed. However, farmer's lung is most typical of dairy farmers who are breaking open bales of hay to feed or bed their barn-enclosed cattle. Acute farmer's lung is thus seen most commonly in winter and spring, before cattle are put out to pasture. Farmer's lung is more prevalent in the north temperate zone.

TODS is seen most commonly following preparation of a conventional upright silo for mechanical unloading. After loading a silo, farmers often place a plastic sheet over the silage, and then add another foot or so of silage to hold this sheet in place. This upper silage "cap" becomes grossly contaminated with microorganisms as it dries. Before starting to feed out the silage, a farmer must climb into the silo, pitch this contaminated silage out of the silo, and lower the mechanical silage unloader into place. High concentrations of microorganisms and their by-products can be inhaled during this task. Farmers are also commonly exposed to clouds of these dusts while shoveling moldy grain in a barn or bin.

How Common Are These Dusts and Resulting Respiratory Diseases?

Disturbance of spoiled plant material can produce spore clouds of very high concentration: breaking open bales of hay in a confined space, such as in a barn, has produced clouds of 1.6×109 spores/m^3 of thermophilic actinomycetes. A person doing light work in this setting may retain 7.5×105 spores/minute in the lungs. Concentrations of 4×109 viable spores/m^3 have been documented in silo openings (written communication, John J. May, MD, August 1985).

The prevalence of resulting disease varies from study to study and is difficult to interpret, but prevalence of farmer's lung usually is well below 5% of the farming population (in the United States, although higher in western England, Scotland, and Finland). For example, 3.9% of one surveyed group of Wyoming farmers and dairy producers gave a history typical of farmer's lung. A population based survey of over 1400 Wisconsin farmers yielded a 0.42% prevalence of confirmed clinical cases. Ten percent of the surveyed population showed serum precipitins to at least one farmer's lung antigen; the highest prevalence was among dairy farmers with the largest farms and largest herds. Some studies demonstrate that a much higher percentage of the exposed population has developed antibodies. Why many farmers with farmer's lung antibodies fail to develop clinical disease is unknown.

TODS resulting from exposure to spoiled plant material has only recently been recognized as a response that is distinctive from farmer's lung; much remains to be learned about this syndrome. However, it probably is far more common than farmer's lung or other illnesses associated with feed storage (such as silo filler's disease). In fact, many cases previously diagnosed as farmer's lung may have been TODS. In a study of New York dairy farmers, 14 of 26 feed-related episodes of respiratory illness were identified as TODS.

Respiratory Problems from Decayed Grain, Hay, and Silage Dusts

Inhalation of organic dusts from spoiled plant material is thought to produce two symptomatically similar, but pathologically distinctive, respiratory responses: hypersensitivity pneumonitis and TODS. Hypersensitivity pneumonitis, also called extrinsic allergic alveolitis, goes by a number of agent-specific descriptive names (see table), including farmer's lung when resulting from occupational exposure to spoiled plant material dusts and occurring in farmers. TODS is sometimes called atypical farmer's lung, silo unloader's disease, or pulmonary mycotoxicosis. Since these two responses result from similar exposures and present in similar fashion, they are often confused. Indeed, much work still needs to be done to define the exact agents inducing each biological response, and the specific mechanisms involved in each type of response.

Farmer's lung is an allergic response of the alveoli, which has variable presentation depending on host factors and specific circumstances of exposure to spoiled plant material. Illness covers a continuum from acute reversible to chronic debilitating disease. Symptoms of acute illness are observed four to eight hours following exposure, with cough, dyspnea, fever and chills, myalgia, and malaise. The acute illness subsides in two to five days, and respiratory impairment resolves completely.

Continuous, low-level exposure can cause chronic subacute illness with weight loss, fatigue, and insidious onset of cough and dyspnea. Lung impairment usually resolves completely if exposure ceases. However, multiple acute attacks or chronic low-level exposure can lead to irreversible, progressive lung damage that can decrease total lung capacity and diffusion capacity. End stages are similar to those of any chronic interstitial pulmonary fibrosis, with death typically resulting from respiratory insufficiency or corpulmonale.

Characteristic physical findings include fine, crepitant rales in the lower two-thirds of both lungs among many patients. Patients may be cyanotic or hypoxemic. Laboratory findings in acute cases may include leukocytosis, sometimes with eosinophilia. Pulmonary function tests of acutely ill patients reveal decreased lung volumes, small airways obstruction, and decreased carbon monoxide diffusing capacity; PO2 may be decreased. Chest films may show a finely nodular infiltrate in the lower two-thirds of peripheral lung fields, but may also be clear. Chronic cases show a spectrum of abnormalities, including pneumonitis, fibrosis, hyperexpansion, or honeycombing of lungs. Serum precipitins to thermophilic actinomycetes are characteristic of farmer's lung patients.

TODS is thought to be a non-allergic, inflammatory reaction of small airways and the alveoli possibly due to mycotoxins or endotoxins. Clinically, acute cases present very much like acute farmer's lung, with cough, fever and chills, fatigue, myalgia, and anorexia occurring four to eight hours following exposure to spoiled plant material. Severity varies from a mild, influenza-like illness to profound illness with severe dyspnea. Symptoms subside in two to five days, and resolve completely within ten days. Chronic illness and presumably permanent lung damage do not appear to occur. Multiple exposures simply produce repeated acute illness. No deaths have been known to result from this syndrome.

A number of features differentiate acute farmer's lung and TODS. These are discussed below. Farmer's lung occurs in only a small subset of any exposed population. Although predisposing factors must exist, these have not yet been defined. Among sensitized farmers, even a small exposure to aerosolized mold and bacteria can elicit an attack. TODS, in contrast, can affect any exposed individual; thus cases often are clustered, with several individuals in a given work situation being affected simultaneously. However, exposure to decayed plant dusts must be massive.

A number of laboratory tests distinguish the two illnesses. Chest radiographs of farmer's lung patients characteristically reveal a finely nodular density in the lower lung fields, while chest radiographs of TODS patients characteristically are clear (although occasionally are abnormal). Blood gas measurements often show decreased PO2 for farmer's lung, but usually no decrease for TODS. Immunoserology of farmer's lung patients is positive, while TODS patients do not typically have antibodies to thermophilic actinomycete antigens. (Note, however, that TODS patients may have previously developed these antibodies, and thus may demonstrate serum precipitins to the thermophilic actinomycete antigens.) Pulmonary function tests, although usually showing marked restriction with farmer's lung, show mild or no restriction with TODS. And, finally, bronchoalveolar lavage (which is done infrequently, and primarily on an investigational basis) yields fluids rich in lymphocytes with farmer's lung, but dominated by leucocytes with TODS, indicative of their respective pathologies. Readers also should note that a symptomatically similar toxic syndrome can be caused among agricultural workers by exposure to moldy plant material, grain dusts that are not necessarily mold-laden cotton dust, and confinement house dusts. These similar responses, referred to collectively as TODS, may or may not be pathologically identical.

Diagnosis

Because presentation of farmer's lung is highly variable, no single factor is diagnostic. Farmer's lung should be suspected in any farmer with an influenza-like pneumonitis or active interstitial lung disease. Normally, the following combination of factors is sufficient for diagnosis: a typical presentation (symptoms of cough, fever, and dyspnea, and possible basal crepitant rales), following a history of exposure to decayed plant material dusts, supported by positive serology to any of the 15 or so fungal or thermophilic antinomycete antigens, an abnormal chest radiograph revealing lung infiltrates, and abnormal pulmonary function tests including restrictive changes and impaired diffusing capacity. However, caution is required for several reasons. Although the presentation and history of exposure alone may be sufficient in acute cases, these are not so helpful in subacute or chronic cases, where continuous low level exposure may be difficult to identify and onset of disease is insidious. And, although farmer's lung patients demonstrate a positive serology, 10% or more of the farming population may possess farmer's lung antibodies and only a small number of these experience clinical illness. Also, care must be taken to use an appropriate battery of farmer's lung antigens. Both chest radiographs and pulmonary function tests may be highly variable, and in some cases either or both may be normal.

Lung biopsy, lung lavage, and bronchoprovocation are not normally required or advised, but may be useful in an exceptional case when a specific diagnosis is needed (for example, for workman's compensation), or with a difficult differential diagnosis. Lung biopsy in farmer's lung reveals a characteristic granulomatous interstitial pneumonitis. Gross thickening of the alveolarcapillary membranes results from mononuclear infiltration into interstitial tissues, resulting in obliteration of the alveoli. Mononuclear cells often form non-caseating granulomata that may occlude bronchioles. Multinucleated Langerhan's giant cells and foreign body type cells that may be birefringent or non-refringent are common in areas of inflammation. Spores of the causative molds usually are not recognized in tissues.

Lung lavage, usually regarded as experimental, may be helpful in ambiguous cases of interstitial lung disease, and demonstrate an increase of lymphocytes, an increase in T to B cell ratios (as compared to peripheral blood), and an increase in IgG and IgM (as compared to albumin).

Bronchoprovocation by farmer's lung antigens has been proposed as a definitive diagnostic test, but can involve significant risk and discomfort to the patient and must be done with care in the hands of experienced physicians.

Acute farmer's lung can be misdiagnosed as influenza, a bad cold, infectious pneumonia, or asthma. An occupational history and the recurrent nature of farmer's lung are helpful in differentiating it from these more common illnesses. Differentiation of most cases of farmer's lung from asthma can be based on lack of wheezing, presence of rales, an abnormal chest radiograph, and pulmonary functions with decreased vital capacity, compliance, and diffusing capacity (rather that reversible obstruction).

Acute farmer's lung may easily be confused with TODS resulting from the same exposure. Although presentation of acute farmer's lung and TODS patients is nearly identical, the two illnesses usually can be separated by considering the following: cases of TODS must follow massive exposures, cases often are clustered, and most patients will not have serum precipitins to farmer's lung antigens. There is no evidence that TODS will progress to chronic disease.

Because acute farmer's lung and TODS may result from exposure within a silo, either may be confused as silo filler's disease resulting from exposure to nitrous oxides. However, this latter disease can be traced to silos filled within the previous two weeks with fresh silage.

Chronic farmer's lung can be misdiagnosed as depression, chronic bronchitis, or any chronic interstitial lung disease. Pulmonary sarcoid may prove an especially difficult differential because of histopathologic and other similarities to farmer's lung. Occupational history and other history of exposure to spoiled plant material are critical in establishing a diagnosis of chronic farmer's lung. Lung lavage or bronchoprovocation may be helpful in exceptional cases.

Treatment

There is no specific treatment for farmer's lung or TODS. Removal from the causative environment is usually self-imposed. Since both TODS and acute farmer's lung are self-limiting, with severe symptoms resolving in two to five days and complete resolution occurring within 10 to 60 days, a physician's help is often not solicited by afflicted persons. In severe cases of acute farmer's lung, with extended duration or extreme hypoxemia, supportive therapy (including oxygen and rehydration) may be needed. Use of corticosteroids is thought to reverse the acute course and shorten the duration of illness. Desensitization is not effective; antibiotics, bronchodilators, and antihistamines are ineffective.

Because a small concentration of antigen can provoke illness in highly sensitive individuals, and continued exposure can lead to permanent impairment, avoidance of spoiled plant material is imperative. Early diagnosis and avoidance are most important in preventing irreversible lung damage.

Prevention

Prevention of exposure to spoiled plant materials is advisable for all farmers; it is imperative for persons sensitized to farmer's lung antigens. This may be accomplished by reducing mold growth in feedstuffs. Capping silage with a plastic sheet held in place by rocks or a heavy chain (rather than additional plant material) reduces the mold and dust in the top layers of silage. Switching to glass-lined, airtight silos (realizing that these silos pose the health risk of asphyxiation) also will reduce mold growth, but may be economically impossible for many farmers. Grain and hay always should be stored when fully dried.

However, elimination of microorganisms from stored fodder is impossible, and thus techniques to prevent aerosolization and inhalation of these particles should be adopted whenever possible. When silo caps are removed, the top layer of silage can be wetted down to prevent spore aerosolization; however, farmers often do not bother to do so. Persons with a history of farmer's lung should never uncap a silo or perform other tasks with a high probability of exposure to massive quantities of plant dusts. Workers uncapping a silo, shoveling grain, or working with feed, especially in any enclosed space, should always wear a certified dust respirator. This respirator should prevent the inhalation of massive amounts of dusts from decayed plant material necessary to cause TODS, and some evidence suggests that spore inhalation is reduced sufficiently to prevent acute farmer's lung in sensitized individuals. The respirator must fit properly and must be properly maintained. In some cases, highly sensitive individuals may need to wear a powered air purifying respirator. Handling dusty fodder mechanically in a manner that keeps the farmer distant from the fodder is a desirable work practice, especially when the fodder is in an enclosed space; the widespread acceptance of large round bales that are transported by a tractor (instead of small, square, hand-carried bales) has probably decreased exposure to moldy hay.

Some dairy farmers with a history of farmer's lung have successfully managed their illness by wearing a respirator regularly and by assigning jobs with the potential of exposure to mold to other individuals. Other such farmers have undertaken more dramatic steps to eliminate exposure to decayed plant materials, including use of glass-lined, airtight silos, completely mechanizing cattle feeding operations, and installing large ventilation systems in the barn (oral communication, James Marx PhD, Feb 1985). Although very expensive, these latter measures have allowed sensitized farmers to stay on the farm.

Monitoring of patients with chronic or repeated acute attacks of farmer's lung should focus on regular testing of pulmonary function and chest radiographs, as well as physical examination and history regarding dyspnea following exposure and on exertion. Measurement of blood gases and exercise tolerance is helpful in assessing impairment. If management and environmental control measures do not prevent the recurrence of farmer's lung, and if pulmonary evaluations indicate progressive respiratory impairment, a farmer may have to leave the farm to prevent permanent impairment.

Section 9.2

Cotton Dust

Occupational Safety and Health Administration (OSHA), Fact Sheet 95-23, http://www.osha-slc.gov/OshDoc/Fact_data/FSNO95-23.html, January 1995.

Introduction

Cotton dust is dust present in the air during the handling or processing of cotton. This dust may contain a mixture of many substances including ground up plant matter, fiber, bacteria, fungi, soil, pesticides, non-cotton matter, and other contaminants.

Health Effects

Exposure to cotton dust can mean serious health problems. The first symptoms of disease are difficulty in breathing or perhaps a tightness across the chest which is particularly noticeable on the first day back at work after a worker has been off for a few days. Workers also cough up phlegm or mucus.

If exposure above the OSHA limit continues, workers may develop byssinosis, also known as "brown lung" disease. While earlier breathing difficulties may be reversible, damage at the advanced stages of the disease is permanent and disabling. Workers who develop brown lung may have to retire early because they are so short of breath they cannot do their normal jobs or even carry out simple tasks. Exposure to cotton dust also leads to increased risk of chronic bronchitis and emphysema.

At the time the final standard was published, as many as 100,000 workers in the cotton industry were "at risk" from cotton dust exposure. An estimated 35,000 individuals are disabled from byssinosis as a result of exposure to cotton dust.

Worker Protection

To protect workers from disabling respiratory diseases, employers are required to limit the amount of respirable cotton dust in the air. The limits—known as permissible exposure limits—are average exposures as measured over an eight-hour workday. For yarn manufacturing the limit is 200 micrograms of cotton dust per cubic meter of air; for textile waste houses, 500 micrograms; for slashing and weaving operations, 750 micrograms; and for waste recycling and garnetting, 1000 micrograms.

Dust Measurement

Employers must measure the workplace cotton dust level at least every six months, or whenever there are any changes in equipment or work practices which might increase the amount of cotton dust in the air. Measurements must be representative of an eight-hour period and be performed for each shift and in each work area. Employers must explain the procedure to their workers and permit them to observe the monitoring. They must notify employees in writing of the findings within five days after measurement. If the levels are above Occupational Safety and Health Administration (OSHA) standards, employers must list in the notice to employees the steps they will take to correct problems.

Dust Controls

Often employers can reduce dust levels by adjusting dust control equipment, such as ventilation systems, and by cleaning and repairing the equipment regularly. An employer's dust control program must include, at a minimum, the following:

1. cleaning floors with a vacuum or another method that cuts down the spreading of dust

2. disposing of dust in such a way that as little dust scatters as possible

3. using mechanical methods to stack, dump or otherwise handle cotton or cotton waste, when possible

4. checking, cleaning, and repairing dust control equipment and ventilation systems

Compressed air may not be used to clean clothing and floors and may only be used to clean equipment if no other methods are possible and workers involved in the cleaning wear respirators. If these measures fail to reduce the cotton dust levels below the OSHA limits, employers must try additional engineering controls and work practices.

Respiratory Protection

Employers must supply employees with respirators, if other measures are not sufficient to reduce exposure. If respirators are necessary, workers are to be fitted for them and instructed in using, cleaning, and maintaining them. An employee who cannot wear a respirator for medical reasons must have the opportunity to transfer to another job where the level of cotton dust is within the OSHA limit, at no loss in pay, seniority, or other rights and benefits, if another position is available.

Medical Examinations

In addition to reducing the dust in the air, employers must provide free annual medical exams, including breathing tests, to workers employed in dust areas. If workers show significant physical changes, more frequent exams must be made available to them. Results are to be provided to workers, and workers may copy exam and test results if they wish. Employers are to maintain the records for 20 years and make them available to workers or to their designated representatives with the consent of the workers and to OSHA and the National Institute for Occupational Safety and Health (NIOSH) on request.

Training Program

To insure that employees are aware of the hazards of cotton dust, employers are required to conduct a training program at least annually. Warning signs must be posted in work areas where the cotton dust level is higher than the OSHA limit.

Chapter 10

A Guide to Respiratory Protection at Work

Exposure Assessment for Your Respiratory Protection Program

You can significantly reduce the incidence of job-related illness or injury from exposure to harmful airborne contaminants such as gases, vapors, dusts, mists, and fumes. The first step is a workplace exposure assessment for identifying harmful exposures, their extent or magnitude, and how to control them.

Employee exposure can be determined by a person who is professionally trained to make workplace hazard exposure assessments. The assessor evaluates the processes, procedures, and hazard communication program, and conducts exposure monitoring to determine the types of controls necessary to protect employee health and safety. The assessor also takes samples in a worksite operator's breathing zone to analyze employee exposure.

A large company may have an industrial hygienist on staff who can conduct an exposure assessment. Smaller businesses may choose to have the hazard assessment and monitoring performed by their insurance carriers, or to contract with an industrial hygiene consulting firm for providing these services.

California Occupational Safety and Health Administration, "Guide to Respiratory" Protection At Work, Pub. No. S-630, http://www.dir.ca.gov/dosh/dosh_publications/respiratory.html, August 1995.

129

Controlling Harmful Exposures

Employers should follow a specified sequence of procedures to control harmful exposures at the worksite.

First, the employer prevents harmful exposures by means of engineering controls, if feasible. Second, the employer initiates administrative controls in addition to feasible engineering controls. Third, the employer prevents harmful exposures through use of personal protective equipment, such as respirators, if the engineering and administrative means do not achieve the desired control level.

Installing ventilation equipment that is designed to remove contaminants from the employee's breathing zone, substituting a non-toxic or less toxic substance for the harmful substance, and isolating or enclosing the work operation are the most widely used engineering controls.

When engineering controls are not feasible, or they fail to reduce employee exposure to acceptable levels, administrative controls are used to reduce the amount of time during which employees are exposed to the harmful substance. Administrative controls have severe limitations and cannot be used where concentration is above the level that must never be exceeded (termed the ceiling limit), or in atmospheres that may be immediately dangerous to life and health, or for specified contaminants such as asbestos.

Respiratory Protective Equipment

Because respiratory equipment that is used to protect employees from exposure to harmful airborne contaminants also has limitations, specific requirements must be met. Respiratory protective equipment can be used only when it is clearly impractical to use engineering and administrative controls for reducing employee exposure to acceptable levels, or while engineering controls are being installed, or in emergency situations.

Respirators are required in an atmosphere that could contain less than 19.5 percent or more than 23.5 percent oxygen, and in atmospheres that could contain dusts, fibers, mists, fumes, gases or vapors at harmful concentrations. General industry employers who must provide respiratory equipment should develop and maintain a respiratory protection program.

Elements of an Effective Respiratory Protection Program

This section summarizes the basic requirements for an effective respiratory protection program.

Written Program

Employers whose employees use respiratory protective equipment should prepare a written program that describes the procedures for operating respiratory protection equipment, as an element of their written injury and illness prevention program. These procedures are the foundation for training employees as well as developing and maintaining an effective respiratory protection program. Written operating procedures include instructions related to:

- selecting and issuing respirators
- training employees
- conducting respirator facepiece fit tests
- conducting facepiece seal fit checks
- inspecting respirators
- cleaning and sanitizing respirators
- maintaining and repairing respirators
- storing respirators
- respirator limitations
- medical surveillance

Respirator Selection

All respiratory protective equipment has use limitations. The type of personal protective equipment an employer selects, including respirators, is dependent upon the type of work being performed, the airborne hazard, and available oxygen. Many different types of respirators are available for a variety of applications. The employer must make sure the proper respirator is selected and used for the kind of work being performed and the hazard involved. Improper selection or using inadequate equipment can lead to serious injury or illness, and under certain conditions could be fatal.

Consider the following when selecting respirators:

- Is protection needed for oxygen deficient or enriched atmospheres? Only air supplying respirators can be used.
- Is protection needed for airborne contaminants?
- What are the contaminants?

- What are the contaminant warnings? Inadequate warning properties—such as not being able to detect the contaminant by smell, taste or irritation below the permissible exposure limits—require air supplying respirators.

- What is the permissible exposure limit, action level, ceiling, short term and/or excursion limits for each contaminant?

- What are the contaminant's physical properties?

- What are the contaminant's chemical properties?

- What health effects can be caused by exposure?

- Is the onset of symptoms delayed?

- What are the employee exposure levels?

- What are the maximum possible exposures?

- How long are employees exposed?

- Where is the work being conducted? Work in a confined space requires air supplying respirators and additional safety precautions.

- What physical work activity is being conducted?

- What other protective equipment is being worn?

- What is the health status of the employees? Some employees may have to be excluded from using respiratory equipment because of pulmonary or other medical disorders.

Respiratory equipment selection is an extremely important element of an effective respiratory protection program. Selection is a very complex issue to be handled only by people trained in this area. It is also very important to adhere to the respiratory equipment selection criteria, and to consider other protective equipment—gloves, eye protection, clothing—to be used for protecting employees at the worksite.

Respirator Approval

Though an employer may select respiratory protective equipment from a variety of types, shapes and manufacturers, the only respirators that can be used in the workplace are those approved by the National Institute for Occupational Safety and Health (NIOSH) and the Mine Safety and Health Administration (MSHA). All approved respiratory protective equipment has an approval number displayed prominently on the equipment. The NIOSH/MSHA approval number always begins with the letters TC, followed by the schedule number for which the respirator is approved. The last numbers identify the manufacturer-designation for the equipment. For example, a respirator with a NIOSH/MSHA approval number TC-21C-XX indicates that it is approved by NIOSH/MSHA for protection against particulates (dust), and the manufacturer identifies it as their unit XX. Alterations, modifications or use of parts not designated for a specific respirator by its manufacturer voids the NIOSH/MSHA approval. Only properly trained personnel are permitted to repair respirators.

Types of Respirators

Respirators are classed in two basic groups: air purifying respirators (APR) and air supplying respirators (ASR).

Air Purifying Respirators

One type of air purifying respirator (APR) removes particles of dust, fibers, fumes or mist from the air as the contaminant moves through a filter. Another type of APR removes certain vapors and gases by absorbing or reacting with the contaminant, and lets clean air enter the facepiece. Combination APRs remove both particulates and vapors.

Contaminated air may be drawn through the APR filter by two different means. The most common means relies on the respirator wearers using their own breathing to cause the air to pass through the filter, by creating a negative pressure inside the respirator facepiece. The other method is to use an air pump that delivers air at a slight positive pressure through the filter to the inside of the facepiece. This type of APR is a powered air purifying respirator (PAPR).

The kind of filter used in an APR depends upon the contaminant it is designed to remove. For example, a filter designed to remove organic vapors usually contains activated charcoal in a cartridge or canister attached directly or by a breathing tube to the respirator facepiece. A filter designed to remove metal fume can constitute the entire facepiece, or be attached directly or by breathing tubes to the respirator facepiece. Some APRs have an end-of-service indicator for when the filter system is expended and the filter must be changed.

133

Air Supplying Respirators

Air supplying respirators (ASR) provide regulated breathing air from a source other than the air in the contaminated work area. An ASR consists of a facepiece and equipment for supplying the breathing air by compressors or pressurized cylinders. An airline ASR provides regulated air to the facepiece through a hose by means of a remotely located pressurized cylinder or compressor. Another type of ASR provides breathing air from a self-contained breathing apparatus (SCBA), which is a pressurized cylinder worn by the respirator wearer.

One type of SCBA cylinder provides enough air to the user for entry into and exit from a contaminated atmosphere to perform work — such as a 30-minute airpack. The other type of SCBA is for escape purposes only, and may contain enough air for five to ten minutes. The SCBA approved for escape only must never be used to enter a contaminated area to perform work, or to enter an area for rescue. An SCBA or airline respirators with auxiliary escape SCBA attached are the only respiratory protective equipment approved for entry into an atmosphere that is immediately dangerous to life and health, such as a confined space, or atmospheres of unknown content or concentration.

No respirator is approved for use in an atmosphere containing more that 25 percent of the contaminant's lower explosive limits.

Respirator Use Limits

Air purifying respirators have limitations and are not approved for use:

- When the contaminant has poor warning properties and is not easily recognized by taste, smell or irritation at or below its permissible exposure limit.

- In oxygen deficient or enriched atmospheres. APRs do not supply oxygen, or filter out high levels of oxygen or other gases.

- When the contaminant concentration exceeds the NIOSH/MSHA maximum designated use concentration for the respirator.

- When the service life indicator shows that the filter system is expended and the filter must be changed, or the shelf-life date for the filter has expired.

- In atmospheres that could become immediately dangerous to life or health: where a short exposure could cause death, injury, illness or delayed reaction.

Leakage

With some APRs the user causes air to enter the filter at each breath. These are called negative pressure APRs because every time the wearer inhales, the pressure created inside the facepiece is negative in relation to the contaminated atmosphere outside the facepiece. If there are leaks around the face seal, the negative pressure inside the respirator can draw contaminated air into the facepiece. When the respirator wearer begins to taste, smell, or experience irritation from contaminated air, this indicates that leakage or a breakthrough has occurred.

In the case of an APR, breakthrough may mean that the filter, canister or cartridge needs replacing, there is mechanical failure of the respirator valves, a breathing tube connection is loose, or there is a leak at the facepiece seal.

In the case of an ASR, breakthrough may mean a failure of valves, regulators, hoses, breathing tubes or fittings, or loose connections or a leak at the facepiece seal.

A poor face seal may be the reason for leakage of contaminants into the facepiece of any APR or ASR. A poor face seal may be caused by weight gain/loss changing the physical features of the wearer's face.

Leakage can also be caused by debris and dirt buildup, excessive perspiration, use of Vaseline, a growth of beard or other facial hair, or wearing any item that interferes with the facepiece seal.

Missing, worn, or deteriorated respirator parts, such as missing exhalation valves or insufficiently tightened cartridges, may cause leakage of a contaminant into the facepiece. Contaminant leakage into the facepiece of an ASR may be due to cracked, deteriorated or loose connections between hoses and breathing tubes, or to malfunctioning regulators or improperly seated facepiece lenses. Additional leakage of contaminants into the facepiece may occur if the wearer overbreathes the regulated air supply, thereby creating a negative pressure inside the facepiece.

Filter Obstruction

All APRs for dust, fumes and mist have filters which become obstructed or clogged by particulates and which must be changed when it becomes hard to breathe through the filter. PAPRs have the same use limitations as negative pressure or non-powered air purifying respirators.

One disadvantage in using PAPRs is that the constant flow of air through purifying filters decreases the amount of time the filter can be used, because the greater air flow and collection of contaminants on the filter cause greater loading on the filter.

Protection Factors

Different respirators offer different levels of protection. NIOSH and MSHA have established protection factors for every type of respirator to indicate how much protection a specific respirator type provides.

The respirator protection factor (PF) is the ratio of contaminant concentration level outside the respirator to the expected possible concentration inside the respirator. The higher the PF value for a respirator, the less contaminant leakage into its facepiece is expected. PFs are approximate values and apply only when the wearer has been properly fitted, tested and trained, and when the respirator is correctly worn and kept in proper operating condition.

As a general rule, when a contaminant has a specific permissible exposure limit (PEL) listed in the regulatory standard, the maximum contaminant level at which a respirator may be used is the lower value of the PEL multiplied by the PF for the respirator, or the maximum use concentration specified on the NIOSH/MSHA approval label.

Some air supplying respirators, such as pressure-demand self-contained breathing apparatus, may be used in atmospheres that are immediately dangerous to life or health—but only when the concentration of contaminants does not exceed 25 percent of the lower explosive limits.

Respirator Training

Once proper respiratory protective equipment is selected, the employer is responsible for making sure that employees who use it are adequately trained. The employee is responsible for correctly using a respirator and making sure it remains in good condition.

Part of training is to encourage employees to ask questions for clarity. An employee who actively participates may have good ideas for work practices and process operations that could enable the employer to limit or control the exposure hazard in a way that reduces the need for respirators.

Employees must receive thorough training in the need, use, sanitary care, proper fit and testing of the equipment, along with its limitations. They also wear the equipment in normal air for a familiarity period, then in a test atmosphere. The training an employee receives will help protect against injury, illness and loss of life. Employees must know how to use respirators correctly and safely.

Respirator training must cover:

- Appropriate hazard communication—why a respirator is needed, the nature of the hazard, and possible consequences if respirators are not used.

- Limitations for the type of respirator being used.

- Procedures for respirator inspecting, maintenance, donning and wearing, and performing fit checks.

- Qualitative or quantitative fit test procedures, as appropriate.

- How to sanitize and store respirators to prevent deterioration and contamination.

- Opportunity to wear respiratory equipment in normal air for an adequate familiarity period, and to wear it in a test atmosphere— such as one generated by smoke tubes or isoamyl acetate.

Respirator training should cover:

- Why engineering controls are not feasible or not adequate to control the hazard, and what efforts are being made to reduce the need for respirator use.

- Opportunity for employees to demonstrate that they fully comprehend the information presented.

Fit Tests

Respirator facepieces are made in a variety of sizes to fit a wide range of face shapes. Some employees, however, are not able to achieve a good fit, and they must not be permitted to use respirators.

Facial scars, beards, whiskers, sideburns, large mustaches, and weight gains/losses interfere with proper fit of a respirator facepiece seal. This problem is especially acute for negative pressure respirators. When respirators are first used, a variety of sizes and manufacturers' brands are tried to achieve both a comfortable and an adequate fit.

A fit test is essentially a challenge test, used to determine whether the respirator fits properly with a good face seal. Two types of fit tests can be conducted: qualitative and quantitative.

Qualitative Fit Test

A qualitative fit test uses irritant smoke, isoamyl acetate or saccharin solution aerosol to estimate the face seal fit, and depends on the wearer's subjective response to the chemical challenge test. If the wearer detects a smell, taste or irritation, or if the concentration inside is above acceptable values, the wearer has failed the fit test. The wearer must re-adjust the facepiece and the test be conducted again. It may be necessary to try several different facepieces to find the respirator with good fit.

The qualitative fit test depends on the wearer's judgment and ability to detect odor, taste or irritation caused by the test substance. Prior to beginning the test, the instructor first determines whether the wearer can distinguish the test substance. The qualitative test gives only a rough measure of leakage within the respirator facepiece. Qualitative fit tests introduce the test substance around the facepiece seal while the wearer performs head and body movements and talks.

Quantitative Fit Test

A quantitative fit test uses particulates or chemicals, such as a monodisperse sodium chloride aerosol, to measure the amount of material inside the respirator facepiece after leakage, compared to the outside concentration. The quantitative fit test numerically measures respirator facepiece fit. This test requires specialized equipment to generate the test substance and to measure its concentration inside and outside the respirator. Conducted only by trained personnel, the quantitative test introduces the substance around the facepiece seal while the wearer is inside a test chamber.

Fit Checks

With the exception of hoods and certain powered air purifying respirators, a fit check is conducted by the wearer every time the respirator is put on. A point-of-use fit check must be made to determine whether respirator valves are working properly, and how well the facepiece fits and seals out contaminants. Positive pressure and negative pressure fit checks are indicators of respirator operability and facepiece fit.

Fit checks are conducted during initial selection and training, and every time an employee puts on a respirator before entering a contaminated atmosphere. The employee must not use a respirator unless the checks have been satisfactorily completed.

Maintenance

Employers must ensure that the respiratory equipment provided for their employees is maintained correctly with proper inspection, cleaning, sanitizing, and storage. Inspection and monitoring records are required for some respiratory protective equipment. The manufacturer's instructions must be followed to ensure proper respirator maintenance, cleaning and sanitation.

Inspecting

Inspections are conducted and repairs performed as needed on all respiratory and associated equipment. The following items, when applicable to the type of respirator being used, are checked before and after each use, during cleaning, or as otherwise required.

- Inspect facepiece, straps, valves, gaskets, gasket seats, breathing tubes, air hoses and other elastomeric parts for cleanliness, cracks, deterioration, distortion.

- Inspect cartridges and filters for dents and cracks.

- Inspect hose clamps and fittings for tightness.

- Inspect regulators for proper working order. Only specifically trained personnel may perform maintenance work on regulators.

- Inspect compressed air cylinder for dents, corrosion, and whether it complies with proper hydrostatic test dates.

- Inspect air compressors, carbon monoxide and/or high temperature detectors, and alarm systems for proper working order.

- Inspect emergency respirators, which must be inspected at least monthly with a record of inspection affixed to the respirator or its storage container.

Cleaning and Sanitizing

Respirators are maintained in a clean and sanitary condition to ensure that contaminants do not cause deterioration or malfunction of parts, and to prevent dermatitis developing among employees using the equipment. A respirator must not be used by another employee until it has been thoroughly cleaned and sanitized.

Procedures for cleaning a cartridge-type respirator are:

1. Remove the cartridge, gaskets, valves and straps from the respirator.

2. Wash the respirator body in a mild soap solution or the cleaning solution recommended by the manufacturer.

3. Immerse the respirator in a sanitizing solution according to the manufacturer's instructions.

4. Thoroughly rinse the respirator to remove any residue. Failure to remove soap and properly sanitize the respirator may cause dermatitis and/or eye irritation.

5. Air dry the respirator in an area away from contaminants. Do not dry respirator at temperatures above manufacturer's recommendation.

Storing

Respirators can be permanently damaged and distorted if they are not properly stored. Respirators stored in the open may become contaminated by materials that shorten the life of the elastomeric parts, cause facial dermatitis, or contribute to body burden by ingestion. Some storage practices may shorten or deplete the life of cartridges, or cause contamination of the respirator's inner portion.

Respirators must be protected from sunlight, dust, moisture, temperature extremes, and contaminants. All respirators are cleaned, sanitized, air dried and stored in a manner that prevents such exposure.

Proper storage in a dust-tight container, such as a resealable plastic bag, prevents contamination that can lead to facial dermatitis, respirator distortion and deterioration.

Repairing

If a respirator needs repair, only the replacement parts approved by the manufacturer for that model can be used. Use of unapproved parts voids NIOSH/MSHA approval for the respirator, and may contribute to its failure. This refers to all respirator parts—including clamps, straps, cartridges, valves, regulators, hoses and seals.

The employer must maintain an adequate supply of repair parts or extra respirators to ensure that only properly maintained respirators are available and in use.

Only specifically trained personnel are permitted to repair respirators. Repair of air supplying respirators and their associated equipment, such as regulators, monitoring and alarm devices, is performed by the manufacturer or other trained person.

Employee Health

Even with appropriate equipment provided and adequate training given, an employee's health status must be considered before allowing respirator use. Medical conditions—such as pulmonary deficiencies, hearing diseases, anemia, hemophilia, and vision correction needs— may affect an employee's ability to wear and work with a respirator. No employee should be assigned work requiring respirators without first receiving a physical examination and approval by a licensed physician. The initial physical exam is followed by annual review of the employee's medical status. Medical approval becomes mandatory when employees are required to work with certain contaminants such as asbestos, cotton dust, and other regulated carcinogens.

The consulting physician determines the medical criteria that apply to employees who wear respirators. These factors are considered during a medical evaluation of an employee:

- medical history pertaining to a condition that could affect the employee's ability to wear a respirator

- physical examination with emphasis on respiratory and cardiovascular condition

- spirometry test for forced vital capacity and forced expiratory volume in one second

The employer provides the following information to assist the examining physician with employee assessment:

- type of respirator required for the work

- duration and frequency of respirator use

- type of work to be performed while wearing respirator

- environmental conditions in workplace

- other personal protective equipment to be worn

Respirator Program Surveillance

The employer should conduct ongoing surveillance of the respiratory protection program to identify deficiencies and make corrections as needed. The employer seeks input from employees, and discusses the program with them to determine whether they are experiencing any difficulties while using the equipment.

The employer should instruct employees to give immediate notification if any respirator users believe they have inhaled a harmful quantity of contaminant or are otherwise affected by harmful contaminants. The employer then investigates the circumstances immediately and takes corrective action.

As part of surveillance, the employer periodically reviews the entire respiratory protection program to make sure that:

- proper respiratory protective equipment is being used, correctly maintained and stored.

- all employees are trained and fit tested.

- employees are medically qualified to continue using respirators.

- environmental factors have not changed, or if they have, other toxic substances or conditions which increase the degree of employee exposure are taken into consideration during review of the worksite respiratory protection program.

Recordkeeping

Employers are required to maintain records relating to employee exposures at the worksite. These records cover such subjects as airborne chemical sample data, monitoring procedures, medical evaluations, emergency respirator inspections, training and fit tests.

Part Three

Skin and Eye Issues

Chapter 11

Occupational Dermatitis

Introduction

Many dermatoses may have occupational relevance, but the overwhelming majority are dermatitic. In current terminology "dermatitis" is used synonymously with "eczema" to describe inflammatory reactions in the skin with a particular spectrum of clinical and histopathological characteristics.

A dermatitis may be entirely endogenous (constitutional) or be entirely exogenous (contact). Exogenous dermatitis may be caused by irritant or allergic contact reactions. A dermatitis often has a multifactorial aetiology and may be aggravated by the presence of pathogens such as Staphylococcus aureus. When considering a hand eczema it is always worth investigating the possible role of contributory factors and assessing the importance of these. Atopic hand eczema is a common example of an endogenous eczema in which exogenous factors normally compound the situation.

An occupational dermatitis is one where the inflammatory reaction is caused entirely by occupational contact factors or where such agents are partly responsible by contributing to the reaction on compromised skin. In most cases occupationally related dermatitis affects the hands alone, though there may be spread onto the forearms. Occasionally, the face may be the prime site of inflammation (for example, with airborne contact factors), and other sites may be affected.

Irritant Contact Dermatitis

Irritant contact dermatitis is caused by direct chemical or physical damage to the skin. Everyone is susceptible to the development of an irritant contact dermatitis if exposure to an irritant (toxic) agent is sufficient. It occurs particularly where the stratum corneum is thinnest. Hence, it is often seen in the finger webs and back of the hands rather than the palms.

There are two main types of irritant contact dermatitis—acute and chronic. The acute form occurs after exposure to an agent or agents causing early impairment in the function of the stratum corneum and an inflammatory reaction. The chronic form follows repeated exposure to the same or different factors causing cumulative damage until an inflammatory reaction ensues that persists even after further exposure is stopped. People with a history of atopic eczema, especially atopic hand eczema, are at particular risk of developing a chronic irritant contact dermatitis. This chronic dermatitis is particularly observed in jobs that include "wet work."

Allergic Contact Dermatitis

Allergic contact dermatitis is a manifestation of a type IV hypersensitivity reaction. The dermatitis develops at the site of skin contact with the allergen. Secondary spread may occur. Contaminated hands may spread the allergen to previously unexposed sites. Trivial or occult contact with an allergen may result in a persistence of a dermatitis. Some allergens are essentially ubiquitous—for example, formaldehyde and sesquiterpene lactones.

There are two phases to the presentation of an allergic contact reaction: induction, during which the state of hypersensitivity to a molecule is acquired, and elicitation, whereby an eczematous reaction follows from subsequent exposure to the substance. Even with potent experimental allergens there is a minimum period of about 10 days from first exposure to the immunological acquisition of hypersensitivity. The probability of developing hypersensitivity depends on the sensitizing capacity of the chemical and exposure to it. Most potential allergens in the domestic and industrial market have low intrinsic potential for sensitization, with the important exception of some biocides. Contact allergens tend to be of low molecular weight (less than 600) and capable of forming covalent bonds with carrier proteins in the skin.

It is not yet possible to determine an individual's susceptibility to developing contact allergy. Hypersensitivity is specific to a particular molecule or to molecules bearing similar allergenic sites. Although hypersensitivity may eventually be lost, the state should be considered to last indefinitely.

Rubber Latex Protein Sensitivity

Of concern is the increasing occurrence of immediate type I hypersensitivity to proteins present in gloves made from natural rubber latex. The problem is seen principally among health workers, but people in other industries where examination gloves are used are also at risk. The Medical Devices Agency has published a bulletin describing the problem.[1]

Primary prevention involves the use of non-powdered gloves with very low protein residues. Affected people need to be provided with synthetic alternatives to rubber.

Management of Occupational Dermatitis

Assessment

Understanding the patient's job is necessary. A job title is not sufficient for this understanding; the question to be asked is not "What do you do?" but "What exactly do you do and how do you do it?" The title "engineer" can mean anything from a desk bound professional to a lathe worker exposed to soluble coolants. From a good job description it may be possible to estimate sources of excessive contact with potential irritant contact factors or with allergens. Data sheets may be helpful in this evaluation, but the information that they contain is often superficial and is only what is needed to meet regulatory requirements. A site visit—watching the patient working—may be necessary.

The history of the dermatitis may provide clues as to the aetiology [cause of the disease]. Irritant contact dermatitis may occur as an "epidemic" in a workplace if hygiene has failed, while allergic contact dermatitis is usually sporadic.

Evaluation of contact factors: The evaluation of irritant factors is always subjective. Evaluation of allergic contact factors is objective and is provided only by diagnostic patch tests. Properly performed, patch tests will show the presence or absence of important allergens. Patch testing is the only method for the objective evaluation of a dermatitis. There are major pitfalls in the use of this essential tool— proper training and experience are essential if it is to provide valid results.

A competent assessment requires all of the above followed by recommendations on reducing or stopping exposure to the offending agent and similar ones.

Diagnosis

Anyone can patch test, but few do it well—if you don't know how to do it, don't do it.

The diagnosis of an occupational dermatitis should describe thoroughly the nature of the condition, including any endogenous or aggravating factors. A medical record in a patient's notes of "Works in a factory, contact dermatitis 2/52" is inadequate as a description of an important disease process, and it could have profound implications for the patient's concept of the problem and employment. Delays in diagnosis that result in continued exposure to relevant irritants or allergens can adversely affect the prognosis.

Early referral to an appropriate dermatology department is vital for a full assessment of a suspected occupational dermatitis. Improper assessment can have a devastating effect on a patient's prospects for future employment, with important medicolegal implications. If in doubt, refer. Also consider contacting the patient's occupational health department if there is one.

Dermatitis of occupational cause may be suspected when

- Dermatitis first occurred while employed.

- There is a history of aggravation by work.

- There may be, at least initially, improvement (or clearance) when not at work.

- There is exposure to irritant factors or potential allergens.

- Work is in an "at risk" occupation.

Examples of Common Irritants

- "wet work"
- solvents
- detergents
- soluble coolants
- vegetable juices
- wet cement

With all of above, skin may be "hit" at several target sites, causing damage by several mechanisms.

Irritant Contact Dermitis [Acute or Chronic?]

1. Acute

   - Severity of reaction depends on dose of irritant agent.

   - Chapping can be considered a minor form and a chemical burn (such as cement burn) an extreme event.

   - Intermediate eczematous reactions are common, and minor reactions are very common.

   - It may occur on the face—for example, low humidity occupational dermatosis, airborne irritant vapors.

   - Once irritant factors have been removed, resolution is usually spontaneous without important sequelae.

2. Chronic

   - Persistent dermatitis [is] the most common cause of continued disability from occupational skin disease.

   - Problem continues for long periods even with avoidance of aggravating factors.

   - Re-exposure to even minor irritant factors can cause rapid flare.

   - Even after apparent healing there may be an indefinitely increased susceptibility to recurrence of dermatitis after exposure to irritants.

Common Occupational Allergens

- rubber accelerating chemicals—such as thiurams, carbamates, mercaptobenzothiazole
- biocides—such as formaldehyde, isothiazolinones
- hairdressing chemicals—such as thioglycolates, p-phenylendiamine
- epoxy resin monomers
- chromate
- plant allergens—such as sesquiterpene lactones

Sensitization to Latex Gloves

- Affected people are usually atopic.

- Presentation may be localized urticarial reaction at sites of skin contact or may be respiratory symptoms when starch powdered gloves have been used.

- Has become an important cause of occupational morbidity in some groups—for example, dental students.

- Anaphylaxis is possible with appropriate exposure.

- Definitive demonstration of hypersensitivity can be made by prick testing with water soluble proteins.

Patterns of Hand Dermatitis

- From distribution and morphology of dermatitis on hands, it is not possible to be definitive about aetiology.

- Thus, vesicular hand dermatitis with classic endogenous distribution may be mimicked by allergic contact dermatitis to isothiazolinone biocides or chromate sensitivity.

- It is a major error to rely on patterns of hand dermatitis alone in making a diagnosis.

Patch Testing

- Properly performed, it requires expertise, time, and proper facilities.

- [It is] difficult to undertake adequately in the workplace—there are no shortcuts.

- [It is a] primarily a hospital based procedure.

- [It] should be performed only by those with proper training who:
    - can prescribe an appropriately comprehensive screen.
    - know what not to test.
    - know what to dilute for testing.
    - can competently read the reactions.
    - can give authoritative advice after interpreting the reactions.

Preventing Occupational Dermatitis

Primary prevention is aimed at providing appropriate information and protection. Employer and employee should be aware of potential risks of exposure.

- education of need for good occupational hygiene.

- adequate provision of suitable and effective means of reducing exposure

- awareness of limitations of personal protection devices

References

1. Medical Devices Agency. "Latex sensitization in the health care setting (use of latex gloves)." London: MDA, April 1996. (Device bulletin MDA DB 9601.)

151

Chapter 12

Skin Care for the Hands

Like all tools, hands must be kept in shape to function correctly. Here's expert advice on skin care for the hands.

We see less and less tolerance in workplaces today for the full range of occupational hazards," says Jeffrey Stull, president, International Personnel Protection, a personal protection specialist within the industrial hygiene community and a member of the Kimberly-Clark Skin Wellness Institute. "Safety consciousness extends not only to serious accidents and acute diseases, but to chronic conditions, such as occupational dermatitis, that can have a lasting effect on a person's health and his ability to do his job."

Occupational skin diseases are common in industrial workplaces where heavy dirt and greases, contact with harsh chemicals, or frequent handwashing are common. The U.S. Bureau of Labor Statistics notes that occupational skin diseases such as allergic and irritant (contact) dermatitis are the second most common occupational malady. In 1997, there were approximately 58,000 reported cases of occupational skin diseases, accounting for slightly more than 13 percent of all occupational diseases. That's more than cases of dust diseases of the lungs, respiratory conditions due to toxic agents, poisoning and disorders due to physical agents combined.

Stull says the prevalence of reported cases of contact dermatitis is due, in part, to the increased use of specialized chemicals in the

From "Helping Hands," by Ian Crassweller, in *Occupational Hazards*, Vol. 61, I. 8, Aug. 1999, pp. 58–61. Copyright 1999 by Penton Media Inc. Reprinted with permission.

workplace and workers' increased sensitization to them. He likens the trend to the increase in latex allergies reported when latex glove use became widespread in the 1980s to protect against bloodborne pathogens. The National Institute for Occupational Safety and Health (NIOSH) has made contact dermatitis a top priority in the National Occupational Research Agenda (NORA). NIOSH notes that "occupational skin diseases are believed to be severely underreported, such that the true rate of new cases may be many fold higher than documented."

NIOSH/NORA observes, "Because the prognosis of occupational irritant and allergic dermatitis is poor, prevention is imperative. This fact is emphasized by one study showing that 75 percent of patients with occupational contact dermatitis developed chronic skin disease."

"One of the biggest issues is the lack of established exposure limits for skin protection," Stull says. "Those exposure limits are hard to quantify, due to the inherent differences in individuals' skin health and resistance to chemicals. Consequently, there are no accurate ways to measure or assess exposures."

In industries where the use of harsh chemicals is common, employers are working to control skin exposure by changing processes, substituting less hazardous chemicals and encouraging the use of protective apparel, such as gloves. Stull cautions against relying solely on gloves to protect hands. "Gloves can irritate skin or become damaged, allowing hazardous chemicals to permeate to the skin, and there are many work situations in which wearing gloves just isn't practical," he says.

To study the problem of skin diseases, NORA Allergic and Irritant Dermatitis Priority Research Area activities have been identified:

- Develop analyses for predicting the irritant contact dermatitis of chemicals and mixtures in the workplace.

- Sponsor scientific meetings focused on irritant and allergic contact dermatitis in the workplace.

- Develop a benchmark database for allergens and irritants.

- Develop alternative methods for identifying workplace irritants.

- Determine the genetic basis of workers' susceptibility to irritants.

- Increase knowledge of the pathophysiology of irritant contact dermatitis.

- Determine the genetic basis of workers' susceptibility to allergens.

- Determine the influence of environmental factors on initiation and elicitation of allergic contact dermatitis.

- Increase the knowledge of the basic pathophysiology of allergic contact dermatitis.

- Develop alternative methods for identifying workplace allergens.

Private industry and other research groups are focusing on issues relating to healthy skin and hands. For example, scientists in the Kimberly-Clark Skin Wellness Institute are researching the role of skin cleansers in contributing to or preventing contact dermatitis. "Most people don't understand the subtle differences among various types of skin cleansers," Stull explains. "However, there is a growing appreciation for different types of skin health products, how they work together and how they are designed for different cleaning tasks and exposure situations."

Skin cleansers are expected to remove deep grime or kill bacteria and leave skin feeling and smelling good. Often, the nature of heavy-duty cleansing or killing bacteria calls for chemicals that can strip the skin of its natural oils, damaging, drying and cracking skin and decreasing its resistance to chemicals and substances that normally wouldn't affect healthy skin.

Gary Grove, Ph.D., director of the Skin Study Center in Broomall, Pa., and a member of the Kimberly-Clark Skin Wellness Institute, notes that traditional soaps and detergents clean skin well, but dry it by removing protective oils because they don't discriminate between dirt on the skin surface and the essential oils that protect skin. Grove implemented a series of blind studies of the effectiveness of various cleansers and skin damage they cause. He washed with different cleansers, then measured the surface hydration state with an electrical conductance meter. In another test, he applied industrial oil-based ink and roofing tar to skin and used a chromameter to measure the amount of dirt before and after cleansing. He found most industrial skin cleansers cleaned skin effectively, but reduced its surface hydration, which can lead to contact dermatitis.

One cleanser tested did not reduce the skin's barrier function when removing dirt. It used liposome micro-encapsulation technology to incorporate a cleaning solvent within a skin conditioner for delivery to the skin. The result was less irritation to the skin. "It's important to remember that the use of the wrong cleanser or the improper use of the right cleanser can have a detrimental effect on the skin. A holistic approach is needed," Grove says.

Barrier creams and post-cleansing moisturizers are key elements in a skin health program. Proper skin health behavior also is important.

According to Kimberly-Clark's Skin Wellness Institute, here's how to clean hands properly:

1. Wet hands and forearms using a stream of warm running water. Excessively hot water is harder on the skin, dries the skin and is too uncomfortable to wash with for the recommended amount of time. Because cold water prevents soap from lathering properly, soil and germs may not be washed away.

2. Apply cleanser. Dispensers deliver the proper amount of cleanser, while protecting the rest from contamination. Use the right cleanser for the task. Use a nickel-size amount of general purpose cleanser or a quarter-size quantity of antimicrobial cleansers. Follow the instructions on the label.

3. Lather thoroughly. Scrub hands and forearms for at least 15 seconds. Use a nail brush, if necessary. Repeat until the skin is thoroughly clean.

4. Rinse thoroughly. Dry hands completely with a paper towel. Leaving soap residue on the skin and incomplete drying contribute to dermatitis.

5. Repeat steps 2–4 if hands are particularly dirty or greasy.

6. Use a paper towel to turn off the faucet without re-contaminating hands.

7. Use hand cream after washing and during the day to restore the skin's natural oils, keeping it resilient. Skin conditioning agents (emollients) soften and smooth skin. Moisturizers reduce shedding of dry skin flakes and inhibit the growth of microorganisms.

"Something as simple as using the right skin cleanser and the right handwashing technique can dramatically improve productivity," Stull concludes. "I encourage industrial hygienists and employers to conduct a cost/benefit analysis of skin care products and programs to determine the best and healthiest approach for their situation."

—by Ian Crassweller

Ian Crassweller, skin care category manager, Kimberly-Clark Away From Home Sector, is executive director of the Kimberly-Clark Skin Wellness Institute in Roswell, Ga.

Chapter 13

Preventing Allergic Reactions to Natural Rubber Latex in the Workplace

Background

Composition of Latex

Latex products are manufactured from a milky fluid derived from the rubber tree, Hevea brasiliensis. Several chemicals are added to this fluid during the processing and manufacture of commercial latex. Some proteins in latex can cause a range of mild to severe allergic reactions. Currently available methods of measurement do not provide easy or consistent identification of allergy-causing proteins (antigens) and their concentrations. Until well accepted standardized tests are available, total protein serves as a useful indicator of the exposure of concern [Beezhold et al. 1996a]. The chemicals added during processing may also cause skin rashes. Several types of synthetic rubber are also referred to as "latex," but these do not release the proteins that cause allergic reactions.

Products Containing Latex

A wide variety of products contain latex: medical supplies, personal protective equipment, and numerous household objects. Most people who encounter latex products only through their general use in society have no health problems from the use of these products. Workers

National Institute for Occupational Safety and Health (NIOSH), Department of Health and Human Services (DHHS), DHHS (NIOSH) Pub. No. 97-135, http://www.cdc.gov/niosh/latexalt.html, June 1997.

157

who repeatedly use latex products are the focus of this chapter. The following are examples of products that may contain latex:

Emergency Equipment

- blood pressure cuffs
- stethoscopes
- disposable gloves
- oral and nasal airways
- endotracheal tubes
- tourniquets
- intravenous tubing
- syringes
- electrode pads

Personal Protective Equipment

- gloves
- surgical masks
- goggles
- rubber aprons
- respirators

Office Supplies

- rubber bands
- erasers

Hospital Supplies

- anesthesia masks
- rubber tops of multi-dose vials
- wound drains
- injection ports
- catheters
- dental dams

Household Objects

- automobile tires
- motorcycle and bicycle handgrips
- carpeting
- swimming goggles
- racquet handles
- shoe soles
- expandable fabric (waistbands)
- dishwashing gloves
- hot water bottles
- condoms
- diaphragms
- balloons
- pacifiers
- baby bottle nipples

Individuals who already have latex allergy should be aware of latex-containing products that may trigger an allergic reaction. Some of the listed products are available in latex-free forms.

Latex in the Workplace

Workers in the health care industry (physicians, nurses, dentists, technicians, etc.) are at risk for developing latex allergy because they use latex gloves frequently. Also at risk are workers with less frequent glove use (hairdressers, housekeepers, food service workers, etc.) and workers in industries that manufacture latex products.

Types of Reactions to Latex

Three types of reactions can occur in persons using latex products:

- Irritant Contact Dermatitis
- Allergic Contact Dermatitis (delayed hypersensitivity)
- Latex Allergy

Irritant Contact Dermatitis

The most common reaction to latex products is irritant contact dermatitis—the development of dry, itchy, irritated areas on the skin, usually the hands. This reaction is caused by skin irritation from using gloves and possibly by exposure to other workplace products and chemicals. The reaction can also result from repeated hand washing and drying, incomplete hand drying, use of cleaners and sanitizers, and exposure to powders added to the gloves. Irritant contact dermatitis is not a true allergy.

Chemical Sensitivity Dermatitis

Allergic contact dermatitis (delayed hypersensitivity, also sometimes called chemical sensitivity dermatitis) results from exposure to chemicals added to latex during harvesting, processing, or manufacturing. These chemicals can cause skin reactions similar to those caused by poison ivy. As with poison ivy, the rash usually begins 24 to 48 hours after contact and may progress to oozing skin blisters or spread away from the area of skin touched by the latex.

Latex Allergy

Latex allergy (immediate hypersensitivity) can be a more serious reaction to latex than irritant contact dermatitis or allergic contact dermatitis. Certain proteins in latex may cause sensitization (positive blood or skin test, with or without symptoms). Although the amount of exposure needed to cause sensitization or symptoms is not known, exposures at even very low levels can trigger allergic reactions in some sensitized individuals.

Reactions usually begin within minutes of exposure to latex, but they can occur hours later and can produce various symptoms. Mild reactions to latex involve skin redness, hives, or itching. More severe reactions may involve respiratory symptoms such as runny nose, sneezing, itchy eyes, scratchy throat, and asthma (difficult breathing, coughing spells, and wheezing). Rarely, shock may occur; but a life-threatening reaction is seldom the first sign of latex allergy. Such reactions are similar to those seen in some allergic persons after a bee sting.

Levels and Routs of Exposure

Studies of other allergy-causing substances provide evidence that the higher the overall exposure in a population, the greater the likelihood that more individuals will become sensitized [Venables and Chan-Yeung 1997]. The amount of latex exposure needed to produce sensitization or an allergic reaction is unknown; however, reductions in exposure to latex proteins have been reported to be associated with decreased sensitization and symptoms [Tarlo et al. 1994; Hunt et al. 1996].

The proteins responsible for latex allergies have been shown to fasten to powder that is used on some latex gloves. When powdered gloves are worn, more latex protein reaches the skin. Also, when gloves are changed, latex protein/powder particles get into the air, where they can be inhaled and contact body membranes [Heilman et al. 1996]. In contrast, work areas where only powder-free gloves are used show low levels or undetectable amounts of the allergy-causing proteins [Tarlo 1994; Swanson et al. 1994].

Wearing latex gloves during episodes of hand dermatitis may increase skin exposure and the risk of developing latex allergy. The risk of progression from skin rash to more serious reactions is unknown. However, a skin rash may be the first sign that a worker has become allergic to latex and that more serious reactions could occur with continuing exposure [Kelly et al. 1996].

Who Is at Risk?

Workers with ongoing latex exposure are at risk for developing latex allergy. Such workers include health care workers (physicians, nurses, aides, dentists, dental hygienists, operating room employees, laboratory technicians, and hospital housekeeping personnel) who frequently use latex gloves and other latex-containing medical supplies. Workers who use latex gloves less frequently (law enforcement personnel, ambulance attendants, funeral-home workers, fire fighters, painters, gardeners, food service workers, and housekeeping personnel) may also develop latex allergy. Workers in factories where latex products are manufactured or used can also be affected.

Atopic individuals (persons with a tendency to have multiple allergic conditions) are at increased risk for developing latex allergy. Latex allergy is also associated with allergies to certain foods, especially avocado, potato, banana, tomato, chestnuts, kiwi fruit, and papaya [Blanco et al. 1994; Beezhold et al. 1996b]. People with spina bifida are also at increased risk for latex allergy.

Diagnosing Latex Allergy

Latex allergy should be suspected in anyone who develops certain symptoms after latex exposure, including nasal, eye, or sinus irritation; hives; shortness of breath; coughing; wheezing; or unexplained shock. Any exposed worker who experiences these symptoms should be evaluated by a physician, since further exposure could result in a serious allergic reaction. A diagnosis is made by using the results of a medical history, a physical examination, and tests.

Taking a complete medical history is the first step in diagnosing latex allergy. In addition, blood tests approved by the Food and Drug Administration (FDA) are available to detect latex antibodies. Other diagnostic tools include a standardized glove-use test or skin tests that involve scratching or pricking the skin through a drop of liquid containing latex proteins. A positive reaction is shown by itching, swelling, or redness at the test site. However, no FDA-approved materials are yet available to use in skin testing for latex allergy. Skin testing and glove-use tests should be performed only at medical centers with staff who are experienced and equipped to handle severe reactions.

Testing is also available to diagnose allergic contact dermatitis. In this FDA-approved test, a special patch containing latex additives is applied to the skin and checked over several days. A positive reaction is shown by itching, redness, swelling, or blistering where the patch covered the skin.

Occasionally, tests may fail to confirm a worker who has a true allergy to latex, or tests may suggest latex allergy in a worker with no clinical symptoms. Therefore, test results must be evaluated by a knowledgeable physician.

Treating Latex Allergy

Once a worker becomes allergic to latex, special precautions are needed to prevent exposures during work as well as during medical or dental care. Certain medications may reduce the allergy symptoms, but complete latex avoidance (though quite difficult) is the most effective approach. Many facilities maintain latex-safe areas for affected patients and workers.

Recommendations

The following recommendations for preventing latex allergy in the workplace are based on current knowledge and a common sense approach to minimizing latex-related health problems. Evolving manufacturing technology and improvements in measurement methods may lead to changes in these recommendations in the future. For now, adoption of the recommendations wherever feasible will contribute to the reduction of exposure and risk for the development of latex allergy.

Employers

Latex allergy can be prevented only if employers adopt policies to protect workers from undue latex exposures. NIOSH recommends that employers take the following steps to protect workers from latex exposure and allergy in the workplace:

1. Provide workers with non-latex gloves to use when there is little potential for contact with infectious materials (for example, in the food service industry).

2. Appropriate barrier protection is necessary when handling infectious materials [CDC 1987]. If latex gloves are chosen, provide reduced protein, powder-free gloves to protect workers from infectious materials. The goal of this recommendation is to reduce exposure to allergy-causing proteins (antigens). Until well accepted standardized tests are available, total protein serves as a useful indicator of the exposure of concern.

3. Ensure that workers use good housekeeping practices to remove latex-containing dust from the workplace:
    *   Identify areas contaminated with latex dust for frequent cleaning (upholstery, carpets, ventilation ducts, and plenums).

- Make sure that workers change ventilation filters and vacuum bags frequently in latex-contaminated areas.

4. Provide workers with education programs and training materials about latex allergy.

5. Periodically screen high-risk workers for latex allergy symptoms. Detecting symptoms early and removing symptomatic workers from latex exposure are essential for preventing long-term health effects.

6. Evaluate current prevention strategies whenever a worker is diagnosed with latex allergy.

Workers

Workers should take the following steps to protect themselves from latex exposure and allergy in the workplace:

1. Use non-latex gloves for activities that are not likely to involve contact with infectious materials (food preparation, routine housekeeping, maintenance, etc.).

2. Appropriate barrier protection is necessary when handling infectious materials [CDC 1987]. If you choose latex gloves, use powder-free gloves with reduced protein content:

   - Such gloves reduce exposures to latex protein and thus reduce the risk of latex allergy (though symptoms may still occur in some workers).

   - So-called hypoallergenic latex gloves do not reduce the risk of latex allergy. However, they may reduce reactions to chemical additives in the latex (allergic contact dermatitis).

3. Use appropriate work practices to reduce the chance of reactions to latex:

   - When wearing latex gloves, do not use oil-based hand creams or lotions (which can cause glove deterioration) unless they have been shown to reduce latex-related problems and maintain glove barrier protection.

   - After removing latex gloves, wash hands with a mild soap and dry thoroughly.

   - Use good housekeeping practices to remove latex-containing dust from the workplace: Frequently clean areas contaminated with latex dust (upholstery, carpets, ventilation ducts, plenums, ventilation filters, and vacuum bags used in latex-contaminated areas).

4. Take advantage of all latex allergy education and training provided by your employer:

   - Become familiar with procedures for preventing latex allergy.

   - Learn to recognize the symptoms of latex allergy: skin rashes; hives; flushing; itching; nasal, eye, or sinus symptoms; asthma; and shock.

5. If you develop symptoms of latex allergy, avoid direct contact with latex gloves and other latex-containing products until you can see a physician experienced in treating latex allergy.

6. If you have latex allergy, consult your physician regarding the following precautions:

   - Avoid contact with latex gloves and other latex-containing products.

   - Avoid areas where you might inhale the powder from latex gloves worn by other workers.

   - Tell your employer and your health care providers (physicians, nurses, dentists, etc.) that you have latex allergy.

   - Wear a medical alert bracelet.

7. Carefully follow your physician's instructions for dealing with allergic reactions to latex.

Additional Information

For additional information about latex allergy, see the organizations listed in the Resources section of this sourcebook.

Acknowledgments

Principal contributors to this Chapter were R.E. Biagini, S. Deitchman, E.J. Esswein, J. Fedan, J.P. Flesch, P.K. Hodgins, T.K. Hodous, R.D. Hull, W.R. Jarvis, D.M. Lewis, J.A. Lipscomb, B.D.

Lushniak, M.L. Pearson, E.L. Petsonk, L. Pinkerton, P.D. Siegal, W.G. Wippel, and K.A. Worthington.

References

Bauer X, Ammon J, Chen Z, Beckman U, Czuppon AB [1993]. Health risk in hospitals through airborne allergens for patients pre-sensitized to latex. *Lancet* 342:1148-1149.

Beezhold D [1992]. LEAP: Latex ELISA for antigenic protein. *Guthrie J* 61:77–81.

Beezhold D, Pugh B, Liss G, Sussman G [1996a]. Correlation of protein levels with skin prick test reactions in patients allergic to latex. *J Allergy and Clin Immunol* 98 (6):1097-102.

Beezhold DH, Sussman GL, Liss GM, Chang NS [1996b]. Latex allergy can induce clinical reactions to specific foods. *Clin Exp Allergy* 26:416–422.

Blanco C, Carrillo T, Castillo R, Quiralte J, Cuevas M [1994]. Latex allergy: clinical features and cross-reactivity with fruits. *Ann Allergy* 73:309–314.

CDC (Centers for Disease Control and Prevention) [1987]. Recommendations for prevention of HIV transmission in health-care settings. *MMWR* 36(S2).

CDC (Centers for Disease Control and Prevention) [1989]. Guidelines for prevention of transmission of human immunodeficiency virus and hepatitis B virus to health-care and public-safety workers. *MMWR* 38(S-6):1–37.

CFR. *Code of Federal regulations*. Washington, DC: U.S. Government Printing Office, Office of the Federal Register.

Heilman DK, Jones RT, Swanson MC, Yunginger JW [1996]. A prospective, controlled study showing that rubber gloves are the major contributor to latex aeroallergen levels in the operating room. *J Allergy Clin Immunol* 98(2):325–330.

Hunt LW, Fransway AF, Reed CE, Miller LK, Jones RT, Swanson MC, et al. [1995]. An epidemic of occupational allergy to latex involving health care workers. *JOEM* 37(10):1204–1209.

Hunt LW, Boone-Orke JL, Fransway AF, Fremstad CE, Jones RT, Swanson MC, et al. [1996]. A medical-center-wide, multidisciplinary approach to the problem of natural rubber latex allergy. *JOEM* 38(8):765–770.

Katelaris CH, Widmer RP, Lazarus RM [1996]. Prevalence of latex allergy in a dental school. *Med J Australia* 164:711–714.

Kelly KJ, Sussman G, Fink JN [1996]. Stop the sensitization. *J Allergy Clin Immunol* 98(5): 857–858.

Liss GM, Sussman GL, Deal K, Brown S, Cividino M, Siu S, et al. [1997]. Latex allergy: epidemiological study of hospital workers. *Occup Environ Med* 54:335–342.

Nasuruddin BA, Shahnaz M, Azizah MR, Hasma H, Mok KL, Esah Y, et al. [1993]. Prevalence study of type I latex hypersensitivity among high risk groups in the Malaysian population preliminary report. Unpublished paper presented at the Latex Allergy Workshop, International Rubber Technology Conference, Kuala Lumpur, Malaysia, June.

Orfan NA, Reed R, Dykewicz MS, Ganz M, Kolski GB [1994]. Occupational asthma in a latex doll manufacturing plant. *J Allergy Clin Immunol* 94(5):826–830.

Ownby DR, Ownby HE, McCullough J, Shafer, AW [1996]. The prevalence of anti-latex lgE antibodies in 1000 volunteer blood donors. *J Allergy Clin Immunol* 97(6):1188–1192.

Rosen A, Isaacson D, Brady M, Corey JP [1993]. Hypersensitivity to latex in health care workers: report of five cases. *Otolaryngol Head Neck Surg* 109(4):731–734.

Seaton A, Cherrie B, Turnbull J [1988]. Rubber glove asthma. *Br Med J* 296:531–532.

Sussman GL, Beezhold DH [1995]. Allergy to latex rubber. *Ann Intern Med* 122: 43–46.

Swanson MC, Bubak ME, Hunt LW, Yunginger JW, Warner MA, Reed CE [1994]. Quantification of occupational latex aeroallergens in a medical center. *J Allergy Clin Immunol* 94(3): 445–551.

Tarlo SM, Wong L, Roos J, Booth N [1990]. Occupational asthma caused by latex in a surgical glove manufacturing plant. *J Allergy Clin Immunol* 85(3):626–631.

Tarlo SM, Sussman G, Contala A, Swanson MC [1994]. Control of airborne latex by use of powder-free latex gloves. *J Allergy Clin Immunol* 93: 985–989.

Truscott W [1995]. Abstracts: new proposals for the increased incidences of immediate type hypersensitivity to latex. *J Allergy Clin Immunol* 95(1, Part 2):252.

van der Walle HB, Brunsveld VM [1995]. Latex allergy among hairdressers. *Contact Dermatitis* 32:177–178.

Vandenplas O, Delwiche JP, Evrared G, Aimont P, Van Der Brempt S, Jamart J, Delaunois L [1995]. Prevalence of occupational asthma due to latex among hospital personnel. *Am J Respir Crit Care Med* 151:54–60.

Venables K, Chan-Yeung M [1997]. Occupational asthma. *The Lancet* 349:1465–1469.

Yunginger JW, Jones RT, Frasway AF, Kelso JM, Warner MA, Hunt LW [1994]. Extractable latex allergens and proteins in disposable medical gloves and other rubber products. *J Allergy Clin Immunol* 93(5):836–842.

Chapter 14

Chemical Burns

Chapter Contents

Section 14.1

Chemical Burns Need Prompt First Aid

Carl R. Metzgar, *Pit & Quarry*, November 1995, Vol. 88, N. 5, p. 56.
Copyright 1995 by Advanstar Communications, Inc.
Advanstar Communication, Inc. retains all rights to this article.
Reprinted with permission.

Chemical burns represent only a small proportion of the burns treated in a hospital burn center. Unfortunately, that safety personnel may have little experience treating chemical burns. However, by considering some of the characteristics of a chemical burn and its first aid treatment, the potential seriousness can be limited.

To get some idea of the size of the problem, in the period from July 1976 to June 1980, there were 857 burn patients treated at the Baltimore Regional Burn Center. Of these, 35 cases were chemical burns. Chemical burns are not a high frequency problem to the public.

Two of the 35 chemical burns were due to portland cement. According to the records, both of the patients mentioned spilled dry cement on the cuffs of work boots and the chemical remained in contact with the skin for more than eight hours. Because little pain was experienced initially, treatment was delayed for three to four days.

The burns were probably due to cement plus moisture from some source. Sweat could have been the source for the moisture. The moisture activates the caustic properties of the lime that is present when portland cement and water are mixed.

The elements involved in cement and concrete burns are:

- direct skin contact
- duration of contact
- enough pressure to keep the cement or concrete in contact with the skin

In the two cases mentioned, the period of time for skin contact was in the range of eight hours. Other sources indicate burns may occur after much shorter exposure times, some as short as 30 minutes with wet concrete.

What Is the First Aid for the Exposure to Calcium Hydroxide in the Moist Cement/Concrete Mixture?

Lavage is a French word that means washing. That is the word doctors use. First aid books say "wash with copious amounts of water." Copious means "furnish plentifully" in this context. Remember— water at low pressure, lots of water at low pressure. Keep the flow going for at least 15 minutes and get medical care. When administering first aid, keep washing until transportation to medical care begins. It's okay to go beyond the 15 minutes.

Note in the two cases mentioned treatment was delayed. There was no washing until the end of the shift. The troublesome part of cement, lime and concrete burns is that by the time there is pain, there is probably a serious chemical burn. Observation is an important part of the prevention/treatment combination.

First aid is simple and inexpensive, yet [treatment is often delayed] because either the patient or the bystanders did not recognize the injury hazard.

What about the two cement cases? Did the workers not know that cement could burn? The report did not indicate where these workers were exposed. Was the exposure in a cement plant, ready mix concrete plant, pre-stress concrete plant, hardware store, concrete block plant or do-it-yourself project in a backyard? It would be reasonable to expect that any one of these locations would have copious amounts of water available within minutes of the exposure. Either knowledge or will was missing. A safety program can and should take care of the knowledge part.

The Occupational Safety and Health Administration (OSHA) requires that customers be provided with an Material Safety Data Sheet (MSDS) sheet. A made-to-order safety meeting for employees is a review of the portland cement MSDS. It is reasonable to go over the portland cement MSDS at stone plants because over the course of the year, concrete gets placed for some construction project and often by operations people.

There is one further consideration that just may have changed since 1980 when the data set was closed. Eighteen of the 35 chemical burns were work-related, 10 of 35 were home accidents and seven of 35 were assaults. Of the seven assaults, six were injuries with lye which is easy to purchase. Chemical burns have a lower mortality rate than gunshot wounds, but the long-term pain and suffering are greater. If a new study were done, the proportion of assaults might be higher.

171

Intentional and unintentional chemical burn injuries may be difficult to prevent, but prompt, appropriate first aid is easy.

— by Carl R. Metzgar

Carl R. Metzgar, CSP, *Pit & Quarry*'s safety editor, trains, consults and writes from Winston-Salem, N.C. He has 25 years experience in the pit and quarry industries. His telephone number is (910) 766-8264.

Section 14.2

Cement Burn

Excerpted from "Cement Burn," Khanh V.Q. Luong; Lan T.H. Nguyen, *Journal of Family Practice*, December 1995, Vol. 41, N. 6, p. 601–602, Copyright 1995 Appleton & Lange. Reproduced with permission from *The Journal of Family Practice*.

People working with cement should be aware of the potential for cement burn. The alkalinity of cement is due to the exothermic reaction of calcium oxide with water, which forms calcium hydroxide. Prolonged exposure of the skin to wet cement may result in a caustic burn.

Cement is one of the most widely used substances throughout the world. The alkalinity of cement is due to calcium oxide. In reported cases of cement burn, most patients were unaware of the hazards of prolonged contact with cement. We report two cases of cement burn.

Case Reports

Case 1

A 35-year-old male construction worker developed minor irritation on his lower legs after wet cement spilled between his boots and legs. Seven days later, his lower legs developed many areas of deep secondary burns, requiring hospitalization for debridement of the necrotic tissue but no skin grafts.

Case 2

A 56-year-old man was admitted to the hospital for a severe leg ulcer. The patient was working in a cement powder plant. Cement leaked through his right boot and came in contact with and irritated his foot. Blisters developed, and his skin lesion began to have serious drainage over the next several days. Wound cultures grew Pseudomonas aeruginosa, for which he was treated with intravenous antibiotics and daily soaks in povidone-iodine. The wound healed a few weeks later.

Discussion

In a study of the dermal chemical response to alkali injury in 60 men, Houck et. al. noticed a decrease in hydroxyproline in the lesions and an increase in hexosamine. The collagen content of the lesion also decreased profoundly within 3 days following injury. Some people seem to have skin that is particularly sensitive to caustics, whereas others have more tolerance. Allergic dermatitis can result from the presence of hexavalent chromates in cement in patients who have become sensitized to metallic salt, but this does not seem to be an important factor contributing to the burn.

Rowe reported that prolonged exposure, usually more than 2 hours, of skin to wet cement can produce third-degree burns. The sand that is added to wet cement to make concrete can potentiate the burn by abrading the skin, particularly by means of the pressure and friction resulting from kneeling or movement within a boot. Hydration of cement is exothermic, but the rise in temperature is slow and, thus, is not responsible for the burns.

People working with cement should be aware of this hazard. The risk of developing skin problems is highest when contact with wet cement is prolonged with pressure or occlusion. In case of contact, the skin should be washed with copious amounts of water. Appropriate antibiotics may be needed for secondary infection.

Chapter 15

Eye Protection

Chapter Contents

Section 15.1

Achieving Safe Sight 24 Hours a Day

From "Achieving Safe Sight 24 Hours a Day," in *Occupational Hazards*,
Vol. 60, N. 4, April 1998, pp. 71–73. Copyright 1999 by Penton Media Inc.
Reprinted with permission.

Did you know that 400,000 cases of occupationally related eye injuries occur annually? That's more than 1,000 eye injuries in the American workplace each day! Some 70 percent of serious injuries are the result of flying or falling objects. Approximately 60 percent of those objects are smaller than the head of a pin. More than 77,000 eye injuries (19 percent) result in lost time, defined as one full day or more out of work. The financial impact to employers in lost time and workers' compensation annually is estimated to be in excess of $300 million.

But eye injuries don't stop at the plant gates. According to Prevent Blindness America, 41 percent of all eye injuries occur after hours in or around the home. Shrub and tree trimming, lawn care, woodworking projects, and chopping wood are just a few examples of how home activities can result in eye injuries.

Any injury to the human eye can have serious consequences, no matter where it occurs, warns Anne Chambers, marketing manager for safety eyewear for Uvex Safety Inc., the Smithfield, Rhode Island-based manufacturer of safety eyewear. Whether it is on the job or in the home, an eye injury can cause an employee to lose time from work and suffer temporary or permanent impaired vision. There can be significant consequences for the employer. Employee injuries result in sick or disability leave, lost productivity, higher workers' compensation costs, and increased medical insurance costs. Everyone loses.

During the past two decades, much attention has been given to establishing stricter guidelines and implementing precautionary measures to reduce the incidence of work-related eye injuries. Some employers have implemented ongoing eye safety training and hazard assessment programs. Despite these efforts, the most recent statistics do not reflect a significant reduction in the number of annual eye injuries. According to OSHA, 90 percent of all occupationally related injuries could have been avoided through the use of proper protective eyewear. In addition, a 1995 market study conducted by Future Technology Surveys Inc. estimates that of the 20 million workers required to wear eye and face protection, only 60 percent are actually in compliance.

Unfortunately, many workers who suffered eye injuries believed protective eyewear was not required in their particular situation. This points out, says Chambers, that employee eyewear training must be ongoing. Employees need to know how and when to use protective eyewear. An excellent source of training materials for preventing eye injuries is Prevent Blindness America, Schaumburg, IL (847/843-2020).

Help for the Asking

Manufacturers of safety eyewear are watchful of these statistics and are doing their part to increase worker compliance, says Chambers. Some manufacturers provide training videos, hazard assessment surveys or other supplemental materials that can be used by an employer to help establish on-the-job training programs.

Eyewear manufacturers continue to make significant technological and design improvements in an attempt to make wearing safety eyewear more appealing to workers. If protective eyewear isn't comfortable, doesn't fit properly or isn't stylish, employees just won't wear it. Safety eyewear that is not worn is obviously not effective. Many safety eyewear manufacturers are now closing the design gap. This means many of the more popular sport and sunglass styles of today will become the basis for tomorrow's protective eyewear. Statistics show 57 percent of workers suffering from an eye injury are between the ages of 20–34 years. This fashion-conscious group must have a choice of eyewear styles to make them feel and look good or they won't wear them. Manufacturers must be quick to provide new styles, or they will be left behind.

Looking good and feeling good are key factors. However, safety should never be compromised for style. Industry leaders are becoming more adept at incorporating both style and protection. Employers should choose a safety eyewear manufacturer that produces a variety of styles and designs to satisfy all of their employees. Sleek, low-profile and wrap-around lens designs are very popular, as are unique frame colors and lens tints. For example, camouflage frames are very popular with employees who enjoy hunting. Unique frame colors offer female employees fun and colorful frames to select from so they aren't limited to masculine-looking eyewear. This year, the industry can expect to see some advancements in coloration technology that will transform an ordinary pair of safety spectacles into a "spectacular" pair.

Comfort and fit are also critical factors. If the protective eyewear is heavy and uncomfortable, it won't be worn, and it will not provide effective protection. Employers should look for features such as lightweight frames (less than 50 grams, if possible) and cushioned, adjustable temples that relieve pressure at the sensitive mastoid area behind the ear.

Many safety spectacles come in a one-size-fits-all style. Unfortunately one size does not fit all employees, Chambers says. She recommends that employers select a manufacturer that offers a variety of sizes. For example: a slim frame fits a slender facial profile; a standard frame is suitable for the majority of employees; custom bridges are for employees with low-profile nasal areas; RX eyewear is for prescription wearers, and OTG (over-the-glass) eyewear is designed for employees who prefer to cover their own prescription glasses with safety spectacles.

Lens fogging is another serious issue because it can blur or distort vision. Many workers remove (even if only temporarily) their safety eyewear when it fogs, and frequently do not replace their spectacles until the task is completed. This contributes to eye injuries. Manufacturers continue to look at new and improved anti-fog coatings to eliminate this occurrence. For example, several months ago, Uvex Safety introduced a new, proprietary anti-fog lens coating called uvextreme[R] AF. This anti-fog coating was developed to minimize fogging in the most extreme work environments. It combines hydrophilic (water absorbing) and hydrophobic (water shedding) features in one permanently bonded, dual-action coating. This new coating has dramatically reduced the incidence of fogged lenses in safety eyewear.

Eye Safety Off the Job

All of the technology and design improvements discussed above should have a positive impact on employee compliance. But what about eye safety off the job and around the home? Employers should make a point of discussing eye safety in both environments. Employers ultimately pay for all eye injuries, regardless of where they occur. It is always best for employers to reinforce proper eye safety habits by encouraging employees to practice safe sight at home.

Company-sponsored family outings or picnics present great opportunities to distribute complimentary pairs of protective eyewear. Colorful frames and shaded lens tints, such as mirrored or gray with a company name or logo imprinted on the temple, are a perfect token of employer appreciation and concern for employee safety, 24 hours a day. Some employers offer employees the opportunity to purchase safety eyewear for home use at a reduced price. Employers should consider the distribution of safety eyewear for home use a natural extension of an overall vision health care package.

Section 15.2

Water Rescues: Showers, Eyewash Units Remedy Chemical Exposure

From "Water Rescues: Showers, Eyewash Units Remedy Chemical Exposure," by Patricia M. Fernberg, in *Occupational Hazards*, Vol. 60, N. 7, July 1998, pp. 73–76. Copyright 1999 by Penton Media Inc. Reprinted with permission.

Drench showers and eyewash units provide a proven first response for eye and skin contact to hazardous chemicals.

What kind of idiot would put acid into bottles like this? The man fumed, pushing his safety glasses up on his brow to get a better look at the problem. He picked up the bottles to show his supervisor on the other side of the yard. Suddenly, the bottle in his left hand slipped. Glancing down, the man was relieved to see that it was unbroken, but from the center of the container, a single drop flew upward into his eye.

His scream drew coworkers, who forced him to his knees, prying his hand from his eye and pulling the eyelid upward. They irrigated the eye with water from a hose as the supervisor called for help. Paramedics continued irrigating en route to the emergency room, and the soaking continued at the hospital. Hours later, the man was sent home. Two weeks later, his vision was as it had been prior to the accident. Decisive action by his coworkers saved his sight.

Consultant Neil Langerman, Ph.D., of Advanced Chemical Safety in San Diego, tells this story to illustrate that accidents are caused by a series of events, any one of which, if it had not occurred, would have prevented the accident. Chemical splash accidents are a sterling example of this theory. Engineering the hazard out of a problem (e.g., properly storing the acid) normally is sufficient prevention. Administrative controls, such as warning other employees away from the improperly stored acid and bringing the hazard to the supervisor's attention (rather than carrying the bottles), also prevent accidents. In this case, training was sloppy: the employee let down his guard, did not have his personal protective equipment (PPE) in place and almost paid with his eyesight.

Despite decades of effort to eliminate them, occupational eye injuries remain a widespread and costly problem. "We have traditionally used the annual figure of 356,000 eye injuries of all types in the workplace," says Tod Turriff, vice president of Prevent Blindness America, a 90-year-old nonprofit organization dealing with health-related vision problems, including safety issues. However, the Chicago-based agency anticipates a NIOSH report, due this summer, that will identify between 650,000 and 700,000 workplace-related eye injuries, based on workers' compensation claims. "One-quarter of those injuries will result in permanent disability," Turriff says. "That's when the individual loses at least one full day of work from dust and debris, from injurious light sources such as welding flashes and electric arcs, and from chemical splashes.

Quantity Counts

When chemicals splash in the eyes, it is natural to close them to avoid further injury, yet closing them is the surest way to destroy eyesight. Acids burn initially when they contact the eye, then precipitate protein in front of the eye. Alkali splashes are potentially more damaging because alkali leaches water from the tissues and continues to burn through them. Closing the eyes seals the chemical under the folds of the lids, allowing the molecules to bond with water, fueling the burn. "Within seconds, the alkali will have penetrated the cornea and reached the iris, the lens, the vitreous humor, and the retina," explains John B. Jeffers, M.D., director of emergency services at the Wills Eye Hospital in Philadelphia. "In some cases, the entire eye is destroyed."

Corrosive gas molecules can combine with as little as 30 percent relative humidity in the air to form mists that irritate the eyes. Likewise, acids, alkali, or solvents that contact unprotected skin burn rapidly through the tissue unless they are rapidly diluted with large quantities of potable liquid and the particulates flushed away.

"If you don't give it [the burn] lots and lots of water, typical water-reactive industrial chemicals will take the water out of the person's system and will continue to do damage by dehydrating and burning," Langerman explains. "The faster you get water on it, the better. A little bit of water is devastating because it activates the chemical, but if you use enough water, it will flush that heat away." Both Langerman and Jeffers strongly advise flushing continuously until the victim is transported because chemical residue continues burning and the pH of the tissue can rise rapidly when flushing is discontinued. Ideally, eyes should be flushed with a sterile, isotonic, pH-balanced solution at a temperature between 60 and 90 degrees F. Drench showers should use clean, uncontaminated water that is near body temperature. "Realistically, the quality of the water doesn't matter," Langerman says. "What matters is that you use lots of it." Both he and Jeffers point out that, in an emergency, any potable fluid, anything you can drink, can be used. "We can treat infections, but there is no way I can recover your sight," Langerman warns.

Helpful Standards

Finding appropriate shower and eyewash equipment may be easier than you thought possible. Robert Hurley, president of Fendall, an Arlington Heights, Ill., manufacturer of eyewash stations, suggests starting with the Occupational Safety and Health Administration's (OSHA) hazard communication standard, 29CFR 1910.1200, which requires employers to identify and evaluate all chemicals used in the workplace. "Look anywhere in your facility where chemicals could splash in the eyes or come in contact with the skin. Then use material safety data sheets (MSDSs) to identify those chemicals that are hazardous," he says. The MSDS should tell you if the potential hazard requires proximity to an emergency shower or eyewash station.

Hurley points out, "Looking at the 1997 OSHA citations, the hazard communication standard was one of the top 10 items cited. Another [prominent] item was the lack of emergency shower and eyewash facilities." The Occupational Safety and Health Administration (OSHA) can cite companies at which hazardous chemicals are in use and in which emergency showers and eyewash stations are not present, accessible to those working with the chemicals, or in proper working condition. OSHA standard 29 CFR 1910.151, Medical Services and First Aid, states: "Where the eyes or body of any person may be exposed to injurious corrosive materials, suitable facilities for drenching or flushing the eyes and body shall be provided within the work area for immediate emergency access."

Having identified the operations in which hazardous chemicals prescribe the need for emergency shower and eyewash units, consult the American National Standards Institute's ANSI Z-358.1-1998 for emergency eyewash and shower equipment. This iteration by the Industrial Safety Equipment Association (ISEA), Arlington, Va., updates the 1981 standard to include eyewash stations, emergency showers, drench hoses, combination units, and personal eyewash bottles and promulgates minimum performance standards for installation and use, training, and maintenance. "The standard is meant to protect the users," says Christine Fargo, ISEA technical projects coordinator. "But it is also a checklist against which manufacturers of this equipment can measure themselves."

What Does the Standard Require for Features?

Plumbed and Self-Contained Emergency Showers

- Shower heads should provide a column of flushing fluid that is, at minimum, 82 in. in height from the floor of the unit, with a minimum diameter of 20 in. at 60 in. from the floor of the unit. The center of the spray pattern should be 16 in. from any obstruction. The heads should deliver a minimum of 20 gallons/minute of fluid at a non-injurious velocity for at least 15 minutes.

- Valve actuators are to be easy to locate and use, and shall be located not more than 69 in. above the floor of the unit.

- Enclosed units will allow a minimum unobstructed area of 34 in. in diameter.

- Plumbed units must be tested weekly. All units are to be inspected annually for compliance with the standard.

Plumbed and Self-Contained Eyewash Equipment

- Flushing fluid should flow in a non-injurious, controlled pattern that reaches both eyes simultaneously at a minimum rate of 0.4 gallons per minute for at least 15 minutes. A suitable flow pattern is 4 in. long with two sets of parallel lines equidistant from the center.

- Nozzles should be protected from airborne contaminants, yet the protection should not impede its immediate use.

- Flushing fluid should be protected from airborne contaminants.

- Eyewash nozzles must be not less than 33 in. nor more than 45 in. from the floor and not less than 6 in. from the wall.

- Plumbed eyewash units must provide an uninterruptible supply of flushing fluid at a minimum flow pressure of 30 pounds/square inch (psi).

- Personal eyewash units must be filled with flushing fluid, should not be injurious when used, and must be regularly inspected and maintained.

- The non-corrosive control valve on both showers and eyewash units should open within one second or less from activation, should remain open without use of the user's hands, and should shut off only when manually deactivated. The control valve should be easy to locate and use.

- Users should be able to reach both showers and eyewash units, unobstructed, within 10 seconds from the site of the hazard. The units should be on the same level as the floor, and should be both easily identified and well-lit. In areas where a strong caustic or acid is present, the eyewash unit must be adjacent to that area.

Training

Every employee who works with hazardous chemicals and every supervisor "should be trained to recognize hazardous materials, to understand where they are, to understand that flushing the eyes is the first step in emergency first aid, to know where the emergency eye stations are, and to properly use eyewash stations," advises Hurley.

Training, says Jim Johnson, business unit manager of shower and eyewash equipment at Encon Safety Products in Houston, should be part of employee orientation. "We recommend that user training on these units be part of your safety training program," he adds. Prevent Blindness America offers information and referral services. Call 800-331-2020 or visit its website at www.preventblindness.org. Safety literature and videos on eye health and safety and the Wise Owl PPE safety program are available.

Maintenance personnel must be trained to test and service all eyewash and shower stations in accordance with the ANSI standard. All manufacturers offer videos or printed information demonstrating proper maintenance techniques. Copies of ANSI Z-358.1 (1998) are available from ISEA by calling 703-525-1695.

Having eyewash and shower stations does not excuse an absence of engineering controls, administrative measures, and PPE for preventing chemical accidents, but they are your best first response for averting permanent injury.

When Chemicals Contact the Eyes

1. Summon help.

2. Find a source of potable fluid.

3. Remove contact lenses, which trap chemicals against the eye surface.

4. Force upper and lower eyelids open (inside-out, if possible) and direct the fluid upward into the eyes and in all directions.

5. Flush continuously until emergency crews arrive.

6. Transport the person to the hospital.

When Chemicals Contact the Skin

1. Summon help.

2. Find a source of potable fluid.

3. Remove the victim's clothes and shoes.

4. Drench the body continuously until help arrives.

5. **Do not** use soap.

6. Transport the person to the hospital.

Prevent Workplace Blindness

1. Different workplace materials have different hazard levels. Look for acceptable substitute chemicals that present less danger to the eyes and body.

2. Make sure individuals who handle chemicals know exactly what it is they are dealing with and how to protect themselves.

3. Make sure employees wear suitable eye and face protection. Safety glasses with side shields are not appropriate for dealing

with chemical hazards. Issue goggles with indirect ventilation. For severe exposure, use face shields. In very hazardous situations, use a full mask and respirator.

4. Prepare for emergencies. If you are dealing with a known hazard in an appropriate location, eye and body wash stations should also be there. Train employees and supervisors in administering first aid and bringing in paramedics in severe medical emergencies.

Chapter 16

Eyestrain

Eyestrain: The Number One Complaint of Computer Users

The most widespread problem in computer use today is not carpal tunnel syndrome, nor is it those nagging problems of the upper back, neck, or shoulders. According to the National Institute of Occupational Health and Safety (NIOSH), the number one cause of high levels of fatigue, errors at work, and lost days of production is eyestrain. NIOSH studies indicate that if you work at a computer for more than three hours a day, you may be among the 88 percent who suffer from eyestrain.

The reasons for eyestrain among computer users include primary and secondary glare, excessive lighting, improper ergonomics, poor-quality or inappropriately adjusted video display terminals (VDTs), uncorrected or improperly corrected vision, and insufficient or non-existent eye care. Each of these reasons will be discussed separately in this chapter.

Unless steps are taken to make the necessary corrections, eyestrain can cause blurred vision, headaches, gritty eye sensation, eye fatigue, neck and shoulder pain, color perception change, decreased visual efficiency, more frequent errors, and reduced efficiency.

This chapter contains text from Rosemarie Atencio "Eyestrain: the Number One Complaint of Computer Users," *Computers in Libraries*, September 1996, Vol. 16, No. 8, pp. 40–44, copyright 1996 by Information Today, Inc. Reprinted with permission. And Jim Seymour, "Your Eyes Come First," reprinted from *PC Magazine*, October 24, 1995, with permission. Copyright © 1995, Ziff Davis Media, Inc. All rights reserved.

As an ergonomic consultant and a specialist in repetitive strain prevention, I have detailed in this chapter some of the common sources of these eyestrain problems. Since these problems have concrete solutions, I have also provided suggestions for correcting the problems.

Primary and Secondary Glare

Primary glare is direct glare. For example, I consulted in an office where a VDT was in front of a window. As the operator looked at her VDT, she was also trying to compensate for the glare of the sun shining in her eyes. In that case, the glare was from natural light, but it can also occur with artificial light.

Secondary glare is reflective glare. This type of glare is very common in libraries where many of the surfaces have a high-gloss finish. In fact, I was invited to conduct workshops at a beautiful new library. This building was right out of the pages of an architectural or interior design magazine. Every surface was covered with a highly reflective material. It was visually interesting to the patrons, but how fatiguing for the staff! Light was bouncing off everything.

In order to cut glare, windows need to have blinds or drapes. (Blinds are better than drapes and vertical blinds are better than horizontal for controlling glare.) Matte-finished, soft-colored walls reflect less than bright or glossy walls. Furniture, equipment, and counters near the VDT need to have non-reflective surfaces. (Also note the placement of mirrors or art work with reflective glass.)

To check for glare on the VDT, place a mirror in front of the screen to identify sources of reflections. If the cause of the reflections cannot be eliminated, move the workstation or configure the workstation in a way to reduce or eliminate the glare. It may be necessary to make or buy a hood for the VDT to shield it from reflection. Glare guards are made specifically for VDTs, but the guards are generally considered a less satisfactory answer than elimination of the reflection. Unfortunately, glare guards may reduce glare at the cost of clarity. Shop carefully. You may be trading off one eyestrain problem for another.

Excessive Lighting

Typically, standard office lighting is provided by bright overhead fluorescent lights. This type of lighting is great for precision work, but is unsuitable for computer users. There are two problems created by this common form of lighting: one is that the light causes a great deal of primary and secondary glare, the other is that it creates harsh shadows. Either way, the computer user's eyes are working harder than necessary.

Using a VDT is equivalent to sitting in the living room watching TV while reading or knitting. In that setting, there is usually some indirect light source of the room and direct light illuminating the task area. The same holds true for a computer area. Therefore, if at all possible, it is better to turn down the overhead lights around the VDT. If there is no way of adjusting the brightness at the light switch, you may need to ask the maintenance department to remove some of the bulbs. Another solution would be to get appropriate diffusers for the overhead lights. If nothing else can be done, the computer station should be placed in between the rows of lights instead of directly underneath them.

Do strive to keep the room softly lit while reserving stronger light only for the task area. It could go a long way toward cutting eyestrain.

Improper Ergonomics

The most common ergonomic VDT problems deal with placement: sitting too close to the VDT, placing the VDT too high or too low, or pushing the VDT too far to one side of the desk or counter.

In order to alleviate the problem of sitting too close to the VDT, allow double your reading distance. The recommended range of distance from the eyes to the VDT is 18 to 29 inches. This distance is necessary not only for better vision, but also to keep dust particles out of the eyes. The VDT is quite a magnet for dust.

There are some differences of opinion about the best height for the VDT. A good rule is to make sure that the top of the VDT (not the screen) is even with your eyes. In this way, your eyes will be able to look slightly down without straining your neck.

Make sure that the VDT is squarely in front of you. In one library where I consulted, the VDT was placed in a very awkward position because, I was told, the person working at the computer needed to be able to keep an eye on the circulation center in case extra help was needed. I convinced the staff to place the VDT squarely on the counter. It was an easy sell once I demonstrated that an overhead mirror would accomplish the necessary view of the circulation desk and would not require anyone to use the computer in such an awkward manner. This is an example of how making a small, inexpensive change can make all the difference in working comfortably. Look at your work area. Ask yourself what small but significant changes you could make.

For the sake of your neck, use a document holder. If you place it right next to the VDT at the same height, you can save yourself a lot of fatigue and unnecessary movement. Wes Francis, of The Ergonomic Office Store, tells me that you can now buy document holders with built-in task lights. That is an excellent idea!

Poor-Quality or Inappropriately Adjusted Video Display Terminals

Raymond Soneira, president of Sonera Technology, a company that manufactures and sells VDT testing devices, told me during a conversation, "The public will take an active role when it comes to reading. They know how to optimize their comfort. They will sit in a comfortable seat, adjust the lighting for better vision, place the reading material in the best position to read it. But people are passive when it comes to the VDT. They will sit down, make no adjustments in the lighting, the background, or the image quality."

Geometric distortion, flicker, contrast, brightness, and color can all lead to problems for the eyes. Glare on the screen can wash out color, thereby forcing the eyes to strain and the neck to push forward.

Just as you take your car in regularly for preventive maintenance, you need to do the same thing with your VDT. Every six months, the VDT needs to be checked to make certain that it is functioning within the manufacturers' specifications. Also, the VDT needs to be regularly maintained as suggested by the manufacturer. Check your manual to learn how to conduct a periodic inspection. Your VDT may be experiencing a flicker problem caused by an internal board or card that may need upgrading.

Sonera Technology sells a software test package to help evaluate the resolution, color, screen distortion, and other diagnostic information so that you can maximize your VDT comfort and avoid subliminal problems.

Another small but important bit of maintenance is to clean the screen of the VDT with an antistatic spray and a lint-free wipe cloth or paper every day. You can also purchase antistatic screens.

Uncorrected or Improperly Corrected Vision

Computer operators need to have their vision checked regularly-NIOSH recommends at least once a year. However, if you sit for long periods of time at the VDT or if there is a lot of stress in your job, you probably would do well to have your eyes checked twice a year. Even if you do not require prescription eyewear for distance or reading, there may be a need for correction just for the specific problems of the computer.

If you are already using prescription eyewear, the lens correction may not take into consideration the distance from your eyes to the VDT. All too often, I have seen computer operators craning their necks in all directions trying to find that perfect place to look through bifocals or trifocals to see the VDT.

It is important to tell your optometrist or ophthalmologist how much time you spend at the computer. It is also a good idea to measure (a string will do) from the bridge of your nose to the VDT to provide your doctor with an accurate measurement of the necessary distance for correction.

There is evidence that the standard black-on-white Snellen chart used for diagnosing eye problems is not appropriate for the problems of VDTs. Dr. Gerald Murch studied the problems of eye fatigue in computer users and made some interesting conclusions. He found that over a number of hours at a VDT, the eye focusing point extends beyond the screen and out to a resting point of accommodation (RPA). Because of the RPA, the VDT viewer must then expend extra effort to make his or her eyes focus on and process visual information. Through the work of Dr. Murch, a new visual diagnostic tool called PRIO was developed for eye professionals. I talked with Jon Torrey, vice president of consumer marketing at PRIO, who said that the company can provide you with information on which eye professionals near you use PRIO diagnostics. [See "Your Eyes Come First" for more information on RPA and PRIO].

Insufficient or Non-Existent Eye Care

There are several eye-health problems specific to using a VDT. First of all, the eyes have evolved to see at a distance. They are also meant to take in a three-dimensional world. By contrast, the VDT presents a close-up, two-dimensional process. The other problem is that the eyes are open wider and less blinking takes place at a VDT. This is the equivalent of running your car without putting sufficient oil in it. No wonder the eyes feel gritty and fatigued after a few hours at the VDT. This is especially important for contact lens wearers.

Vacations for Your Eyes

To maintain eye health, you need to rest your eyes from time to time. NIOSH recommends a break every two hours from the VDT. In my books I refer to this time as a "mini-vacation." I define it as a small rest, an exercise, or another task that breaks up the cycle of repetition for the body.

There are many things that you can do with this time. Here are some ideas:

- Rub your hands together until your hands are warm and tingling. Close your eyes and cup the warm palms of your hands over your eyelids while resting the heel of your hand on your cheekbones. Breathe deeply and visualize black.

- Scan a distant horizon or follow the lines of a tree or a cloud.

- Wash your eyes free of dust particles using an eyecup and distilled water. Eye rinsing is especially important for contact lens wearers. (Avoid regular use of vasoconstricting drops.)

- Apply steady finger pressure (acupressure) to these points. Take three deep breaths at each point. 1) Press your index finger at the cheek ridge just below the middle of the eye; 2) press the indentation just at the outside corner of the eye; 3) press on both sides of the root of the bridge of the nose.

- With your eyes closed, slowly move your eyes to the right, to the left, up, and then down. Do it three times.

Using any of these techniques may also relieve your feelings of fatigue and stress. Try them and see what works for you.

—by Rosemarie Atencio

Rosemarie Atencio is the president of Health & Wellness Dynamics, Inc. (HWD), which specializes in consulting and training in repetitive strain prevention and stress management. She is also a holistic health practitioner, ergonomic consultant, lecturer, and author. Her books include *Carpal Tunnel Syndrome: How to Relieve & Prevent Wrist BURNOUT!* and *Shoulders, Upper Back & Neck: Free Yourself from PAIN!* Contact her at 800/935-7323 or hhwd@teleport.com. Contact Rosemarie Atencio at (800) 935-7323, (541) 935-1608, hhwd@teleport.com, or write to her at HWD, Inc., P.O. Box 220, Vaneta, OR 97487.

Your Eyes Come First

PC Specs

For more than a decade I've used special eyeglasses optimized for the working distance from my eyes to the monitor, based on my desk setup, posture, and so on. These computer glasses have made a noticeable difference.

But until recently, not enough of a difference. Because until recently optometrists didn't know how to prescribe glasses correctly for the glowing phosphors of computers and the virtual image they present to the eye.

When the eye focuses on sharp, black-on-white type on a conventional eye-testing chart, it tends to hold focus on that plane. So testing your vision with the ubiquitous Snellen card—used in virtually every optometrist's office—is fine for determining the correct prescription for reading glasses or sewing glasses. But it doesn't work very well for glasses for computer users.

The villain is a physiological phenomenon called the lag of accommodation. Simply put, when the eye attempts to focus on the inevitably softer image on a computer monitor's cathode-ray tube, or on a notebook's LCD screen, it is unable to hold focus on that virtual image plane.

Instead, the eye's focus almost immediately starts drifting outward toward a point called the resting point of accommodation (RPA). You subconsciously force the eye's focus back onto the monitor image, but the eye quickly begins drifting its focus back out to that RPA once again.

The difference between the point at which you want the eye to focus—the plane of the computer screen—and that RPA point is your lag of accommodation. And it is that constant refocusing, not found in any other environment or human action, that leads to the many manifestations of eyestrain.

There has been no good way to determine an individual's specific RPA—the distance varies a good deal from one person to the next—nor to devise a prescription to correct for each person's lag of accommodation. As a result, "computer glasses," no matter how carefully prescribed, no matter the competence of the person conducting the eye exam, have been rough approximations, inherently flawed because they were based on that unrealistic, black-ink-on-white-paper Snellen-card test.

But for the past two months I've been wearing a new pair of computer glasses that have gone a long way to overcome the lag-of-accommodation problem. The magic isn't in the glasses themselves, which are ordinary single-vision glasses ground to a conventional prescription, but in the way that the prescription was determined.

Dr. Cosmo Salibello has been working on this problem for more than a decade. Convinced that an active, "Gaussian stimulus" test card was the only valid way to simulate the eye's reaction to a computer display, he and colleagues at a little Portland, Oregon company,

PRIO, developed a device that lets optometrists accurately determine an individual's RPA and build correction for that distance into prescriptions.

The PRIO Vision Tester is a backlit box, about 5 by 7 by 1 inch, that attaches to the doctor's side of the eye-examination system. It displays green and amber text against a black background, and green text against a white background. The process is quick: You read the text over and over for a couple of minutes, to start your eyes' focus-swapping routine, and then the doctor measures your ocular movement.

Before and After

My new computer glasses were produced from the results of a PRIO exam, and in direct comparisons with another pair based on an ostensibly correct prescription derived from a Snellen-chart test, I see a real difference.

But the most important difference isn't detected in a quick test between PRIO-based correction glasses and conventional close-work correction lenses. It comes over time: Even after long sessions at the computer, I no longer have the weary, red-eyed, blurry vision I once blamed on the computer.

The PRIO technique and equipment are new, and it can be hard to find an optometrist in your area using the device. You (and your optometrist and your employer) can contact PRIO at 800-621-1098 or priojt@teleport.com for more information.

I rarely offer such unqualified endorsements. But I have little choice here: My vision and yours are too important to put at risk. And PRIO can make a big difference.

References for "Eyestrain: the Number One Complaint of Computer Users"

Godnig, Edward C., and John S. Hacunda. *Computers and Visual Stress*. Charlestown, RI: Seacoast Information Services, 1990.

Harwin, Ronald, and Colin Haynes. *Healthy Computing*. New York: Amacom, 1992.

Hutchinson, R. Anthony. *Computer Eye-Stress*, New York: M. Evans, 1985.

Stigliani, Joan. *The Computer User's Survival Guide*, New York: O'Reilly & Associates, 1995.

Bass, Steve, "New Sight for Sore Eyes" *PC World* 14 (Feb., 1996) 334.

Lewin, David I., "Preventive Medicine at Work" (Small Business Computing) Nation's Business 83 (March, 1995): 33-35.

Murch, Gerald, "How visible is your display?" *Electro-Optical Systems Design* 14 (1982): 43-49.

Seymour, Jim, "Your Eyes Come First" *PC Magazine* 14 (Oct., 24, 1995): 93-94.

"Industry, science clash on monitor location" (CTD Clinic) *CTD News* 4 (June, 1995): 8-9.

"Terminally Dry Eyes (News from the World of Medicine)" *Reader's Digest* 144 (March, 1994): 20.

Health and Safety Guidelines for Video Display Terminals in the Workplace. Oregon: Oregon Department of Insurance and Finance, 1991.

Working Safely with Video Display Terminals. Washington, DC: U.S. Department of Labor, 1991.

Part Four

Noise and Hearing Issues

Chapter 17

Work Related Hearing Loss

Work related hearing loss continues to be a critical workplace safety and health issue. The National Institute for Occupational Safety and Health (NIOSH) and the occupational safety and health community named hearing loss one of the 21 priority areas for research in the next century. Noise-induced hearing loss is 100 percent preventable but once acquired, hearing loss is permanent and irreversible. Therefore, prevention measures must be taken by employers and workers to ensure the protection of workers' hearing.

Magnitude

Approximately 30 million workers are exposed to hazardous noise on the job and an additional nine million are at risk for hearing loss from other agents such as solvents and metals.

Noise-induced hearing loss is one of the most common occupational diseases and the second most self-reported occupational illness or injury. Industry specific studies reveal:

- 44% of carpenters and 48% of plumbers reported that they had a perceived hearing loss.

- 90% of coal miners will have a hearing impairment by age 52 (compared to 9% of the general population); 70% of male, metal/nonmetal miners will experience a hearing impairment by age 60.

National Institute for Occupational Safety and Health (NIOSH), Centers for Disease Control and Prevention (CDC), undated fact sheet, http://www.cdc.gov/niosh/hpworkrel.html.

While any worker can be at risk for noise-induced hearing loss in the workplace, workers in many industries have higher exposures to dangerous levels of noise. Industries with high numbers of exposed workers include: agriculture; mining; construction; manufacturing and utilities; transportation; and military.

Costs

There is no national surveillance or injury reporting system for hearing loss. As such, comprehensive data on the economic impact of hearing loss are not available. Some estimates find that occupational hearing loss compensation costs alone are in the hundreds of millions of dollars per year. The following examples provide an indication of the economic burden of occupational hearing loss.

Washington State, workers' compensation disability settlements for hearing-related conditions cost $4.8 million in 1991. This figure does not include medical costs or personal costs which can include approximately $1500 for a hearing aid and around $300 per year for batteries. Moreover, workers' compensation data are an underestimate of the true frequency of occupational illness, representing only the tip of the iceberg.

In British Columbia, in the five-year period from 1994 to 1998, the workers' compensation board paid $18 million in permanent disability awards to 3,207 workers suffering hearing loss. An additional $36 million was paid out for hearing aids.

Through their hearing conservation program, the U.S. Army saved $504.3 million by reducing hearing loss among combat arms personnel between 1974 and 1994. Between 1987 and 1997, as a result of military efforts to reduce civilian hearing loss, the Department of Veterans Affairs saved $220.8 million and the Army an additional $149 million.

Prevention

Removing hazardous noise from the workplace through engineering controls (e.g. installing a muffler or building an acoustic barrier) is the most effective way to prevent noise-induced hearing loss. Hearing protectors such as ear plugs and ear muffs should be used when it is not feasible to otherwise reduce noise to a safe level. NIOSH recommends hearing loss prevention programs for all workplaces with hazardous levels of noise. These programs should include noise assessments, engineering controls, audiometric monitoring of workers' hearing, appropriate use of hearing protectors, worker education, record-keeping, and program evaluation.

Chapter 18

Curing the Noisy Office

While office noise rarely threatens workers' health, it can have a damaging effect on your company's productivity. The following expert advice can help you successfully handle noise problems in office buildings.

This office is so noisy that I can't even think!" A complaint heard, in one form or another, every day in offices around the world. While these complaints are often dismissed as frivolous or a nuisance, you want to satisfy your customers. Is the noise harmful? Is there a quick fix?

Office noise is rarely loud enough to damage hearing. The Occupational Safety and Health Administration (OSHA) regulates noise exposures when the sounds are above 85 decibels (dBA).

This is about the level of noise when you have to raise your voice to hold a conversation with someone standing next to you. If people are exposed to noise this loud for an 8-hour day, OSHA requires that a formal hearing conservation program be developed. This program includes noise measurements, engineering controls to reduce noise, hearing examinations for exposed employees, and personal protective equipment.

Although there are no regulations concerning office noise below the 85 dBA level, a series of sound pressure level curves has been recommended to describe acceptable noise levels in various indoor settings.

William E. Hemp, Michael Glowatz Jr., *Occupational Hazards*, August 1995, Vol. 57, N. 8, pp. 36–40. Copyright 1999 Penton Media Inc. Reprinted with permission.

The American Society of Heating, Refrigeration and Air Conditioning Engineers (ASHRAE) suggests that an open-plan office have a noise criterion range of 40–50 that corresponds to 49–58 dBA. Noises above this level can interfere with voice communications and, for some people, even thought processes. If productivity is adversely affected, someone will want to know why. Safety officials and building managers needs a plan to deal with obtrusive, non-regulated office noise.

The Typical Office

Typical offices are large, open areas with many employees working at individual work stations. The open plan office should be designed to include spaces for noisy devices and conferences. Consideration is given to barriers of adequate height and sufficient absorption to prevent direct sound paths. All interior surfaces, including walls, ceilings, light fixtures and office furnishings, need treatment to prevent reflections. For private offices or cubicles, on the other hand, high levels of ambient noise are controlled by the transmission loss through partitions.

Common noise sources in the office are copying machines and printers, computers, fax machines, air conditioners, dehumidifiers, humidifiers, piped-in music or personal radios and fans. Most important is people-generated noise such as talking, laughing and walking. Noises from outside the office can also affect office workers. Trucks, airplanes or highway noise may present a problem in some office buildings. Noise may originate from one local source or may be diffuse and spread throughout the office.

Characteristics of Noise

Several factors affect how obtrusive or annoying a sound can be. Frequency is a major annoyance factor for typical office noises. While an adult with good hearing can hear frequencies between 20 and 20,000 hertz (Hz), frequencies between 2000 Hz and 8000 Hz are perceived as the most annoying. For noises of the same sound level, those below 500 Hz or above 10,000 Hz are considered less annoying. Frequency is also important when determining what type of noise control is needed, if any.

The loudness or sound level is also a factor, but there is a no critical sound level below which nobody will be annoyed and above which everybody will be annoyed. In general, a tone whose sound level fluctuates is more annoying than one whose level is constant.[1]

Noise duration also affects how obtrusive a noise is perceived; intuitively, long-duration noises are more obtrusive than short-duration noises. However, continuous noise can be ignored. Many complaints of noise involve intermittent, short-duration noise.

Two other factors can also explain why some noises are more bothersome than others: predictability of the noise, and value of the noise. If employees know that at 10 a.m. and 4 p.m. a tractor trailer leaves the loading dock, they may not perceive the noise as being as obtrusive as the dehumidifier that kicks on and off every so often. The value of the noise is also important in determining how obtrusive a noise is perceived. People using the copier feel that the noise they are generating is necessary while the other employees may be annoyed by the noise coming from that machine again.

Noise Control Plan

Identifying an obtrusive noise is the first step in dealing with noise complaints. Respond to the complaint by visiting the area where the complaint originated. Meet with people and ask for their opinions. Show genuine concern about the "problem." Appear interested and willing to help. This appearance is often overlooked but is critical. People perceive that management is concerned enough about them that the Hawthorne effect creates an attitude of lessened noise interference with any change in work environment.

Employees may sense the noise in two ways. First, the employees hear the noise as it travels through the air from the noise generating source. Second, less frequently, the employees may "feel" the noise as the noise source vibrates and sends vibrations through the building structure. Sound measurements may be useful to show that harmful sound levels do not exist. Octave band measurements are essential to develop an effective control strategy in complex situations. The obtrusive noise is usually obvious and a quick investigation will often identify the offending noise source.

The next step is to determine why the noise is a problem. Try to identify which specific characteristic of the noise is offensive. This is necessary to determine which noise control measures are warranted. Is the noise too loud, too unpredictable, too high-pitched?

With the objections documented, the safety director or building manager can then develop a noise control strategy. Noise control is an intricate science based on many factors. While we can't review all those factors here, we can take a look at a greatly simplified strategy based on many of the factors of noise control engineering.

Eliminating Noise

Consider eliminating the noise first. Maintenance for building equipment can often reduce noise from neglected equipment. Typically, this means attention to the Heating, Ventilation, and Air Conditioning (HVAC) system (low duct velocity, attention to disturbances in the ductwork, isolation of fans and motors from vibrating surfaces, etc.). Enclosing or isolating noisy office equipment is also helpful. The copier in the center of the office floor may be very disruptive to the people nearby. By moving it to another location, such as a copier room or even the side of the room, you can minimize the number of employees affected by the noise.

Isolating Noise

Isolating a noise source is done effectively by moving it far away from people. For point sources, sound levels drop off with distance in accordance with the "inverse square law," which yields a 6 dB sound level reduction for each doubling of the distance from the source. In open plan offices, there are reflections and multiple noise sources to consider, so noises are often isolated by enclosing them. When computer printers became prevalent, a market developed for computer printer noise enclosures. The noise reduction achieved by enclosing a copy machine in a separate room can reduce the noise level by more than 15 dBA. Many open offices insist on a remote room for copiers and fax machines; however, this is becoming less prevalent as more and more individuals have personal computers with printers at their desks.

When noise sources are diffuse, you may consider isolating the people. Room dividers have limited use because they do not extend from the floor to the ceiling, which is necessary to block noise waves from traveling from one side of the room to the other. Dividers should be as large as practical and not less than 5 feet high to optimize sound attenuation. Noise will bend around partitions and even under them if they are not placed as close to the floor as possible.

A separate remote conference room where employees can retire for speech privacy is needed for confidential conversations. Noise will penetrate drop ceilings, traveling long distances above ceilings before reentering the work space through transfer grills or other openings. For this reason, conference rooms should have slab-to-slab walls and appropriate sound absorptive interiors. If speaker phone conferences are common, many conference rooms should be available. Raised voices are common for speaker phone conversations. Open plan office design assumes workers in open plan spaces would learn to speak with lowered speech levels.

Absorbing Noise

In an office, noise generated from a source travels through the air and through the building structure. As the noise travels through the air, it reflects off hard objects and is absorbed by soft objects. Sound-absorbing material should be used on all surfaces near the sound generator that can reflect sound.

Absorbing the noise with "sound soak" is most effective for higher frequency noise (peaking at or above 1000 Hz). With each frequency of noise having an identifiable wavelength, different sound-absorbing materials will absorb some wavelengths better than others. Sound absorption coefficients have been determined for many building materials.

Office furnishings will affect the sound propagation in an office. Softer materials will absorb more sound. Window treatments and wall coverings can help reduce noise in an office if they are properly selected. Carpet applied directly to walls is not a suitable solution. Generally, about 1 inch of fiberglass under a decorative fabric will provide a suitable sound-absorbing treatment.

Sometimes, maintenance can adversely affect the noise-control properties of some building materials. Re-painting an acoustical ceiling can reduce the sound-absorption properties of some ceilings. Perforated or slotted acoustical ceilings can be repainted often without reducing their sound absorption quality unless a considerable number of perforations are covered over. Fissured acoustical ceilings need more care when repainting to avoid covering over too many large fissures. Acoustical ceilings without openings depend entirely on the porosity of the material for sound absorption. Re-painting this type of ceiling will reduce its ability to absorb noise.

Active Noise Control Systems

Active noise control systems are used for two purposes: to silence an obtrusive noise or to generate a desirable noise. The systems are termed "active" because sound is added to achieve the result. To silence a noise, the system produces a sound that is out-of-phase and cancels the noise. Systems also produce background noise, sometimes called "white noise," to mask other noises or for privacy.

Active HVAC silencers have been designed into new construction plans of major office buildings. Silencers are comprised of four major components: downstream microphone, loudspeaker, upstream microphone and controller. The downstream microphone picks up the characteristics of the fan noise and transmits that information to the controller. The controller determines an opposite phase, equal amplitude and frequency sound for the loudspeaker to play. The upstream microphone completes the feedback loop, picking up any errors for the controller to correct. Active noise control systems can also detect noise that is characteristic of worn fan belts or bearings, a sort of backup to preventive maintenance. Measured noise levels in completed office buildings have met acoustical specifications.[2]

Background noise, a type of active control, is useful as a masking sound in an open office environment. Open plan offices must consider two, often conflicting goals: speech privacy and speech intelligibility. Background noise for speech privacy makes it difficult to hear conversations and noises from other areas. However, the background noise should not interfere with the ability to hold a face-to-face or telephone conversation, which is speech intelligibility.

- Music is acceptable but rarely used because musical tastes are so diverse that an acceptable musical selection, even "elevator music," is often impossible to achieve.

- Ventilation systems can provide a masking effect, but if they are not constantly on, their unpredictability can be more disruptive than helpful.

- Electronic masking systems are available and have proven effective in many instances. These systems generate white noise, a tone with equal energy across all band widths from say, 20 Hz to 20,000 Hz. The white noise is then tailored to the environment to achieve noise reductions of 5 dB per band width.

Determining the level of the background noise is often a compromise. The level of noise needed for privacy may be louder than the level needed to hold a normal conversation.

Summary

So, what should you do when the noise complaints come in? First, determine if the noise is above 85 dBA and possibly hazardous, or below 85 dBA and just obtrusive, a problem for local management to correct. If it is a hazardous noise situation, OSHA requirements are explicit. If it is obtrusive and affecting the proficiency of employees, corrective action is usually deemed necessary even though no safety and health regulations are broken.

You have a noise control strategy to follow: investigate, identify, characterize and abate. Abatement can involve several options: eliminating noise, absorbing noise, isolating noise and even adding complementary sounds to reduce the overall noise.

By acting on noise complaints and following such a strategy, you have taken the initiative and shown concern for employees' well being. You have also taken steps to ensure productivity is not reduced by factors under your control. The corrective action may require some remediation and that is when the management decisions enter the picture. But money wisely spent to improve the work environment is rarely wasted.

References

1. John A. Molino, *Handbook of Noise Control*, 2nd Edition, ed. by Cyril M. Harris (New York: McGraw-Hill, 1979), pp. 16–3, 16–5.

2. Howard K. Pelton, Steven Wise, and William S. Sims, "Active HVAC Noise Control Systems Provide Acoustical Comfort," *Sound & Vibration*, XXVIII (July 1994), 14.

— by William E. Hemp, CIH, CSP

William E. Hemp, CIH, CSP, is a safety engineer for AT&T Bell Laboratories. Prior to working at AT&T, he worked as a safety engineer for the Naval Air Engineering Center, Lakehurst, N.J. He has over 10 years experience in the health and safety field. Michael Glowatz, Jr., CIH, CSP, is the manager of industrial hygiene & safety for AT&T Bell Laboratories. His past experience includes working as an OSHA compliance officer. He has published numerous articles on safety and health topics. Charles P. Lichtenwalner, CIH, CSP, is a member of the technical staff at AT&T Bell Laboratories and a member of the Institute of Noise Control Engineers. He also has published widely on current safety and health issues.

Chapter 19

Does OSHA's Noise Standard Really Protect People's Hearing?

In Brief

The noise standards set by the Occupational Safety and Health Administration (OSHA) fail to protect workers from hearing loss and other extra-auditory effects of loud noise. The reduced 85-decibel allowable noise still affects the hearing capacity of workers exposed to long hours at this noise level. Protection measures implemented by various agencies using engineering controls were also eliminated by an OSHA guideline suggesting the use of less efficient methods to reduce costs.

Introduction

Everybody knows that if you're exposed to loud enough noise for a long enough time, you'll lose your hearing. But few people know that hearing loss is just one of the problems associated with noise exposure. Noise affects our ability to react to warning signals, and some research suggests that it may adversely affect vision, increase stress levels and raise blood pressure. These effects are called extra-auditory because they go beyond just experiencing a hearing loss.

From "Does OSHA's Noise Standard Really Protect People's Hearing?" by John F. Rekus, in *Occupational Hazards*, Vol. 60, N. 5, May 1998, pp. 71–76.

Extra-Auditory Effects

- *Speech interference*. A mechanic working on an overhead crane fumbles a socket wrench. He yells down to warn you out of the way, but you can't hear him over the background noise. Today's your lucky day. The wrench lands with a clank two feet in front of you. But what about the next time? Can you act on warnings you don't hear?

- *Color perception*. Noise affects some people's ability to differentiate between red and green. Because red and green are used to indicate stop and go, safe and unsafe, on and off, and similar conditions, the inability to tell them apart could lead to a fatal injury.

- *Peripheral vision*. Another extra-auditory effect is reduced peripheral, or side, vision. Not being able to detect movement out of the corner of your eye might result in your being run over by a forklift or slapped on the side of the head by a moving crane load block.

- *Increased stress*. Did you ever want to strangle a neighbor who blared his stereo at night when you were trying to get some sleep? If so, you're aware of yet another extra-auditory effect of noise—increased stress and irritability. It's fairly well established that people who are distracted, stressed out and irritable are more likely to make mistakes that could lead to injuries.

- *Blood pressure changes*. Some people's blood pressure increases upon exposure to noise. If they have pre-existing cardiovascular problems, exposure to excessive noise could make things worse.

- *Startle response*. The startle response occurs when someone sneaks up behind you and yells "boo." Now you probably won't lose your hearing from someone sneaking up behind you to yell in your ear, but you could be fried, when in your startled state, you inadvertently touch that high-voltage circuit you were testing with your voltage probe.

OSHA Noise Standard

Curiously, OSHA's noise standard doesn't address any of these extra-auditory effects. It is only concerned with occupational hearing loss, and even in that respect, it doesn't do a very good job protecting workers. In fact, OSHA knows that significant number of workers will lose their hearing, in spite of the standard! How can this be?

OSHA allows people to be exposed to a level of 90 decibels (dB) for up to eight hours. As the noise level goes up, the exposure time must be reduced. Ninety decibels is pretty loud. It is comparable to the noise of a fast-moving freight train about 10 feet away. Even though OSHA knew that some people exposed to 90 dB noise would develop a permanent hearing loss, this limit was chosen as a political compromise that considered economic concerns as well as employee protection.

Later, OSHA attempted to address the shortcomings with another compromise of sorts—the hearing conservation amendment to the noise standard. In that March 1983 revision, OSHA called for noise monitoring and protective equipment in 85-decibel environments, if employees experience a standard threshold shift (STS) in their hearing capacity. Absent an STS, hearing protection is not required unless noise levels reach 90 decibels as an 8-hour time-weighted average.

In short, these were the best that OSHA could do given the political influences of the day. But here's the bottom line: contrary to popular belief, following the OSHA standard won't keep some workers from developing a hearing loss.

Some health professionals who recognized that the OSHA standard was not adequately protective took the initiative of setting voluntary lower limits. For example, for more than two decades, the Department of Defense (DOD) has used an exposure threshold of 85 decibels. DOD policies also require that both civilian and military personnel wear ear protection above this limit regardless of how long they are exposed.

Engineering Controls

OSHA standard 29 CFR 1910.95(a) (Code of Federal Regulations) stipulates that "[w]hen employees are subjected to sound levels exceeding those listed in Table G-16, feasible administrative or engineering controls shall be utilized." Engineering controls are things that can reduce the noise level or eliminate it all together. For example, scrap grinders used in the plastics industry typically have sound levels over 100 dB. To control this noise, many plastics plants have built sound-absorbing rooms around their grinders. Because the enclosure absorbs the noise, sound levels in the rest of the plant are low enough that people don't need to wear ear protection. Other examples of engineering controls include: installing mufflers on air exhausts; using plastic gears instead of metal gears; doing simple things like tightening machine guards so they don't rattle; or putting people in booths or control rooms that isolate them from the noise.

During the Reagan era, OSHA pulled a nasty trick on the working people it was supposed to be protecting. It issued an administrative enforcement directive which in essence torpedoed the universally accepted industrial hygiene principal of using engineering controls before relying on other, widely acknowledged, less effective controls, such as employee work practices and personal protective equipment. OSHA's internal compliance document CPL 2-2.35A, titled 29 CFR 1910.95(b)(1), Guidelines for Noise, and dated Dec. 19, 1983, stipulated that if average 8-hour sound levels were less than 100 dB, employers had the option of doing a cost-benefit analysis to see if a hearing conservation program was less expensive than engineering controls. Unlike the standard, this administrative policy was an executive fiat not subject to public comment. Although most of the CPL has been withdrawn, its spirit has been incorporated into Chapter III of OSHA's Field Instruction Reference Manual (FIRM), which you can find on the OSHA CD-ROM or on OSHA's web page, http://www.osha. gov. Paragraph C.3.b of the FIRM states:

> Current enforcement policy regarding 29 CFR 1910.95(b)(1) allows employers to rely on personal protective equipment and a hearing conservation program rather than engineering and/or administrative controls when hearing protectors will effectively attenuate the noise to which the employee is exposed to acceptable levels as specified in Tables G-16 or G-16a of the standard.

Given that safety and health professionals generally agree that protective equipment is the last line of defense for controlling hazards, I've been perplexed why there has not been public outcry about this arbitrary and capricious policy.

Noise Reduction Rations

Many people do not understand the labels on ear protection that indicate the noise reduction rating or NRR. Take, for example, a foam plug that has a published NRR of 27 dB. Now, good old common sense tells you that if you've got a noise level of 107 dB, and earplugs with an NRR of 27 dB, when you put the plugs on, the noise level at your ear level should drop to 80 dB (107 dB-27 dB = 80 dB). That's just common sense right? Well, actually this is just another safety myth (see "Safety Myths: What Everybody Knows Is Simply Wrong," Occuaptional Hazards, OH, October 1996).

Don't believe me? Check it out. If you consult OSHA's Figure II:5-1, Calculating Hearing Protector Attenuation of the OSHA Industrial

Hygiene Technical you will find that the agency instructs its compliance industrial hygienists to first subtract 7 dB from the NRR to compensate for spectral uncertainty. This is because the acoustical spectrum of industrial noise is not a pure tone like that used during a hearing test. That means that our original 27 dB NRR now becomes: 20 (27 dB-7 dB = 20 dB).

But we're not done yet. The technical manual then tells us to apply a safety factor. Now, in many scientific and engineering applications, safety factors of four to seven are pretty common, but OSHA requires a safety factor of only two. In other words, we divide 20 dB by our safety factor of 2 and wind up with 10 dB. So we've now gone from a published NRR of 27 to an effective level of protection of only 10 dB.

All of this complexity creates a public misperception as to the meaning of NRR. What people fail to understand, and some experts fail to communicate, is that the testing protocol uses a test panel that in essence receives two hearing tests: one without ear protection and one with it. The NRR is then calculated based on the results of these two tests.

Summary

- Noise exposure may produce extra-auditory effects such as interference with speech, changes in vision, increased stress, and high blood pressure.

- Even if you comply with the OSHA standard, many of your employees may still suffer a permanent hearing loss. Even though OSHA's noise standard stipulates that engineering controls be used to reduce noise exposure, the enforcement policy ignores this requirement when sound levels are less than 100 dB.

- Finally, remember that the NRR on a package of earplugs might not provide the protection you think it does. Find out what it means and protect your workers accordingly.

How We Hear

The ear consists of three sections: the outer ear, which is the part we can see; the middle ear, which is behind the ear drum; and the inner ear, which is deep inside our head. Sound waves enter the outer ear and travel down the ear canal to the eardrum, which is attached to three small bones called the hammer, the anvil and the stirrup.

When sound waves strike the eardrum, it flexes back and forth in response to the changes in pressure. This flexing moves the hammer, which bangs the anvil, which in turn pushes the stirrup in and out on a membrane in the inner ear called the oval window.

As the oval window moves back and forth, it applies pressure to a fluid in the inner ear. The fluid is contained inside a snail-shaped bony structure called the cochlea. The cochlea contains a membrane with lots of hair cells sticking out. When the fluid in the inner ear is compressed and released, it causes the hair cells to move, sort of like sea weed moving back and forth with the surf. When the hair cells move, they generate nerve impulses that are sent to the brain. The brain then interprets these impulses as sound.

When we are exposed to excessive levels of noise, the hair cells inside the cochlea are damaged. The damage takes place gradually and we don't even know that it is happening. In a way, it's a lot like stomping on blades of grass. You stomp on the grass and the blades will bend. However, given enough time they will eventually spring back. But if lots of people keep walking on them over and over again, they will eventually be beaten down to the point where they won't be able to spring back.

The same thing happens to the hair cells in our ears. When they are exposed to a little noise, they get tired, and our ability to hear goes down. This is called a temporary threshold shift. Given some rest, our hair cells recover just like the blades of grass. But with exposure to very high noise levels or extended periods of loud noise, the damage is permanent. In other words, once you lose your hearing, you can never get it back. It damages your hearing without you even knowing it.

Types of Ear Protectors

Ear protection is generally divided into three categories: earmuffs, which go over your ears; earplugs, which go in your ears; and canal caps. which cover the ear canal.

Earmuffs

Earmuffs have two cup-like covers connected by a stiff metal or plastic head band. The cups are lined with a sound-absorbing material and fit over your ears to from a noise barrier. They also have foam- or fluid-filled cushions around the edge of the cups. Because the cushions are flexible, they adjust to the shape of your head to form a reasonably good seal around your ears. Many people think that because they are bigger, earmuffs provide a higher level of protection than earplugs or canal caps. In reality, some earplugs provide as much or more protection as muffs.

Earmuffs are a good choice if you are exposed to noise intermittently. They are easy to put on and take off, easy to store, and unlike earplugs, they are large enough that they aren't easily misplaced. On the down side, some people who wear muffs for extended periods of time find that after a while, they begin to feel hot, tight and bulky. Earmuffs can also get in the way if you've got to move your head around in a small space.

Earmuffs will generally fit a wide range of workers, but some people's heads might be a little too big or too little small for a few brands to fit well. In addition, some people's ears might be too large to fit entirely inside some muffs. Although these situations are rare, they can occur.

If you wear glasses, be aware that the temple piece passing under the cushion can reduce the muff's effectiveness by three to seven decibels. This reduction can be offset by using glasses with thinner temple pieces.

Another thing you should know is that position of the headband may influence the level of noise reduction. Even though most people wear the headband over the top of their head, a few people prefer to wear it behind their neck or under their chin. Each of these positions may cause variation of a few decibels, so you had better check the package or product data sheets to see what effect each of these other positions has.

Earplugs

Earplugs are usually a little more comfortable than muffs, especially if you wear ear protection for a long time. In addition, unlike earmuffs, their fit is not affected by the temple pieces of eye glasses, and they won't get in the way if you stick your head into a tight space.

Molded plugs made from a soft, pliable plastic were the first generation of earplugs. Inserted into the ear canal, they block noise from reaching the inner ear. Although they are reasonably effective, some people find them uncomfortable after a few hours.

Formable plugs are made from specially treated cotton, mineral wool and slow-recovery plastic foams. The big advantages of formable plugs are that they are soft, lightweight and conform to the shape of your ear. As a result, they are comfortable to wear for long periods of time.

The two most common types of formable plugs are either plastic foam cylinders or fiberglass balls surrounded with a thin, flexible, plastic skin. Because formable plugs are a little bigger than our ear canals, they must be compressed a little before they are inserted. To do this, you simply hold the plug between your thumb and forefinger and roll it back and forth to form a cone shape. Make sure your hands are clean before you do this because you don't want grease, oil, chemicals or abrasive materials to enter your ear canal.

Canal Caps

Canal Caps are sort of a cross between earmuffs and earplugs. They consist of a soft, pliable plastic pod attached to a flexible head band. The headband is placed over your head and the pods are positioned over the ear canal openings. The pods are not inserted into the canal like earplugs, but instead they simply block the ear opening.

People who only have to wear ear protection intermittently, or for short periods of time, often find canal caps to be a good choice. For example, maintenance workers who have to go in and out of noisy areas throughout the day often find that it's easier to slip on a pair of canal caps rather than having to mess around with plugs. They also find that because of their lower profile, canal caps don't get in the way as much as muffs. Supervisors who are in and out of high-noise areas all day long also find that caps are convenient, as do people who have to walk through high-noise areas to get to work stations where they are not affected by noise.

Although canal caps are great for these short-duration uses, many people find that the firm, steady pressure on their ear canals becomes a nuisance after a while. Canal caps generally are not a good choice for people who have to wear ear protection all day long.

—by John Rekus

John Rekus is an independent safety consultant and author of the *Complete Confined Spaces Handbook*. With more than 20 years of OSHA regulatory experience, he specializes in conducting OSHA compliance surveys and providing safety training for workers and managers. He lives near Baltimore and may be reached at (410)583-7954 or via his web site at www.jfrekus.com.

Chapter 20

Protective Hearing Equipment

Introduction

In 1972, the National Institute for Occupational Safety and Health (NIOSH) published *Criteria for a Recommended Standard: Occupational Exposure to Noise*, which provided the basis for a recommended standard to reduce the risk of developing permanent hearing loss as a result of occupational noise exposure [NIOSH 1972]. NIOSH has now evaluated the latest scientific information and has revised some of its previous recommendations. The 1998 recommendations go beyond attempting to conserve hearing by focusing on preventing occupational noise-induced hearing loss (NIHL).

The NIOSH recommended exposure limit (REL) for occupational noise exposure (85 decibels, A-weighted, as an 8-hour time-weighted average [85 dBA as an 8-hr TWA]) was reevaluated using contemporary risk assessment techniques and incorporating the 4000-hertz (Hz) audio-metric frequency in the definition of hearing impairment. The new risk assessment reaffirms support for the 85-dBA REL. With a 40-year lifetime exposure at the 85-dBA REL, the excess risk of developing occupational NIHL is 8%—considerably lower than the 25% excess risk at the 90-dBA permissible exposure limit (PEL) currently enforced by the Occupational Safety and Health Administration (OSHA) and the Mine Safety and Health Administration (MSHA).

Excerpted from "Criteria for a Recommended Standard, Occupational Noise Exposure," National Institute of Occupational Safety and Health, DHHS (NIOSH) Pub. No. 98-126, http://www.cdc.gov/niosh/98-126f.html, June 1998.

NIOSH previously recommended an exchange rate of 5 dB for the calculation of time-weighted average (TWA) exposures to noise. However, NIOSH now recommends a 3-dB exchange rate, which is more firmly supported by scientific evidence. The 5-dB exchange rate is still used by OSHA and MSHA, but the 3-dB exchange rate has been increasingly supported by national and international consensus.

Hearing Protectors

A personal hearing protection device (or hearing protector) is any device designed to reduce the level of sound reaching the eardrum. Earmuffs, earplugs, and ear canal caps (also called semi-inserts) are the main types of hearing protectors. A wide range of hearing protectors exists within each of these categories. For example, earplugs may be subcategorized into foam, user-formable (such as silicon or spun mineral fiber), premolded, and custom-molded earplugs. In addition, some types of helmets (in particular, flight helmets worn in the military) also function as hearing protectors. Refer to Nixon and Berger [1991] for a detailed discussion of the uses, advantages, and disadvantages of each type of protector. Items not specifically designed to serve as hearing protectors (e.g., cigarette filters, cotton, and .38-caliber shells) should not be used in place of hearing protectors. Likewise, devices such as hearing aid earmolds, swim molds, and personal stereo earphones must never be considered as being hearing protective.

Ideally, the most effective way to prevent NIHL is to remove the hazardous noise from the workplace or to remove the worker from the hazardous noise. Hearing protectors should be used when engineering controls and work practices are not feasible for reducing noise exposures to safe levels. In some cases, hearing protectors are an interim solution to noise exposure. In other instances, hearing protectors may be the only feasible means of protecting the worker. When a worker's time-weighted noise exposure exceeds 100 dBA, both earplugs and earmuffs should be worn. It is important to note that using such double protection will add only 5 to 10 dB of attenuation, or protection against high noise levels [Nixon and Berger 1991]. Given the real-world performance of hearing protectors [Berger et al. 1996], NIOSH cautions that even double protection is inadequate when TWA exposures exceed 105dBA.

How much attenuation a hearing protector provides depends on its characteristics and how the worker wears it. The selected hearing protector must be capable of keeping the noise exposure at the ear below 85 dBA. Because a worker may not know how long a given noise exposure will last or what additional noise exposure he or she may incur later in the day, it may be prudent to wear hearing protectors whenever working in hazardous noise. Workers and supervisors should periodically ensure that the hearing protectors are worn correctly, are fitted properly, and are appropriate for the noise in which they are worn [Helmkamp et al. 1984; Gasaway 1985; Berger 1986; Royster and Royster 1990; NIOSH 1996].

Historically, emphasis has been placed on a hearing protector's attenuation characteristics—almost to the exclusion of other qualities necessary for it to be effective. Although those who select hearing protectors should consider the noise in which they will be worn, they must also consider the workers who will be wearing them, the need for compatibility with other safety equipment, and workplace conditions such as temperature, humidity, and atmospheric pressure [Gasaway 1985; Berger 1986]. In addition, a variety of styles should be provided so that workers may select a hearing protector on the basis of comfort, ease of use and handling, and impact on communication [NIOSH 1996; Royster and Royster 1990]. Each worker should receive individual training in the selection, fitting, use, repair, and replacement of the hearing protector [Gasaway 1985; Royster and Royster 1990; NIOSH 1996]. What is the best hearing protector for some workers may not be the best for others [Casali and Park 1990]. The most common excuses reported by workers for not wearing hearing protectors include discomfort, interference with hearing speech and warning signals, and the belief that workers have no control over an inevitable process that culminates in hearing loss [Berger 1980; Helmkamp 1986; Lusk et al. 1993]. Fortunately, none of these reasons present insurmountable barriers. Given adequate education and training, each can be successfully addressed [Lusk et al. 1995; Merry 1996; Stephenson 1996].

Workers and management must recognize the crucial importance of wearing hearing protectors correctly. Intermittent wear will dramatically reduce their effective protection [NIOSH 1996]. For example, a hearing protector that could optimally provide 30dB of attenuation for an 8-hr exposure would effectively provide only 15 dB if the worker removed the device for a cumulative 30 min during an 8-hr day. *The best hearing protector is the one that the worker will wear.*

Several methods exist for estimating the amount of sound attenuation a hearing protector provides. In the United States, a single number descriptor (NRR) is required by law [40 Code of Federal Regulations (CFR) 211] to be shown on the label of each hearing protector sold.

The NRR was designed to function as a simplified descriptor of the amount of protection provided by a given device. When its use was first proposed, the most typical method used to characterize sound attenuation was the real ear attenuation at threshold (REAT) method, as described by the American National Standards Institute in ANSI S3.19-1974 [ANSI 1974]. Sometimes called the octave-band or long method, this method was believed to provide too much information to be useful for labeling purposes; thus a single-number descriptor (NRR) was devised.

One problem inherent to using single-number descriptors of sound attenuation is the need to ensure that the resulting value does not sacrifice the estimated protection for the sake of simplicity. Thus these calculations will typically underestimate laboratory-derived "long methods" for estimating sound attenuation. To get around some of the limitations associated with NRR calculations, other methods have been developed for estimating hearing protector performance. The single-number rating method and the high-middle-low method may be used when a person needs to estimate performance more accurately than possible with the NRR but does not want to resort to octave-band descriptions of sound attenuation. Detailed descriptions of these methods are in The NIOSH Compendium of Hearing Protection Devices [NIOSH 1994].

Both NRR and the other hearing protector ratings referred to above are based on data obtained under laboratory conditions in which experimenters fit hearing protectors on trained listeners. As such, these ratings may differ markedly from the noise reduction that a worker would actually experience in the real world. Specifically, studies have repeatedly demonstrated that real-world protection is substantially less than noise attenuation values derived from experimenter-fit, laboratory-based methods. In the late 1970s and early 1980s, two NIOSH field studies found that insert-type hearing protectors in the field provided less than half the noise attenuation measured in the laboratory [Edwards et al. 1979; Lempert and Edwards 1983]. Since the 1970's, additional studies have been conducted on real-world noise attenuation with hearing protectors [Regan 1975; Padilla 1976; Abel et al. 1978; Edwards et al. 1978; Fleming 1980; Crawford and Nozza 1981; Chung et al. 1983; Hachey and Roberts 1983; Royster et al. 1984; Behar 1985; Mendez et al. 1986; Smoorenburg et al. 1986; Edwards and Green 1987; Pekkarinen 1987; Pfeiffer et al. 1989; Hempstock and Hill 1990; Berger and Kieper 1991; Casali and Park 1991; Durkt 1993]. In general, these studies involved testing the hearing thresholds of occluded and unoccluded ears of subjects who wore the hearing protectors for the test in the same manner as on the job. The tests attempted to simulate the actual conditions in which hearing protectors are normally used in the workplace. The laboratory NRRs consistently overestimated the real-world NRRs by 140% to 2,000% [Berger et al. 1996]. In general, the data show that earmuffs provide the highest real-world noise attenuation values, followed by foam earplugs; all other insert-type devices provide the least attenuation. From these results, it can also be concluded that ideally, workers should be individually fit-tested for hearing protectors. Currently, several laboratories are exploring feasible methods for this type of fit testing [Michael 1997].

Royster et al. [1996] addressed problems associated with the use of the NRR. These researchers demonstrated that relying on the manufacturer's instructions or the experimenter to fit hearing protectors may be of little value in estimating the protection a worker obtains under conditions of actual use. The Royster et al. [1996] study reported the results of an interlaboratory investigation of methods for assessing hearing protector performance. The results demonstrated that using untrained subjects to fit their hearing protectors provided much better estimates of the hearing protector's noise attenuation in the workplace than using the experimenter to fit them. This method has since been adopted for use by ANSI in ANSI S12.6-1997 [ANSI 1997]. Furthermore, the method has subsequently been endorsed by the National Hearing Conservation Association (NHCA) Task Force on Hearing Protector Effectiveness as well as numerous other professional organizations.

OSHA [1983] has instructed its compliance officers to derate the NRR by 50% in enforcing the engineering control provision of the OSHA noise standard. However, NIOSH concurs with the professional organizations cited above and recommends using subject fit data based on ANSI S12.6-1997 [ANSI 1997] to estimate hearing protector noise attenuation. If subject fit data are not available, NIOSH recommends derating hearing protectors by a factor that corresponds to the available real-world data. Specifically, NIOSH recommends that the labeled NRRs be derated as follows:

- *Earmuffs*: Subtract 25% from the manufacturer's labeled NRR.

- *Formable earplugs*: Subtract 50% from the manufacturer's labeled NRR.

- *All other earplugs*: Subtract 70% from the manufacturers labeled NRR.

For example, measure noise exposure levels in dBC or dBA with a sound level meter or noise dosimeter.

- When the noise exposure level in dBC is known, the effective A-weighted noise level (ENL) is:

$$ENL = dBC - derated\ NRR$$

- When the noise exposure level in dBA is known, the effective A-weighted noise level is:

$$ENL = dBA - (derated\ NRR\text{-}7)$$

To summarize, the best hearing protection for any worker is the removal of hazardous noise from the workplace. Until that happens, the best hearing protector for a worker is the one he or she will wear willingly and consistently. The following factors are extremely important determinants of worker acceptance of hearing protectors and the likelihood that workers will wear them consistently:

- convenience and availability
- belief that the device can be worn correctly
- belief that the device will prevent hearing loss
- belief that the device will not impair a workers ability to hear important sounds
- comfort
- adequate noise reduction
- ease of fit
- compatibility with other personal protective equipment

Part Five

Preventing Work-Related Musculoskeletal Disorders

Chapter 21

Back Injuries and Their Prevention

Chapter Contents

Section 21.1

Prevention of Back Injury/Disability

From "Back on Track," by S.L. Smith, in *Occupational Hazards*, Vol. 58, N. 3 March 1996, pp. 75–78. Copyright 1999 by Penton Media Inc. Reprinted with permission.

Nearly everyone will have a back ache at some point in his or her life. Our experts tell how to keep that ache from turning into a permanent pain in the disability file. Aching backs are a medical provider's Valhalla. As much as $100 billion each year is spent treating low back pain.

Medical experts believe that while low back pain may manifest itself suddenly, it actually develops slowly over time for the vast majority of sufferers. Some 80 percent of Americans will experience at least one bout of low back pain before the age of 65. Researchers like Stover Snook, Ph.D., assistant vice president and director of laboratories, Liberty Mutual Research Center for Safety and Health, admit that they cannot pinpoint the cause of back pain. They do not know if it originates in the muscles, vertebrae, ligaments or discs of the back. They do know that the effects are cumulative, becoming more apparent as we age.

Predictors of Pain

A popularly held belief is that back pain is caused by workplace conditions. A more accurate view is that back disability is caused by workplace conditions, say experts, while back pain has other causes. In fact, a recent groundbreaking study, published in the journal *Spine* by an international team of researchers, found that similar lumbar disc degeneration was found among sets of identical twins, even when one twin had a sedentary job and the other twin had a job in an occupation traditionally associated with low back pain, such as material handling. The researchers, led by Michele Crites Battie, Ph.D., from the Department of Physical Therapy, University of Alberta, concluded that occupation accounted for relatively little of the lumbar disc degeneration they found. Genetics, and to a lesser degree, age, determined disc degeneration.

What that means, said Snook, is that low back pain "is impossible to prevent. Low back pain is an age and genetic disorder... [Disability is] triggered by workplace factors." There is some good news: While low back pain might be an inevitable condition for most of us, disability is not. "We can reduce the incidence of disability from low back pain through job design and management response," said Snook. According to Snook and other experts, a problem which is costing industry almost $12 billion in workers' compensation costs—back disability—can be virtually eliminated through job and workstation design, disability management, control over psychosocial factors such as employee/supervisor relationships, and training and exercise.

Workstation Design

Low back pain can be triggered by jobs which involve repetitive motion and tasks such as lifting, bending and stretching. Redesign of the job or workstation when repetitive motion is a problem can greatly reduce strain on the lower back, said Pat McDermott-Caine, president of ErgoWorks Inc., Medford, Ore. She helps companies design workstations which provide proper ergonomic support for employees. According to her, workstations tend to be designed for people who are a standard size of 5 feet 6 inches to 5 feet 10 inches. Everyone else could potentially have a problem with that workstation. If only one employee uses a workstation, then customize it as much as possible to fit that employee's needs. Raise or lower task lighting; tilt, raise or lower work surfaces; move equipment so the employee does not have to stretch or bend down; and place all tools within easy reach.

When a workstation is used by several different shifts, McDermott-Caine suggests making workstations adjustable so that the work surfaces can be raised or lowered and equipment and tools moved to different locations. A common mistake made by companies, McDermott-Caine said, is buying the same chair for all employees, even though people come in all heights and sizes. "The worst situation is when companies buy the same nonadjustable chair for everyone. That's just folly," she said. "I tell them, the more comfortable the chair, the longer the worker will stay in it."

Not all improvements have to cost a small fortune. An older chair can be improved with a lumbar support pillow, McDermott-Caine noted. Similarly, a leaner board placed at the edge of a workbench to support the weight of employees who sort materials does not have to be fancy, just functional. "The point is to develop creative solutions," she said, "ones which allow you to fit workstations to many individual workers."

Design of Job Tasks

Fixing the workstation is usually only part of the battle in the workplace, said Eric Farabaugh, a physical therapist at The Workplace, a worker rehabilitation organization in Pittsburgh. Sometimes, the job tasks—and matching them with employees—are the problem.

"A NIOSH study found that 10 percent of existing employees are not physically capable of performing their jobs and that 75 percent of injuries occur within that group of 10 percent," said Farabaugh.

Pre-placement, post-offer screenings, to determine if workers can physically perform their required job tasks, would go a long way in eliminating back pain and disability, according to Farabaugh. Once employees are given the green light for a job, think twice before tossing them right into the work pool, said Farabaugh. Especially for jobs which require significant lifting, a work-hardening period, to build strength and tolerance, is suggested. Start out with the employee lifting lighter loads and gradually work up to heavier ones. Information and demonstrations in the proper way to lift—with loads held closely to the body; no twisting while lifting; and avoiding wet or slippery floors while carrying objects—should be a part of the training process, he explained.

Farabaugh said he uses a checklist to determine if job tasks need a redesign. He looks for repetitive motion, lifting of heavy loads, prolonged sitting, and high-pressure, fast-moving work situations as predictors of back pain and disability.

Redesigning jobs can cost little or no money. One company changed the size of transport boxes, so that they were too large (although they weigh the same) for one employee to lift alone. A second set of handles was added, silently reminding employees that two people are needed to lift the 50-pound boxes. Another firm added a small section of aluminum to the end of one conveyor belt and attached it to the beginning of the next belt. Workers can slide boxes along, rather than having to pick them up and carry them to the next station.

Although the jury is still out on the benefits of job rotation in the prevention of back pain, some managers swear by it. A small midwest manufacturing company rotates employees in a parts packaging operation among five work-stations every two weeks. Employees sort parts, check them for flaws, package them into groups of 100, box them up and load the boxes onto skids. The job rotation has not only benefited the employees physically, but professionally: they are now trained in four job tasks in addition to the one for which they were hired.

What works for one company and employee population might not work for another. Whenever decisions must be made about job or workstation redesign, Farabaugh suggests including employees in the process. After all, he notes, they are the people most interested in the outcome of the redesign. "Their back is their responsibility. I tell them, 'Don't expect doctors to take the pain away once you've injured your back.' Get involved in preventive measures, like job design, training and strengthening," he said.

Exercise and Stress Reduction

The benefits of fitness and exercise for the human body have been widely reported. Whether or not they have an impact on recovery from back pain is unclear. Liberty Mutual's Snook, for example, said that he knows of no studies which show that exercise has reduced low back pain. "What exercise does do is build up tolerance for back pain and reduce disability," said Snook.

Some health practitioners claim that stretching and strengthening programs in the workplace can help prevent injuries and disability. The discs in the back lose most of their blood flow by the time we reach the age of 20, and stretching programs help "feed" the discs by moving fluids in and out, said Richard W. Bunch, Ph.D., P.T., president of the Industrial Safety and Rehabilitation Institute Inc., Harahan, La. He suggests that employees think of the discs as resembling jelly donuts. Often, people bend or hunch over into postures which force the jelly in the disc to press up against the back wall of the disc, which is the weaker wall. Eventually, discs can bulge or rupture.

Bunch recommends a stretching program which includes back and neck stretches and a few partial sit-ups. The exercises are designed to build strength, provide nourishment to the discs, and relieve stress, cited by some experts as a cause of back disability.

Veronica E. Brooke, M.T., a massotherapist and director of the Lakewood Massotherapy Center, Lakewood, Ohio, often receives referrals from Cleveland-area physicians who support massage as one type of therapy to relieve stress and reduce back pain. "People tend to hold a lot of stress in their backs and shoulders and necks. Our lives are more stressful, and if a person has a job that puts a lot of pressure on his or her back, then he or she often ends up in a doctor's office," said Brooke.

Her job is to help those people relax and to teach them to listen to their bodies. Jobs which require repetitive movement leave muscles stuck in a pattern, she claimed. Some muscles become overused and stressed, while others are underused and become weak. Brooke said that a skilled therapist can find those misused muscles and let the client know what's going on with his or her body. "It's all about awareness. Being aware of your body and what makes it feel better and work better," said Brooke. She counsels her clients not to ignore those little twinges which could foreshadow full-blown back pain.

A muscle spasm, said Brooke, is "the body's way of telling us to stop what we're doing. Those muscles have either been overworked, or are overcompensating for other muscles which are not working properly." She said she has more clients in the winter, not as the result of slips and falls or from the cold weather, but because people are not as active and are not "working out the kinks" when they come home from work.

Brooke encourages her clients to stay as physically active as possible, even if they suffer from back pain. Exercise is a great way to relieve tension, she noted. "A few stress-reducing exercises while sitting at work—shoulder rolls, neck rolls, toe touches—can really make a difference and keep muscles more relaxed." Just walking into work is traumatic for some employees, leading to tight muscles and tense attitudes, so Brooke advocates reducing stress wherever and however possible. "Whatever physical activity works for you—running, yoga, walking—get out and do it," she advised.

Psychosocial Factors

A research team led by Stanley J. Bigos, M.D., studied work perceptions and psychosocial factors affecting the reporting of back injuries among 3,000 workers. Other than a history of back problems, the biggest predictor for the reporting of back injury was job satisfaction. Employees who claimed to "hardly ever" enjoy their job tasks were 2.5 times more likely to report a back injury than employees who "almost always" enjoyed their jobs. The study also found that employee/supervisor relationships and positive or negative family and co-worker relationships influenced the reporting of back injuries.

According to the Bigos report: "Perhaps normally expected back pain is the final straw that breaks the already burdened camel's back."

A change in the work situation, such as layoffs or a change in work responsibilities, can be predictors of back disability, warns Donald Chaffin, Ph.D., director of the University of Michigan's Center for Ergonomics, as can an unsympathetic response from supervisors or the medical community after an injury. "When employees feel like they've lost control to the medical community or they are in an unsympathetic work environment, then pain becomes more disabling," said Chaffin.

Experts suggest having a system in place to deal with injured employees that starts within three days of an injury report. The system should include a person from the company, preferably someone the worker knows, who remains in touch with the worker and his family, reassuring them of management's concern and support. A case manager, either within the firm or from an outside provider, should maintain close contact with health care providers and the worker.

Health care providers should be familiar with the work environment and the job tasks for which the employee is responsible. If he can no longer perform that job, then a team—including company management, the employee, the employee's supervisor, the doctor and physical therapist—needs to come up with alternative choices. Whatever solution is chosen, it must be one the employee endorses, said Chaffin.

"People get used to working with the same people. They become friends with their co-workers. It is added stress on an injured employee when he or she is expected to learn new job skills and work with a new peer group," he commented. Spend time with that employee helping him adjust to the new job, said Chaffin, and you stand a better chance of keeping him on the payroll. Ignore his pain or concerns, and you can start counting out those disability payments.

No worker, given a choice, would be doubled over in pain, Chaffin points out. Once he or she is in pain, it is up to management to start eliminating as many causes of that pain and reasons not to return to work as it can find. Experts say that the majority of all disability claims can be eliminated through factors such as workstation and job task design over which management has some or total control. The first step is for management to believe that workers want to return to work, and to take steps to help them reach that goal.

"Workers have a great motivation to return to their previous lifestyle. Back pain doesn't just affect them at work. I let them know that we're not here just to patch them up to return to work. The goal is not to be disabled and living with pain," said Farabaugh. "The goal is to be able to return to their lives."

Section 21.2

Back Belts: Do They Prevent Injury?

National Institute of Occupational Safety and Health Centers for Disease Control and Prevention (OSHA DHHS), Pub. No. 94-127, January 1, 1994. Despite the age of this document, readers seeking an understanding of back injuries will still find the information useful.

Introduction

Back injuries account for nearly 20% of all injuries and illnesses in the workplace and cost the nation an estimated 20 to 50 billion dollars per year. The National Institute for Occupational Safety and Health (NIOSH) believes that the most effective way to prevent back injury is to implement an ergonomics program that focuses on redesigning the work environment and work tasks to reduce the hazards of lifting.

However, in response to the increasing human and economic costs of back injury, companies have implemented numerous other measures, either in conjunction with or in place of sound ergonomics programs. For instance, there has been a dramatic increase in the use of industrial back belts.

The decision to wear a back belt is a personal choice; however, NIOSH believes that workers and employers should have the best available information to make that decision. This chapter outlines the current state of scientific knowledge on back belts and stresses the importance of an overall ergonomics program. Companies should not rely on back belts as a "cure all" for back injury, but should begin to undertake prevention measures which reduce the risks of lifting tasks.

Do Back Belts Prevent Injury?

In recent years, there has been a dramatic increase in the number of workers who rely on back belts to prevent injury during lifting. Back belts, also called "back supports" or "abdominal belts," are currently worn by workers in numerous industries, including grocery store clerks, airline baggage handlers, and warehouse workers. As their use has risen, NIOSH has increasingly been asked for advice on back belt selection. In response to these inquiries, the Institute decided to address a more fundamental question. Rather than ask "Which belt will best protect workers?" NIOSH researchers began with the question—"Do back belts protect workers?"

A Lack of Scientific Support

Employers relying on back belts to prevent injury should be aware of the lack of scientific evidence supporting their use. After a review of the scientific literature, NIOSH has concluded that, because of limitations of the studies that have analyzed workplace use of back belts, the results cannot be used to either support or refute the effectiveness of back belts in injury reduction. Although back belts are being bought and sold under the premise that they reduce the risk of back injury, there is insufficient scientific evidence that they actually deliver what is promised.

The Institute, therefore, does not recommend the use of back belts to prevent injuries among workers who have never been injured. Because the Institute's primary focus is on the prevention of injury, NIOSH did not address the use of back belts as medical treatment during rehabilitation from injury. If you or your workers are wearing back belts as protective equipment against back injury, you should be aware of the lack of scientific evidence supporting their use.

How Did NIOSH Come to These Conclusions about Back Belts?

NIOSH systematically reviewed published, peer reviewed scientific literature on back belts to determine if they actually reduce the risk of back injury. Because there were few studies on the association between workplace use of back belts and injuries, NIOSH also reviewed studies of the relationship between back belt use and forces exerted on the spine during manual lifting. In other words, much of the existing research is based on theories of what causes back injury, rather than on the actual rates of workplace injury with and without back belt use. For a detailed technical report on the studies, please refer to "Workplace Use of Back Belts: Review and Recommendations" (Publication No. 94-122). Contact information for NIOSH can be found in the Resources section of this sourcebook.

233

What about the Claims That Back Belts...

- reduce internal forces on the spine during forceful exertions of the back?
- increase intra-abdominal pressure (IAP), which may counter the forces on the spine?
- stiffen the spine, which may decrease forces on the spine?
- restrict bending motions (range of motion)?
- remind the wearer to lift properly?
- have reduced injuries in certain workplaces?

While all of these claims have been put forth as support for the use of back belts, they remain unproven. There is currently inadequate scientific evidence or theory to suggest that back belts can reduce the risk of injury. Moreover, even if back belts produced the biomechanical effects listed above, there is no proven link to injury prevention.

NIOSH searched the peer-reviewed literature for studies investigating these claims and evaluated the scientific evidence they produced. A summary of the findings is provided on the following pages.

I Heard That Back Belts...

Reduce Forces on the Spine

Lifting may produce a variety of forces within the body which contribute to the pressure on the spine, termed "loading." Many of the studies NIOSH reviewed sought to examine the impact of back belt use on loading. None of the studies provide sufficient data to indicate that industrial back belts significantly reduce loading during lifting. In fact, there is little evidence to suggest that these forces could be reduced with a back belt.

Increase Intra-Abdominal Pressure (IAP)

While this theory remains controversial, some believe that if the pressure is increased within the abdomen, it will counterbalance the compressive force being exerted downward on the spine. The studies NIOSH reviewed were inconclusive, and the relationship between IAP and spinal compression is not well understood. Therefore, even if a back belt increased IAP, there is, as yet, no evidence that it would reduce forces on the spine or decrease back injury.

Remind Workers to Lift Properly

At this point, there is little scientific evidence that back belts remind workers to avoid awkward postures and heavy loads.

Stiffen the Spine

Numerous ligaments, tendons, and other soft tissues surround the spine and help hold it in place. The theory is that if back belts increase this support, they would decrease the motion allowed between segments of the spine, and therefore decrease damage to the discs in the lower back. There is no conclusive evidence that back belts increase the stiffness of the spine, and no proven relationship between this stiffness and the reduction of injury.

Reduce Bending Motions

Loading on the spine increases when a person has to bend as far forward as possible. If the ability to bend this far forward could be restricted by a back belt, the risk of injury would possibly be decreased. It would appear that abdominal belts help restrict the range of motion during side to side bending and twisting. However, they do not have the same effect when the worker bends forward, as in many industrial lifting situations.

Reduce Injuries in Certain Workplaces

There have been anecdotal case reports of injury reduction in workplaces using back belts. However, many companies which have instituted back belt programs have also implemented training and ergonomic awareness programs. The reported injury reduction may be related to these or other factors. On the basis of available evidence, the potential effectiveness of back belts in reducing the occurrence of low back injuries remains unproven.

Why Is So Little Known about the Utility of Back Belts?

Back belts were initially used in medical settings. These belts, termed "orthoses," resemble the corsets worn by women in the nineteenth century and are typically used to provide additional back support during rehabilitation of injuries. Subsequently, athletes began using leather belts for weight-lifting. Only in recent years has the "industrial back belt" been widely used. While there are more than 70 types of industrial back belts, the typical abdominal support used in workplaces today is a lightweight, elastic belt worn around the lower back, sometimes held in place with suspenders.

Because of the recent emergence of back belt use in the workplace, there have been few published studies of the rate of injury among workers using the belts. These studies suffer from design flaws and have not produced sufficient support for or against the use of back belts. NIOSH encourages efforts to more adequately determine the association between back belt use and the prevention of low back injury and is committed to supporting further research in this area.

Could Wearing a Back Belt Increase the Potential for Injury?

At this point, there are no definitive studies on either the beneficial or harmful effects of wearing back belts. Just as there is speculation that back belts may help, there is also concern that they may harm workers. As a result of the NIOSH review, the Institute is concerned with the potentially harmful effects associated with a false sense of security that may accompany back belt use.

There is some research showing that workers believe they can lift more when wearing a back belt. If workers falsely believe they are protected, they may subject themselves to even greater risk by lifting more weight than they would have without a belt.

How Should Workers Be Protected?

Rather than relying solely on back belts, companies should begin to implement a comprehensive ergonomics program that strives to protect all workers. The most effective way to prevent back injury is to redesign the work environment and work tasks to reduce the hazards of lifting. Training in identifying lifting hazards and using safe lifting techniques and methods should improve program effectiveness.

If you are putting all your prevention resources into back belts, you are not adequately protecting your workers.

How Can an Ergonomics Program Be Implemented?

A first step in implementing an ergonomics program would be to evaluate jobs that require frequent lifting; twisted or bent postures; or pushing or pulling. Redesign these tasks so that:

236

- the load is close to the body.

- the load is between shoulder and knuckle height.

- twisted lifts are eliminated.

- gravity moves the load when possible.

- slides, chutes, hoists, and hand trucks are used to move heavy loads.

- weight is reduced to the lowest feasible level.

What If I Still Decide to Use Back Belts?

NIOSH believes that the decision to use back belts should be a voluntary decision by both employers and employees. Back belt use should not be a mandatory job requirement. If your workforce continues to wear back belts, you should remember the following points:

- There is a lack of scientific evidence that back belts work.

- Workers wearing back belts may attempt to lift more weight than they would have without a belt. A false sense of security may subject workers to greater risk of injury.

- Workers and employers should redesign the work environment and work tasks to reduce lifting hazards, rather than rely solely on back belts to prevent injury.

- The research needed to adequately assess back belt effectiveness will take several years to complete. In the interim, workers should not assume that back belts are protective.

Have Other Groups Questioned the Effectiveness of Back Belts?

NIOSH is not alone in questioning the effectiveness of back belts. Other institutions issuing similar statements include the American Industrial Hygiene Association, the Army Office of the Surgeon General, the State of Washington Department of Labor and Industries, the Alberta Ministry of Occupational Health and Safety (Canada), the United Brotherhood of Carpenters, and the Construction Safety Association of Ontario.

Chapter 22

Carpal Tunnel Syndrome (CTS)

Chapter Contents

Section 22.1

Causes of CTS

"Carpal Tunnel Syndrome," National Institute of Occupational Safety and Health, Doc. N. 705001, June 1997.

In recent years, reports of repetitive motion injuries have risen dramatically in workplaces across the country. These problems, frequently termed "Cumulative Trauma Disorders" are being reported at alarming rates in all types of workplaces—from meatpacking plants to newspaper pressrooms. According to the Bureau of Labor Statistics, "disorders associated with repeated trauma" account for about 60% of all occupational illnesses. Of all these disorders, carpal tunnel syndrome is the condition most frequently reported.

What Is Carpal Tunnel Syndrome (CTS)?

The carpal tunnel receives its name from the 8 bones in the wrist, called carpals, that form a tunnel-like structure. The tunnel is filled with flexor tendons which control finger movement. It also provides a pathway for the median nerve to reach sensory cells in the hand. Repetitive flexing and extension of the wrist may cause a thickening of the protective sheaths which surround each of the tendons. The swollen tendon sheaths, or tenosynovitis, apply increased pressure on the median nerve and produce Carpal Tunnel Syndrome (CTS).

What Are the Symptoms of CTS?

The symptoms of CTS often first appear as painful tingling in one or both hands during the night, frequently painful enough to disturb sleep. Accompanying this is a feeling of uselessness in the fingers, which are sometimes described as feeling swollen, even though little or no swelling is apparent. As symptoms increase, tingling may develop during the day, commonly in the thumb, index, and ring fingers. A decreased ability and power to squeeze things may follow. In advanced cases, the thenar muscle at the base of the thumb atrophies, and strength is lost.

Many patients with CTS are unable to differentiate hot from cold by touch, and experience an apparent loss of strength in their fingers. They appear clumsy in that they have trouble performing simple tasks such as tying their shoes or picking up small objects.

What Causes CTS?

As stated earlier, swelling of the tendons that line the carpal tunnel causes CTS. Although there are many reasons for developing this swelling of the tendon, it can result from repetitive and forceful movements of the wrist during work and leisure activities. Research conducted by the National Institute for Occupational Safety and Health (NIOSH) indicates that job tasks involving highly repetitive manual acts, or necessitating wrist bending or other stressful wrist postures, are connected with incidents of CTS or related problems. The use of vibrating tools also may contribute to CTS. Moreover, it is apparent that this hazard is not confined to a single industry or job but occurs in many occupations, especially those in the manufacturing sector. Indeed, jobs involving cutting, small parts assembly, finishing, sewing, and cleaning seem predominantly associated with the syndrome. The factor common in these jobs is the repetitive use of small hand tools.

Prevention

NIOSH recommendations for controlling carpal tunnel syndrome have focused on ways to relieve awkward wrist positions and repetitive hand movements, and to reduce vibration from hand tools. NIOSH recommends redesigning tools or tool handles to enable the user's wrist to maintain a more natural position during work. Other recommendations have involved modified layouts of work stations. Still other approaches include altering the existing method for performing the job task, providing more frequent rest breaks, and rotating workers across jobs. As a means of prevention, tool and process redesign are preferable to administrative means such as job rotation.

The frequency and severity of CTS can be minimized through training programs that increase worker awareness of symptoms and prevention methods, and through proper medical management of injured workers.

Treatment

Treatment of CTS may involve surgery to release the compression on the median nerve and/or use of anti-inflammatory drugs and hand splinting to reduce tendon swelling in the carpal tunnel. Such medical interventions have met with mixed success, especially when an affected person must return to the same working conditions.

Section 22.2

Dissecting the CTS Debate

From "Dissecting the CTS Debate," by Susannah Zak Figura, in *Occupational Hazards*, Vol. 57, Nov. 1995, pp. 28–32. Copyright 1999 by Penton Media Inc. Reprinted with permission.

Why do workers get carpal tunnel syndrome, and what can employers do to prevent it? While experts search for answers, victims straddle a line between complete recovery and permanent disability.

Graciela Landivar worked piece-rate in a New York City bridal dress shop for 25 years. After 16 years of assembling two satin gowns every hour, 40 hours a week, she began noticing numbness and tingling in both hands. Now, she can't do simple household chores and even has trouble holding a telephone to her ear. She closes doors with her shoulder because she can't clasp a door handle. "People look at me as if I am a useless person," she said.

Juanita Bresson, a supervisory nurse in an Ohio home care agency, never had a job requiring repetitive wrist and hand motions as Landivar did, but she developed similar symptoms, severely in her right hand and mildly in her left. Already an arthritis sufferer, Bresson self-diagnosed her hands as arthritic and lived with the symptoms for a year and a half. Before she finally had corrective surgery in the right hand, Bresson couldn't take lids off jars, comb her hair or handle books. "Every night, my hand fell asleep before I did," she said.

Extent of the Problem

Landivar and Bresson are victims of carpal tunnel syndrome (CTS). In 1993, CTS caused 41,019 private industry workers to miss days on the job, according to the Bureau of Labor Statistics (BLS). That's a drop in the bucket when compared to the nearly 2.3 million total ill-nesses and injuries that kept workers home, but the numbers are on the rise. In 1992, the first year for which BLS collected CTS-specific data, there were only 33,042 lost work day cases associated with CTS.

Why the increase? In part, experts say, the rise is due to the ex-tensive media attention CTS has received in recent years. As more people learned about the disorder, more people reported symptoms they used to live with quietly. In turn, as public awareness increased, so did the tendency of state workers' compensation boards to consider cumulative trauma disorders (CTD)—of which CTS is but one type—compensable, making workers more likely to report their symptoms.

Also at play, at least in assembly line work, are faster production lines manned by fewer workers, said Adrienne Joy Markowitz, indus-trial hygienist for the Retail, Wholesale and Department Store Union, AFL-CIO, whose members include poultry processing plant workers. "The pace of the work is getting faster, but there's no relief, no breaks," she said, adding that in many workplaces there is little opportunity to rest sore, aching hands and other upper extremities.

Kennith Brock, senior vice president for loss prevention for work-ers' compensation giant Liberty Mutual Insurance Group, believes the CTS problem has been blown out of proportion, and suggests BLS fig-ures may be inflated. In 1992, for example, BLS reported that 4.1 percent of all lost work day injuries and illnesses could be attributed to CTDs. For the same year, he noted, only 2.1 percent of Liberty's claims were for CTDs.

Back injuries caused by lifting, pushing or lowering heavy objects, on the other hand, accounted for 33 percent of Liberty's claims and 40 percent of its costs. "CTDs [related to the hands and arms] are important, but they're not the universal problem that [people have been] led to believe they are," Brock said.

The Victims

There is little argument, however, that CTS is a problem in indus-tries which demand long hours of repetitive motion work such as meatpacking, dressmaking and telecommunications. Nearly 25 per-cent of the Union of Needletrades, Industrial and Textile Employees' (UNITE) 355,000 members suffer from upper extremity disorders, the most prevalent being CTS, reports UNITE safety and health special-ist Laurie Kellogg.

Kellogg suspects the rate is much higher because many women working in the garment industry don't speak English and so don't feel confident seeking treatment through the health care or workers' compensation systems. "They're more likely to suffer in silence," she said, adding that by the time they come to the UNITE health clinic, their cases are very far advanced.

Kellogg recalled one immigrant garment worker who came to her office two years ago with CTS in both hands. "She couldn't hold anything, but was afraid to take time off work to seek medical treatment for fear of losing her job." One year later, Kellogg saw the woman again and noticed black scars on her fingertips. "She said she burned her fingers when she cooked for her family because she couldn't feel the fire."

In the telecommunications industry, 66 percent of telephone operators experience numbness or tingling of fingers, and 12 percent have been medically diagnosed with CTS, according to a recent survey of Communications Workers of America (CWA) union members. Just six years ago, only half reported numbness or tingling in their hands and 6 percent had been diagnosed with CTS.

Cumulative trauma disorders such as CTS, tendonitis and cysts represent CWA's "biggest safety and health issue," said David LeGrande, director of occupational safety and health for CWA. Although LeGrande insists CTS hasn't been blown out of proportion, he concedes that "it has been [reported on] in an alarmist way."

Work-Related or Not?

With the relatively small body of research on CTS generating mixed conclusions, a consensus about its precise causes has yet to be reached. Especially contentious is whether the illness is work-related, a prospect that could ultimately cost industry billions of dollars in workers' compensation expenses and product liability suits. "There's still quite a lot we don't know about how CTS develops," said George Piligian, M.D., occupational medicine physician at the Mount Sinai Irving J. Selikoff Occupational Health Clinic in New York. Work-related forceful repetitive motion contributes to CTS, Piligian said, but so can diabetes, arthritis, pregnancy and a low thyroid hormone level. Colorado orthopedic surgeon Willard Schuler, M.D., added that some people are prone to developing CTS while others are not. "If you're prone to nerve entrapment, you'll get CTS," and work-related repetitive motion is only one of many factors that can aggravate it, he said.

Peter Nathan, M.D., surgeon at the Portland Hand Surgery and Rehabilitation Center, agreed that some people are predisposed to the problem. After conducting 12 years of personally funded research on the subject, Nathan also believes that CTS is only peripherally related to workplace activities and is more closely associated with a body's general health. The older you are, the fatter you are and the less you exercise, the more prone to CTS you are, according to Nathan's findings.

"There's no question that all of those personal factors play a role," said ergonomist Marilyn Joyce, but work is also a factor. Joyce believes Nathan may have weighed personal factors too heavily in his calculations.

CWA's LeGrande also agrees that there may be non-work contributors to the development of CTS, but he insists the primary factor is the workplace. When people spend at least 7 hours a day at work and do no excessively repetitive activities at home, the workplace must be considered, he said.

Diagnosis and Treatment

The first signs of possible CTS, says Mount Sinai's Piligian, are numbness, tingling or pain in the thumb, index and middle fingers, as well as in part of the ring finger. To determine whether and to what extent the symptoms are related to the median nerve, patients undergo an electromyography study (EMG) to test hand muscle strength and response capability, as well as a nerve conduction study (NCS), to test the speed at which a nerve carries a sensory message.

If test results suggest a mild case of CTS, Piligian recommends "conservative" treatment comprised primarily of physical therapy and decreasing the number of repetitive, forceful hand motions a patient does each day. The treatment can go on for weeks or even months, depending on the patient.

Other physicians also suggest CTS sufferers take non-steroidal anti-inflammatory drugs and wear a splint to keep the wrist straight at night, when symptoms are most severe. Still others have had patients respond to steroid injections in the wrist and regular doses of vitamin B-6. These forms of conservative treatment, however, should not be considered substitutes for physical therapy and a reduction of repetitive motion, Piligian noted.

If conservative treatment fails, or if EMG and NCS tests suggest a moderate or severe CTS case, Cleveland plastic and hand surgeon Teresa Ghazoul, M.D., recommends a carpal tunnel release. This surgical procedure opens the transverse carpal ligament, thereby releasing pressure and allowing more room in the carpal tunnel for the median nerve and blood vessels. For those who have let symptoms go untreated for years and have permanent nerve damage, Ghazoul noted that surgery probably won't reverse their condition completely, but it can help keep the problem from getting worse. For supervisory nurse Bresson, a recent carpal tunnel release on her right hand relieved all her symptoms. Although it took six months for a full recovery, Bresson says she is "amazed" at how much better her hand feels. "I am so happy to have it work right." She occasionally still wears a brace on her left wrist, but her symptoms remain mild.

According to Schuler, Bresson's experience with the carpal tunnel release is common. "Surgery for carpal tunnel syndrome is about 90 percent effective," he said. If the procedure is not successful, then the problem probably wasn't CTS in the first place, he said.

Because appropriate protocols and methodologies are not always followed when testing for CTS, however, there can be misdiagnoses, warned Howard Sandler, M.D., president of Sandler Occupational Medicine Associates Inc. Sometimes, a nerve conduction study comes back negative because the physician did not test the right area, he said. At the same time, other nerve entrapment disorders with similar symptoms to CTS can be overlooked and wrongly classified as CTS, he added. Joyce told of one person who had carpal tunnel surgery only to discover afterward that CTS wasn't the problem, but that thoracic outlet syndrome, which affects the chest and shoulder area and can impact the hands, was.

Quick to Operate?

UNITE's Kellogg criticizes surgeons for being too quick to operate on suspected CTS cases. "We see it all the time and it's so upsetting," because there may have been a misdiagnosis, she said. "[But surgery] is where the money is [for doctors]." Carpal tunnel surgery bills out at about $2,000 just for the surgeon's fees, while physical therapy costs between $100 and $200 an hour and typically calls for six 1-hour sessions, according to Susan Mackinnon, M.D., professor of surgery at Washington University School of Medicine in St. Louis. In Mackinnon's view, surgery for CTS is over-prescribed and rarely relieves a patient's most serious symptoms. "The patients tell us they have a little bit of numbness or tingling, but that's not the main reason they're here," she said. "Their major complaint is pain in the neck, shoulders and upper back that makes it difficult to carry out daily activities."

Working with physical therapist Christine Novak, Mackinnon tested a hypothesis that unnatural postures people assume at work, at home or during sleep increase pressure on nerves and cause muscles to become too weak or too strong. Through physical therapy, Mackinnon and Novak teach patients how to get their muscles back into balance. A small percentage of patients may still benefit from carpal tunnel surgery, Mackinnon said, but only those whose hand tingling and numbness truly interfere with their work. In a 1994 study of 64 of Mackinnon's CTD patients, 90 percent said conservative treatment relieved their most troublesome symptoms—neck and shoulder pain—and 63 percent of those reported relief of finger tingling and hand numbness. "Based on our [study] results, surgery often is not necessary, nor recommended," Mackinnon said. "This translates into tremendous cost savings for patients and insurance companies."

Long-Term Changes

Once CTS symptoms are relieved, whether by conservative or surgical treatment, experts say that if a person returns to a work situation which may have prompted the conditions, the CTS will likely return. Since patients are usually unwilling to give up their jobs, preventing the recurrence of CTS often depends on employers minimizing risks by reorganizing workstations to make the worker more comfortable and reducing repetitive motion tasks by rotating the worker through various jobs.

Afraid her pleas for better work equipment and job rotation wouldn't be taken seriously, Graciela Landivar said she won't be returning to her bridal shop job which she left last January, at least not if she can help it. She filed for workers' compensation two and a half years ago and still awaits approval for surgery. In the meantime, she has an appointment with a vocational school to pursue a different job. "The last two years have been horrible," Landivar said. "I have five children.... I want to work."

5 Steps to Preventing CTS

The employee must also do his part, ergonomist Joyce noted. Preventing CTS is a "shared responsibility" between workers and employers, she said.

1. Be sure work stations (tables, chairs and equipment) are at the appropriate height to minimize musculoskeletal stress.

2. Redesign jobs to reduce the amount of repetitive motion.

3. Provide workers with opportunities for adequate rest periods.

4. Keep production expectations realistic.

5. Teach workers the importance of taking breaks and of using tools correctly.

Wrist Rests: Do They Help Prevent CTS?

Computer keyboard wrist rests, used by many office workers to help prevent CTS, do not relieve pressure in the carpal tunnel, according to Alan Hedge, director of the Human Factors and Ergonomics Laboratory at Cornell University.

According to Hedge, who has done several studies on the effectiveness of various wrist rests, the pressure within the carpal tunnel when wrists sit on keyboard rests is the same as when they are resting on desk tops. Both put pressure on the underside of the wrist, one of the most sensitive parts of the body. "Putting weight on that part of your wrist is bad news for all fingers and nerves," Hedge said. Palm rests, however, "can offer some benefit if used in the right orientation," he added. A palm rest is a wider version of a flat wrist rest that allows the hand to rest on the two major palm muscles (one is below the thumb, the other below the small finger) rather than on the wrist.

The best position overall for typing on a keyboard, according to Hedge's research findings, is with the keyboard slightly above lap level with a broad palm rest to use between periods of typing. When CTS sufferers tested this setup, they lost their symptoms, he said.

Thomas Votel, president of ergonomic product manufacturer Ergodyne, agrees that pressure on the palm is preferable to pressure on the wrist. But the difference between "wrist rests" and "palm rests" is a semantic one, he said, adding that Ergodyne produces a "wrist rest" that actually supports the palm.

Whatever the rests are called, they should encourage a neutral wrist posture and be comfortable for the user, he said. In this growing area of study, Votel added, no one has definite answers.

Ergonomist Marilyn Joyce, who agrees there are many unanswered questions relating to wrist rests, recommends pushing a keyboard far enough away so that a worker can rest his forearms on the work table. If that is not possible, wrist rests should be used only while resting, Joyce said.

Chapter 23

Understanding Neck and Arm Disorders

Chapter Contents

Section 23.1

Neck and Arm Disorders

Mats Hagberg, *British Medical Journal*, August 17, 1996, Vol. 313, N. 7054, pp. 419–423. Copyright 1996 by British Medical Association. Reprinted with permission.

Characteristics of Non-Specific Musculoskeletal Pain in Neck and Shoulder

History

- Pain and stiffness gradually increase during work and are worst at end of working day and week.

- Pain localized to cervical spine and angle between neck and shoulder.

- Usually no radiation of pain.

- Symptoms improved by heat and worsened by cold draughts.

Signs

- tenderness over neck and shoulder muscles

- reduced range of active movement of cervical spine (normal passive movement)

- no neurological deficits

Differential diagnosis

- thoracic outlet syndrome and other nerve entrapments

- systemic diseases

Terms and Definitions

Over recent years the use of terms such as repetitive strain injury (RSI) and cumulative trauma disorder have been strongly criticized.

Sometimes the terms have even been used synonymously with disease terms such as carpal tunnel syndrome (compression of the median nerve at the wrist) and de Quervain's disease (inflammation of the tendons to the long thumb abductor and the short thumb extensor at the wrist). Neither carpal tunnel syndrome nor de Quervain's disease is necessarily related to repetitive strain or cumulative trauma.

Use of these terms to describe work related musculoskeletal disorders has been criticized because they suggest a pathological mechanism that is usually not proved. A work related musculoskeletal disorder may be caused by a single strain or trauma, not necessarily a repetitive or cumulative one. Furthermore, both psychological and social factors play an important role in the genesis and perpetuation of work related musculoskeletal disorders.

The World Health Organization considers the cause of work related musculoskeletal diseases to be multifactorial. The work environment and the work performed are important but are not the only factors to be considered. The preferred term for conditions that may be subjectively or objectively influenced or caused by work is work related musculoskeletal disorder. This umbrella term neither defines the pathological mechanism nor the diagnostic criteria.

Specific Risk Factors

Risk Factors for Work Related Neck and Arm Disorders

- posture
- repetitive motion
- handling loads

- psychological and social factors
- task invariability
- individual susceptibility

Certain occupations are associated with a high risk for neck and arm pain. Some risk factors can be identified, but the interaction between different risk factors is not understood and there is not enough data yet to set accurate exposure limits for disease effects.

It is important to recognize that personal characteristics and other environmental and sociocultural factors usually play a role in these disorders. A patient with neck pain may be exposed to an awkward posture at work but also to social stress at home—both factors contribute to sustained contraction of the trapezius muscle, inducing pain and stiffness. The cause of a work related disorder can sometimes be attributed to a specific exposure in a job, but there is often simultaneous exposure to several different factors. Individual factors must also be considered when assessing the history of a patient with a work related disorder and when redesigning a job before such a patient returns to work.

Posture

Working with the hands at or above shoulder level may be one determinant of rotator cuff tendinitis. Industrial workers exposed to tasks that require working over shoulder level include shipyard welders, car assemblers, and house painters. In one study the prevalence of rotator cuff tendinitis was 18% among shipyard welders compared with 2% among male office workers, corresponding to an odds ratio of 13.

The pathogenesis of rotator cuff tendinitis is mainly impingement—the compression of the rotator cuff tendons when they are forced under the coracoacromial arch during elevation of the arm. The supraspinatus tendon is forced under the anterior edge of the acromion, causing both a compression that impairs blood circulation through the tendon and a mechanical friction to the tendon. Reduced blood flow to the tendons because of static muscle contraction may contribute to degeneration of the rotator cuff tendons.

Abduction and forward flexion of more than 30° may constitute a risk factor since the pressure within the supraspinatus muscle will be greater than 30 mm Hg, impairing blood flow. The vessels to the supraspinatus tendon run through the muscle, and so the pressure in the muscle can affect tendon vasculature.

Among players of musical instruments, unnatural and constrained postures are common. Pain in the neck and arm have been related to gripping an instrument and awkward posture. Pain in the left shoulder and arm in professional violinists can be due to static holding of the violin in the left hand.

Neck flexion while working at a visual display terminal may be associated with non-specific neck and shoulder symptoms. An exposure-response relation has been found for neck pain and angle of neck flexion among keyboard operators—neck pain was more prevalent among operators who flexed their necks more acutely. Incorrect glasses or need for glasses when working at a visual display terminal may result in neck and shoulder pain.

The development of non-keyboard input devices, such as the computer mouse, has resulted in new postures that may cause a combination of symptoms of the wrist and shoulder. Work tasks of long duration with flexed and, to some extent, extended wrists have been reported as risk factors for carpal tunnel syndrome.

Motion

Repetitive motions of the shoulder may constitute a risk for rotator cuff tendinitis. An experimental study showed that women performing repetitive forward flexions of the shoulder developed shoulder tendinitis. Clinical signs of tendinitis were present up to two weeks after the experiments. Repetitive motions by industrial assembly workers (truck making, meat packing, and circuit board assembly) have been associated with the development of shoulder tendinitis, lateral epicondylitis, and tendinitis at the wrist (de Quervain's disease).

Repetitive motion being a causal factor for tendinitis is consistent with the high risk of shoulder tendinitis among competitive swimmers and epicondylitis among tennis players.

Handling Loads

Only a few studies have investigated the effect of handling loads on symptoms of the neck and arms. Handling heavy loads seems to be related to osteoarthrosis and cervical spondylosis. A high risk of acromioclavicular osteoarthrosis and shoulder tendinitis among rock drillers has been attributed to both handling loads and exposure to hand and arm vibration.

Psychological and Social Factors

Psychological and social factors are generally more strongly associated with back pain than shoulder pain. Furthermore, the association is stronger for non-specific pain than for pain with a specific diagnosis. This means that a diagnosis of general cervicobrachial pain may be more strongly related to psychological and social factors than carpal tunnel syndrome or shoulder tendinitis. Highly demanding work and poor work content (that is, repetitive tasks with short cycles) have been identified as risk factors for neck and shoulder pain. Psychological factors and personality type may be determinants of muscle tension and the development of myofascial pain.

Piece work is associated with neck and arm disorders when compared with work paid by the hour. This effect may be due to an increased work pace in addition to high psychological demand and low control in the work situation. Management style, in terms of social support to employees, is claimed to be associated with reporting of neck and shoulder symptoms. Social support from management obviously affects turnover of workers and sick leave.

Task Invariability

It used to be argued that to prevent work related musculoskeletal disorders it was necessary to minimize the load that workers were exposed to. This concept has led to the creation of jobs with low external load, but some of these are still not healthy. Poor work content usually leads to a job with invariable tasks, resulting in constrained postures and a low static load for the neck and arms. Ergonomists now try to design jobs that are not only physically variable but are psychologically variable and stimulating.

The health problems caused by task invariability may be due to prolonged static contraction of the trapezius muscle during work or daily activity resulting in an overload of type I muscle fibers, which might explain neck myalgia. At a low level of muscle contraction, the low threshold motor units (type I fibers) are used. A low static contraction during work may result in a recruitment pattern in which only the type I muscle fibers are used, causing selective fatigue of motor units and damage to the type I fibers. Biopsies of the trapezius muscle from patients with work related trapezius myalgia show enlarged type I fibers and a reduced ratio of area of type I fibers to capillary area.

Individual Susceptibility to Musculoskeletal Disorders

Age

- For most musculoskeletal disorders, risk increases with age.

Sex

- Among both the general population and industrial workers, women have a higher incidence of carpal tunnel syndrome and muscular pain in the neck and shoulder than men.

- Whether this is due to genetic factors or to different exposures at work and at home is not clear.

Anatomical Differences or Malformations

- A rough surface and sharp edge of the intertubercular sulcus on the humeral head increase wear on the tendon of the long head of biceps muscle, which may make person more prone to biceps tendinitis.

- A cervical rib is a common cause of neurogenic thoracic outlet syndrome: a repetitive task may be the occupational exposure that triggers clinical disease.

- Width of carpal tunnel has been proposed as a risk factor for carpal tunnel syndrome, but there is no consensus.

Table 23.1. Work Related Musculoskeletal Disorders Found in Blue Collar and White Collar Workers

	Assembly line worker	Keyboard operator
Shoulder pain	Usually shoulder tendinitis due to working with hands above shoulder height.	Usually myofascial pain, which may be caused by task invariability leading to static tension of trapezius muscle.
Hand and Wrist Pain	Repetitive power grips may cause repetitive strain of extensor tendons and tendinitis. Carpal tunnel syndrome may also be related to repetitive power grips.	Intensive keying may cause repetitive strain of extensor tendons and tendinitis. Carpal tunnel syndrome may also be related to intensive keying.

Individuals may have increased vulnerability to injury because of disease, genetic factors, or lack of fitness. This individual susceptibility may result in a lower than normal threshold for a given exposure to cause a work related musculoskeletal disorder. Furthermore, exposure may trigger symptoms early and at an unusual location because of local strain in a person with a pre-clinical systemic disease. For example, a worker exposed to repetitive flexion in the shoulder developed tendinitis one year before developing rheumatoid arthritis. An electrician exposed to repetitive power grips and vibration developed symptoms and signs of carpal tunnel syndrome—at surgery, these were found to be due to amyloidosis.

For work related musculoskeletal disorders, individual factors usually have a low magnitude of risk compared with relevant ergonomic factors.

Prevention and Management

Management of Work-Related Neck and Arm Disorders

Clinical Management

- Non-steroidal anti-inflammatory drugs can reduce pain and inflammation.

- Acupuncture can be used to reduce pain.

- Corticosteroids—single subacromial injection of corticosteroid mixed with local anesthetic may cure a shoulder tendinitis. For tennis elbow and carpal tunnel syndrome, corticosteroids should be used by specialists only.

- Heparin (15000 IU/day in a single intravenous dose) given for three to four days is effective treatment for acute crepitating peritendinitis.

- Surgery—Surgical division of the carpal ligament is the first choice of treatment for carpal tunnel syndrome. For chronic severe shoulder tendinitis, surgical removal of the lateral part of the acromion may relieve pain at night.

- Splints—Whether splints should be used to treat early hand and wrist tendinitis and carpal tunnel syndrome is still debatable.

Modifications to Working Environment

- Job analysis—To assess work relatedness of a patient's symptoms it is necessary to evaluate posture, motion, handling of loads, psychological and social factors, and task invariability.

- Job redesign—Job enlargement can reduce duration and frequency of stressful postures and load handling. Job enrichment can reduce poor work content and task invariability. Introduce new layout of workplace and technical aids.

- Technique training—Ergonomists and supervisors can improve working technique to reduce stressors of postures, motion, and load handling.

- Rests and breaks should be organized to allow recovery.

The overall objective of management is to get a healthy patient and an early return to work by medical means and by modifying the patient's working environment.

Clinical treatment should be targeted towards relieving any pain and inflammation and restoring a patient's range of movement. Physical conditioning by strength and aerobic training may reduce pain and increase a patient's work capacity, while psychological conditioning by stress management techniques may increase a person's ability to cope with work related stressors.

Patients should be encouraged to remain at work. Sick leave may develop into chronic disability. Try to find work tasks that the patient can perform at least on a part time basis. Otherwise make sure the patient has contact with the workplace at least once a week. Time off work is a powerful predictor of disability pension.

Repetitive Stress Injuries (RSI)

Principles of managing hand and arm pain in keyboard operators:

- Exclude clear pathological causes such as carpal tunnel syndrome.

- Reassure patient that the condition is curable.

- Keep patient at work if possible but away from keyboard work if necessary.

- Monitor patient's progress with regular follow up.

- When symptoms have subsided advise gradual reintroduction of precipitating factors.

- Explore psychological profile, including attitudes to work and support from management and colleagues.

- Liaise with patient's workplace, if possible with an occupational physician or nurse.

- Ensure that workstation ergonomics have been evaluated and are satisfactory and that patient has been taught to use the equipment properly and has the right glasses.

- Inquire about variation of work tasks, work intensity, and whether there are rules or opportunities for breaks from keyboard work or job rotation.

- Hospital admission is rarely needed, and specialized physiotherapy is of dubious benefit.

- Those few patients who do not respond to this multidisciplinary management may eventually have to be trained to use voice activated word processors, etc.

In the middle and late 1980s there was an epidemic of compensation claims for so called RSI—work related pain of the arm and wrist—from keyboard operators in Australia. This coincided with the widespread replacement of typewriters with computer keyboards. At one extreme, this was thought to be a genuine overuse syndrome, while, at the other, it was regarded as mass hysteria with an element of bandwagoning. RSI also appeared in other countries, while its incidence progressively declined in Australia, where claims had grown to such a size that the government changed the compensation system so that symptoms associated with using keyboards were no longer compensated.

A country's compensation system has a great effect on the reporting and control of work related disorders. In Sweden there has been a substantial decrease in reported work related diseases, probably due to an increased demand for evidence of work relatedness before compensation is approved. This conjecture is supported by statistics showing that rates of reported work related musculoskeletal symptoms in national surveys are constant. A generous compensation system can lead to patients becoming medicalized and lacking the motivation to attempt rehabilitation. However, a compensation system that facilitates reporting of work related disorders allows early identification of hazards that may constitute a serious risk to a workforce.

The existence of RSI as a clinical entity has been challenged medically and legally. Many sufferers have won compensation, but very few have secured damages by means of civil litigation—almost all claims are settled out of court. The diagnosis of RSI (a completely unsatisfactory term as explained earlier) is usually one of exclusion, there being, by definition, no physical signs. Whatever the true nature of the condition, almost every doctor will see patients who relate their pain syndrome to keyboard work, and management is seldom easy or straightforward. Ideally, it should be multidisciplinary.

Section 23.2

Are Your Workers Vulnerable to Vibration Hazards?

Donald Wasserman, *Occupational Hazards*, May 1998, Vol. 60, N. 5, pp. 99–101. Copyright 1999 Penton Media Inc. Reprinted with permission.

Introduction

All too often, hazards can remain unknown until workers begin to exhibit symptoms from years of working with dangerous equipment or materials. Hand/Arm Vibration Syndrome (HAVS) is one of those under-recognized hazards that now seems to be gaining increased awareness as more workers discover that their illness is a result of years of using vibrating tools on the job.

Donald Wasserman, a human vibration consultant in Cincinnati, notes that from 1.5 million to 2 million people are exposed to occupational vibration in the United States today. "Left untreated, results may affect workers in many different forms. One common result is what's known as 'white-finger disease,' or HAVS," he states.

It is easy to understand why occupational vibration is a difficult hazard to recognize. It's not as apparent as, say, toxic chemicals or fumes, or the possibility of falling from scaffolding. Results of vibration, however, can be just as detrimental. Early neurological stages of HAVS are usually reversible if further exposure to vibration is reduced or eliminated, but that is not the case for its advanced stages, and worst vascular stages. Treatment is palliative at best; hence, prevention is critical.

The Problem

Occupational vibration has been around for many years—at least since the very early 1900s, when pneumatic tools were introduced. Gradually, the link was made, and in 1918 Hand/Arm Vibration Syndrome was discovered. Since that time, the problem has been studied continuously worldwide, but it continues to get less attention than it deserves.

259

HAVS is a chronic progressive disorder with a white-finger latency period that can vary from a few months to several years. The development of HAVS in a population of workers and the length of the latency period depend on many interacting factors, including vibration level produced by the tool, hours of tool use per day, environmental temperature, type and design of the tool, manner in which the tool is held, vibration tolerance of the worker, and tobacco and drug use by the worker.

There are numerous pneumatic tools commonly associated with HAVS: for example, grinders, drills, fettling tools, jackhammers, riveting guns, impact wrenches, chainsaws, powered hammers, chisels, sanders, breakers, compactors, sharpeners, shapers, etc. You'll find this hazard in many industries—from a power saw operator in the woodworking field to a riveter in an automotive or aerospace facility. Any application involving some type of vibrating hand tool should be assessed.

The exposure time necessary may range from 1 month to 30 years, depending on the intensity of the vibration source, the transmissibility and absorption of vibration to the hand, and individual susceptibility. In high-risk work situations, the incidence and prevalence of HAVS can be 90 percent or higher.

Symptoms

The major health problems associated with the use of vibrating tools are peripheral vascular and peripheral neural disorders of the fingers and hands. Symptoms include:

- numbness
- pain
- blanching of the fingers
- loss of finger dexterity
- discomfort and pain in upper limbs

Cold temperatures many times seem to set off these symptoms. Frigid temperatures also worsen the effects of vibration.

Hand/Arm Vibration Syndrome can damage blood vessels, reducing blood supply; and damage nerves in the fingers, causing a permanent loss of feeling. The bones and muscles may also become damaged. Flexibility and grip strength may be lost, as well. HAVS can lead to gangrene if left untreated.

Diagnosis

The diagnosis of HAVS is based initially on a battery of objective tests, on a history of vibration exposure, and the exclusion of other causes of Raynaud's phenomenon (a similar illness, although not necessarily resulting from vibration). After the diagnosis is confirmed, the severity in each hand is assessed and categorized by stage (i.e. 1,2,3), based on the results of tests. The stage of severity helps determine the type and need for treatment and degree of impairment for compensation, when appropriate. In the initial stages, the syndrome often is classified as a neurological ailment, but as it develops, it usually becomes a vascular problem.

Prevention and Control

How can you control HAVS? Because its development is progressive, i.e., related to dose (time plus intensity), you need to apply control measures first, to reduce the intensity of vibration at the source. Just as important, isolation and damping techniques need to be used to reduce transmission to the hands.

Ergonomically designed and special anti-vibration tools can make a significant difference in vibration levels that reach the user. There are a variety of anti-vibration tools that conform to recommended safety limits. Some qualities you should look for in equipment include ergonomic design, a high power-to-weight ratio, low torque, a cutoff rather than slip-clutch mechanism, and non-slip handles to reduce the need for excessive grip force.

Damping techniques, such as wearing gloves at all times, are recommended. Anti-vibration gloves primarily decrease the transmission of high frequency vibration from the tool to the body. Additionally, they help keep the hands warm and dry, further reducing the chances of vibrational harm. They also reduce the risk of cuts and abrasions.

Glove materials must be selected carefully. A common material used in anti-vibration gloves is visco-elastic, which is available in numerous formulations and brands. Another material used in anti-vibration gloves is Gelfom, available in Ansell Edmont products. This composite material meets tough European material testing standards.

Treatment and Management

Once HAVS is recognized, several procedures should immediately be put in place. Hand and body temperature should be maintained in the workplace, smoking should be avoided, and, ideally, further vibration exposure should be eliminated.

If avoidance of the inflicting tool is impossible, a modified work routine, with frequent work breaks or job rotation, should be introduced. Rotation jobs should consist of vibration-free tasks. For workers who have the later stages of HAVS, alternative vibration-free work should be considered, full-time.

In the latter stage(s) of HAVS, drug therapy may be recommended. The necessity for this increases with the severity of the symptoms and the age of the subject. There is no cure for HAVS; the medications simply reduce the pain and suffering.

Awareness and education are the keys to preventing Hand/Arm Vibration Syndrome. When causes and effects of this occupational hazard are known and workers are protected appropriately, precautionary measures go a long way toward reducing the effects of vibration. Workers save themselves a lot of pain and possible loss of finger dexterity in the future, and they can save their company from the threat of high indemnity costs.

Donald Wasserman, past chief of Occupational Vibration at the National Institute for Occupational Safety and Health (NIOSH), currently is working as a human vibration consultant in Cincinnati. For further information, call 513/891–9084.

Source: *Journal of Family Practice*, Feb. 1994 v38 n2 p180–186, Hand-arm vibration syndrome, Peter L. Pelmear; William Taylor.

Chapter 24

Ergonomics

Chapter Contents

Section 24.1

An Ergonomics Program Guideline

"Fitting the Job to the Worker," Consultation and Compliance Services Division, Washington State Department of Labor and Industries, F417-110-000, http://www.lni.wa.gov/wisha/ergo/veg/vegch3.htm, August 1994. Despite the age of this document, readers seeking an understanding of ergonomics will still find the information useful.

This section covers two types of controls for designing ergonomically sound workplaces:

- engineering controls
- work practice controls

Hazard prevention and control is the part of your ergonomics program in which changes are made so the jobs, workstations, tools, and environment fit the worker. It is the active process of eliminating or reducing the risk of injury by changing the things that contribute to the risk factors. After you evaluate the job and identify the specific problems, you can eliminate or reduce the risk of injury through the use of these controls. Personal characteristics of the workers, such as size, physical condition or medical history, may need to be accommodated to make the best fit.

Engineering Controls

Engineering controls involve making changes to workstations, tools, or equipment used on the job, or changing the way a job is done to avoid work-related musculoskeletal hazards. These controls are preferred over all others because they make permanent changes that eliminate hazards at the source. Although they can be more expensive to implement than other controls, their effect is often more significant.

Because of the importance of engineering controls, we include here a comprehensive list of types and examples. Engineering controls include workstation design, work methods design, tool and equipment design, controls and displays, connectors, fasteners and valves, and product design. Following are descriptions and examples of each.

Workstation Design

Aspects of workstations you can change with engineering controls include workspace layout, work surfaces, standing and walking surfaces, seating, storage, work fixtures, materials handling/movement and work environment.

Workspace Layout

Workspace layout and arrangement should allow:

- adjustability to fit each worker's size
- the worker to maintain neutral posture and avoid awkward or extended reaches and jerky movements while performing the tasks
- a variety of working positions to avoid static postures
- full range of motion and adequate leg room
- adequate space for and access to all necessary tools and equipment
- frequently used work items within easy arm's reach
- unobscured line of sight

For example, in a packing operation, boxes being packed with parts could be placed at waist level in front of the worker, rather than behind, below or on an overhead shelf.

Work Surfaces

Work surfaces should be at the proper height and angle for the individual worker's size, tools, and equipment used. They should permit neutral postures and be adjustable, especially where different kinds of tasks are performed or the workstation is shared. For example, where workers inspect or assemble small parts, or perform other visually intensive tasks, work surfaces could be tilted to reduce neck, shoulder and arm strain.

Walking and Standing Surfaces

Surfaces on which people stand for long periods should be designed to prevent slipping and provide adequate traction and comfort. Anti-fatigue floor mats, sit-stand stools, and footrests can help make workers more comfortable.

Seating

Seat-height adjustability and lower back support are important for work done for a long time while seated. Some workers may choose to sit part of the time and stand other times to reduce stress on the body from working in one position too long. Chairs or seating should:

- adequately support the back and legs
- have padded seats
- have separately adjustable back and seat cushions
- permit feet to be supported either on the floor or with a footrest
- be easily adjustable while seated
- have swivel seats for most tasks
- isolate workers from whole-body vibration
- have adjustable arm support when appropriate

Storage

Storage areas should be organized so that workers maintain good body positions, reduce muscular forces and avoid excessive reach. Store heavy items between knee and shoulder height and frequently used items closest to the worker.

Work Fixtures

Workers should not have to use their hands or bodies as a vise to hold objects; mechanical devices do this much better. Tooling fixtures and jigs should be set up to avoid awkward postures and excessive forces.

Materials Handling Movement

Lifting, carrying, pushing or pulling objects can strain the back, arms and shoulders. Strength and lifting limits should not be exceeded; extreme muscular exertion can cause injury. The following steps will make materials handling/movement easier:

- Do not exceed the physical ability of the worker doing the lifting.
- Provide adequate recovery time for tasks that require frequent lifting.
- Provide easy access so the load is in front of the person lifting.

- Eliminate twisting by changing the start or end point of the lift.
- Put items to be lifted between knee and shoulder height.
- Provide handles or cutouts to make grasping easier, permit a closer lift, and allow items to be carried near the body.
- Change an object's shape to make it easier to grasp.
- Decrease the weight of objects.
- Decrease the distance or height over which the object must be moved.
- Distribute a load evenly within a container.
- Use hand carts or hand trucks.
- Use a vacuum-assisted hoist or integrated conveyors.
- Use loaders, cranes and motorized material pallets to help move loads that are larger or heavier than one or two people can safely handle. (By handling materials mechanically in larger packages, you can enhance productivity and recover your initial investment.)

Work Environment

Here are some ways you can minimize work-environment hazards:

- Isolate equipment or operations that produce loud or distracting noise.
- Make lighting bright enough without causing glare so workers can see clearly (See special requirements for computer workstations as listed in the section titled "Designing Ergonomically Sound Offices").
- Isolate hands and feet from cold.
- Reduce whole-body vibration while riding in a vehicle or standing near equipment.
- Isolate workers from excessive heat; provide adequate cooling and ventilation.

Work Methods Design

Work methods should be designed so work can be completed safely and comfortably, and factors contributing to work-related musculoskeletal disorders are minimized. Here are several risk factors and examples of how you can change work methods to reduce them:

Static or Awkward Postures

Prolonged static or awkward postures can rapidly cause fatigue. Work should be done so neutral postures are maintained, stoops and reaches are avoided, and time working overhead is minimized. For example, tasks should be organized so that workers at a conveyor belt don't have to lean over the belt.

Mechanical Stress

Nerves, tendons, and blood vessels can be damaged by exposure to hard or sharp edges, such as a table edge. Equipment should be moved so a worker doesn't touch the edge, or edges should be padded to minimize contact. For example, in packing boxes, the position of the box could be changed so a worker doesn't have to contact a sharp table edge to place the contents in the box.

Repetitive-Motion Tasks

Tasks involving repetitive motion are major contributors to cumulative-trauma disorders. You can minimize repetition by:

- using automation, such as in stapling, sorting, labeling or filling operations
- changing the job to include tasks that don't use the same muscle groups

For example, in a check-sorting operation, instead of having one person open mail, another take checks out of envelopes, another stamp them and yet another record the figures, each worker could do each of those tasks.

Excessive Force

Workers must use excessive force when objects are difficult to grasp or control, equipment and tools are poorly maintained, or tasks require awkward postures. You can eliminate the use of excessive force by:

- improving friction on slippery objects
- using mechanically assisted devices for awkward lifts
- choosing tools that better fit the hand

- keeping equipment properly maintained to prevent jamming and sticking

- providing adequate work room to perform tasks

Work Rates

The capacity of workers should be considered in establishing production goals. Increased work rates, excessive overtime, and incentive programs for piece work can cause fatigue, increasing the chance for injury.

Tool and Equipment Design

Tools and equipment should fit the individual user and be chosen for the specific demands of the task. Tools should be designed to maintain neutral body positions. Take extra care to avoid twisting, vibration, static muscle loading, and pressure on tissues and joints. Factors that can be modified to prevent risks include tool size, weight, and balance; handle size and position; and power control design.

Tool size, weight and balance. You should select tools just heavy enough to accomplish the task. You can do these things to minimize risks:

- Use counterweights or supports to minimize the weight of a tool; extra force should not be required to counteract the balancer.

- Select tools that can bend or are shaped to prevent awkward wrist or shoulder postures.

- Select balanced tools that can be held at the center of gravity.

Handle size and position. The size of the handle influences the amount of force that can be exerted without straining the muscles and tendons. A handle that is too large or too small requires more force to accomplish the same amount of work as a tool with a correctly-sized handle. Handles should:

- fit the individual user's hand and be long enough so they don't press into the palm or wrist.

- have rounded (not sharp) edges, a positive stop or flanged end, and no fluting.

- be made of material that is non-conductive, compressible, and doesn't feel slippery.

- minimize vibration transferred to the hand. For example, some screwdrivers prevent repeated motion in an awkward position by means of a pistol grip, and a "yankee drill" mechanism rotates the bit when the tool is pushed forward.

Power control. Workers should be able to turn a tool off and on or keep it running without using extra force. Auto-start/stop tools are preferred. You can do these things to reduce hazards:

- Minimize rotational forces with variable torque settings.

- Avoid high-tension and one-finger triggers.

Controls and Displays

The location of equipment/machinery controls and indicators should take into account their importance, frequency, and sequence of use, and the height of workers. Controls and displays need to be visible and accessible while in use, and easy to operate in relation to equipment functions. Spacing should be adequate to accommodate gloves or other protective equipment.

Connectors, Fasteners, and Valves

Components, connectors, valves and fasteners should be located to allow neutral postures during work. The following can help reduce risks:

- Quick-release connectors and fasteners that require few turns with little force can reduce strain.

- Connectors should be positioned to allow easy access.

- Connectors should be labeled and set up to make connection easy and prevent cross-connection.

Product Design

Product designers should take into account ergonomic considerations, not only for the people who use products, but also for those who fabricate, assemble and perform maintenance on them. Form, materials, means of assembly, packaging, disassembly, and disposal should be considered. Designers should ask these questions to reduce hazards in product design:

- Does material handling or assembly require awkward postures, excessive, repetitive movements, or extreme force during assembly or manufacturing?

- If sharp edges are a hazard, can they be removed?

- Can materials be changed to help fabrication or assembly?

- Could assembling parts in a different order eliminate musculoskeletal hazards?

- Could the product's size or shape be changed to make manufacturing easier and make the product more acceptable to the user?

Work Practice Controls

Work practice controls are procedures for safe and proper work that are used to reduce the duration, frequency, or severity of exposure to a hazard. Standard operating procedures should allow for enough workers to complete the tasks and should be a regular part of the way you do business. When defining safe work practice controls, it is a good idea to ask workers for their ideas, since they have firsthand experience with the tasks. These controls should be understood and followed by managers, supervisors, and workers.

- *Work methods training*. Employees should be taught how to perform their jobs with the lowest physical stress and best posture, as well as how to handle materials, tools and equipment safely.

- *Gradual introduction to work*. New and returning employees in jobs involving risks, such as prolonged repetitive motion, should be introduced gradually to a full workload to improve work capacity and prevent injury.

- *Monitoring*. Review all jobs regularly to see if specified safe work practices are being used. Work techniques should be reviewed periodically to ensure that they reduce risks.

- *Recovery pauses*. Regular recovery pauses can help prevent eye strain, headache, neck, back, shoulder, arm or hand pain. Employees can perform activities that involve different muscle groups during these pauses.

- *Job rotation*. If possible, job rotation should be used to prevent injury, not as a response to it. Also, job rotation should generally be used as an intermediate solution while you work on

271

other solutions. Workers should be rotated into jobs using different muscle-tendon groups to prevent fatigue.

- *Job design*. Your company should look at ways that jobs can be (re)designed to incorporate good ergonomic practices. These include providing relief from frequent repetitive motions, static or awkward postures, excessive forceful exertions, and mental and muscular fatigue.

- *Maintenance and housekeeping*. Regular maintenance is critical to ensure that your employees have tools and equipment that are in proper working order and perform to expectations. Equipment that is not maintained and cleaned can make regular operations more difficult. Worn-out tools should be replaced; dull tools should be sharpened. Housekeeping should be done as often as necessary to reduce musculoskeletal hazards.

Section 24.2

Ergonomically Designed Tools

Roberta Carson, *Occupational Hazards*, September 1995, Vol. 57, N. 9, pp. 49-54. Copyright 1999 Penton Media Inc. Reprinted with permission.

Give workers the wrong hand and power tools, and the result could be costly: cumulative trauma disorders. Here's how to choose the right tool for the job.

Although ergonomic principles have been widely applied to work station design and to material handling tasks throughout industry, ergonomic tool design is one area which has not received the attention it deserves. Injuries such as tendinitis, carpal tunnel syndrome, trigger finger and epicondylitis have been associated with the use of hand and power tools. Most of these injuries are caused by employees using poorly designed tools or from employees using the wrong tool for the job.

Employers must simultaneously consider the ergonomic qualities of a tool and the task for which the tool will be used before a tool order is written.

Causes of Cumulative Trauma Disorders (CTD)

In order to prevent costly and painful CTDs associated with the use of tools, it is important to understand what can cause these injuries. That is easier to do if you first have a basic understanding of hand and arm anatomy.

The thumb is controlled by strong, short muscles in the hand. In contrast, the fingers are controlled by muscles in the forearm which are connected to the fingers via long finger flexor tendons which go through the hand and wrist into the forearm. These flexor tendons, some blood vessels and the median nerve (which feeds the thumb, index finger, middle finger and part of the ring finger) pass through the carpal tunnel in the wrist. This tunnel is formed by small bones held together by a ligament stretched across the tunnel. Cumulative trauma injuries can occur when the tendons and nerves become stressed from repetitive use and/or awkward postures and high exertions of force.

Tool Selection Criteria

All tools should be easy to use and comfortable to hold with a secure grip. Tools should not produce pressure points, cause unnecessary exertions of force, or require the use of awkward postures. When selecting a tool for a job, it is important to consider how the tool is designed and what postures are required for operating the tool in each specific task.

Wrist deviation. A tool should be selected which will allow the operator to keep the wrist straight. Work performed with unnatural, deviated wrist postures can lead to tendinitis, tenosynovitis or carpal tunnel syndrome. When choosing a tool, you must consider the orientation of the work piece and how it will affect wrist positioning. If work is done in both the horizontal and vertical planes, more than one tool may be necessary.

Shoulder deviation. Some tools may force the operator to raise his elbows, thus abducting the shoulder, which can cause muscle fatigue and pain and can lead to tissue degeneration. Proper tool selection and workplace design allows the elbows to be kept close to the body.

Guidelines for Manual and Power Tools

- *Distribute grip force.* Select tools which distribute the grip forces over as wide an area as possible. The grip force should not be concentrated on one or two fingers or in the center of the palm. Any concentration of pressure in one area can lead to tendinitis, tenosynovitis or carpal tunnel syndrome. Choose tools with handles which span the hand and extend beyond the palm. Be sure that even the larger employees can hold the tool without the handle digging into the center of the palm.

- *Do not use pinch grip.* Tools should not require employees to use the pinch grip. Maintaining the pinch grip, such as when holding tweezers or pencils, forces the hand to work 4-5 times harder than when gripping with the entire hand. The pinch grip combined with wrist deviation can lead to carpal tunnel syndrome. Whenever possible, select a tool which can be held with the entire hand or power grip.

- *Do not exert forces on sides of fingers.* The tool handle should not exert forces on the side of the fingers. The nerves and blood vessels are very close to the skin and can be damaged easily. Select tools with rounded edges at all areas of potential contact.

- *Hands should not be exposed to sharp edges or corners.* No part of the hand should be exposed to sharp edges or corners of the tool. This includes the sides of the fingers, and the palm and side of the hand. As mentioned above, the nerves and blood vessels are very close to the skin and can be damaged by this kind of external pressure.

- *Be sure there is ample finger and hand room in the handle.* If employees will be putting their fingers and/or hand into the tool's handle, such as with scissors or handsaws, be sure that all users can easily fit their hands or fingers into the handles of the tools. Also, consider the thickness of gloves when applicable. Selections should be made based on at least the 95th percentile male hand and finger sizes.

- *No finger grooves in handles.* Avoid finger grooves or scallops in the handles; these indentations do not fit a wide range of hand sizes. If the user's hand is "too big" for the scallops, the fingers will rest on the edges of the grooves, possibly causing nerve or blood vessel damage. Conversely, if the user's hand is "too small" for the scallops, more than one finger will be squished into a scallop, causing discomfort and the risk of nerve or blood vessel damage. Instead of scalloped handles, select tools with knurled or textured surfaces which will make it easier to hold the tool and will reduce the grip force requirements.

- *Handles should be covered in semisoft, nonslip, compressible materials.* Avoid tools with hard metal or plastic handles. Tools that are covered in semisoft, nonslip, compressible materials will be easier to hold and use. The cushioned handles are comfortable and easy to hold with no hard or sharp edges. Additionally, coated handles tend to be less slippery when wet, thereby reducing the amount of force necessary to hold a slippery or greasy tool in place.

- *Metal handles transfer heat to and from the hand faster than a coated handle.* In cold environments, a tool with a metal handle feels much colder in the hand than a coated tool. Likewise, in hot workplaces, the metal handles feel hotter than the coated handles. When selecting tools, be sure the material is not so soft that it can become embedded with small pieces of wire, etc. which can be dangerous. Additionally, handles which are too soft diminish the feedback to the hand, which may result in an unnecessary increase in pressure being exerted to complete the task.

- *Tool should be designed for right- and left-handed users.* Tools which are designed only for either the right or left hand are often held in the wrong hand or wrong configuration, which can cause discomfort or injury.

- *If a large downward force is required, tool should have a flange.* Tools which will be used to exert large downward forces, such as a screwdriver, should have a flange at the base of the handle. This flange will keep the hand from slipping off the tool and becoming injured and/or damaging the product.

- *Job-specific tools should only be used for jobs for which they were designed.* Specially designed job-specific tools may not be applicable to all industrial tasks. Using a tool for a job other than that for which it was designed can force the body into awkward postures and lead to pain and injury.

- *Select only high quality tools.* If an employee is not using a high quality tool, it may break or malfunction, causing injuries or product damage. Also, poorly designed cutting tools may dull over time, requiring an increase in force to complete each task. Although it is tempting to purchase less expensive tools, it is important to realize that these tools usually do not last as long as higher quality tools. In the long run, it may be cheaper to make the initial investment in high-quality tools.

- *Tools should be well-balanced in hand.* To determine if a tool is well-balanced, simply hold the tool in your hand in the same posture you would use if you were working with it. A well-balanced tool will easily stay in the proper position with no effort required by your hand to balance the tool. Well-balanced tools avoid the extra exertions required to hold an unbalanced tool (e.g. top heavy) in place while operating it.

- *Metal parts should have non-glare matte finishes.* Glare can be caused by a bright light being reflected off a polished metal surface into the eye. Glare can be annoying and may cause difficulty in seeing the task being performed. In order to avoid the problem of glare from shiny metal surfaces, all metal parts of tools should have non-glare matte finishes.

Guidelines for Power Tools

- *Minimize vibration.* Vibrating tools can damage the blood vessels, nerves, bones, joints and muscles. The effect of vibration depends on frequency, amplitude, acceleration, duration, direction, point of application and body factors. Reducing exposure to the vibration can relieve the symptoms. This can be achieved by: Covering the tool handle with a rubber housing; providing padded gloves; purchasing vibration-dampened tools; directing the cold air exhaust away from the hand; interjecting rest periods; and job rotation.

- *Cords should be flexible and not interfere with the job.* When purchasing power tools, be sure all power and air cords are flexible and can be easily manipulated. Additionally, be sure the cords will not interfere with the job. If necessary, suspend the cord on a ring above the head of the employee.

- *All power tools should be suspended on an overhead balancer.* This eliminates the need for the user to support the weight of the tool. These balancers allow the user to easily move and activate the tool without having to support its weight.

- *Use torque arms whenever necessary.* Studies have shown that using torque arms with torque-controlled tools will reduce the grip force and torque reaction to the worker's hand. Torque-controlled tools shut off automatically when a preset torque is reached. When the tool shuts off, the inertia is absorbed by the hand, resulting in torque reaction or kickback. Some power tools may not be available with internal torque control, making a torque reaction bar essential.

- In either circumstance, the torque reaction in right-handed users causes wrist extension. For left-handed users, wrist flexion is the result. In addition to the sudden change in wrist posture, most employees grip the tool tighter during torque reaction in an effort to control the tool. This increase in grip force, combined with the awkward wrist postures, can lead to CTDs.

- Torque arms, which are attached to the bench, hold the tool in order to absorb the torque reaction. Although these arms can limit the movement of the tool somewhat, it is worth the effort for a user to become accustomed to using a torque arm.

Guidelines for Specific Tools

- *Pliers and cutters.* Ergonomically designed pliers and cutters should be designed with handle lengths of at least 4 in. They should have a grip span of 3–4 in. when the tool is open, and 2–3.5 in. when the tool is closed in hand. These tools should have a spring return and no finger grooves. Handle curvature. should be no more than 1/2 in. over its entire length. Handles should be mirror images. Pliers and cutters should be usable by right- and left-handed workers. Use tools with a high-quality cutting blade.

- *Manual screwdrivers.* Ergonomically designed screwdrivers should have handles at least 5 in. long. The handle diameter for medium and large blade screwdrivers that will be used to exert force should be in the range of 1.0–1.35 in., indicating a circumference of 3.1–4.2 in. Handle diameter of the small, thin blade tools used for precision work should be in the range of 0.7–0.8 in., translating to a circumference of 2.2–2.5 in. Flanges should be on the base of the handle to prevent the hand from slipping off the tool. The tool should not have fluted handles, finger grooves or large indentations on the handles.

- *Power tools (screwdrivers, etc.).* Whenever possible, tools should be equipped with push-to-start mechanisms which will eliminate the need to activate a trigger. If push-to-start is not possible, then use a thumb trigger or a long trigger which can be operated by two or more fingers.

- *The handles should be long enough* (at least 4 in.) to avoid the end of the tool digging into the palm. Handles should be rounded with no deep indentations and no finger grooves or scalloping. All areas of potential contact should be rounded. Handle breadth should measure 2–3 in. for pistol grip tools. Handle diameter should be 2–2.5 in. for cylindrical tools. The handle should be located close to the tool's center of gravity so it feels well-balanced in hand. Torque control settings should be used whenever applicable. Power and air cords should be flexible and not interfere with the job.

Proper Tool Maintenance

An organized and thorough tool maintenance program is essential. All tools should be checked regularly, and employees should be encouraged to trade in old, worn tools. The ergonomic qualities of a tool can be defeated if the tool is not working properly.

Sharpen or replace cutting blades if they begin to dull. Teach employees to quickly report any dulling of blades. Using a dull cutting blade requires the employee to exert more force to complete the task than when using a sharp blade.

Springs on two-handled tools, such as pliers and cutters, must be in good working condition. Tools without properly working springs require the employees to open the tool with their pinkies after each use. Replace tools with defects such as worn handles and broken parts immediately.

To minimize the risk of employees losing or stealing tools, insist that employees return the used tool before getting a new one. This also allows the employer to recondition old tools, which can result in large financial savings.

Training

To ensure that all employees can perform their jobs safely, it is important to provide training. Each employee should understand the basics of ergonomics, and should receive job-specific training covering the proper methods and tools to be used. This training is especially important when new tools or methods are introduced.

Without proper training, employees may perform a task with the wrong tool or improper posture, putting them at risk for CTDs. During the training session or break-in period, be sure each employee has ample time to practice before being expected to meet production goals.

Providing the correct ergonomically designed tool can significantly reduce the risk of employees developing painful and costly CTDs. However, tools are only one part of the process. Be sure to consider all other aspects of the job, and to train all employees properly.

Prevention of CTDs Associated with Tools

There are four major steps that can be taken to reduce the incidence and severity of CTDs related to the use of tools:

1. Use anthropometric data.

2. Reduce the number of repetitions.

3. Reduce the force required.

4. Eliminate awkward postures.

Anthropometry

Knowing the varying body dimensions of the people performing jobs in a facility is an important aid to selecting tools and designing jobs to fit their physical capabilities.

Anthropometry is the study of human body measurements. Ergonomists aim to design for 90 percent of the population—all those falling between the 5th and 95th percentiles. (5th percentile means 5 percent of the population is smaller, and 95th percentile means 5 percent of the population is larger.)

When designing and selecting tools, use anthropometric data to provide tools that are comfortable for all users and will not cause injuries. These data are useful when determining handle length, grip span, tool weight, trigger length and other pertinent factors.

Reduce the Number of Repetitions

Tasks which require high repetition rates require more muscle effort and therefore allow less recovery time, which can lead to fatigue and injury, Because there are no current guidelines for safe numbers of repetitions, it is best to try to reduce the number of repetitions as much as possible. Methods to reduce the repetition rate include:

- decrease production rates
- limit overtime
- change method

- provide mechanical assists

- automate whenever possible

- change product design

- rotate employees

- encourage employees to take frequent mini-breaks and perform relief exercises

- increase the number of employees assigned to a particular task

- expand the number of tasks each employee performs to minimize the constant repetition of a particular sub-task

Reduce the Force Required

If the force requirements are too high, the soft tissues are strained and may not recover, causing injury. Additionally, tendons and nerves are stressed when held in contact with sharp and/or hard edges. Reduce the required force as much as possible by:

- using power tools and assists wherever possible

- using the stronger power grip instead of the weaker pinch grip

- spreading the force over as wide an area as possible

- providing adequate gripping surfaces which are not slippery, sharp or excessively hard

- using jigs and fixtures to avoid the pinch grip whenever applicable

Minimize Awkward Postures

Jobs should not require employees to work in awkward postures which stress the joints and tissues, causing injuries. To minimize awkward postures while using tools, design jobs so that they:

- keep the wrist in the neutral position

- keep elbows close to the body and bent 90-110 degrees

- avoid reaching over shoulder height

- avoid reaching behind body

- minimize forearm rotation

References

Chaffin, D.B. and Andersson, G., *Occupational Biomechanics*, John Wiley and Sons, Inc., New York, 1984.

Kroemer, K.H.E., "Cumulative Trauma Disorders: Their Recognition and Ergonomics Measures to Avoid Them," *Applied Ergonomics*, 1989, 20.4, 274–280.

Putz-Anderson, V., *Cumulative Trauma Disorders—A Manual For Musculoskeletal Diseases Of The Upper Limbs*, NIOSH, Taylor and Francis, New York, 1988.

—by Roberta Carson

Roberta Carson is the founder and principal of ErgoFit Inc., a Newton, Mass.-based ergonomics consulting firm. She has an M.S. in industrial engineering from the University of Michigan and has served in ergonomics positions with AT&T Technologies and General Motors Corp.

Section 24.3

Designing Ergonomically Sound Assembly Workstations

Torsten Bunning, "Designing Ergonomically Sound Assembly Workstations," *Occupational Hazards*, August 1998, Vol. 60, N. 8 pp. 63–66, Copyright 1999 Penton Media Inc. Reprinted with permission.

Work environments affect the bottom line in terms of both product quality and worker productivity. In the workplace, the primary aim of ergonomics is to provide an environment that matches workers' physical characteristics to the tasks being performed. In manufacturing industries, manual assembly operations represent a broad spectrum of task variables. Traditionally, these task variables tended to be viewed on a relatively short term basis. Today, such variables are being looked at in terms of their long-range impact. For example, a small stretch to pick up a part may not be a problem for a worker in the short term. However, if that worker has to do this for a long time, the movement may cause a cumulative and harmful effect.

To illustrate the point, imagine spending six hours in the middle seat of a coach-class flight. You have your laptop with you and have been working on an important project since takeoff. The flight will land in two hours and you are still working to complete your project. Do you suppose your work during the last two hours of the flight will be as incisive and productive as when you first took off? Now, imagine the physical and mental fatigue of having to take this same flight day-in and day-out, five days a week, 50 weeks a year.

One incentive to provide an ergonomically sound workplace is related to government regulatory requirements. But an equally valid case can be made on the basis of economic justification: a significantly improved bottom line. Manual assembly workstations that are properly designed in accordance with proven ergonomic principles can help maximize worker efficiency, safety, morale, and overall productivity. It is estimated that the return on investment for every $1 spent to improve ergonomic conditions is approximately $6.

Task Analysis

As the starting point, it's essential that the designer of an ergonomic workstation fully understands the function(s) to be performed at the station. Key questions to be answered:

- What are the characteristics of the piece being worked on?
- How is it moved?
- What parts are added, and how?

The work throughput must be considered up front, in order to design the most ergonomically effective workstation. A designer should also have a basic understanding of the ergonomic principles that will be incorporated into the station. In this regard, software is available that greatly simplifies the design of ergonomic workstations, while verifying the validity of the design.

Seven-Step Design Protocol

Robert Bosch Corp., has placed strong emphasis on furnishing people-oriented work environments in all of its assembly facilities worldwide. To meet these requirements, the company has conducted in-depth research to determine all work-relevant anthropometric data such as typical body sizes and movement ranges. As a result, Bosch has developed a seven-step ergonomic protocol that serves as the basis for assembly workstation design company-wide. The steps, in logical sequence, are:

1. consider work height

2. consider size of grab area

3. optimize part container layout

4. avoid work above heart-level

5. consider fields of vision

6. match light intensity to the work task

7. properly adjust work equipment to the task

Worktable Surface Height

The first step in design of an ergonomically optimized workstation is the determination of proper worktable surface height. The worktable surface height must accommodate the postures, movements, and chair heights for a wide range of employees body sizes; i.e., body height from the 5th percentile of female workers to the 95th percentile of male workers. Additional factors that should be considered include:

- A worker's arms should be below the shoulder; back and neck at less than a 20 degree to 30 degree incline.

- Ample leg room should be provided beneath the worktable top: approximately 1 in. between legs and the bottom of the work top. Also, there should be no obstructions, such as drawers between the legs and the bottom of the work top.

- Height of the workpiece on top of the worktable has a major influence on worker posture. For precision and close inspection, the workpiece should be 2 in. above the worker's elbows. For light assembly tasks (up to 5 lbs.) the workpiece should be 2 in. to 4 in. below the worker's elbows. For heavy work requiring force during assembly (5 lbs. to 10 lbs.), the workpiece should be 4 in. to 8 in. below the worker's elbows.

Size of Grab Area

There are three grab areas for a worker: maximum, optimum and two-hand. All parts, supplies, and tools should be placed within easy reach of the worker. Placing items within easy reach helps avoid body and arm twisting and continuous wrist flexing when reaching for parts. This, in turn, reduces repetitive motion injuries. In determining the size of the grab area, the following guidelines should be observed:

- a maximum grab area in general, 25 in., with the worker leaning forward at the trunk, using the shoulder joint as the reference point for the measurement

- optimum grab area in general, 12 in., with the worker leaning forward at the trunk, using the shoulder joint as the reference point

- optimum work area 10 in. should be a 10 in. box measured 5 in. from the front of the worker's body

- two-handed extended reach with grip, in general, 22.5 in., with the worker leaning forward at the trunk, using the shoulder joint as the reference point for measurement

Parts Container Layout

Grab containers should be located so that grab distances are as short as possible. In addition, the following guidelines should be considered:

- Container layout should always be within easy reach and should require a minimum amount of motion—no farther than 15 in. from the front edge of the workstation at any angle.

- Heavy parts should be placed in bottom containers on the worktable surface. Reason: less exertion is required to move parts from the container in a parallel line to the work surface than would be needed to move parts in a top bin downward to the work surface.

- Position containers with parts used most often as close as possible to the worker.

- Position all containers in the optimum grab area (12 in., with the worker leaning forward at the trunk, using the shoulder joint as the reference point). Containers mounted on adjustable articulating arms should follow the sweep of the optimum grab range, rather than containers mounted flat at the back of the workstation.

Avoid Work above the Heart

When designing a workstation, avoid placing workers in the following conditions:

- *Work positions above the heart*. This reduces blood circulation, causing a worker's performance to decline rapidly.

- *Statis holding during assembly*. This reduces blood flow to the muscles, increasing muscle fatigue. This, in turn, reduces coordination, which is a leading cause of poor product quality.

Consider Fields of Vision

The surroundings observed by a worker's eyes, when the eyes and head don't move, is defined as the field of vision. It is desirable to minimize movement of the eyes and head during assembly or inspection operations. Reason: It takes approximately three seconds for the head to rotate and the eyes to refocus. During this process, piecepart throughput is reduced. When locating grab containers on the work top, consider the following:

- A 15 degree view angle requires no worker head or eye movement to grab parts. As a result, piecepart throughput should be at maximum.

- A 35 degree view angle requires only the worker's eyes to move to grab parts. As a result, piecepart throughput is only slightly reduced.

- Position grab containers at equal vision range. This makes it unnecessary for a worker's eyes to adjust to varying distances every time he/she shifts viewing angles.

Match Light Intensity to the Task

Proper lighting is extremely important. The correct lighting for a task reduces errors and increases worker performance. These are the basic guidelines for matching light intensity to the task:

- 500 lux for simple assembly tasks such as telephones, small motors, printers and automotive components

- 1,000 lux for testing electrical equipment and for assembling delicate electronics such as TVs and printed circuits

- 1,500 lux for adjusting and testing electrical equipment, assembling delicate electronics and sorting assemblies for quality

Properly Adjust Work Equipment to the Task

Tables, chairs, grab container tool shelves, material shuttles and parts case lifters should be adjustable in order to fit the worker to the work task. In general, modular workstation systems provide the greatest flexibility for fast and accurate adjustment of these components. For adjustability, the following are key components that deserve careful attention:

- worktable frames and material shuttles that allow easy adjustment of accessories or container shelves to the desired position

- work chairs with a height adjustment range for proper fit from the 5th percentile female to the 95th percentile male seated worker at the workstation

- material shuttles mounted on wheels to move parts around the workstation for easy part accessibility and quicker piecepart throughput

- grab container tool shelves that allow workers to quickly adjust parts. Select grab containers to fit the task.

- case lifters with operator-selectable height ranges—typically between 25 in. and 43 in.—to lift heavy parts to the desired work height. An optimally designed ergonomic workstation with adjustable components will be of little or no benefit, however, unless workers are trained to make the proper adjustments to their work equipment. Yet, this may be one of the most overlooked aspects of workplace ergonomics. By spending a few minutes adjusting chair, table surface, grab containers, shuttles and the like at the beginning of a shift, the worker will create a much more comfortable and productive work area.

The seven-step protocol represents only the basic, preliminary design of an ergonomically sound assembly workstation. Clearly, workstations should be tailored to the specific assembly tasks they are to accommodate. For this reason, modular components that can be readily adjusted, modified and/or reconfigured should be used.

Many assembly tasks in the electronics industry, for example, require provision for adequate electrostatic discharge (ESD) protection. In such cases, the modular components of a workstation, such as work surfaces and seating units, should be available with ESD protection as an option.

Moreover, ergonomically designed hand tools are as important to a workstation as any other accessory, if not more so. While the workstation can provide the proper work environment (i.e., work surface and location of the workpiece being assembled), it's the tool in the hands of a worker that performs the actual assembly. If the tool(s) is not ergonomically designed and is not used in an ergonomic manner, the chances of developing a cumulative trauma disorder (CTD) are greatly increased.

Manual assembly workstations that meet sound ergonomic criteria can be thought of as an investment in productivity. For manual assembly operations, an obsolete production environment can be compared to obsolete production equipment, such as machine tools: both can seriously weaken a company's productivity and competitive posture.

—by Torsten Bunning

Torsten Bunning is an ergonomics designer with Robert Bosch GmbH in Stuttgart, Germany.

Section 24.4

Designing Ergonomically Sound Offices

From "Guidelines for Office Ergonomics," Consultation and Compliance Services Division, Washington State Department of Labor and Industries, 6105-T1, http://www.cebaf.gov/ehs/manual/EHSbook-241.html, October 15, 1999.

Introduction

Ergonomics is the matching of the work environment, tools, and the people who use them. Good ergonomics help comfort, productivity, and reduce the risk of injury and illness. The recommendations listed below are based in part upon information developed by the National Safety Council, the Food and Drug Administration and the National Institute of Occupational Safety and Health.

Computer Equipment

Keyboard

Height

A keyboard at correct height will allow the operator's upper and lower arms to be at a ninety-degree angle while typing. A prolonged period of work with angles more than 15 percent either way from this optimum position can cause pain in the shoulders, back, neck, arms and wrist.

Angulation

The keyboard should be sloped in a manner which places the operator's wrist in a natural bend, with the hand slightly tilted back. Keyboards may have built-in feet which allow for angulation adjustment. There are a number of retrofit devices available that will aid in proper angulation.

Position

The keyboard should be squarely to the front of the operator. Even a slight misalignment causes torsional stress on the upper body which results in fatigue and pain in the neck, shoulders and back.

Wrist Support

The wrists should be supported while typing. If the keyboard is well designed, the workstation surface may offer proper wrist support. Most keyboards, however, cannot be properly angled without also needing some type of supplementary wrist support. Ideally, the support needs to be soft and to allow skin to "breathe." There are a number of wrist support devices on the market, including some that combine a tilted platform for the keyboard for proper angulation.

Use of Keyboard

Typing force has an effect on the strain to your wrists and hands. Most people type with excessive force, and people with chronic wrist/hand strain injuries often type with the greatest force. Use a light touch, and be conscious of the angle of your wrists as you type.

Video Display Terminal (VDT) or Monitors

Height

The top of the screen should be at or slightly below eye level, with the operator's head in a normal, erect position. This is a very important parameter. If the operator is forced to look downwards or upwards for prolonged periods, neck, back, and shoulder strain are likely. There are a number of platforms or stands available which alter height and provide storage space for the keyboard or other items. There are also pivoting support brackets that hold the VDT off of the work surface altogether. Note that an incorrect VDT height is almost certain to contribute to other posture problems as the operator unconsciously compensates his or her position.

Angulation

Ideally, the screen surface should be perfectly vertical. This offers the best compromise between glare prevention and elimination of optical distortion.

Position

As with the keyboard, the screen should be directly to the front of the operator. Twisting or turning motions during typing contribute to neck, shoulder, and back discomfort. Materials which are being read during typing should also be directly to the front. This usually necessitates the use of a document holder of some description.

Distance

The screen surface (which is not necessarily the front edge of the VDT) should be within 18 to 24 inches from the operator's face. In part, the size of the screen (and therefore the display's character size) influences this measurement. Operators should not position the screen to compensate for vision problems; they should wear their corrective lenses and position the screen at the proper distance.

Brightness and Contrast

Most VDT's and monitors have both brightness and contrast adjustment controls. The screen should be sufficiently bright to overcome incidental glare from lighting and windows, but excessive brightness can cause blurred screen characters and eye strain. Contrast may need to be adjusted for different software to make best use of background formats.

Image

All cathode-ray-tube devices—televisions, VDT's, etc.—eventually lose image quality. This usually takes years of normal use, but in time the phosphor coating on the screen deteriorates, causing loss of character resolution. Also, prolonged display of unchanged images causes these to be "burned" into the screen. Screen-saver features help prevent this. Turning off the VDT when not in use is also helpful. A VDT or monitor with a deteriorated image should be replaced.

Color

Various opinions have been put forth as to what color and type screens are best for long-term viewing. This may actually be a personal preference item. Color monitors offer the advantage of variety and selectability over monochrome devices. Certain color combinations are obviously distracting and will cause eye strain. Good contrast and image resolution are important no matter what color.

Screen Maintenance

Cleanliness of the screen is important. Smudges, dust, scratches, and so forth, cause the eye to attempt to focus in two planes simultaneously, causing strain. This is particularly noticeable if a glare filter is used over the front of the screen, and it is blemished. These should be virtually undetectable to the eye when in use.

Document Holders

Documents which are being read during typing should not be flat on the desk. They should be in a near vertical position, in the same focal plane as the VDT screen. Avoid any need to turn the head or change eye focus while typing. There is a wide selection of devices to hold paper and/or books in proper position, and price is not a good predictor of their suitability.

Corrective Lenses and VDT Use

Many visual problems associated with the use of VDT's can be traced directly to poor eye care. Uncorrected or improperly corrected vision problems are more likely to cause visual fatigue, and fatigue affects how well you can see, which in turn may make your work more difficult. The purpose of corrective lenses is to bring your vision back into an acceptable range. The use of corrective lenses should have no effect on your ability to use a VDT. Lenses recommended for VDT use, in usual order or preference, include:

- the monofocal
- the full-width bifocal, the flat-top bifocal
- the progressive addition lens

Bifocals can be a problem for VDT operations. Conventional reading-type bifocals may not be appropriate. If you must tilt your head back or into an uncomfortable position to see the screen, your glasses should be changed.

It is an important health measure for everyone to have periodic eye examinations to make sure any vision problems are discovered and quickly corrected. Operating a VDT, like performing any other close work, can be hard on the eyes.

Chairs

The single most important piece of office work station equipment is the chair. Various studies have shown that 25 to 50 percent of workers who habitually sit in incorrect chairs suffer from back problems.

A poorly designed or improperly selected chair will defy all attempts to achieve proper posture. If more than one person uses a computer work station, the chair should be easily adjustable; pneumatic-type adjustments are best for this.

Height

An actual measurement is important to determine proper chair height. The operator sits with both feet flat on the floor and with thighs and shins exactly perpendicular. Measure the distance from the hollow of the knees to the floor and subtract two inches. This is the correct height for the chair seat from the floor.

If the chair height is less than this optimum, the knees are elevated, preventing the thighs from supporting the proper amount of torso weight. This places stress on the buttocks and lower back. (Note than an average adult has over 100 pounds of torso weight; the greater the load-bearing surface, the better.)

If, on the other hand, the chair is too high, excessive pressure is placed on the thighs at the front edge of the seat, possibly causing loss of circulation to the lower legs. Chairs with worn-out cushions can cause this also, even at the correct height. A downward-turned front edge on the seat is a good design feature.

Adjustability

Most people will use whatever chair they are given. If it is not adjustable or can only be adjusted with great difficulty, they will use it as found. Loss of productivity is almost guaranteed due to back, leg and foot discomfort.

Back Rest

The lower curve of the back (the lumbar area) should be well supported by the chair back. The spine's normal, erect curvature should be maintained by the chair. Since people are proportioned differently, the chair-back elevation should also be adjustable. The best chairs have the capability to allow the back to be adjusted vertically and horizontally with respect to the seat.

Arm Rests

Arm rests are somewhat misnamed. They actually offer rest to the upper body by supporting the arms. Many people do not care for arm rests, although they are very beneficial. These objections often are related to experiences with full-length "executive chair" arm rests which prevent chairs from being positioned close enough to the desk. Proper arm rests need not be very long, but their height should be adjustable if more than one person uses the chair. The arm should be supported slightly while typing in the position described under "Keyboard Height."

Stability

Older office chairs usually were equipped with four legs and casters. These are potentially unstable and may tip if the person leans forward between two legs. Newer chairs have five legs. Casters should be selected for the type of floor surface. Carpet casters on a hard floor make for an "elusive chair" which may roll away from the sitter as he or she sits. Chair mats are needed for carpeted floors to prevent carpet wear and to make chair movement easier while seated.

Foot Support

Most people who must sit for prolonged periods find it more comfortable to have their feet in a slightly upward tilted position. This can be accomplished with homemade foot rests, but there are commercial products which offer adjustable angle and heights. Many people with chronic lower back problems are helped by using some type of foot support.

Desk/Workstation

Height

The desk height should allow proper arm alignment for keyboard use. Note that most conventional desks are made with work surfaces higher than this, and although they may be ideal for writing and other functions, they will put a keyboard much higher than it should be. Computer workstations usually provide a lower surface for a keyboard. There are retrofit, roll-out shelves available for conventional desks which put the keyboard at the proper height.

Work Area

At a minimum, the available surface area should accommodate the computer enclosure, the VDT or monitor, the document holder, and the keyboard, observing good position parameters. Flat-finish or non-glare surface colors help reduce reflected glare and associated eye strain.

Leg Room

Most people are comfortable if they have about 25 to 28 inches vertical distance from the underside of the work surface to the floor. Very tall individuals will need more distance. There should be sufficient space for some lateral leg movement, and the front-to-back space beneath the desk should allow for periodic stretching of legs. Storage of materials beneath the desk should be discouraged.

Office Environment

Noise

Noise is an unavoidable component of most offices. It does have a serious penalty, however. Stress, loss of concentration, and reduced productivity are all associated with noise. It is important to remember, too, that one person's music can be another's noise. In general, every effort should be made to keep nuisance noise to a minimum: phone ringing volume, office machinery, door slamming, etc. Many older computer printers generate excessive noise. Resilient padding underneath and in enclosures can help make them quieter. Office partitions often can help isolate or attenuate noise. Carpeting, drapery, and upholstery all absorb considerable noise energy.

Traffic

Traffic (as in people) in the work area is a powerful distraction. Visual barriers are often needed to screen people with high-concentration tasks from passersby. Some workstations have integral partitions. Arrangement of the office can reduce traffic in the vicinity of desks and workstations. Of course, a private office has certain advantages, too.

Wall Coverings

Wall paint or covering is a very effective means of controlling VDT screen glare. Basic white is a poor choice for an office where computers are in frequent use; light grays, tans, blues and greens are usually a better choice. Reflectivity is a specifiable item in paint selection. Textured wall coverings may be preferable to paint altogether in some settings.

Lighting

Lighting can enhance or hinder office operations. VDT screen glare is known to cause eye strain, headaches, loss of concentration, and loss of productivity. Unfortunately, computers often live in environments where other tasks are performed and where high illumination levels are needed. Lighting measurement is not always a straightforward process either. The most up-to-date guidelines for light levels address a number of variables such as reflectivity of the work surface, tasks performed, and so on. If you suspect a problem, ask your Environmental Health and Safety staff to evaluate the lighting in your work area.

Unless the VDT can be given its own room, it will likely be subject to excessive ambient light levels and glare. Windows are especially troublesome. Evaluate glare with the VDT turned off; the black screen offers the best potential surface for glare. Occasionally, a hood will be needed on a VDT to reduce stray light and glare on the screen.

Room lighting for computer-only operations can be much lower than for general offices: 20 to 50 foot-candles as opposed to 80 or more. Be aware, however, that many people feel uncomfortable at first in environments with this lower level of illumination.

Task lighting is often the best solution. Whole-room or ambient light level is kept to a safe (for walking) minimum, while individual work areas are lighted by desk lamps to the necessary levels. This usually offers considerable energy savings as well. New, modular office workstation systems carry this concept to an advanced degree.

Fluorescent Lighting

Usually, general-purpose fluorescent lighting is not the best choice for computer environments. It is usually installed with excessive illumination levels, and its light is well diffused, which promotes screen glare. This does not mean that all fluorescent lighting is unsuitable. It will likely benefit from some "fine tuning," however.

Tube Color. There are several choices of light hue in florescent tubes: cool white, warm white and full spectrum. There is some evidence that full spectrum causes less glare and is more pleasing to the average eye.

Diffusers. The grid or lens in a florescent fixture has a great deal of influence on glare properties. Egg-crate-types are often more desirable than prismatic types. Parabolic diffusers are perhaps best of all, although more expensive. They minimize lateral glare.

Windows

Nearly everyone wants a window near his or her desk. Natural light, however, diffusing through a window, is a powerful glare source. Try to locate the VDT to minimize glare. Windows near VDT's should have opaque blinds, and screens should be turned away from the window.

Glare is produced when light reflects onto the screen. Although its original source may have been overhead lights or a window, walls and other reflective surfaces can contribute.

Another related problem occurs when there is an illumination source within the field of vision of the operator while she attempts to focus on the screen or document. The pupils adjust their dilation for the eyes' total light field, and that may not be consistent with the illumination in the focus field: the screen and document. Eye strain and headaches are possible. Light-blocking partitions or repositioning the VDT are potential solutions.

Temperature and Humidity

The ideal office temperature is in the range of 72 to 75 degrees, with a relative humidity of 50 to 60 percent. Unfortunately, there are many possible reasons why these conditions cannot always be maintained. There are also biological differences in individuals' comfort levels, and majority rule is sometimes the only resolution.

Humidity is more important than many people realize—both for comfort and health. Excessive humidity, especially in warm weather, causes discomfort. Very low humidity, on the other hand, can cause irritation of mucous membranes, even to the extent of nose bleeds. Low humidity also promotes static electricity which can damage electronic devices.

Ventilation

All offices need fresh air to prevent normal indoor pollutants from reaching objectionable concentrations and to replenish oxygen we use in respiration. Fresh air is usually introduced into larger buildings by mechanical means: fan systems that blend outside air with heating or cooling supply air, and by exhaust fans which draw air through an area to replace the amount removed. The fan systems were designed for a certain number of occupants. If changes to space use and occupancy occur, the original ventilation design may be inadequate. It is important to coordinate space-use decisions with plant engineering to prevent problems later on with poor air quality.

Persistent or recurring odors may be an indication that an area is not getting sufficient fresh air. Mold and mildew growth is also a warning sign. Call plant engineering if you suspect there is a problem with your ventilation.

Radiation

In recent years, there has been a great deal of speculation and publicity about possible human health effects from radiation emitted from computer VDTs. Early cathode-ray tubes, including those used in televisions, could emit X rays: ionizing radiation. For many years, however, product manufacturing safety standards have made this problem negligible.

All electrical equipment can produce electromagnetic fields: non-ionizing radiation. Research to date has not established what, if any, low-level health effects are associated with this type of radiation. Even though VDTs have internal shielding, there can be detectable electromagnetic fields close by. The energy of these fields diminishes quickly with distance, so that an operator sitting at the typical distance from the VDT gets an extremely low exposure. Radiation from computer equipment is not a problem unless the shielding or case has been damaged or removed. Even in that instance, electrical shock is a much greater concern. Never use a piece of electronic equipment that you suspect is damaged.

Part Six

Infectious Disease Issues

Chapter 25

Occupational Infections in Health-Care Workers

As employers, hospital staff members or patient care providers, family physicians may be consulted about occupational exposures in health-care workers. Pathogens transmitted by blood and/or air have received considerable attention because of the initiatives for health-care workers enacted by the Occupational Safety and Health Administration (OSHA) in recent years. This chapter focuses on recent developments concerning the prevention of certain infections in health-care workers, as well as interventions that may be effective following exposure.

Blood-Borne Pathogens

Human Immunodeficiency Virus

By 1996, the Centers for Disease Control and Prevention (CDC) had documented 51 confirmed cases of occupational transmission of the human immunodeficiency virus (HIV) in health-care workers and 108 possible cases of transmission.[1] Most of the confirmed cases were caused by percutaneous injuries with used sharp instruments.

The CDC recently issued provisional guidelines for the chemoprophylaxis of health-care workers following an occupational exposure to blood or body fluids known to be infected with HIV.[2] These guidelines were recently reviewed in *American Family Physician*.[3]

Marian Swinker, "Occupational Infections in Health-Care Workers: Prevention and Intervention," used with permission from the December 1999, issue of *American Academy of Family Physicians*. All rights reserved.

The risk of seroconversion is generally estimated to be about 0.3 percent following a needle stick with HIV-positive blood, 0.1 percent after a mucous membrane splash and slightly less than 0.1 percent for a cutaneous splash on non-intact skin. The risk of seroconversion after an occupational exposure increases with the quantity of blood received and the source patient's viral load.[4] After a health-care worker has been exposed to HIV, surveillance for seroconversion should be continued for a minimum of six months.

Hepatitis B

An estimated 5 percent of the U.S. population carries antibody evidence of past hepatitis B virus (HBV) infection, and between 0.1 and 0.5 percent of Americans are chronic HBV carriers.[5] In recent years, the number of hepatitis B cases has declined only slightly in the general population.

The sequelae of hepatitis B infection are well known. Between 5 and 10 percent of HBV-infected adults develop chronic hepatitis with persistent infectivity, and 15 to 25 percent of chronically infected persons eventually develop cirrhosis or hepatocellular cancer.[5]

In the past, up to 30 percent of health-care workers in high-risk specialty areas (e.g., dialysis units) were infected by HBV.[6] However, the number of reported hepatitis B cases in health-care workers has declined significantly in recent years, from 12,000 cases in 1990[6] to 5,100 cases in 1995.[7] This decline occurred because of widespread adoption of preventive immunization, increased adherence to universal precautions, and use of personal protective equipment by health-care workers.

Standards established by OSHA require that hepatitis B vaccine be offered to all health-care workers who may be exposed to blood and body fluids as part of their job duties.[8] This protection should also be offered to other workers at risk for HBV infection, including hospital housekeeping personnel who clean up blood spills or encounter needle sticks from improperly discarded syringes, as well as plumbers and other maintenance personnel who dismantle the drains into which blood and body fluids are discarded.

The risk of HBV infection after percutaneous exposure varies from 2 percent if the patient is negative for the hepatitis B early antigen (HBeAg) to 40 percent if HBeAg is present. Overall, the estimated risk of HBV infection after an occupational exposure ranges from 20 to 30 percent.[9]

Hepatitis B vaccine can be highly effective, with 95 percent seroconversion rates cited in initial studies.[10] In practice, the vaccine is less effective, with reported seroconversion rates of 73 to 88 percent;[11,12] persons at risk for decreased seroconversion include males, smokers, the elderly and the very obese.

In health-care workers, post-vaccination testing for hepatitis B surface antibody (HbsAB) is helpful if it is performed within one to six months after the vaccine series has been completed.[13] However, post-vaccination testing is not required by OSHA and is not recommended for the general population.

In occupationally exposed patients, the results of post-vaccination testing are useful in determining who needs a booster (as part of the initial series) because of failure to seroconvert and who needs hepatitis B immune globulin (HBIG) after an exposure. Workers who initially seroconverted after vaccination do not need to be given HBIG following exposure to a patient who is positive for either HBeAg or hepatitis B surface antigen (HbsAg), even if the titer of antibody is undetectable at the time of the incident.[6] Antibody titers decline with time, but previous seroconverters should generate antibody if they are exposed to hepatitis B.[14]

While some persons fail to seroconvert after a three-shot hepatitis vaccine series, most convert after receiving four, five or even six doses. If no antibody response occurs after six injections, the general practice is to discontinue vaccine administration.

Hepatitis B vaccine is injected into the deltoid muscle because gluteal injection has been associated with failure to develop antibody. The vaccine is very safe, although anaphylactic reactions (one case per 600,000 doses) have been reported recently.[15] At present, routine booster doses of hepatitis B vaccine are not recommended.

Since the hepatitis B vaccine contains no infectious material, its administration is not contraindicated in pregnant women. However, few data are available on the actual use of the vaccine during pregnancy. Thus, its elective administration for general prevention is usually delayed until after delivery.[16] Vaccination may be considered if an infectious exposure occurs during pregnancy and the benefits of the vaccine are considered to be greater than the potential risk to the fetus.

Health-care workers who receive an occupational exposure to a blood-borne pathogen should receive a specific plan for treatment and follow-up care. [6]

Hepatitis C

While the prevalence of hepatitis B in health-care workers is diminishing, the relative proportion of blood-borne hepatitis C virus infections is increasing. Hepatitis C constitutes the majority of infections previously termed "non-A, non-B hepatitis."

Hepatitis C can lead to chronic hepatitis in 50 to 60 percent of cases and to persistent infection in 85 percent of cases. Clinically overt disease occurs in less than one third of infected persons.[7,15] Primary risk factors for hepatitis C include intravenous drug use and the receipt of blood transfusions before 1990. However, nearly one half of infected persons have no recognized risk factors.

The estimated prevalence of hepatitis C infection is about 1.0 percent in health-care workers [16] and less than 1 percent in the general population.[5] The prevalence of hepatitis C infection in hospitalized patients may be as high as 18 percent.[16] The risk of hepatitis C transmission from a needle stick has been found to be about 4 percent using antibody to hepatitis C for follow-up and about 10 percent using the more sensitive but less available HCV-RNA test.[15]

A hepatitis C-exposed health-care worker can be offered little prophylactically, since gamma globulin is ineffective, and interferon is used for treatment only. Surveillance for the development of hepatitis C after a valid blood- or body-fluid exposure should continue for six to nine months to detect hepatitis C antibody.

Airborne Pathogens

Tuberculosis

Tuberculosis may be considered both a nosocomial and an occupational infection. The incidence of *Mycobacterium (M.) tuberculosis* infection in health-care workers varies widely, depending on such factors as practice, location, patient population, and local prevalence of tuberculosis. The baseline prevalence of past tuberculous infection in health-care workers ranges from 1 to 28 percent.[17]

From 4 to 70 percent of health-care workers exposed to *M. tuberculosis* develop a positive skin test, with the risk being higher for those who perform bronchoscopy.[18] Without a known exposure, the yearly conversion rate for health-care workers averages from 0.1 to 5.0 percent.[17]

Nationally, the number of reported cases of tuberculosis increased by 14 percent from 1985 to 1993. Consequently, concern about this disease has increased, and more attention is now being given to control measures. To protect health-care workers and to reduce the risk of tuberculosis exposure, OSHA adopted the 1994 CDC guidelines for the prevention of *M. tuberculosis* transmission in health-care facilities.[19]

In 1997, OSHA published (in the Federal Register) a proposed rule for preventing occupational exposure to tuberculosis. This standard will supersede the CDC guidelines in January 1998.[20]

OSHA mandates that health-care facilities conduct a risk assessment, perform tuberculosis skin testing at least yearly and develop isolation procedures for potentially infectious tuberculosis patients in hospitals and in some outpatient settings.[19] When providing care for patients with tuberculosis, health-care workers must use respiratory protective devices, such as high-efficiency particulate filters (or other approved masks) or helmet-type, powered air-purifying respirators. The protective masks must be individually fitted to each worker.

Multiple drug-resistant strains of *M. tuberculosis* are an increasing occupational concern among health-care workers. These strains are frequently present in HIV-infected patients, and they are associated with a high mortality rate. Hospitals and other health-care facilities may be settings for the nosocomial transmission of drug-resistant strains of *M. tuberculosis*. Employee health practices may be affected in facilities where isoniazid (INH; Laniazid, Nydrazid) resistance occurs. If a health-care worker exposed to a drug-resistant strain of *M. tuberculosis* experiences a skin test conversion, the typical isoniazid prophylactic regimen may need to be modified or supplemented with one or more drugs to which the infecting organism is susceptible.

The purified protein derivative (PPD) skin test is the recommended instrument for tuberculosis screening in health-care workers.[19]

Health-care workers whose PPD tests have recently become positive should be evaluated for isoniazid prophylaxis after a chest radiograph is obtained to rule out active disease. Isoniazid is typically given prophylactically for six months to adults, nine months to children and 12 months to HIV-infected patients. Prophylactic therapy should be considered for health-care workers whose PPD test converts to positive during yearly surveillance, regardless of age, because these persons are at high risk for tuberculosis (i.e., recent conversion and contact with active tuberculosis).

Bacille Calmette-Guerin (BCG) vaccine is not routinely recommended for preventive use in health-care workers.[19] However, vaccination may be considered in unusual circumstances, such as for a health-care worker with significant repetitive exposure to patients with multidrug-resistant tuberculosis, when isoniazid prophylaxis could be ineffective.

The CDC recommends that health-care workers who have previously received BCG vaccine be screened with a yearly PPD skin test. The skin test is contraindicated only of the worker has experienced a large necrotic reaction to past PPD testing. This recommendation represents a change from past practice, which suggested no skin testing after the receipt of BCG vaccine.

Skin test reactions related to BCG vaccine typically decline in severity with time, and the vaccine is not completely effective in preventing infection. If a PPD skin test response increases in size during yearly surveillance, a new infection is suggested, rather than a reaction to previous BCG vaccination. PPD skin test results are interpreted no differently in BCG recipients than in non-vaccinated persons.

OSHA guidelines mandate the use of two-stage testing for tuberculosis in all new employees at risk for *M. tuberculosis* exposure who have not had a PPD skin test in the past year.[21] This two-stage procedure is used to detect a possible "boosting" effect that can occur when the first (falsely negative) PPD test leads to a "recall" of the immune response. A positive second test (given one to three weeks after the first test) constitutes a true positive if the CDC criteria are met.[19] A positive test indicates past tuberculosis exposure or infection and thus requires further evaluation. The boosting effect can persist for many months and can lead physicians to falsely consider a person enrolled in a yearly testing program to be a recent converter when tested for a second time. In actuality, the second text is a "booster-effect positive." This situation is the rationale for the two-step test requirement.

Boosting is most likely to occur in persons over 55 years of age or in BCG vaccine recipients. It can occur in 2 to 10 percent of the general population.[22,23] The overall incidence of boosting in health-care workers is not known.

The CDC guidelines allow decisions about the use of two-stage testing to be based on institutional data concerning the incidence of boosting in the facility. However, OSHA has chosen to enforce the use of the two-step procedure for new employees regardless of age or immune status, or the facility's data on boosting incidence.

No evidence exists showing that pregnancy affects the accuracy of PPD skin testing. The PPD test is safe and valid throughout pregnancy, and it has no known teratogenic effects.[19]

Varicella

Varicella (chickenpox) exposure in a non-immune health-care worker can be a significant problem. If infected, the worker will be contagious for one or two days before onset of the rash, during which time the varicella-zoster virus can be spread to non-immune or immunocompromised persons.

Varicella-zoster infection is almost always more severe in adults than in children. However, congenital varicella syndrome, which may occur after a maternal infection, can cause low birth weight, cutaneous scarring, limb hypoplasia, chorioretinitis, cataracts, and other anomalies. The risk of congenital varicella syndrome is highest in the first trimester of pregnancy (0.7 to 2.0 percent).[24] A non-immune pregnant woman who develops chickenpox near term can also transmit the varicella-zoster virus to her newborn. This infection can be severe or fatal.

The CDC recommends that non-immune employees be removed from work from days 10 through 21 following varicella exposure. Varicella-zoster immune globulin (VZIG) generally is not recommended for healthy workers, because it can prolong the incubation period by more than one week and is not 100 percent effective in preventing infection.[24]

Most adults have developed an immunity to varicella. A history of chickenpox is a very reliable indicator of this immunity. Furthermore, between 71 and 93 percent of adults with a negative or uncertain history are actually seropositive and thus are immune to varicella.[24] On the other hand, previous infection and antibody development are not 100 percent protective against re-infection with the varicella-zoster virus or recurrence of the infection as zoster. Chickenpox in an immune person may be mild and slightly atypical, with few lesions and minimal fever.

Varicella vaccine is recommended in health-care workers with no history of chickenpox who have tested negative for varicella antibody. The two shots in the vaccine series are delivered four to eight weeks apart, and 99 percent of recipients are reported to develop antibody. Following vaccination, health-care workers generally do not need to be removed from patient care, since the risk of viral transmission from a healthy vaccine recipient is minimal. However, 1 to 5 percent of adult vaccine recipients develop a varicella-like rash that sheds the virus at a low titer. A health-care worker who develops this rash should be removed from patient contact.[25]

Varicella vaccine is not recommended for use in pregnant women, HIV-positive persons, or persons with immune suppression or malignancy. Vaccination should be delayed for five months following the receipt of blood, plasma, immune globulin or VZIG.[24]

Pertussis

Over the past five years, the reported incidence of pertussis (whooping cough) has increased beyond recent historic limits.[26,27] Pertussis can be a life-threatening illness in infants, but childhood immunization has eliminated much of the morbidity and mortality in young children. However, pertussis vaccine is not given after the age of seven. Since immunity wanes with time, adolescents and adults can be susceptible to pertussis and serve as a reservoir of infection for children.

In adults, pertussis presents as a mild, atypical respiratory illness, usually without the characteristic whoop. Up to 25 percent of coughs lasting more than one week have been attributed to pertussis.[28] An estimated 50 million U.S. adults are susceptible to Bordetella pertussis infection, and 20 to 60 percent of the infections are asymptomatic.[29]

Pertussis can create serious problems in health-care settings. Mini-epidemics have occurred in hospitals where adults have transmitted pertussis to pediatric patients. The organisms that cause this illness are spread by direct contact with respiratory secretions. Caretakers can acquire the infection and perpetuate the cycle. The incubation period for pertussis is six to 20 days. If untreated, the illness can last four to eight weeks.[5]

Since specific testing of nasopharyngeal secretions is required, pertussis is seldom diagnosed in adults. The presence of a positive nasopharyngeal culture on Bordet-Gengou or Regan-Lowe medium is helpful, but the organisms that cause pertussis can be difficult to recover, especially in the later, paroxysmal-cough stage of the illness. Alternatively, direct fluorescent antibody testing of secretions can be used to make a presumptive diagnosis, but it is not especially sensitive or specific for pertussis. While polymerase chain reaction testing and enzyme-linked immunosorbent assay serology are more accurate, these tests are not widely available.

If an outbreak of pertussis occurs in a health-care setting, prophylactic treatment of health-care workers should be considered to stop the spread of disease, especially to children. For asymptomatic health-care workers, prophylaxis consists of a 14-day course of erythromycin, 500 mg four times per day, or a 14-day course of trimethoprim with sulfamethoxazole (Bactrim DS, Septra DS), one tablet twice daily. Prophylaxis should be started within three weeks of the pertussis exposure.[5,29] Azithromycin (Zithromax), 500 mg on the first day and 250 mg per day for the next four days, is a new alternative.[29] For all of these agents, treatment and prophylactic doses are the same.

If a health-care worker is symptomatic, a nasopharyngeal swab for culture is obtained. The person is removed from work, and antibiotic therapy is initiated. After a minimum of five days of treatment and if the person is asymptomatic, he or she may return to patient care.

Unfortunately, the nonspecific symptoms of pertussis in adults are similar to those of many other respiratory infections. Pertussis vaccine is not used in adults because of the high incidence of associated side effects. The new acellular pertussis vaccine is not officially recommended for adults. However, the administration of this vaccine to employees in one hospital effectively terminated a persistent pertussis outbreak.[30]

Final Comment

This chapter has reviewed only a few of the many blood-borne and airborne occupationally acquired infections that present problems for health-care workers.[31] Certain groups of health-care workers have been found to be at increased risk for acquiring specific infections (Table 25.1).[32] Other infections may be acquired by oral-fecal transmission (Table 25.2).[32]

OSHA has established guidelines for reducing the risk of occupational exposure to pathogens and for the treatment of health-care workers after an exposure. Control measures that can help to protect both workers and patients include immunizations, prophylactic antibiotic therapy (when indicated), the removal of potentially infectious persons from the work setting, work practices to reduce the risk of pathogen transmission and the use of personal protective equipment by health-care workers. Hand washing, vaccination, and the prompt and appropriate isolation of potentially infectious patients are simple, cost-effective strategies that help prevent occupationally acquired infections.[31]

How Can I Keep Myself from Getting an Infection at Work?

As a health-care worker, you may be exposed to many different sources of infection. Infections may be transmitted by blood or body fluids, by air or respiratory secretions, or by direct contact with other infectious materials. You can protect yourself from infection by following the infection control guidelines in your workplace, by using personal protective equipment like gloves and masks, and by following universal precautions (that is, handling all blood and body fluids as though they are infectious). This section discusses some of the infections that may be transmitted in your workplace and ways you may keep yourself from getting them.

What Are Blood-Borne Pathogens, and How Can I Protect Myself from Infection with Them?

Many infections can be spread by blood or body fluids. The human immunodeficiency virus (HIV) and the hepatitis B virus are common

Table 25.1. Occupationally Acquired Infections Encountered in Specific Groups of Health-Care Workers

Groups Affected	Infections
Laboratory workers	Neisseria meningitidis infection, brucellosis, Q fever, hepatitis, typhoid fever, tularemia, tuberculosis, dermatomycosis, Venezuelan-equine encephalitis, psittacosis, coccidioido-mycosis, rickettsiosis, arenavirus infection
Animal workers—includes veterinarians and animal laboratory workers	Cryptosporidiosis, cutaneous larvamigrans, toxocaral infection, lymphocytic choriomeningitis
Primate handlers	Simian B virus infection, hepatitis A, yellow fever, Marburg virus infection, tuberculosis, simian immunodeficiency virus infection, shigellosis
Pregnant health-care workers	Rubella, parvovirus B19 infection, cytomegalovirus infection, varicella, echovirus infection, coxsacidevims infection
Pregnant veterinarians	Brucellois, tuberculosis, cryptococcosis, listeriosis, lymphocytic choriomeningitis, Q fever, toxoplasmosis, Venezuelanequine encephalitis
Pathology workers	Tuberculosis, human immunodeficiency virus infection, hepatitis B, Creutzfeldt-Jakob disease, Legionnaires' disease, Lassafever virus infection, anthrax, group A streptococcal-infection, tetanus, typhoid fever
Surgery workers	Hepatitis B, other infections caused by blood-borne pathogens
Dentists	Hepatitis B, hepatitis C, herpetic whitlow, mumps, tuberculosis
Anesthesia workers	Hepatitis B, rhinovirus infection
Laundry workers	Smallpox, salmonellosis, hepatitis A, scabies, Q fever

examples. However, infections caused by other viruses and bacteria, such as syphilis and hepatitis C can also be spread by blood or body fluids. The guidelines below can help you protect yourself from blood-borne infections:

- Follow universal precautions. Consider every patient to be infected.

- Avoid contact with the blood or body fluids of all patients.

- Avoid risky behavior when using needles and other sharp instruments, including scissors, scalpels, blades and knives. For example, don't recap needles. Carefully dispose of sharp instruments in appropriate containers.

- Wear protective equipment, including gloves and face shields, to avoid getting blood on your skin or in your eyes when you're performing procedures that may cause splashes or spills.

- Be certain you are immunized against hepatitis B (this vaccine should be offered to you in your workplace).

Table 25.2. Occupationally Acquired Infections Resulting from Oral-Fecal Transmission

Infectious agent	Outbreak-associated attack rate	Health-care workers most affected
Salmonella	5 to 20	Nurses, laundry workers
Hepatitis A	20	Neonatal nurses
Shigella	Low	Nursery nurses
Cryptosporidium	31 to 67	Animal workers
Helicobacter pylori	Seroprevalence rate twice that of the general population	Endoscopy personnel
Clostridium difficile	Very low	None
Norwalk virus	30 to 50	Nurses, care attendants

Do All Body Fluids Transmit Blood-Borne Pathogens?

Body fluids such as tears, sweat, saliva, urine and vomitus are not thought to transmit blood-borne pathogens unless they are visibly contaminated with blood. (Urine or fecal material may contain bacteria or infectious agents that are not considered blood-borne pathogens, but you may wish to avoid them.) Most other body fluids, such as semen, vaginal secretions and pericardial, peritoneal, joint, amniotic and cerebrospinal fluids, can transmit blood-borne pathogens.

What Should I Do If I'm Exposed to Blood by a Cut, a Needle-Stick or a Splash?

If an incident occurs, tell your employer or the employee health service right away. If your skin is broken (by a needle-stick) or fluid has splashed into your eyes, your mouth or onto broken skin, both you and the source patient will be tested. Blood tests should verify that you're immune to hepatitis B and don't currently have a bloodborne infection. The source patient's current and past infections will also be checked.

If the source patient is infected with hepatitis B and, despite immunization, you never developed immunity to hepatitis B, you will be given hepatitis B immune globulin. If the source patient has syphilis, you will be offered antibiotics. If the source patient has HIV infection, you may take preventive medicines for four weeks. These medicines should be started within hours of the accident. You will have repeat blood tests for six to nine months, depending on the risks posed by the source patient. Thus, if any infection develops, it will be found as soon as possible.

What about a Splash of Blood on My Skin?

If your skin has no breaks, cracks, or rashes, you have virtually no risk of getting a blood-borne infection despite the splash of blood. If you do receive an exposure to your skin, immediately wash the affected area thoroughly.

How Can I Protect Myself from Tuberculosis Infection?

Tuberculosis is an infection caused by slow-growing bacteria. These bacteria can infect the lungs or any other body structures, including the brain, the skeleton, and the lymphatic system. You could catch tuberculosis by breathing in infected droplets that get into the air when infected people cough. It's important to know which patients might have tuberculosis. Infected patients may have symptoms such as a chronic cough (lasting for weeks and bringing up mucus or blood), weight loss, fever, or night sweats. If you work around these patients, wear a protective mask. Have these patients wear a mask also, to contain their secretions, and isolate them from other patients (that is, get them out of the waiting room in an office setting, or into isolation in the hospital setting).

How Will I Know If I Have Contracted Tuberculosis?

As a health-care worker, you should have a tuberculosis skin test once or twice a year. The test will determine if you have picked up the bacteria that causes tuberculosis, but the test won't tell if you have disease or active infection. A negative skin test means that you have not picked up the bacteria (unless you are HIV-positive or immunosuppressed). If you have any illnesses or take medicines that keep you from reacting to the tuberculosis skin test, you may need to have additional skin tests to see, if you are able to react to the test.

What Does a Positive Skin Test Mean?

If you have a positive reaction to the tuberculosis skin test, it usually means that you have been exposed to the bacteria, but there is a better than 90 percent chance that your body's immune system has suppressed the infection. When your skin test is found to be newly positive, you will have a chest radiograph to make sure that you don't have an active infection. If your chest radiograph is negative and your skin test reaction is recent, you may be given an antituberculous medicine for six to 12 months. This medicine is used to prevent any activation of the infection in the future, but you are not infectious to others.

What Does It Mean to Have Active Tuberculosis?

If you have a positive skin test and an abnormal chest radiograph or symptoms of tuberculosis, you'll be treated for active disease. When you're diagnosed with active disease, you're infectious to others. You may be treated with three or four medicines for nine to 12 months. You'll need to take precautions with your family, and you'll be kept out of work until you're no longer infectious. Active tuberculosis is much less common than skin test conversion.

313

If I Had Bacille Calmette-Guerin (BCG) Vaccine, Do I Need to Have a Skin Test?

If in the past you received BCG vaccine to prevent tuberculosis, you may have a mild reaction to the tuberculosis skin test, but you should still be tested. Usually, BCG reactions related to the tuberculosis skin test become less severe over time. If your skin test increases in size and intensity, it may indicate that you have been infected with tuberculosis, and you need to be treated. The BCG vaccine is not 100 percent protective, so you could still get tuberculosis even if you had the vaccination.

What Should I Do If I Learn That a Patient I Cared for Had Active Tuberculosis?

Unless you recently had your yearly tuberculosis test, you should have a baseline tuberculosis skin test if you are exposed to a patient with active tuberculosis, especially if the disease wasn't recognized, and isolation and masks were not used. A follow-up test in three months will show if the exposure resulted in infection.

If I Have a Positive Skin Test, Should I Continue to Be Tested?

Once you have had a positive skin test, you shouldn't continue to have skin tests because the tests almost always will be positive. Once you have a positive skin test, it's necessary to rely on symptoms to determine if you have tuberculosis. A chest radiograph should be obtained if you have a cough lasting for two to three weeks, if you are bringing up mucus with blood in it or if you have fever or weight loss. Routine yearly chest radiographs usually are not necessary.

If I Have a Positive Tuberculisis Skin Test, Should I Continue to Use Precautions?

Some people think that once they've been infected with the bacteria that causes tuberculosis, they don't need to take precautions or wear a mask when dealing with tuberculosis patients. Since there have been rare instances of persons being re-infected with a new tuberculosis strain, however, you should continue to take precautions.

If I Haven't Had Chickenpox, Should I Get the Varicella Vaccine?

Even if you don't have a history of chickenpox (varicella) infection, you should have a blood test to check for immunity. Most adults are immune to varicella, even if they have no history of the disease. If your test is negative, you should have the two-shot varicella vaccine series. If you aren't vaccinated, you're at risk of getting chickenpox and spreading it to patients.

I Have Had Chickenpox—Can I Get the Disease Again?

A history of chickenpox infection usually means that you are immune. However, some people do get chickenpox a second time. This can happen even if a blood test is positive for immunity. There is no 100 percent certain way to avoid this, but it happens only rarely. The disease is usually milder the second time. If you have a second round of chickenpox infection, tell your supervisor as soon as you find out you have the disease so you can avoid patient contact.

Why Is Whooping Cough a Concern? Isn't This Disease Prevented by Immunization?

Pertussis (whooping cough) can be life-threatening to unimmunized infants. After children are immunized, the immunity only lasts until they are teenagers. Because pertussis vaccine has side effects in older people, it's not given to adults and teenagers. This means teenagers and adults can get pertussis. Pertussis is responsible for some coughs or bronchitis that seem to "hang on" longer than the usual cold.

References

1. "Number of health-care workers with AIDS rose in 1996." *Occ Safety Health Reporter* 1996;26:659.

2. "Update: provisional Public Health Service recommendations for chemoprophylaxis after occupational exposure to HIV" MMWR *Morb Mortal Wkly Rep* 1996;45:468–80.

3. Perlmutter B, Harris BR. "New recommendations for prophylaxis after HIV exposure." *Am Fam Physician* 1997;55:507–12,515–7.

4.   "Case-control study of HIV seroconversion in health-care workers after percutaneous exposure to HIV-infected blood— France, United Kingdom, and United States, January 1988– August 1994." MMWR *Morb Mortal Wkly Rep* 1995;44:929–33.

5.   Benenson AS, ed. *Control of communicable diseases manual: an official report of the American Public Health Association. 16th ed.* Washington, D.C.: American Public Health Association, 1995.

6.   "Protection against viral hepatitis. Recommendations of the Immunization Practices Advisory Committee (ACIP)." MMWR *Morb Mortal Wkly Rep* 1990;39(RR-2):1–26.

7.   Chester TJ, Fedoruk MJ, Langley RL, Wilkinson C. "The hazards of working in health-care." *Patient Care* 1996;30(3):94–8.

8.   Occupational Safety and Health Administration. "Occupational exposure to bloodborne pathogens—final rule." *Fed Regis* 1991;56(235):64004–182.

9.   "Guidelines for prevention of transmission of human immunodeficiency virus and hepatitis B virus to health-care and public-safety workers." MMWR *Morb Mortal Wkly Rep* 1989;38 (Suppl 6):1–37 [Published erratum appears in MMWR *Morb Mortal Wkly Rep* 1989;38:7461.

10. "Update on hepatitis B prevention." MMWR *Morb Mortal Wkly Rep* 1987;36:353–60.

11. Roome AJ, Walsh SJ, Cartter ML, Hadler JL. "Hepatitis B vaccine responsiveness in Connecticut public safety personnel." *JAMA* 1993;270:2931–4.

12. Wood RC, MacDonald KL, White KE, Hedberg CW, Hanson M, Osterholm MT, et al. "Risk factors for lack of detectable antibody following hepatitis B vaccination of Minnesota health-care workers." *JAMA* 1993;270:2935–9.

13. Frymoyer CL. "Preventing the spread of viral hepatitis." *Am Fam Physician* 1993;48:1479–86.

14. Gerberding JL. "Management of occupational exposures to bloodborne viruses." *N Engl J Med* 1995;332:444–51.

15. "Update: vaccine side effects, adverse reactions, contraindications and precautions. Recommendations of the

Advisory Committee on Immunization Practices (ACIP)." MMWR *Morb Mortal Wkly Rep* 1996:45(RR-12):1–35 [Published erratum appears in MMWR Morb Mortal Wkly Rep 1997;46:7].

16. Davis GL. "Hepatitis C virus infection among health-care workers." *JAMA* 1996;275:1474.

17. Bowden K, McDiarmid M. "Occupationally acquired tuberculosis: what's known." *J Occup Med* 1994;36:320–5.

18. Sbarbaro JA. "Tuberculosis: yesterday, today, and tomorrow [Editorial]." *Ann Intern Med* 1995;129:955–6.

19. "Guidelines for preventing the transmission of Mycobacterium tuberculosis in health-care facilities, 1994." MMWR *Morb Mortal Wkly Rep* 1994;43(RR-13):1–132.

20. Occupational Safety and Health Administration. "Occupational exposure to tuberculosis—proposed rule." The Agency, 1977. 29 CFR Part 1910, docket no. H-371, RIN 1218-AB46:54160.

21. "Enforcement procedures and scheduling for occupational exposure to tuberculosis." Occupational Safety and Health Administration Instruction CPL 2.106, February 9, 1996. U.S. Department of Labor Office of Health Compliance Assistance: http://www. osha-sic.gov/oshdoc/directive data/ CPL_2_106.html.

22. Menzies R, Vissandjee B, Rocher 1, St Germain Y. "The booster effect in two-step tuberculin testing among young adults in Montreal." *Ann Intern Med* 1994;120:190–8.

23. Manusov EG, Bradshaw RD, Fogarty JR "Tuberculosis screening in medical students." *Fam Med* 1996;28:645–9.

24. "Prevention of varicella. Recommendations of the Advisory Committee on Immunization Practices (ACIP)." MMWR *Morb Mortal Wkly Rep* 1996;45(RR-11):1–36.

25. American Academy of Pediatrics Committee on Infectious Diseases. "Recommendations for the use of live attenuated varicella vaccine." *Pediatrics* 1995; 95:791–6 [Published erratum appears in *Pediatrics* 1995;96(1 Part 1): preceding 151 and fo llowing 171].

26. "Selected notifiable disease reports." MMWR *Morb Mortal Wkly Rep* 1996;45:1021.

27. "Pertussis—United States, January 1992–June 1995." MMWR *Morb Mortal Wkly Rep* 1995;44:525–9.

28. Herwaldt LA. "Pertussis in adults. What physicians need to know." *Arch Intern Med* 1991;151:1510–2.

29. Weber DJ, Rutala WA. "Management of health-care workers exposed to pertussis." *Infect Control Hosp Epidemiol* 1994; 15:411–5.

30. Shefer A, Dales L, Nelson M, Werner B, Baron R, Jackson R. "Use and safety of acellular pertussis vaccine among adult hospital staff during an outbreak of pertussis." *J Infect Dis* 1995;171:1053–6.

31. Sepkowitz KA. "Occupationally acquired infections in health-care workers. Part I." *Ann Intern Med* 1996;125:826–34.

32. Sepkowitz KA. "Occupationally acquired infections in health-care workers. Part 11." *Ann Intern Med* 1996;125:917–28.

—by Marian Swinker, M.D., M.P.H.

Marian Swinker, M.D., M.P.H. is professor in the Division of Occupational and Environmental Medicine at East Carolina University School of Medicine, Greenville, North Carolina, where she is also director of the Office of Prospective Health Residency. Dr. Swinker received her medical degree from Pennsylvania State University College of Medicine, Hershey, and her master of public health degree from the University of Pittsburgh (Pennisylvania) school of Medicine. In addition, she completed a residency in preventive/occupational medicine and family medicine at West Virginia University, Morgantown.

Chapter 26

Occupational Exposure to Tuberculosis

Introduction

The number of tuberculosis (TB) cases in the U.S. had been declining for decades until 1985, when TB rates suddenly began to surge upward. Today, TB has re-emerged as a major occupational health problem and a threat to public health.

The fight to stop the increase in TB had some successes in New York City by 1992, when the number of new cases began to fall. This promising trend has continued since then, but the World Health Organization (WHO) warns that the world remains on the verge of a tuberculosis pandemic. New York city is particularly vulnerable to such a threat, due to widespread homelessness and poverty, as well as high rates of immigration from areas where tuberculosis is common. As a result, many workplaces in the city continue to be high-risk settings for TB.

Fortunately, TB is preventable. This chapter explains what TB is, how to protect yourself against it and what your employer must do to eliminate or minimize the risk of TB transmission in the workplace.

Excerpted from "Occupational Exposure to Tuberculosis (TB)," New York Committee for Occupational Safety and Health (NYCOSH), from an undated web page, http://www.nycosh.org/tuberculosis.html. Reprinted by permission of the New York Committee for Occupational Safety and Health, www.nycosh.org.

What Is Tuberculosis (TB)?

TB is an infectious disease that is caused by a microscopic bacteria, which is spread from one person to another through the air. TB usually affects the lungs. TB can infect other parts of the body such as the brain or spine, but such cases are rare.

How Is TB Spread?

TB is spread when a person with active TB disease coughs, sneezes, speaks, or sings and releases tiny airborne droplets into the air, where they may remain suspended until they are inhaled. Prolonged exposure to airborne droplets in confined areas is particularly hazardous. TB is not spread through the skin, blood, or saliva. You cannot catch TB from food or any object. It is safe to touch utensils, clothing, furniture, books, telephones, etc. that have been in contact with someone who has TB.

What Is the Difference between Active TB Disease and TB Infection?

A person can have a TB infection and not have active TB disease. A person with TB bacteria living in his or her body has a TB infection, but if the person does not have any TB symptoms, they do not have active TB disease and they cannot give TB to anyone else. Only a person with active TB symptoms can transmit the disease to others.

Most people who are infected with TB will never develop active TB disease. Between 10 and 15 million people in the US are infected with TB, but 90% of them will never develop active disease.

Who Is Most at Risk for Getting Active TB Disease?

It is possible to get active TB disease shortly after the germs enter the body if the body is weak. It is also possible, even after many years, for inactive TB germs to become active when the body's immune system is weakened. This may be due to certain diseases or conditions such as:

- substance abuse
- serious illness such as diabetes or cancer
- human immunodeficiency virus (HIV) infection
- poor nutrition
- inadequate medical care

- certain types of medical treatment such as chemotherapy or organ transplants

Certain groups of people are also at increased risk of developing active disease including:

- people from countries with high rates of TB
- residents or workers in long term care facilities
- prisoners or staff of correctional facilities
- anyone in close prolonged contact with people with active TB disease

What Is the Test for TB?

A TB infection is identified by means of a skin test known as the Mantoux PPD test. A small needle is used to inject some harmless testing material, called tuberculin (purified protein derivative) just under the skin of the forearm. Within 48 to 72 hours, the skin test must be read by a trained health-care worker. A positive reaction means that you are infected with TB. This does not mean you have active disease.

What Happens If the Test Is Positive?

If you have a positive Mantoux PPD test, a chest x-ray will be done to see if the TB germs have started to damage the lungs. If the x-ray is normal, and there are no symptoms present, no other medical tests need to be done at this time. If the x-ray is normal and there are symptoms, or the x-ray is abnormal and there are no symptoms, more testing must be done.

What Are the Symptoms of Active TB Disease?

- a cough lasting longer than three weeks
- coughing up blood or sputum
- pain in the chest
- weakness or fatigue
- loss of appetite
- unexplained weight loss
- fever
- night sweats

How Is TB Treated?

Active TB disease can almost always be treated with the proper medication. Active TB disease is contagious, so people with active TB disease need to be isolated. This may occur in a hospital where they are isolated from other patients and health-care workers in a specially equipped and ventilated room. Or, they may be told to stay home for a few weeks, and follow special precautions, while taking medication.

The medication is a series of antibiotics which must be taken together for about six months to kill the TB bacteria. After taking the antibiotics for two to three weeks, if the drugs are working, the person generally need no longer be isolated. Despite feeling better, the patient must continue to take the medication every day for the six or more months it is prescribed.

What Is Multi-Drug-Resistant (MDR) TB?

MDR-TB is TB that is not responsive to multiple drug therapies. Nationally, about 15% of TB cases are resistant to at least one conventional TB drug. MDR-TB develops when patients start taking their medications and then stop before they are cured. When this happens, TB germs are not completely killed and will become active again and could become harder to treat. When that happens, people develop resistance to the standard TB drugs and then they must be treated with other medications, making it more difficult to fully recover. People with weakened immune systems, such as those with HIV infection, are also susceptible to multi-drug resistance. An MDR-TB strain can then be transmitted to others in the same manner that any TB is passed— through airborne droplets. Many communities have hired workers who watch TB patients take their medications to ensure that they are taking it all. This practice is known as directly observed therapy.

How Can the Transmission of TB Be Prevented?

- Education about how to recognize the symptoms of active TB disease is crucial to preventing its spread.

- Covering the mouth and nose of the infected person with a tissue can prevent infectious droplets from entering the air.

- Good ventilation prevents TB germs from remaining suspended.

- Ultraviolet light (which is found naturally in sunlight) kills TB bacteria in a few hours.

Is There a Vaccine for TB?

Some people from outside the U.S. have received a vaccine called Bacille Calmette-Guerin (BCG). Those who have received a BCG vaccine may have a positive reaction to the Mantoux Purified Protein Derivative (PPD) test. It is difficult to know if the positive reaction is due to the BCG vaccine or to real TB infection. Therefore, even if a person has had the BCG vaccine, a positive Mantoux PPD test should be handled the same as a TB infection.

Who Is at Risk of Occupational Exposure to TB?

Workers who come into close contact with people with undiagnosed or untreated active tuberculosis in their lungs are at high risk of acquiring TB infection. Workers in correctional facilities, homeless shelters, long-term care facilities, drug treatment centers, and health-care institutions have been identified by the Occupational Safety and Health Administration (OSHA) as being in the most danger. Certain workers within those facilities may be performing activities which put them at higher risk for TB. Other workers may also be at high risk despite the fact that they have not been included in OSHA's high-risk list. Workers in offices where low-income clients are serviced, such as public assistance offices, may be at risk. Institutions where there is poor ventilation and large numbers of people may also pose risks, such as schools, stock market trading floors, and gaming casinos. Outbreaks of TB have occurred in all those locations.

Occupational Exposure and the Law

Are There Legal Protections for Workers Exposed to TB?

There is a proposed OSHA standard (regulation) designed to protect high-risk workers from exposure to TB. It is not yet a law but is expected to become law by the end of the year 2000. Until then, OSHA has issued a directive: "Enforcement Procedures and Scheduling for Occupational Exposure to Tuberculosis" for use by its inspectors when determining if a workplace is at risk for TB exposure. This enforcement directive is based on guidelines published by OSHA. If employers who fall under the scope of the Enforcement Directive have not implemented the OSHA guidelines, the inspector may cite and fine the employer using the OSHA General Duty Clause, along with any other specific regulations which may be applicable. (The General Duty

Clause may be used by OSHA inspectors to cite and fine employers, if no specific OSHA standard exists to address the hazard.)

Below are some of the basic requirements of the OSHA Directive on Enforcement Procedures on Tuberculosis (used for implementing the OSHA Guidelines):

Coverage. The following workplaces/workers are covered by the Directive on Enforcement Procedures Tuberculosis:

- health-care facilities—where patients with confirmed or suspected TB are treated or housed

- correctional institutions

- long-term care facilities for the elderly

- homeless shelters

- drug treatment centers

- workers performing high-hazard procedures on suspect or active TB patients in non-hospital health-care settings such as doctors' offices, clinics, dental offices and home health-care activities

Inspections. OSHA will inspect workplaces to enforce this directive based on:

- employee complaints

- fatalities or catastrophes

- scheduled inspections of high-risk workplaces

Once in the workplace, OSHA will examine the records of the employer. They will conduct an inspection only if the facility has had a suspected or confirmed TB case within the previous six months, which OSHA believes confirms that a potential exposure exists. Then, upon inspection, OSHA will issue citations if it believes workers have potential exposure to exhaled air of an individual with suspected or confirmed active TB disease. They will also issue citations if workers are exposed to a high-hazard procedure performed on an individual with suspected or confirmed TB and which has the potential to generate infectious germs.

OSHA will ask for the employer's infection-control plan to determine what, if any, controls are in place to prevent workers from TB exposure. Citations and fines will be issued if the infection control plan is not protective enough of the workers. If the employer does not have an infection-control plan, OSHA will require that the employer develop the following program (based on the OSHA guidelines):

Methods for early identification of TB. Early recognition of signs and symptoms of active TB disease is a crucial step in preventing its spread.

Medical program.

- *Testing*. All workers covered by this directive must be offered the Mantoux PPD skin test free of charge and at a time and place convenient to them. All newly hired workers must also be tested. Follow-up testing must be conducted every three months, six months, or yearly depending of the level of risk faced by each worker.

- *Medical follow-up*. The employer must evaluate and provide medical follow-up to those workers who test positive showing they have TB infection as well as those who show symptoms of active disease. If a worker has an incident where they have been exposed to a potentially infectious TB patient, they must be tested immediately following the exposure and then again 12 weeks later—at the employer's expense.

Isolation rooms. Individuals with suspected or confirmed cases of active TB disease must be placed in isolation rooms (known as AFB rooms). High-hazard procedures being performed on these persons must also be conducted in isolation rooms. These rooms must be maintained under negative air pressure with the exhaust vented either directly to the outside or through properly designed, installed, and maintained high efficiency particulate air (HEPA) filters.

Training and education. Workers must be trained on TB transmission, its signs and symptoms, medical testing and treatment and site-specific programs regarding the purpose and use of certain protective devices.

Respiratory protection. The law requires that respirators be provided when necessary to protect worker health. The employer must develop a complete respiratory protection program which must insure that workers are using the correct respirators, that the respirators are properly fitted to the worker and that the respirators are properly maintained.

Respirators must be used under the following circumstances:

- when workers enter rooms housing individuals with suspected or confirmed active TB

- when workers are present during the performance of high hazard procedures on individuals with suspected or confirmed active TB

- when emergency-medical-response personnel or others transport, in a closed vehicle, an individual with suspected or confirmed active TB

Employers must provide respirators which have been certified by the National Institute for Occupational Safety and Health (NIOSH) which is the research arm of OSHA. The certified respirators for use against TB are High Efficiency Particulate Air (HEPA) respirators which are 99% effective against TB or Type N95 respirators which are 95% effective against TB.

Recordkeeping. The employer must record any case of TB infection or active TB disease which is found by workplace TB testing. Reporting must be done on the OSHA 200 logs or, for public sector workers, Division of Safety and Health (DOSH) 900 logs.

Tips for Unions

- Fight to insure the OSHA guidelines are enforced.

- Use your health and safety committee to request and evaluate your employer's infection-control plan for TB.

- Encourage the employer to provide HEPA respirators which are more protective than the Type N95 which are also allowed by the OSHA directive.

- Push the employer to develop a TB control plan with input from the union. If the workplace is not covered by the enforcement directive, unions should strive to force the employer to put policies in place to prevent the transmission of TB. The plan should include:

  - education of workers about the symptoms of active TB disease and how it is transmitted, to assist them in identifying TB in the workplace

326

- allowing workers to insist that patients, clients, students or customers who exhibit the symptoms of TB cover their mouths with a tissue to avoid exposing others

- periodic examination of the ventilation systems to insure it is in good working order to reduce the possibility of transmitting disease

- availability of Mantoux PPD testing for workers

The text in this chapter was excerpted from "Occupational Exposure to Tuberculosis (TB)," New York Committee for Occupational Safety and Health (NYCOSH), from an undated web page, http://www.nycosh.org/tuberculosis.html, used with permission. The NYCOSH website (http://www.nycosh.org) contains news and information about on-the-job safety and health, plus hundreds of links to more information you can use to enhance occupational safety. Feedback about the website should be directed to webmanager@nycosh.org.

New York Committee for Occupational Safety and Health (NYCOSH)
275 7th Avenue
New York, NY 10001
Phone: (212) 627-3900
E-mail: nycosh@nycosh.org
Website: http://www.nycosh.org

Chapter 27

Risks and Recommendations for Human Immunodeficiency Virus (HIV) Occupational Exposures

General Information on Occupational Exposures to Human Immunodeficiency Virus (HIV)

Introduction

Health-care workers are at risk for occupational exposure to the human immunodeficiency virus (HIV). Exposures occur through needle-sticks or cuts from other sharp instruments (percutaneous exposures) contaminated with an infected patient's blood or through contact of the eye, nose, or mouth (mucous membrane) or skin with a patient's blood.

Most exposures do not result in infection. The risk of infection varies with the type of exposure and factors such as:

- the amount of blood involved in the exposure
- the amount of virus in the patient's blood at the time of exposure
- whether post-exposure treatment was taken.

Your employer should have in place a system for reporting exposures in order to quickly evaluate the risk of infection from the exposure, counsel you about recommendations for treatments available to prevent infection, and monitor you for side effects of treatments and

"Occupational Exposure to HIV," National Center for Infectious Diseases Centers for Disease Control and Prevention, http://www.cdc.gov/ncidod/hip/faq.htm, January 2000.

determine if infection occurs. This may involve testing your blood and that of the source patient and offering appropriate post-exposure treatment.

How Can Occupational Exposures Be Prevented?

Many needle-sticks and other cuts can be prevented by using medical devices with safety features designed to prevent injuries, by using safer techniques (e.g., not recapping needles by hand), and by disposing of used needles in appropriate sharps disposal containers. Many exposures to the eyes, nose, mouth, or skin can be prevented by using appropriate barriers (e.g., gloves, eye and face protection, gowns) when contact with blood is expected.

If an Exposure Occurs

What Should I Do If I Am Exposed to the Blood of a Patient?

1. Immediately following an exposure to blood:

   - Needle-sticks and cuts should be washed with soap and water.

   - Splashes to the nose, mouth, or skin should be flushed with water.

   - Eyes should be irrigated with clean water, saline, or sterile irrigants.

No scientific evidence shows that the use of antiseptics for wound care or squeezing the wound will reduce the risk of transmission of HIV. The use of a caustic agent such as bleach is not recommended.

2. Following any blood exposure you should:

   - Report the exposure to the department (e.g., occupational health, infection control) responsible for managing exposures. Prompt reporting is essential because, in some cases, HIV post-exposure treatment may be recommended and it should be started as soon as possible—preferably within 1–2 hours.

   - In addition to HIV, discuss the possible risks of acquiring hepatitis B and hepatitis C with your health care provider. You should have already received hepatitis B vaccine, which is extremely safe and effective in preventing hepatitis B.

Risk of Infection after Exposure

What Is the Risk of HIV Infection after an Occupational Exposure?

While the risk is very low, it is not zero. HIV infection has been reported after occupational exposures to HIV-infected blood through needlesticks or cuts; splashes in the eyes, nose, or mouth; and skin contact.

- Exposures from needle-sticks or cuts cause most infections. The average risk of HIV infection after a needle-stick/cut exposure to HIV-infected blood is 0.3% (i.e., three-tenths of one percent, or about 1 in 300). Stated another way, 99.7% of needle-stick/cut exposures do not lead to infection.

- The risk after exposure of the eye, nose, or mouth to HIV-infected blood is estimated to be, on average, 0.1% (1 in 1,000).

- The risk after exposure of the skin to HIV-infected blood is estimated to be less than 0.1%. A small amount of blood on intact skin probably poses no risk at all. There have been no cases of HIV transmission documented due to an exposure involving a small amount of blood on intact skin. The risk may be higher if the skin is damaged (e.g., by a recent cut) or if the contact involves a large area of skin or is prolonged.

Risk from all exposures is probably increased if the exposure involves a larger volume of blood or a higher amount of HIV in the patient's blood. (Source-patients near death with AIDS or patients with symptoms of acute HIV infection usually have higher amounts of HIV in their blood.)

How Many Health-Care Workers Have Been Infected with HIV Occupationally and under What Circumstances?

As of December 1996, the Centers for Disease Control and Prevention (CDC) had received reports of 52 documented cases and 111 possible cases of occupationally acquired HIV infection among Health Care Workers in the United States.

The 111 possible cases were in health-care workers who reported an occupational exposure to blood, body fluids, or HIV-infected laboratory material, and who did not have any other identifiable behavioral or transfusion risk for HIV infection. However, for these workers, infection specifically resulting from an occupational exposure was not documented.

Treatment for the Exposure

Is Treatment Available after an Occupational Exposure to HIV?

Yes. Results from a small number of studies suggest that the use of zidovudine (ZDV) and other antiviral drugs after certain occupational exposures may reduce the chance of HIV transmission. In one study the use of ZDV after HIV exposure from a needle-stick or cut reduced the risk of HIV infection by almost 80%.

Will Treatment after Exposure Prevent HIV Infection?

These studies suggest that post-exposure treatment may prevent infection with HIV. However, because there have been at least 12 reported cases of ZDV failing to prevent HIV infection in health-care

Table 27.1. Health-Care Workers with Documented Occupationally Acquired HIV Infection

Type of occupational exposure	Number
Needle-stick or cuts	45
Eye, nose, or mouth, and/or skin	5
Both injury and mucous membrane	1
Unknown	1
TOTAL	52

Table 27.2. Type of Fluid Involved in Exposure

Type of fluid involved in exposure	Number
Blood	47
Concentrated virus in a laboratory	3
Visibly bloody fluid	1
Unspecified fluid	1
TOTAL	52

workers, post-exposure treatment will probably not prevent all cases of infection transmission.

Is Post-Exposure Treatment Recommended for All Types of Occupational Exposures to HIV?

No. Because most occupational exposures do not lead to HIV infection, the chance of possible serious side effects (toxicity) from the drugs used to prevent infection may be much greater than the chance of HIV infection from such exposures. Both risk of infection and possible side effects of drugs should be carefully considered when deciding whether to take post-exposure treatment. Exposures with a lower infection risk may not be worth the risk of the side effects associated with these drugs.

What about Exposures to Blood for Which the HIV Status of the Source Person is Unknown?

If the source individual cannot be identified or tested, decisions regarding follow-up should be based on the exposure risk and whether the source is likely to be a person who is HIV positive. Follow-up HIV testing should be available to all workers who are concerned about possible HIV infection through occupational exposure.

Treatments Available

What Specific Drugs Are Recommended for Post-Exposure Treatment?

In June 1996, the Public Health Service recommended that zidovudine (ZDV), lamivudine (3TC), and a protease inhibitor, preferably indinavir (IDV), be used as follows:

- ZDV should be considered for treatment of all exposures involving HIV-infected blood, fluid containing visible blood, or other potentially infectious fluid or tissue.

- 3TC should be added to ZDV for increased effectiveness and for use against ZDV-resistant types of virus. Used in combination, ZDV and 3TC are very effective in treating HIV infection, and considerable information shows that they are safe when used for a short time.

- IDV should be added for the highest risk exposures, such as those involving a larger volume of blood with a larger amount of

HIV. IDV is a potent antiviral drug that appears to be safe when taken for a short period, although less information is available about the safety of this drug.

Can Other Antiviral Drugs Be Used or Substituted If These Drugs Are Not Available?

These recommendations are intended to provide guidance to clinicians and may be modified on a case-by-case basis. Whenever possible, consulting an expert with experience in the use of antiviral drugs is advised, especially if a recommended drug is not available, if the source patient's virus is likely to be resistant to one or more recommended drugs, or if the drugs are poorly tolerated.

Should Zidovudine Ever Be Used Alone?

ZDV alone may be considered for some lower risk exposures when the virus is likely to be sensitive to the drug.

How Soon after Exposure to HIV Should Treatment Start?

Treatment should be started promptly, preferably within 1–2 hours, after the exposure. Although animal studies suggest that treatment is not effective when started more than 24–36 hours after exposure, it is not known if this time frame is the same for humans. Starting treatment after a longer period (for example, 1–2 weeks) may be considered for the highest risk exposures; even if HIV infection is not prevented, early treatment of initial HIV infection may lessen the severity of symptoms and delay the onset of AIDS.

How Long Do the Drugs Need to Be Taken?

The optimal course of treatment is unknown; because 4 weeks of ZDV appears to provide protection against HIV infection, if tolerated, treatment should probably be taken for 4 weeks.

Has the Food and Drug Administration (FDA) Approved These Drugs to Prevent HIV Following an Occupational Exposure?

No. The FDA has approved these drugs for the treatment of HIV infection, but not for preventing infection. However, physicians may prescribe any approved drug when, in their professional judgment, the use of the drug is warranted.

Safety and Side Effects

What Is Known about the Safety and Side Effects of These Drugs?

Most of the information known about the safety and side effects of these drugs is based on studies of their use in HIV-infected individuals. For these individuals, ZDV and 3TC have usually been well tolerated when taken in the doses recommended. There is less information about IDV, but it also may be well tolerated when used for a short period. IDV should not be used in combination with certain other drugs, including some prescription antihistamines (consult your health-care provider). Some of the more frequent side effects reported in HIV-infected patients include the following:

- upset stomach (for example, nausea, vomiting, diarrhea), tiredness, or headache for people taking ZDV

- upset stomach and, in rare instances, pancreatitis for people taking 3TC

- jaundice and kidney stones in people taking IDV, although these side effects are infrequent when IDV is taken for less than one month. The risk of kidney stones may be reduced by drinking 48 oz of fluid per 24-hour period.

There is some information about ZDV use by health-care workers as post-exposure treatment. ZDV is usually tolerated, but reported side effects have included upset stomach, tiredness, and headache, all of which stopped when the drug was stopped. There is little information on the side effects of 3TC or IDV in uninfected individuals.

Should Pregnant Health-Care Workers Take These Drugs?

Based on limited information, ZDV taken in the second and third trimesters of pregnancy has not caused serious side effects in mothers or infants. There is very little information on the safety of ZDV when taken during the first trimester or on the safety of other antiviral drugs taken during pregnancy. If you are pregnant at the time you have an occupational exposure to HIV, you should consult a physician about the use antiviral drugs for post-exposure treatment.

Follow-Up after the Exposure

What Follow-Up Should Be Done after an Exposure?

- You should be tested for HIV antibody as soon as possible after exposure (baseline), and periodically for at least 6 months after the exposure (e.g., at 6 weeks, 12 weeks, and 6 months).

- If you take antiviral drugs for post-exposure treatment, you should be checked for drug toxicity, including a complete blood count and kidney and liver function tests just before starting treatment and 2 weeks after starting treatment.

- You should report any sudden or severe flu-like illness that occurs during the follow-up period, especially if it involves fever, rash, muscle aches, tiredness, malaise, or swollen glands. Such an illness or symptoms may suggest HIV infection, drug reaction, or other medical conditions.

- You should contact your health-care provider if you have any questions or problems during the follow-up period.

What Precautions Should Be Taken during the Follow-Up Period?

During the follow-up period, especially the first 6–12 weeks when most infected persons are expected to show signs of infection, you should follow recommendations for preventing transmission of HIV. These include refraining from blood, semen, or organ donation and abstaining from sexual intercourse. If you choose to have sexual intercourse, using a latex condom consistently and correctly may reduce the risk of HIV transmission. In addition, women should not breast-feed infants during the follow-up period to prevent exposing their infants to HIV in breast milk.

HIV Post-Exposure Prophylaxis Registry

What is Being Done to Learn More about the Use of Antiviral Drugs for Treatment after an Occupational Exposure to HIV?

Because information is limited about the side effects/toxicity of antiviral drugs in uninfected people, like you, the Centers for Disease Control and Prevention, Glaxo Wellcome Inc., and Merck and Co., Inc., have begun the HIV Post-exposure Prophylaxis (PEP) Registry, to collect information about the safety, tolerability, and outcome of taking antiviral drugs for post-exposure treatment.

What Kind of Information Will Be Collected by the Registry?

If you give permission, your health-care provider will provide information to the Registry about the exposure, the antiviral drugs taken, abnormal laboratory findings, and physical symptoms associated with the use of these drugs. Participation is voluntary and confidential. No information that would identify you will be collected.

How Can I Learn More about or Enroll in the Registry?

Ask your health-care provider; he or she can obtain information about the Registry by calling toll-free 1-888-PEP4HIV (1-888-737-4448).

Other Sources of Information

Please see the Resources section of the sourcebook for information on how to learn more about health-care workers and occupational exposures to HIV.

Part Seven

Toxins, Hazardous Chemicals, Electromagnetic Fields, and Cancer in the Workplace

Chapter 28

Occupational Lead Poisoning

Lead

What Is Lead?

Lead is a naturally occurring bluish-gray metal found in small amounts in the earth's crust. It has no special taste or smell. Lead can be found in all parts of our environment. Most of it came from human activities like mining, manufacturing, and the burning of fossil fuels. Lead has many different uses, most importantly in the production of batteries. Lead is also in ammunition, metal products (solder and pipes), roofing, and devices to shield x-rays.

Because of health concerns, lead from gasoline, paints and ceramic products, caulking, and pipe solder has been dramatically reduced in recent years.

What Happens to Lead When It Enters the Environment?

- Lead itself does not break down, but lead compounds are changed by sunlight, air, and water.

This chapter includes text from "Lead," an Agency for Toxic Substances and Disease Registry (ATSDR) fact sheet, CAS. No. 7439-92-1, http://www.atsdr. cdc gov/tfacts13.html, April 1993, and "Substance Data Sheet for Occupational Exposure to Lead—1910.1025 App A," Occupational Safety and Health Administration (OSHA), http://www.osha-slc.gov/OshStd_data/1910_1025_APP_A.html, May 31, 1991. Despite the age of this document, readers seeking an understanding of occupational lead poisoning will still find the information useful.

- When released to the air from industry or burning of fossil fuels or waste, it stays in air about 10 days.

- Most of the lead in soil comes from particles falling out of the air.

- City soils also contain lead from landfills and leaded paint.

- Lead sticks to soil particles.

- It does not move from soil to underground water or drinking water unless the water is acidic or "soft."

- It stays a long time in both soil and water.

Has the Federal Government Made Recommendations to Protect Human Health?

- The Centers for Disease Control and Prevention (CDC) recommends all children be screened for lead poisoning at least once a year. This is especially important for children between 6 months and 6 years old.

- The Environmental Protection Agency (EPA) requires lead in air not to exceed 1.5 micrograms per cubic meter (1.5 $\mu g/m^3$) averaged over 3 months. The sale of leaded gasoline was illegal as of December 31, 1995. EPA limits lead in drinking water to 15 micrograms per liter (15 $\mu g/L$).

- The Consumer Product Safety Commission (CPSC), EPA, and the states control the levels of lead in drinking water coolers. Water coolers that release lead must be recalled or repaired. New coolers must be lead-free. Drinking water in schools must be tested for lead.

- The Department of Housing and Urban Development (HUD) requires that federally funded housing and renovations, public housing, and Indian housing be tested for lead-based paint hazards. Hazards must be fixed by covering the paint or removing it.

- The Occupational Safety and Health Administration (OSHA) limits the concentration of lead in workroom air to 50 μg/cubic meter for an 8-hour workday. If a worker has a blood lead level of 40 $\mu g/dL$, OSHA requires that worker to be removed from the workroom.

Substance Data Sheet for Occupational Exposure to Lead

Uses of Lead

Exposure to lead occurs in at least 120 different occupations, including primary and secondary lead smelting, lead storage battery manufacturing, lead pigment manufacturing and use, solder manufacturing and use, shipbuilding and ship repairing, auto manufacturing, and printing.

Ways in Which Lead Enters Your Body

When absorbed into your body in certain doses lead is a toxic substance. Lead can be absorbed into your body by inhalation (breathing) and ingestion (eating). Lead (except for certain organic lead compounds such as tetraethyl lead) is not absorbed through your skin. When lead is scattered in the air as a dust, fume, or mist it can be inhaled and absorbed through your lungs and upper respiratory tract. Inhalation of airborne lead is generally the most important source of occupational lead absorption. You can also absorb lead through your digestive system if lead gets into your mouth and is swallowed. If you handle food, cigarettes, chewing tobacco, or make-up which have lead on them or handle them with hands contaminated with lead, this will contribute to ingestion.

A significant portion of the lead that you inhale or ingest gets into your blood stream. Once in your blood stream, lead is circulated throughout your body and stored in various organs and body tissues. Some of this lead is quickly filtered out of your body and excreted, but some remains in the blood and other tissues. As exposure to lead continues, the amount stored in your body will increase if you are absorbing more lead than your body is excreting. Even though you may not be aware of any immediate symptoms of disease, this lead stored in your tissues can be slowly causing irreversible damage, first to individual cells, then to your organs and whole body systems.

Effects of Overexposure to Lead

Short-Term (Acute) Overexposure

Lead is a potent, systemic poison that serves no known useful function once absorbed by your body. Taken in large enough doses, lead

343

can kill you in a matter of days. A condition affecting the brain called acute encephalopathy may arise which develops quickly to seizures, coma, and death from cardiorespiratory arrest. A short term dose of lead can lead to acute encephalopathy. Short term occupational exposures of this magnitude are highly unusual, but not impossible. Similar forms of encephalopathy may, however, arise from extended, chronic exposure to lower doses of lead. There is no sharp dividing line between rapidly developing acute effects of lead, and chronic effects which take longer to acquire. Lead adversely affects numerous body systems and causes forms of health impairment and disease which arise after periods of exposure as short as days or as long as several years.

Long-Term (Chronic) Overexposure

Chronic overexposure to lead may result in severe damage to your blood-forming, nervous, urinary, and reproductive systems. Some common symptoms of chronic overexposure include loss of appetite, metallic taste in the mouth, anxiety, constipation, nausea, pallor, excessive tiredness, weakness, insomnia, headache, nervous irritability, muscle and joint pain or soreness, fine tremors, numbness, dizziness, hyperactivity and colic. In lead colic there may be severe abdominal pain.

Damage to the central nervous system in general and the brain (encephalopathy) in particular is one of the most severe forms of lead poisoning. The most severe, often fatal, form of encephalopathy may be preceded by vomiting, a feeling of dullness progressing to drowsiness and stupor, poor memory, restlessness, irritability, tremor, and convulsions. It may arise suddenly with the onset of seizures, followed by coma, and death. There is a tendency for muscular weakness to develop at the same time. This weakness may progress to paralysis often observed as a characteristic "wrist drop" or "foot drop" and is a manifestation of a disease to the nervous system called peripheral neuropathy.

Chronic overexposure to lead also results in kidney disease with few, if any, symptoms appearing until extensive and most likely permanent kidney damage has occurred. Routine laboratory tests reveal the presence of this kidney disease only after about two-thirds of kidney function is lost. When overt symptoms of urinary dysfunction arise, it is often too late to correct or prevent worsening conditions, and progression to kidney dialysis or death is possible.

Chronic overexposure to lead impairs the reproductive systems of both men and women. Overexposure to lead may result in decreased sex drive, impotence, and sterility in men. Lead can alter the structure of sperm cells raising the risk of birth defects. There is evidence of miscarriage and stillbirth in women whose husbands were exposed to lead or who were exposed to lead themselves. Lead exposure also may result in decreased fertility and abnormal menstrual cycles in women. The course of pregnancy may be adversely affected by exposure to lead since lead crosses the placental barrier and poses risks to developing fetuses. Children born of parents either one of whom were exposed to excess lead levels are more likely to have birth defects, mental retardation, behavioral disorders, or die during the first year of childhood.

Overexposure to lead also disrupts the blood-forming system resulting in decreased hemoglobin (the substance in the blood that carries oxygen to the cells) and ultimately anemia. Anemia is characterized by weakness, pallor and fatigability as a result of decreased oxygen carrying capacity in the blood.

Prevention of Lead Poisoning

Prevention of adverse health effects for most workers from exposure to lead throughout a working lifetime requires that worker blood lead (PbB) levels be maintained at or below forty micrograms per one hundred grams of whole blood (40 μg/100g). The blood lead levels of workers (both male and female workers) who intend to have children should be maintained below 30 μg/100g to minimize adverse reproductive health effects to the parents and to the developing fetus. The measurement of your blood lead level is the most useful indicator of the amount of lead being absorbed by your body.

Blood lead levels (PbB) are most often reported in units of milligrams (mg) or micrograms (μg) of lead (1 mg=1000 μg) per 100 grams (100g), 100 milliliters (100 ml) or deciliter (dl) of blood. These three units are essentially the same. Sometime PbB's are expressed in the form of mg% or μg%. This is a shorthand notation for 100g, 100 ml, or dl.

PbB measurements show the amount of lead circulating in your blood stream, but do not give any information about the amount of lead stored in your various tissues. PbB measurements merely show current absorption of lead, not the effect that lead is having on your body or the effects that past lead exposure may have already caused. Past research into lead-related diseases, however, has focused heavily on associations between PbBs and various diseases. As a result, your PbB is an important indicator of the likelihood that you will gradually acquire a lead-related health impairment or disease.

Once your blood lead level climbs above 40 μg/100g, your risk of disease increases. There is a wide variability of individual response to lead, thus it is difficult to say that a particular PbB in a given person will cause a particular effect. Studies have associated fatal encephalopathy with PbBs as low as 150 μg/100g. Other studies have shown other forms of diseases in some workers with PbBs well below 80 μg/100g. Your PbB is a crucial indicator of the risks to your health, but one other factor is also extremely important. This factor is the length of time you have had elevated PbBs. The longer you have an elevated PbB, the greater the risk that large quantities of lead are being gradually stored in your organs and tissues (body burden). The greater your overall body burden, the greater the chances of substantial permanent damage.

The best way to prevent all forms of lead-related impairments and diseases—both short term and long term—is to maintain your PbB below 40 μg/100g. The provisions of the Occupational Safety and Health Administration's (OSHA) lead standard are designed with this end in mind. Your employer has prime responsibility to assure that the provisions of the standard are complied with both by the company and by individual workers. You as a worker, however, also have a responsibility to assist your employer in complying with the standard. You can play a key role in protecting your own health by learning about the lead hazards and their control, learning what the standard requires, following the standard where it governs your own actions, and seeing that your employer complies with provisions governing his actions.

Reporting Signs and Symptoms of Health Problems

You should immediately notify your employer if you develop signs or symptoms associated with lead poisoning or if you desire medical advice concerning the effects of current or past exposure to lead on your ability to have a healthy child. You should also notify your employer if you have difficulty breathing during a respirator fit test or while wearing a respirator. In each of these cases your employer must make available to you appropriate medical examinations or consultations. These must be provided at no cost to you and at a reasonable time and place.

References

Agency for Toxic Substances and Disease Registry (ATSDR). 1993. "Toxicological profile for lead." Atlanta: U.S. Department of Health and Human Services, Public Health Service.

Agency for Toxic Substances and Disease Registry (ATSDR). 1993. "Case studies in environmental medicine: Lead toxicity." Atlanta: U.S. Department of Health and Human Services, Public Health Service.

Chapter 29

The New Occupational Neurotoxins: Are They for Real?

All of us have had, from time to time, what my mother-in-law refers to as a "senior moment." Whether it is missing an exit on a highway we have taken a hundred times previously, briefly forgetting the name of a loved one, being unable to recall the spelling of a common word, or simply forgetting how to do something which we could perform effortlessly in years past, we all experience memory lapses.

Similarly, we routinely experience a plethora of behavioral and constitutional symptoms such as depressed mood, irritability, headache and fatigue. And, from time to time, we may have trouble with our ability to perform on various tests, learn new things, or successfully complete in a timely manner common, everyday work tasks. Anyone who has had a couple of beers can easily identify the acute symptoms of intoxication. Many others who did inhale will also recognize other altered behavior, sensation and cognitive functions.

Over the past several decades, there has been increasing interest in neurotoxic effects, primarily long-term problems from potential workplace, consumer product, and environmental exposures. In 1990, the U.S. Congress' Office of Technology Assessment reported that relatively few of the thousands of chemicals in the stream of commerce had been adequately tested for neurotoxicity. It has been estimated by one researcher that 3 to 5 percent of chemicals have neurotoxic potential. Legislative and regulatory actions in this area have been

Howard M. Sandler, *Occupational Hazards,* July 1998, Vol. 60, N. 7, pp. 89–92, Copyright 1999 Penton Media Inc. Reprinted with permission.

limited, although the Federal Insecticide, Fungicide and Rodenticide Act (FIFRA) and the Environmental Protection Act's (EPA) activities in handling pesticides are prominent exceptions.

Neurotoxins Old and New

Neurotoxins can affect both the central nervous system and the peripheral nerves. Some of the more well-known neurotoxins include metals, such as lead and mercury. Lead, for example, can lead to extensor motor paralysis in the forearm (a peripheral nerve effect) and also, in high doses, produce acute encephalopathy and eventually death. Mercury causes dementia, i.e., "Mad as a Hatter." Arsenic can produce a peripheral neuropathy, potentially causing a permanent loss of nerve functioning in certain extremity nerves. Wood alcohol, in sufficient doses, will produce blindness, while manganese exposure is associated with a Parkinsonian-like presentation. Various drugs and plants are hallucinogenic.

More recently, complaints have arisen surrounding such unlikely candidates as poor indoor air quality, fragrances (cacosmia: exaggerated response to odors) and routine building pesticide applications. Such complaints have also alleged exposure to electromagnetic fields and biologic agents, including allergic sensitizers. These newer complaints differ from the more severe and well-recognized problems in that frequently all one has to go on are a wide range of vague complaints and the puzzling results of neuropsychological test batteries.

For these new complaints, many questions remain unanswered. What substances produce neurotoxic effects? What levels of which substances produce acute effects? Chronic effects? Are short-term, high-exposure effects reversible? Is there an effect from long-term, high-exposures? Is it permanent? Is there an effect from long-term, low-level exposures? Does it last?

Determining a Threshold Dose

Many of the questions center around exposure to commonly used solvents and other concerns such as indoor air pollution. There is evidence that long-term high exposures can produce debilitating neurotoxicity, such as in glue sniffers who receive massive toluene exposures. But the extent to which lower level exposures produce effects is unclear. That is: what is the threshold dose?

Does one have to become "high" and consistently exposed at that level for chronic health problems to occur? Researchers looking at painters in Europe in the 1970s and 1980s reported a number of symptoms and abnormal neuropsychometric test results. In the case of lead exposure in children, some experts have opined that there is no safe dose and that doses over 50 percent lower than what was the average exposure in the United States in decades past produce IQ, behavioral and other neurotoxic effects which are alleged to be irreversible. Other substances, such as ethylene oxide, have been reported under the Toxic Substances Control Act to produce neurobehavioral effects.

While the effects appear reversible, complaints reportedly may take many months or even a year or two to fully resolve, depending on the exposure. National Institute for Occupational Safety and Health (NIOSH) scientists have reported that, in general, acute solvent neurotoxicity is short-lived.

Testing

Many neuropsychological tests have been developed over the years to measure brain dysfunction. A number of these tests have been validated. Traditionally performed by clinical neuropsychologists, these tests were first used to identify and shape rehabilitation for problems following stroke, head trauma and other Central Nervous System (CNS) problems. They can grossly identify areas of the brain affected, as well as assess the relative level of dysfunction. In the neurotoxicity area, their use is much more recent.

Some test batteries were devised specifically for the study of neurotoxic effects and focus on visuospatial function, memory and other particular CNS functions which have been potentially identified as neurotoxic in nature. To date, neuropsychological tests have not been routinely used for purposes of medical monitoring and surveillance in the workplace. There are numerous limitations and problems with these tests which limit their usefulness in the evaluation of workers' compensation and litigation cases.

Neuropsychological tests address a range of functional performance areas:

- grip strength
- intellectual processes, e.g., verbal and performance
- receptive and expressive speech
- sensory perception, e.g., tactile, auditory, visual
- short and long-term memory
- emotional functioning

- attention and concentration
- academic abilities

In assessing whether a worker suffers from neurobehavioral effects, there are many testing considerations:

- choosing the right test battery
- correlating symptoms and reported functional deficits
- predicting the worker's pre-exposure functional level
- utility of objective tests such as MRI, CT, NCV, or EEG
- accounting for confounders, such as patient psychiatric state or drugs
- appropriate examiner interpretation
- testing environment, instructions and methodology

One of the more difficult problems is interpretation of test results for a given individual. Most of us will score poorly on one or more tests or subtests within a validated battery. As test results are dependent on subject effort, motivation, and other factors, it is left to the examiner to assure the validity of the test as well as the impact of other factors which can account for test result abnormalities.

These factors include failure to explain or understand test instructions, fatigue, anxiety, depression, malingering, and hysteria. Other factors include litigation, ethnicity/culture, native language, attentional difficulties, alcoholism, and substance abuse. Still others involve low blood sugar, time of day, antagonism toward examiner, underlying medical/neurological disorders, emotional stressor, pain, allergies, or a history of head trauma.

Once results are tallied, the clinical neuropsychological assessment must be performed in context with other factors ranging from childhood development to medical history to observations of coworkers and family members.

These limitations also greatly impact the ability to interpret the test results of a group of workers. For example, what do these tests mean in regard to everyday functioning? It is hardly surprising that severity is often increased in the litigation setting, where motivation, depression, or the stress of legal involvement may account for all or part of the abnormal test findings. This difficulty is underscored by the vast difference in test results frequently found between the examining neuropsychological experts.

Be Aware

While formal testing for neurotoxic effects should not be a routine part of preventive occupational health practice, safety and health staff should become familiar with:

- potential neurologic agents in their workplace

- the need to monitor possible exposures to such agents

- recognition of potential relationship of injury to neurotoxicity, e.g., loss of attention due to narcosis

- strengths and limitations of neurological and neuropsychological testing tools

- need for appropriate individual testing or group screening

It is critical to note that the ability to "test for" outstrips our current understanding of what the results of various neurological testing means. For example, certain clinicians employ neuro-ophthalmologic testing or SPECT scans or other sophisticated approaches in assessing patients. Such tests frequently have limited assessment potential, e.g., cerebral blood flow. None of these tests are specific for neurotoxic effects. Over all, they should be utilized only in a research capacity for workplace and environmental exposure investigations.

While many workplace agents have the potential to affect the nervous system, we are a long way from understanding and documenting the impact of such exposures. Areas for research include effect type, effect reversibility, dose, objective testing capabilities, and differentiation of neuropsychological effect etiologies. Careful research will help prevent neurotoxic exposures, prevent unnecessary concern, and manage current neurotoxicity problems.

—by Howard M. Sandler, MD

Contributing Editor Howard M. Sandler, M.D., is President of Sandler Occupational Medicine Associates, Inc., a Melville, N.Y., occupational and environmental health consulting firm. Dr. Sandler is a former medical officer with NIOSH. He has designed and evaluated occupational health programs for many corporations.

Chapter 30

Pesticide Use and Disposal

Introduction

Pesticides are used to protect crops and stored grains, control household pests and nuisance insects, and eliminate vectors (organisms that carry pathogens from one host to another) of human and animal diseases. Over the past four decades, production and use of pesticides have increased steadily throughout the world. Each year at least two million metric tons of pesticide products are used to control pests and diseases. This trend has been accompanied by growing human health and ecological problems associated with misuse, accidents and improper disposal. As many as 3 million pesticide poisonings, including 220,000 deaths, occur each year throughout the world. While immediate diagnosis and treatment of pesticide poisonings can help prevent fatalities, safe pesticide handling and disposal practices would sharply reduce the risk of exposure.

Pesticides Defined

Pesticides are toxic (poisonous) chemicals used to control pests. Classes of pesticides are commonly named after the pests which they help to control (insecticides control insects; herbicides control weeds; fungicides control fungi; and rodenticides control rodents). The biological component of a pesticide which kills or otherwise controls the

Excerpted from an undated publication produced by the Environmental Protection Agency, http//:www.epa.gov/oia/tips/pestint.htm.

target pest is called the active ingredient. The active ingredient usually has to be diluted with inactive (inert) ingredients for use because:

1. The physical properties of active ingredients are generally unsuitable for field use.

2. Pesticides are highly toxic in their pure form.

3. Required doses are difficult to disperse in high concentrations.

The mixture of active and inactive ingredients is called a formulation. Some formulations include: pesticides mixed with water or oil (wettable powders or emulsifiable concentrates), dry applications (dusts or granules), and gases or vapors (fumigants, aerosols, pressurized sprays). A formulation's inactive ingredients usually have no effect on pests, but might pose a potential risk to human health and the environment.

Avoiding Pesticide Misuse

Pest control can be accomplished by either non-chemical or chemical methods, or through a combination of both. Biological control, such as using natural predators and parasites, and manual control, such as mulching to reduce weed growth, are two examples of non-chemical pest control. If the choice is made to use a chemical pesticide, hazards can be minimized by:

1. Choosing the right pesticide for the pest problem

2. Carefully reading the product label

3. Determining the right amount of pesticide to purchase and use

4. Applying the pesticide in the manner and with the equipment and precautions required by the label

5. Storing and disposing of pesticides and containers as directed on the label

Avoiding the Need for Disposal

Use the following guidelines to help minimize pesticide disposal problems:

*   Purchase small quantities and avoid overstocking and stockpiling.

- Evaluate pesticide requirements in advance and do not accept donations in excess of these requirements.

- Avoid accepting donations of unsolicited pesticides from third parties.

- Do not accept damaged pesticide containers.

- Keep detailed records of stocks and clearly label the containers to avoid the problem of unidentified pesticides.

- Handle pesticide containers properly.

- If possible, store pesticides in a cool place out of direct exposure to sunlight.

- Use "first in-first out" inventory practices.

- These measures can help reduce health risks, save money by reducing damage to pesticide stock, and reduce the need to dispose of unwanted stocks.

Potential Environmental Impacts

Some potential environmental impacts associated with the misuse or overuse of pesticides are:

- *Bioaccumulation*. Those animals at the end of the food chain, such as carnivorous mammals, predatory fishes, and birds of prey, can be killed by bioaccumulation of persistent types of pesticides.

- *Pest resurgence*. Misuse of pesticides can cause the elimination or suppression of natural predators which help to control pests. When pesticides kill or harm these predators, a pest resurgence might occur.

- *Pest resistance*. The misuse of pesticides has led to the build-up of resistance in insect pests, pathogens, and weeds. Over time, target pests can develop resistance, thereby requiring the purchase of more potent and expensive formulations. Pest resistance has economic as well as ecological consequences since increasing amounts of pesticides must be used to achieve control, and since alternative pesticides or control methods might become necessary. In some areas of the world, pesticide overuse has created a population of resistant pests which threaten both subsistence and cash crops.

Public Health Concerns

In 1995, the World Health Organization (WHO) estimated that approximately 3 million cases of pesticide poisonings occur annually, including approximately 220,000 pesticide-related deaths. In 1991, WHO estimated that as many as 25 million agricultural workers in developing countries would suffer an episode of pesticide poisoning each year (Jeyaratnam, 1990). Unsuitable application, overuse of pesticides, or the neglect of safety periods between application and harvest often results in high pesticide residues in food and in unnecessary exposure by agriculture workers and their families. Pesticide residues are known to contaminate clothing, thereby poisoning the wearer. Pesticides can also poison fish, cattle, beneficial insects, pollinators, and soil organisms.

Human exposure to pesticides can occur by way of swallowing the pesticide or its residue (oral exposure), through skin contact (dermal exposure), or by breathing in the pesticide (inhalation contact). The toxicity of exposure to pesticides can be acute (rapid poisoning produced by a single or few exposures) or chronic (effects produced by long-term exposure). Toxicity varies with both the type and concentration of the formulation and with the route of exposure. Also, metabolism and kinetics have a significant influence on a pesticide's ultimate toxicity; some pesticides are activated by metabolism while others are readily deactivated.

Major categories of pesticides include organochlorines, organophosphorus compounds, carbamates, nitrochlorophenols, bipyridyls, and pyrethroids. Examples of organochlorine compounds include endrin, dieldrin, lindane, and toxaphene. Some organochlorine compounds are stored in the body's fatty tissues without causing any apparent adverse effects. Most, however, are persistent in the environment and may affect non-target wildlife adversely. For this reason, the use of persistent pesticides (such as DDT) is strongly discouraged. Currently, approximately 100 countries are participating in negotiations with the United Nations Environment Program (UNEP) to prepare a global treaty to reduce or eliminate persistent organic pollutants (POPs), including the pesticides DDT, aldrin, dieldrin, endrin, chlordane, hexachlorobenzene, mirex, toxaphene, heptachlor, and PCBs. More information is available on UNEP's POPs Home Page.

Organophosphorus compounds are less persistent in the environment and are not stored in the body. Examples of these are parathion, diazinon, and malathion. Of the two groups, organophosphorus compounds are more acutely toxic but less hazardous since they are less persistent in the environment.

A pesticide container's label should indicate the pesticide's hazard class and toxicity level. The label should also include clear application instructions.

Effects on the Human Body

Pesticides can produce injuries internally or externally, depending on the type of pesticide and on the frequency and type of exposure. Dermal exposure can result in simple skin irritation (e.g., redness, itching, or pimples), or in an allergic reaction producing redness, swelling, or blistering. The mucous membranes of the eyes, nose, mouth, and throat are especially sensitive to chemicals.

Internal injuries may occur depending upon where a chemical is transported in the body. Symptoms will depend upon the organ or organs affected. For instance, lung damage from pesticide exposure might result in shortness of breath, clear saliva, or rapid breathing. Damage to the gastrointestinal tract could cause nausea, abdominal cramps, or diarrhea. Excessive fatigue, sleepiness, headaches, muscle spasms, and a loss of sensation can result from injury to the nervous system.

Often, pesticides inhibit or alter the action of certain key enzymes. In this way, exposure to pesticides can cause damage to a internal organs. Organophosphorus compounds, for example, can inhibit enzymes in red blood cells, plasma, the brain, and other organs. Some pesticides—such as chloro/nitro compounds—can stimulate metabolism and cause unusually high body temperatures. Laboratory studies conducted on animals have also linked chronic exposure to certain types of pesticides with birth defects, tumor development, cancers, and endocrine disruption.

Pesticide Residues in Food

With pesticides, farmers can grow more and greater varieties of food more cheaply; home owners can control pests in their gardens; and public health officials can control pests which might spread disease. However, these significant societal benefits should be weighed against potential adverse risks from occupational exposure and against exposure from residues remaining on food.

Regulatory efforts throughout the world have attempted to protect consumers from the potential dangers of pesticide residues in the food supply. To regulate pesticide residues, a legal limit known as the maximum residue limit (MRL) is developed for each pesticide. The MRL is the maximum level of residue that is legally permitted to remain in or on a crop in commerce. This limit is used to provide reasonable assurance that no adverse effects to the consumer will result over a lifetime of dietary exposure. Although strict adherence to MRLs might not be feasible for some countries because of economic constraints, those countries relying on food export profits should monitor for and comply with these MRL levels in order to maintain credibility as responsible exporters.

Control

Regulation of pesticides can help protect against adverse human and environmental health effects while not denying society access to benefits of pesticide use. Registration enables authorities to control quality, use levels, efficacy claims, labeling, packaging and advertising. Registration also helps to ensure that the interests of end-users are well protected. Data required for registration include chemical and physical properties, effectiveness, toxicity for assessment of human health hazards, and prediction of environmental effects.

Selecting Application Methods

The selection of pesticide formulations should take into consideration local environmental conditions, the mode of application, availability of protective clothing and the baseline knowledge of the workers who will be applying the pesticide.

Hand spraying is probably the most common application method for insecticides and herbicides in economically-developing nations. Machine sprayers, usually drawn by a tractor, are particularly useful for spraying trees or large areas of land. Aerial spraying is effective at covering large areas of land, but should be reserved for when speedy application of a pesticide is essential, such as in emergency control of migratory pests.

Low concentration granular, seed dressing, bait formulations, and pheromone traps generally present the least hazard to users and are especially suitable for small-scale farmers who might be unfamiliar with pesticide use. Note, however, that the use of granular formulations can present a hazard to birds and other wildlife.

Training is critical to safety and to the cost-effective application of pesticides. Monitoring of occupational and environmental impacts should be a standard component of pesticide use programs, which should also include water quality testing to ensure that drinking and bathing water is fit for human use.

Applying Pesticides Safely

Use of protective clothing should be mandatory for anyone handling pesticides. Since the clothing can become saturated with pesticides, which greatly increases absorption through the skin, it is important to wash protective clothing well after each use. It is also important to wash the hands and face thoroughly with soap and clean water after using pesticides and prior to eating, drinking, or smoking.

Individuals who handle concentrated pesticides (e.g., a "mixer" or a person who is bagging pesticides) must take extra care. Such workers should wear overalls, gloves, boots, aprons, and respirators or clean cloths over their mouths and noses. For mixing highly toxic pesticides, glasses and a respirator containing a cartridge (replaced at least daily) are essential.

Anyone mixing pesticide formulations should use a long paddle (rather than stirring with only the hands), stir slowly enough to avoid splashing, pour carefully, and properly dispose of empty containers. Baggers should always

1. Weigh the pesticide carefully.

2. Put the pesticide in the bag gently to avoid dust.

3. Avoid contaminating the outside of the bag.

4. Put the bag on a clean surface for closure

5. Keep the surrounding area clean.

When spraying a crop with a pesticide of moderate or low toxicity, the user should wear a protective outer garment such as overalls, boots, and a brimmed hat (if the crop is high). If the user is spraying a pesticide of high toxicity, he should wear rubber or plastic gloves, a rubber or plastic apron, and a pair of glasses. When spraying inside buildings, the user should wear an overall, boots, a brimmed hat and a pair of eyeglasses. The goal of the overall is to cover 85% of the skin on the torso and limbs. A scarf is also needed if the head and neck are not covered. The lower legs and feet should be protected with boots. Anyone handling pesticides should wear gloves which extend to within 5 centimeters of the elbow.

Anyone applying pesticides outdoors should hold the wand away from the body and never spray into the wind (although it is best to spray on windless days). The worker should spray to one side and avoid walking through freshly sprayed areas. Leaking equipment must be repaired immediately. Should any pesticide fall on exposed skin, the user should wash off the pesticide immediately. When possible, anyone applying pesticides should wash between applicator pump charges.

Similar procedures must be exercised when spraying buildings. The user should always:

1. Hold the wand away from the body (especially when spraying upper walls and eaves).

2. Avoid spray drift from door and window drafts.

3. Spray slowly and systematically.

If the nozzle of a pesticide applicator becomes blocked, do not attempt to blow it clear by mouth. Instead, remove the nozzle and blow it clear with the pressure release valve of the pump. Blocked nozzles can also be cleared using either a thin grass stem or stick or can be cleaned with soap and water.

Pilots applying pesticides by plane must also take precautions to avoid contact with pesticides as much as possible. Ventilators should be closed while spraying and the pilot should avoid flying back through the pesticides or over sprayed areas.

Upon terminating pesticide application for the day, each worker should wash himself and his clothes with clean water. Clothes worn while applying pesticides should be washed separately from normal household laundry.

Public Protection

All pesticides must be stored safely away from children, animals, and anyone who might misuse them. Pesticides must be stored in clearly-labeled containers: storage in the original containers is preferable. Containers should be kept in a safe storehouse that is well-ventilated and can be closed off to prevent unauthorized entry. The storehouse should be located away from populated areas, on well-drained land, and away from domestic water supplies. It should be constructed with non-combustible material, and have a leak-proof floor and emergency exits. Any pesticide spillage should be cleaned thoroughly with large amounts of water. Pesticide users must strive to protect other people, their animals, and property from exposure. Pesticides and food should never be transported in the same vehicle.

Groundwater Contamination

Many human disease vectors are controlled by spraying or treating surface waters with insecticides. Additionally, herbicides are often applied to water in tropical areas to control aquatic weeds. Both practices can result in the contamination of groundwater. Other avenues for pesticide contamination of water include:

1. discharges of surplus pesticide

2. improper disposal of water used for washing spraying equipment

3. spraying of crops planted close to water bodies

4. accidental spillage of pesticide formulations

5. run-off, leakage, and erosion from treated soil

6. fall-out of pesticides from polluted air

7. indiscriminate aerial application of pesticides to soils/crops

Within the last decade, groundwater contamination by agricultural chemicals has been documented throughout the United States. The widespread occurrence of pesticides in groundwater and the toxicity of many of these chemicals have caused concern over the potential for adverse health effects from chronic exposure via contaminated drinking water. Groundwater is the only source of drinking water in many rural areas. Significant contamination may occur because of the extensive use of agricultural chemicals and the shallow depths of aquifers.

The agricultural practices most likely to affect groundwater quality are pesticide selection and application rate, nitrogen fertilizer application rate, and crop rotation. Use of less persistent and less mobile compounds can reduce the potential for groundwater contamination. Pesticide application rates directly influence the amount available for leaching (movement of substances with water through the soil). Crop rotations usually reduce the need for application of insecticides and may reduce the need for herbicides. The processes affecting movement of pesticides into groundwater include plant uptake, volatilization (evaporation) to the atmosphere, chemical or microbial degradation (breakdown), adsorption by the soil, and transport by water.

The amount of a chemical that is stored, transformed, or transported is controlled by several factors:

1. the amount and properties (such as solubility and persistence) of the chemical

2. soil properties

3. timing and intensity of precipitation

4. hydrogeologic conditions.

Disposal Options

There are usually several options available for disposing of pesticides safely:

1. Use the pesticide as intended. It is usually preferable to use pesticides as they were designed to be used rather than to dispose of them, as long as the application rate does not exceed the maximum application rate listed on the label. In this way, the pesticides will be subjected to degradation processes, such as reaction with sunlight or microorganisms, that help break down the chemicals. Additionally, it may be possible to identify an alternative use (as long as it is consistent with recommended uses listed on the label) other than the one for which the product was obtained.

2. Return the excess pesticide stocks through your local supplier or agency to the manufacturer. With the permission of the manufacturer or supplier, this option is suitable for all types and quantities of unwanted pesticides. Precautions must be taken to avoid problems during transportation, however. These precautions include:

   • contacting and informing the manufacturer of the pesticide and quantity to be returned

   • properly packing and transporting the pesticides

   • consulting regulatory authorities in your country, transit countries, and the recipient country to determine requirements for shipping the wastes

3. If a pesticide cannot be used as intended or returned to the manufacturer, another suitable disposal method must be found. Several alternative methods are discussed below. Ideally, a method should be chosen that minimizes human exposure, does not damage surface water or ground-water quality, and

makes minimal contributions to the problems of air pollution and solid waste disposal. The method should be easily carried out using local expertise, and the materials needed should be inexpensive and readily available. In addition, precautions must be taken to ensure that pesticide containers are not reused for any purpose other than storing the original pesticides.

Land Treatment (Biodegradation in/on the Soil)

Land treatment is appropriate for small quantities of pesticides which can be diluted and applied to land at the label rate. Some pesticides are biodegradable—that is, they break down through the action of naturally occurring microorganisms in soil, along with natural physical and chemical processes. Land treatment is suitable for pesticides that are susceptible to biodegradation in a short period of time (less than 26 weeks), under either aerobic (in the presence of oxygen) or anaerobic (without oxygen) conditions. The action of the soil microorganisms can be enhanced through the addition of biologically active material like compost, sewage sludge, or night soil.

Land treatment sites should be remote from homes or other buildings, crops, and livestock, and should not be in erosion gullies, sinks, dry water courses, or quarries. Protection of ground and surface waters should be a major consideration in determining the suitability of land treatment. Persistent and basically non-biodegradable pesticides are not suitable for land treatment.

Disposal in Carefully Managed Landfills

A disposal option for small amounts of some solid pesticides, or small amounts of some liquid pesticides that have been converted into a solid product, is burial in a well-managed municipal solid waste landfill. The landfill operator must be notified of the identity of the pesticide waste prior to disposal.

In a well-managed landfill, the waste deposited each day is covered with a layer of soil, and the soil layer is packed using machinery. Microorganisms in the soil layer, and in other organic materials in the landfill, promote the breakdown of pesticide wastes. The landfill should be sited to ensure that ground water will not be contaminated (as determined by a hydrogeologic survey) or it must have a clay or synthetic liner. Landfills should not be located in areas of seismic instability, in flood plains, or in any site where the integrity of the liner system could be adversely affected. Disposal in a landfill is usually not a desirable option for liquid pesticides or for some highly mobile and toxic wastes. In some cases, inorganic pesticides or liquid pesticide wastes containing about 5 percent organic material can be solidified or stabilized prior to disposal in a landfill. Mercury, lead, cadmium, and arsenic, as well as inorganic compounds that are highly mobile in soil, can be encapsulated in concrete or other stable material. Encapsulation will retard mobility and will contain the wastes in a small area that can be recorded for future reference. Significant concentrations of organic substances may retard solidification and affect its mechanical strength; water soluble pesticides may tend to leach from the matrix.

Incineration

When carried out properly, incineration at a facility approved to accept hazardous wastes is a suitable disposal option for many pesticides. Incineration is especially attractive when disposal of large quantities of pesticides is necessary. Well-designed and well-operated combustion processes can almost completely destroy the organic chemical compounds in many pesticides. An incinerator which provides proper combustion of pesticides must have a flame temperature of 900 to 1,200 degrees Centigrade, a fire box in which the chemical will have a residence time of at least 10 seconds, and adequate turbulence.

The incineration process can convert organic pesticides into carbon dioxide, water, sulfur oxides, hydrochloric acid, and other simple compounds. Metals in pesticide wastes are not destroyed by incineration, and may become part of the ash or slag, may vaporize and become part of stack gas, or may oxidize and become ash, particulate, or condensate in the stack or scrubber. Pollution control devices must trap the acids and other substances formed during combustion to prevent environmental pollution or damage to the incinerator.

High-temperature kilns are used in the production of cement, and most countries have at least one cement factory. Pesticides can be used to meet part of the fuel requirements for producing cement, provided the kiln has been evaluated by specialists, found to be suitable for burning such waste, and adapted to ensure consistent high temperatures and prevention of toxic emissions, such as dioxin. Although cement kilns have been successfully used in several countries for incineration of obsolete pesticides, such operations are opposed by some environmental organizations and must be carefully planned with community involvement. Pesticides can also be up to 1 to 2 percent of the fuel in high-temperature boilers.

Other Treatment Methods

Some pesticides can be broken down by appropriate chemical treatment techniques (e.g., treatment with alkalis, acids or oxidants) that change the pesticide into a substance which is less toxic or into one which can be disposed of safely. It is important to exercise extreme caution when using chemical treatment techniques. In some cases, the use of the wrong chemical on a pesticide can produce a more toxic or explosive mixture, or can generate toxic vapors from an ordinarily nonvolatile pesticide. Certain pesticides break down when exposed to sunlight. Small amounts of a few pesticides may be disposed of by release to the air.

Centralized Temporary Storage/Containment

As an interim solution to the problem of unwanted pesticide stocks, the pesticides can be centralized in one or a few secure, monitored locations. If done properly, this will minimize the danger of exposure to people and the environment. The chemical can then be retrieved when a suitable disposal method is available.

Disposal of Containers

After pesticide containers have been emptied, they will still contain a small amount of pesticide and must be properly disposed. It is strongly recommended that all pesticide containers be crushed and/or punctured to prevent their reuse. Serious illnesses and deaths have resulted from reuse of "empty" pesticide containers to store food or water. In general, all used pesticide containers first should be rinsed at least three times immediately after emptying. This procedure will not make any container suitable for storage of food, feed, or drinking water as residuals will always be present. If the triple-rinsing procedure cannot be used, it may be possible to neutralize liquid pesticide remaining in the container by adding an alkaline substance.

For combustible containers (those made of paper, cardboard, fabric, plastic, or wood) disposal may be by incineration or in a carefully managed landfill after the container is crushed or punctured to prevent reuse. Containers made of plastic, metal, or glass should be triple-rinsed, disposed of by returning them to the supplier or a reconditioning center; sending the metal containers to a smelter (if a sufficient number of containers is available to make this cost-effective); or sending them to a carefully managed landfill. Any containers which will be placed in a landfill should first be crushed or broken, and the landfill operator should be informed of the pesticide residues.

Chapter 31

Waste Anesthetic Gasses

Waste Anesthetic Gasses—Introduction

Anesthesia is as common to medical care as is antiseptic care of wounds. However, for too long exposure to and control of waste anesthetic gases (WAGs) and vapors during surgical procedures have put health-care workers in jeopardy. At any given time more than 250,000 people who work in hospitals, operating rooms, dental offices and veterinary clinics, might be exposed unnecessarily to harmful levels of WAGs.

The waste anesthetic gases and vapors of concern are nitrous oxide and halogenated agents (vapors) such as halothane, enflurane, methoxyflurane, trichloroethylene, and chloroform. The list of workers with potential for exposure to WAGs includes nurses, physicians, surgeons, obstetricians, gynecologists, operating room technicians, and recovery room personnel; dentists and veterinarians and their assistants; and other auxiliaries. Hospital emergency room personnel may also be exposed, but not on a regular basis.

This chapter contains text from "Waste Anesthetic Gasses," Occupational Safety and Health Administration (OSHA), Fact Sheet 91-38, http://www.osha-slc.gov/OshDoc/Fact_data/FSNO91-38.html, January 1991, and "Controlling Exposures to Nitrous Oxide During Anesthetic Administration," National Institute for Occupational Safety and Health (NIOSH), Department of Health and Human Services (DHHS) (NIOSH) Pub. No. 94-100, http://www.cdc.gov/niosh/noxidalr.html1994, updated August 5, 1996. Despite the age of these articles, readers seeking an understanding of waste anesthetic gasses will still find the information useful.

The Occupational Safety and Health Administration (OSHA), therefore, has developed technical instructions designed to give guidance for coping with exposure to WAGs. The instructions cover sampling methods, leak test procedures, medical surveillance, disposal methods, training, and exposure to WAGs.

No worker should be exposed to concentrations of WAGs greater than 2 parts per million (ppm) of any halogenated anesthetic agent, based on the weight of the agent collected for a 45-liter air sample by charcoal adsorption over a sampling period not to exceed one hour.

Controlled agents and their respective weights corresponding to 2 ppm are: chloroform, 9.76 mg/cu m; trichloroethylene, 10.75 mg/cu m; halothane, 16.15 mg/cu m; methoxyflurane, 13.5 mg/cu m; enflurane, 151 mg/cu m; fluroxene, 10.31 mg/cu m.

When such agents are used in combination with nitrous oxide, levels of the halogenated agents well below 2 ppm are achievable. In most situations, control of nitrous oxide to a time weighted average concentration of 25 ppm during the anesthetic administration period will result in levels of about 0.5 ppm of the halogenated agent.

The occupational exposure to nitrous oxide, when used as the sole anesthetic agent, should be controlled so that no worker is exposed at eight-hour time-weighted average (TWA) concentrations greater than 25 ppm during anesthetic administration.

A complete WAGs management program includes at the outset the application of a well designed WAGs scavenging system. Such a system will consist of a collecting device (scavenging adapter) to collect WAGs and vapors from breathing systems at the site of overflow; a ventilation system to carry WAGs from the operating room; and, a method or device for limiting both positive and negative pressure variations in the breathing circuit which may be used by the scavenging systems. Most anesthesia equipment being manufactured today includes scavenging systems.

The remainder of the WAGs management program should include work practices minimizing gas leakage, the application of a routine equipment maintenance program so that gas leaks are minimized, and periodic exposure monitoring and provision for adequate general ventilation.

- *Work Practice Controls.* Steps that can be taken to reduce gas leakage can include:

  1. Make sure that waste gas disposal lines are connected.

  2. Avoid turning on nitrous oxide or vaporizer until the circuit is connected to the patient. Switch off the nitrous oxide and

vaporizer when not in use. Maintain oxygen flow until scavenging system is flushed.

- *Personal Sampling.* The primary method of evaluating WAG concentrations in air is by collecting a quantity of air in a sampling bag and then introducing the sample to an infrared analyzer. Sampling should be conducted based on the particular anesthetic agent in use. Nitrous oxide can be sampled by using devices such a large plastic bag pump or the Landauer nitrous oxide monitor. Halogenated compounds should be collected in charcoal tubes 107-110 using two tubes in series.

- *Engineering Controls.* A scavenging nasal mask consists of a compact double mask system. It must consist of a shroud large enough to capture exhausted/escaping nitrous oxide exiting from a patient's mouth. An inner mask is contained within a slightly larger outer mask and a slight vacuum is present in the space between the masks. The vacuum scavenges gases exhaled by the patient as well as any excess gas from the anesthesia machine that could leak from around the edges of the inner and outer masks. Two small hoses lead to the space between layers and are for scavenging.

- *Medical Surveillance.* A medical surveillance program should be made available to all employees who are subject to occupational exposure to WAGs. The program should contain:

  - Comprehensive pre-placement medical and occupational histories which should be maintained in the employees' medical records with special attention given to the outcome of pregnancies of the employee or spouse, and to the hepatic, renal and hematopoietic systems which may be affected by agents used as anesthetic gases

  - preplacement and annual physical examination of employees exposed to anesthetic gases

  - employees should be advised of the potential effects of exposure to WAGs, such as spontaneous abortions, congenital abnormalities in children, and effects on the liver and kidneys

- the records of any abnormal outcome of pregnancies exposed to WAGs and vapors should be documented and maintained for at least the duration of employment plus 30 years.

Controlling Exposures to Nitrous Oxide During Anesthetic Administration

Background

Nitrous Oxide (N2O) is used as an anesthetic agent in medical, dental, and veterinary operatories. This gas is also used as a foaming agent for whipped cream, an oxidant for organic compounds, a nitrating agent for alkali metals, and a component of certain rocket fuels. In dental operatories, agents that cause conscious sedation (such as N2O) are commonly referred to as "analgesic agents."

In 1977, the National Institute for Occupational Safety and Health (NIOSH) published a technical report entitled "Control of Occupational Exposure to N2O in the Dental Operatory." This report presented methods for limiting the concentration of waste N2O to 50 parts per million (ppm) during administration, a limit based on the technical feasibility of existing controls. Since publication of this technical report, data collected by NIOSH have shown occupational exposures as high as 300 ppm in hospital operating rooms and exposures higher than 1,000 ppm in dental operatories equipped with scavenging systems (properly operating scavenging systems have been shown to reduce N2O concentrations by more than 70%).

To determine why occupational exposures to N2O are excessive even when scavenging systems are used, NIOSH has studied work practices (procedures followed by employers and workers to control hazards) and engineering controls (hazard controls designed into equipment and workplaces) for dental operatories. This work environment was chosen because N2O is frequently used as the sole anesthetic agent in dental operatories and exposures there tend to be more difficult to control than in general operating theaters. Control is more difficult in dental operatories because only the patient's nose is covered during anesthetic administration and scavenging, but both the nose and mouth can be covered in general operating theaters.

Health Effects

Animal studies have shown adverse reproductive effects in female rats exposed to airborne concentrations of N2O. Data from these studies indicate that exposure to N2O during gestation can produce adverse health effects in the offspring.

Several studies of workers have shown that occupational exposure to N2O causes adverse effects such as reduced fertility, spontaneous abortions, and neurologic, renal, and liver disease. A recent study reported that female dental assistants exposed to unscavenged N2O for 5 or more hours per week had a significant risk of reduced fertility compared with unexposed female dental assistants. The exposed assistants had a 59% decrease in probability of conception for any given menstrual cycle compared with the unexposed assistants. For dental assistants who used scavenging systems during N2O administration, the probability of conception was not significantly different from that of the unexposed assistants. Since environmental exposures were not measured during these epidemiologic studies, no dose-effect relationship could be established.

Workers Exposed

More than 424,000 workers (i.c., dentists, dental assistants, and dental hygienists) practice dentistry in the United States. In 1983, the American Dental Association (ADA) reported that 35% of all dentists used N2O to control pain and anxiety in their patients. The ADA 1991 Survey of Dental Practice indicated that 58% of dentists reported having N2O anesthetic equipment, and 64% of those practitioners also reported having a scavenging system. The percentage of pediatric dentists using N2O increased from 65% in 1980 to 88% in 1988.

Occupational Exposure Limits

The Occupational Safety and Health Administration (OSHA) does not currently have a standard for N2O. The NIOSH recommended exposure limit (REL) for N2O is 25 ppm as a time-weighted average (TWA) during the period of anesthetic administration. This REL is intended to prevent decreases in mental performance, audiovisual ability, and manual dexterity during exposures to N2O. An REL to prevent adverse reproductive effects cannot be established until more data are available. The American Conference of Governmental Industrial Hygienists (ACGIH) threshold limit value (TLV) for N2O is 50 ppm as an 8-hour TWA. The 1991 Documentation of the Threshold Limit Values and Biological Exposure Indices states that "control to this level should prevent embryofetal toxicity in humans and significant decrements in human psychomotor and cognitive functions or other adverse health effects in exposed personnel."

Conclusions

A large population of health-care workers is potentially exposed to N2O, and NIOSH has documented cases in which exposures substantially exceed existing RELs. NIOSH has concluded that exposure to N2O causes decreases in mental performance, audiovisual ability, and manual dexterity. Data from animal studies demonstrate that exposure to N2O may cause adverse reproductive effects. Studies of workers exposed to N2O have reported adverse health effects such as reduced fertility, spontaneous abortion, and neurological, renal, and liver disease. The recommendations in this chapter should therefore be followed to minimize worker exposures.

Recommendations

Engineering controls, work practices, and respirators (when necessary) should be used to minimize the exposure of workers to N2O. Employers should ensure that their workers are adequately protected from N2O exposure by taking the following steps:

- Monitor airborne concentrations of N2O.

- Implement appropriate engineering controls, work practices, and maintenance procedures.

- Institute a worker education program that
    - describes standard operating procedures for all tasks that may expose workers to N2O, and
    - informs workers about proper work practices, controls, equipment, and protective gear that should be used when working with N2O.

Use the guidelines in the following section to minimize worker exposures to N2O.

Guidelines for Minimizing Worker Exposures

Exposure Monitoring

Exposure monitoring should be the first step in developing work practices and worker education programs, since measurements of N2O are needed to determine the type and extent of controls that are necessary. Follow the guidelines below to minimize worker exposures:

- Monitor for N2O when the anesthetic equipment is installed and every 3 months thereafter.

- Include the following types of monitoring:
    - leak testing of equipment

- monitoring of air in the worker's personal breathing zone

- environmental (room air) monitoring

- Prepare a written monitoring and maintenance plan for each facility that uses N2O. This plan should be developed by knowledgeable persons who consider the equipment manufacturers' recommendations, frequency of use, and other circumstances that might affect the equipment.

- Perform air monitoring by gas-bag sampling or real-time sampling.

- When real-time sampling is conducted to obtain personal exposure data, attach the sampling train to the lapel of the worker on the side closest to the patient; N2O concentrations in this location are most representative of those in the worker's breathing zone. Diffusive samplers (referred to as passive dosimeters) are commercially available and may be useful as initial indicators of exposure.

Engineering Controls and Maintenance Procedures

The following engineering controls and maintenance procedures have been shown to be feasible and effective in reducing exposure to N2O during anesthetic administration.

Anesthetic Delivery

Excessive exposure to N2O may occur as a result of leaks from the anesthetic delivery system during administration. The rubber and plastic components of the anesthetic equipment are potential sources of N2O leakage because they may be degraded by the N2O and the oxygen as well as by repeated sterilization.

The following figure illustrates sources of possible leaks from anesthetic delivery systems in dental operatories. These sources include leaks from the high-pressure connections that is, from the gas delivery tanks, the wall connectors, the hoses connected to the anesthetic machine, and the anesthetic machine (especially the on-demand valve). Low-pressure leaks occur from the connections between the anesthetic flowmeter and the scavenging mask. This leakage is due to loose-fitting connections, loosely assembled or deformed slip joints and threaded connections, and defective or worn seals, gaskets, breathing bags, and hoses.

Take the following steps to control N2O exposure from anesthetic delivery systems:

- Use connection ports with different-diameter hoses for N2O and O2 to reduce the possibility of incorrectly connecting the gas delivery and scavenging hoses.

- Check all rubber hoses, connections, tubing, and breathing bags daily and replace them when damaged or when recommended by the manufacturer.

- Following visual inspection, perform leak testing of the equipment and connections by using a soap solution to check for bubbles at high-pressure connections. For a more thorough inspection of all connectors, use a portable infrared spectrophotometer (such as a Miran 1A or 1B) calibrated for N2O detection.

- Check both high- and low-pressure connections (such as O-rings) regularly, as they may become worn; replace them periodically, according to the manufacturer's recommendations.

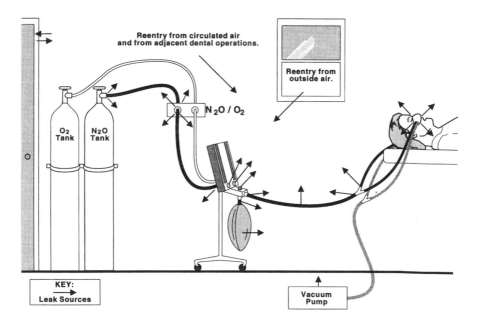

Figure 31.1. Sources of Leaks from Anesthetic Delivery Systems in Dental Operatories

- Evaluate the N2O and oxygen mixing system for leaks when it is first installed and periodically thereafter, according to the manufacturer's recommendations.

- Ensure that gas cylinders are safely handled, used, and stored as specified by the National Research Council and as required by OSHA.

Scavenging Systems

Control of N2O at the scavenging mask is the next priority after control of N2O leakage from the anesthetic equipment. Leakage from the scavenging mask can be one of the most significant sources of N2O exposure because the breathing zone of a dentist or dental assistant is within inches of the mask. NIOSH research has reported breathing-zone concentrations of N2O above 1,000 ppm.

Take the following steps to control N2O exposure from anesthetic scavenging systems:

- Supply scavenging masks in a variety of sizes so that the mask always fits comfortably and securely over the patient's nose or face.

- Use an automatic interlock system to assure that the N2O cannot be turned on unless the scavenging system is also activated. N2O should never be used without a properly operating scavenging system.

- Make sure that the scavenging system exhaust rates (flow rates) are approximately 45 liters per minute (L/min) to minimize leakage of N2O. Flow rates of less than 40 L/min may result in significant leakage around the mask. Monitor the flow rate with a flowmeter that is

  - validated to measure air flow within 5% of actual air flow

  - permanently connected to the scavenging system vacuum line, and

  - positioned so that it is always visible to the operator

- Maintain the flowmeter by cleaning and recalibrating it according to the manufacturer's recommendations.

- Use scavenging vacuum pumps that are powerful enough to maintain a scavenging flow rate of at least 45 L/min at each nasal mask regardless of the number of scavenging units in use at one time.

- Vent N2O from all scavenging vacuum pumps to the outside of the building away from fresh air intakes, windows, or walkways. Scavenging system exhaust should not be vented into a recirculating ventilation system.

Room Ventilation

Take the following steps to assure that the ventilation system effectively removes waste N2O:

- If concentrations of N2O are above 25 ppm in work areas, increase the air flow into the room or increase the percentage of outside air to allow for more air mixing and further dilution of the anesthetic gas. Maintain a balanced air supply and exhaust system so that N2O does not contaminate adjacent areas.

- If concentrations of N2O are still above 25 ppm, use supplementary local ventilation (a hood or duct to capture N2O at the source) in conjunction with a scavenging system to reduce N2O exposure in the operatory. The effectiveness of this ventilation depends on its location with respect to the patient and the airflow rates. Do not work between the patient and the exhaust duct, where contaminated air would be drawn through the worker's breathing zone.

- Dilute N2O and remove contaminated air from the work area by placing fresh-air vents in the ceiling; direct the supply of fresh air toward the floor and the operating area. Place exhaust-air vents at or near the floor.

Work Practices

Use the following work practices to control N2O exposures:

- Inspect the anesthetic delivery systems and all connections before starting anesthetic gas administration. Make sure that breathing bags, hoses, and clamps are in place before turning on the anesthetic machine.

- Connect the scavenging mask properly to the gas delivery hose and the vacuum system.

- Do not turn on the machine delivering N2O until
  - the vacuum system scavenging unit is operating at the recommended flow rate of 45 L/min, and

378

- the scavenging mask is secured over the patient's nose or face.

- Fasten the mask according to the manufacturer's instructions to prevent leaks around the mask during gas delivery.

- Do not fill the breathing bag to capacity with N2O; an over-inflated bag can cause excessive leakage from the scavenging mask. The breathing bag should collapse and expand as the patient breaths. This bag activity shows that the proper amounts of N2O and air are being delivered to the patient.

- Flush the system of N2O after surgery by administering oxygen to the patient through the anesthetic equipment for at least 5 minutes before disconnecting the gas delivery system.

- Encourage patients to minimize talking and mouth-breathing during dental surgery. When mouth-breathing is apparent, avoid the patient's breathing zone to the extent possible.

Respiratory Protection

Workers should wear respiratory protection when N2O concentrations are not consistently below 25 ppm; however, practical considerations may prevent them from wearing such protection. Therefore, it is essential that employers use the engineering controls and work practices described in this chapter to reduce N2O concentrations below 25 ppm.

When N2O concentrations are not consistently below 25 ppm, workers should take the following steps to protect themselves:

- Wear air-supplied respirators. Air-purifying respirators (that is, respirators that remove N2O from the air rather than supply air from a clean source) should not be used because respirator filters do not efficiently remove N2O. As specified by the NIOSH Respirator Decision Logic, the minimum level of protection for an air-supplied respirator is provided by a half-mask respirator operated in the demand or continuous-flow mode. More protective air-supplied respirators are described in the NIOSH Respirator Decision Logic. The assigned protection factor (APF) for this class of respirator is 10. The APF indicates the level of protection provided by a class of respirator. An APF of 10 means that the respirator should reduce the air concentration of N2O for the wearer by a factor of 10 (or to 10% of the concentration without respiratory protection).

- When respirators are used, the employer must establish a comprehensive respiratory protection program as outlined in the NIOSH Guide to Industrial Respiratory Protection and as required by the OSHA respiratory protection standard. Important elements of this standard are

  - an evaluation of the worker's ability to perform the work while wearing a respirator

  - regular training of personnel

  - periodic environmental monitoring

  - respirator fit testing

  - maintenance, inspection, cleaning, and storage

  - selection of proper NIOSH-approved respirators

- The respiratory protection program should be evaluated regularly by the employer.

Acknowledgements

Barbara L. Dames and James D. McGlothlin, Ph.D., were the principal contributors to this chapter. Comments, questions, or requests for additional information should be directed to the following:

Dr. Laurence J. Doemeny
Acting Director, Division of Physical Sciences and Engineering
NIOSH
4676 Columbia Parkway
Cincinnati, OH 45226
Telephone: (513) 841-4321

Chapter 32

Occupational Exposure to Formaldehyde

Formaldehyde (FAH) is a colorless, flammable gas with a strong, pungent odor. It is widely used in hospitals, in disinfectants, in carpet and furniture glues, and in a large number of other products. FAH is used in liquid form as a water and methanol solution called Formalin, which has a clear to milky appearance, and in solid form as a white powder called Para-formaldehyde. Formaldehyde gas may be given off by either liquid Formalin or Paraformaldehyde powder.

Formaldehyde's odor may be detected by some people. Many others, however, may not be able to smell it at all. Therefore, the sense of smell can not be relied upon to warn workers. Rather, irritation of the eyes, nose and bronchial tubes and watering eyes may indicate exposure to FAH or formaldehyde-containing substances more often than the sense of smell.

Uses

Formaldehyde products have a wide variety of uses in hospitals including:

- tissue preservatives and in embalming fluids in autopsy rooms and the pathology department

"Formaldehyde," from the American Federation of State, County, and Municipal Employees (AFSCME) website, http://www.afscme.org/health/faq%2Dfah.htm, May 1993. Despite the age of this document, readers seeking an understanding of occupational exposure to formaldehyde will still find this information useful.

- in kidney dialysis units and central supply as a sterilizing agent

- in operating rooms as a disinfectant

Many detergents, disinfectants, and cleaning agents used by custodians may contain FAH. It is very important for custodial and housekeeping workers to become familiar with the products they use, how to work with those products safely, and when safer substitutes may be available. Read the label. Ask questions. And be careful when handling any product containing formaldehyde.

Formaldehyde is also used in carpet and furniture glues and can contaminate office air, especially where there is already a building ventilation problem. Formaldehyde is also a byproduct of engine exhaust, photochemical smog, and incinerator and cigarette smoke.

Acute (Short-term, Immediate) Effects

- *Low Exposure Levels (0.1–5 parts per million [ppm])*: Burning, tearing of eyes; skin irritation.

- *Moderate Exposure Levels (10–20 ppm)*: Burning of eyes, nose and trachea; severe coughing; severe difficulty in breathing; and intense tearing of the eyes.

- *High Exposure Levels (50–100 ppm)*: Tightening in the chest; irregular heartbeat; severe headache; pulmonary edema (fluid in the lungs); inflammation of the lungs; possibly even death.

Chronic (Long-term, Delayed) Effects

- *"Sensitization."* Some workers may be especially sensitive to formaldehyde and may develop an "allergic" reaction to very low-level exposures. This is called "sensitization" and can occur suddenly, even after an employee has worked with FAH for years with no reaction.

  - Sensitization to formaldehyde may occur in other environments outside the hospital setting. Many office products such as glues used in office furniture and rugs, carbonless copy paper, and the inks used by some copy machines contain formaldehyde. Where ventilation is poor, exposure to formaldehyde in offices can lead to "Tight Building Syndrome," or "Indoor Air Pollution," where workers develop allergies and flu-like symptoms.

- Where facilities have in-house print shops to publish newsletters, menus, and other materials, employees must also expect to find products which contain formaldehyde and may present a health risk.

- *Eczema.* Workers exposed to formaldehyde solutions or resins can develop eczema (flaking and itching skin), which may involve the eyelids, neck, hands, arms, armpits and scrotum. The condition may also be caused by contact with clothing contaminated with formaldehyde.

- *Dermatitis.* Contact with formaldehyde or contaminated clothing can also cause a severe form of skin disease called "dermatitis." Dermatitis may range from simple reddening of the skin to severe cracking and blistering. Prolonged exposure may cause the fingernails to turn soft and brown-colored.

- *Eye Damage.* Direct contact with the eye will cause severe burning and tearing, and may damage the cornea.

- *Cancer.* Formaldehyde is known to cause nasal cancer and may be associated with other respiratory cancers and cancer of the brain. The National Institute for Occupational Safety and Health (NIOSH) has recommended that FAH be treated as a potential human carcinogen. The American Conference of Governmental Industrial Hygienists (ACGIH) also calls formaldehyde a suspected human carcinogen.

- *Reproductive System.* There is also evidence that women workers exposed to formaldehyde experience menstrual disorders. Other studies have found that FAH can damage the genetic make-up of certain cells, which means it may cause birth defects.

Safe Work Procedures

Training

All employees working with formaldehyde or formaldehyde-containing products should be given comprehensive training which should include specific information about the product, how to use it safely, the hazards associated with it, personal protective equipment required, and procedures to follow in an emergency situation.

Material Safety Data Sheets

Material Safety Data Sheets (MSDS's) should be made available to each employee assigned to work with FAH or FAH-containing products. The MSDS should be provided to the employer by the manufacturer and should contain complete and detailed information on the chronic and acute health effects, fire and explosion hazards, and safety precautions. Training and MSDS's are usually required under Right-to-Know laws.

Engineering Controls

Substitution. One of the most effective methods of controlling exposure to formaldehyde is to substitute a safer, less toxic material where possible. For example, a dilute bleach may be used to disinfect the exterior of dialyzers and is much safer to use than cleaning agents containing formaldehyde.

Extreme care must be used when selecting possible substitutes. The alternative should be thoroughly evaluated for possible health effects prior to selection. In many cases, phenols, glutaraldehyde and other cold sterilants may be used as safer alternatives for formaldehyde.

Enclosure. Enclosure of the process is another preferred method of controlling worker exposure. The employee is prevented from coming into direct contact with the formaldehyde. The enclosure should be designed with a slight vacuum so that any leaks will result in the flow of external air into the enclosure. The enclosure should be tested regularly to make sure that it is operating properly and that formaldehyde gas is not escaping into the general room air.

Local exhaust ventilation. Local exhaust ventilation—where FAH is removed from the worker's breathing area—should be used to control worker exposure if formaldehyde and associated products must be used. Laboratory work with formalin or specimens preserved in formalin should be done under a fume hood or in a biological safety cabinet. Alternatively, local ventilation with moveable ducting and adjustable air inlets may be used. However, these systems are often less effective because they depend upon being properly adjusted and are more easily tampered with.

All local exhaust ventilation systems should be checked at installation to ensure that the system is working properly at three month intervals and whenever there is a change in process or operations.

All ventilation systems provided to control contaminants should be exhausted separately from general room air to the outdoors to prevent exposure of other hospital workers to the contaminated air.

General dilution ventilation means providing an adequate number of air exchanges per hour to keep air moving in a work area. In a hospital setting, the use of floor fans and blowers in the ceiling will not protect workers from exposure to formaldehyde.

Respiratory Protection

Respirators should be available for emergency use but they should not be used to protect workers from exposure to formaldehyde on a day-to-day basis. In selecting the proper respirator, it is important to know all of the hazards to which workers may be exposed. The respiratory protection must be carefully selected with a complete understanding of the hazards present.

Improper use of respirators is dangerous. Such equipment should only be used if the employer has a written program that takes into account work place conditions, requirements for worker training, and respirator fit testing. The program should also include medical exams, with emphasis on lung function, to determine an employee's ability to work under the additional strain of wearing a respirator (particularly a negative pressure respirator) as described in Occupational Safety and Health (OSHA) standard 29 Code of Federal Regulations (CFR) 1910.134.

Protective Clothing

Employees working with liquid formaldehyde should be provided with impervious clothing, heavy-duty waterproof gloves, face shields (8 inch minimum), aprons, boots and other protective clothing necessary to prevent skin contact with formaldehyde. Employees should wear splash-proof safety goggles where FAH may come into contact with the eyes.

Personal Hygiene

Workers should wash thoroughly any areas of the body which may have come in contact with formaldehyde:

* after exposure and at the end of each workday
* before lunch breaks and rest periods
* before eating, smoking or using toilet facilities

Special Precautions

Formaldehyde is flammable and explosive but only in higher concentrations. Explosive concentrations may build up in improperly ventilated storage rooms and fume hoods. Formaldehyde should *never* be stored near or used with hydrochloric acid because the two chemicals combine to form Chloromethyl Ether (BCME), a very powerful cancer-causing agent.

Medical Surveillance

Physical symptoms such as respiratory irritation or dermatitis should be an alarm that an employee is being overexposed to formaldehyde. A physician who knows the complete background of the nature of the worker's exposure should perform an examination. Monitoring of the employee's condition should continue as any treatment program is carried out. In addition, any other employees who may also be exposed to formaldehyde in the workplace or may show any symptoms of exposure to FAH should be examined. Medical examinations should be performed on an annual basis with special emphasis on the skin and the respiratory tract, and should include a medical history.

Workplace Exposure Limits

OSHA has issued a revised standard on formaldehyde. It reduces the Permissible Exposure Limit (PEL) from 1 part per million (ppm) to 0.75 as an 8-hour Time-Weighted Average (TWA) with a 2 ppm 15-minute Short Term Exposure Limit (STEL). Finally, the new standard establishes an "Action Level" at 0.5 ppm (8-hour TWA). At the action level, the employer is required to institute a monitoring and abatement program which must include the following:

- *Monitoring*. Initial monitoring must be performed by every employer covered by the standard. If the initial monitoring indicates an exposure at or above the action level, the employer must continue monitoring periodically, but at least every 6 months. Monitoring must continue until the results of two consecutive sampling periods taken at least 7 days apart show the exposure level has been reduced to below the action level. Employees must be notified of the results of such monitoring and affected employees or their union representative may observe any monitoring.

386

- *Regulated areas.* The new standard requires the employer to establish regulated areas where monitoring indicates a level of formaldehyde which exceeds either the PEL (0.75 ppm) or the STEL (2 ppm). The areas must be signed and posted: DANGER... FORMALDEHYDE... IRRITANT AND POTENTIAL CANCER HAZARD... AUTHORIZED PERSONNEL ONLY. Entry into the area must be restricted.

- *Compliance methods.* The employer is required to use engineering controls (described above) and work practice controls, except while such controls are being installed, during maintenance and repair activities for which such controls are impossible, and in work situations where engineering and work practice controls do not reduce exposure to below the PEL or STEL.

- *Respiratory protection.* Respirators are required to be worn while engineering controls are being installed, during maintenance, and repair activities for which such controls are impossible, in work situations where engineering and work practice controls do not reduce exposure to below the PEL or STEL, and in emergencies. The standard further specifies the types of respirators which are to be used for varying levels or contamination and requires that such use must be in compliance with 29 CFR 1910.134 (b)(d)(e) and (f), the OSHA Respiratory Protection Standard.

- *Protective clothing and equipment.* The standard includes requirements for clothing which is impervious to formaldehyde, gloves, safety goggles, face shields, and other personal protective equipment which may be required under 1910.132 and 1910.133. The employer is also responsible for maintaining all personal protective equipment, including laundering of contaminated clothing.

- *Hygiene protection.* The standard requires change rooms for employees who must wear protective clothing, emergency quick drench showers, and emergency eyewash stations.

- *Housekeeping.* The standard requires surveying for leaks or spills (including visual inspections), proper maintenance of equipment, spill clean-up procedures, and waste disposal methods.

- *Medical surveillance.* The standard requires medical surveillance for all employees exposed at levels above the action level or the STEL.

- *Hazard communication.* The requirement under the standard for the hazard communication program is to be in compliance with the requirements of 29 CFR 1910.1200. This includes employee Right-to-Know training (repeated at least annually). Material Safety Data Sheets (MSDS), product labeling, and all other requirements under the Hazard Communication Standard (or, where applicable, state Right-to-Know laws.)

- *Recordkeeping.* The standard requires the employer to establish and maintain accurate records of all monitoring of employee exposure to formaldehyde.

ACGIH (American Conference of Governmental Industrial Hygienists) is a standard-setting organization made up of industrial hygienists from governmental agencies and educational institutions. ACGIH has eliminated the old eight hour Time Weighted Average and the 2 ppm Short Term Exposure Limit and adopted a ceiling limit TLV 0.3 for FAH in June 1992. ACGIH has classified formaldehyde as a suspected carcinogen. That designation implies that there may be *no safe level of exposure* to formaldehyde.

NIOSH (National Institute for Occupational Safety and Health) recommends a ceiling limit of 0.1 ppm. NIOSH further recommends that formaldehyde be treated as a human carcinogen.

Chapter 33

Carbon Monoxide Poisoning

What Is It?

Carbon monoxide—a colorless, odorless, tasteless gas—is one of the most common industrial hazards. Mild poisoning can cause such symptoms as nausea, dizziness or headaches, while severe poisoning can result in brain or heart damage or even death. This poisonous gas is produced by the incomplete burning of any material containing carbon, such as gasoline, natural gas, oil, propane, coal, or wood. Forges, blast furnaces, and coke ovens all produce carbon monoxide, but one of the most common sources of exposure in the workplace is the internal combustion engine.

Be suspicious of carbon monoxide poisoning if you develop headache, flushed face, dizziness, or weakness. Bear in mind that although carbon monoxide has no telltale odor, it may mix with gases which do have an odor. Thus, the smell of other gases doesn't mean an absence of carbon monoxide.

Are You Likely to Be Poisoned?

If you have a heart condition, your condition may be aggravated by carbon monoxide. Ingestion of barbiturates and alcohol may increase

Occupational Safety and Health Administration, Fact Sheet No. OSHA 92-11, http://www.osha-slc.gov/OshDoc/Fact_data/FSNO92-11.html, January 1992. Despite the age of this document, readers seeking an understanding of occupational carbon monoxide poisoning will still find the information useful.

the gas' health effects. Further, smokers will have higher carboxyhe-moglobin than non-smokers, and therefore face higher risk from carbon monoxide exposures on the job.

Harmful levels of carbon monoxide are a potential danger to: acety-lene workers, blast furnace workers, boiler room workers, brewery workers, carbon black makers, coke oven workers, customs workers, diesel engine operators, dock workers, garage mechanics, metal oxide reducers, miners, organic chemical synthesizers, petroleum refinery workers, pulp and paper workers, steel workers, toll booth and tunnel attendants, and warehouse workers.

How Does Carbon Monoxide Harm You?

Large amounts of carbon monoxide can kill in minutes. The more carbon monoxide in the air and the longer you are exposed to it, the greater the danger. Any one or more of the following symptoms can signal carbon monoxide poisoning: headaches, tightness across the chest, nausea, drowsiness, inattention, or fatigue. As the amount of carbon monoxide in the air increases, more serious symptoms develop such as lack of coordination, weakness and confusion.

The poisoning can be reversed if caught in time. But even if you recover, acute poisoning may result in permanent damage to the parts of your body which require a lot of oxygen, such as the heart and brain.

There is a significant reproductive risk involved with carbon monoxide. An *American Journal of Industrial Medicine* article quotes two studies showing that acute carbon monoxide exposures that were non-lethal to the mother were associated with fetal loss.

What Can You Do about Carbon Monoxide?

If you suspect carbon monoxide, get out of the area and into the open fresh air. Remove anyone overcome by the gas immediately, and give the person artificial respiration. Call for a doctor, and continue the artificial respiration until the doctor arrives, or the person recovers. Prompt action can make the difference between life and death.

How Can Poisoning Be Prevented?

Suggestions for Employers

1. Install an effective ventilation system to remove poisonous carbon monoxide from the area.

2. Maintain appliances and equipment in good order, adjusting flames, burners, and drafts to reduce the formation of carbon monoxide.

3. Consider switching from fossil fuel-powered equipment to battery-powered machinery when possible.

4. Provide approved respirators for emergency use. Regular respirators (negative pressure) will not work in this atmosphere. If necessary, provide an independent air supply to workers.

5. Install carbon monoxide monitors or regularly test air in areas when carbon monoxide is generated or used.

6. Provide pre-placement and periodic medical examinations for workers who may be exposed to carbon monoxide. If possible, transfer affected workers to other jobs.

7. Instruct workers in the hazards of carbon monoxide and train them in the proper use of respirators.

Suggestions for Workers

1. Report to your employer any condition which might make carbon monoxide form or accumulate.

2. Be alert to ventilation problems, especially in enclosed areas where gases of burning fuels may be released.

3. Report complaints early. Don't overexert yourself if you suspect carbon monoxide poisoning. Physical activity increases the body's need for oxygen and thus increases the danger of poisoning.

4. If you get sick, don't forget to tell your doctor about the possibility of exposure to carbon monoxide.

5. Think carefully about your smoking habits. Tobacco, when burned, releases carbon monoxide which reduces the oxygen-carrying ability of the blood, even before any industrial exposure is added.

What Are the Federal Standards?

The Occupational Safety and Health Administration (OSHA) standard for exposure to carbon monoxide prohibits workers' exposure to more than 35 parts of the gas per million parts of air (ppm), averaged over an 8-hour workday. There is also a ceiling limit of 200 ppm (as measured over a 15-minute period).

Chapter 34

Chloroform

What Is Chloroform?

Chloroform is a colorless liquid with a pleasant, non-irritating odor and a slightly sweet taste. It will burn only when it reaches very high temperatures. In the past, chloroform was used as an inhaled anesthetic during surgery, but it isn't used that way today. Today, chloroform is used to make other chemicals and can also be formed in small amounts when chlorine is added to water. Other names for chloroform are trichloromethane and methyl trichloride.

What Happens to Chloroform When It Enters the Environment?

- Chloroform evaporates easily into the air.
- Most of the chloroform in air breaks down eventually, but it is a slow process.
- The breakdown products in air include phosgene and hydrogen chloride, which are both toxic.
- It doesn't stick to soil very well and can travel through soil to groundwater.

Agency for Toxic Substances and Disease Registry (ATSDR), http://www.atsdr.cdc.gov/tfacts6.html, September 1997.

- Chloroform dissolves easily in water and some of it may break down to other chemicals.

- Chloroform lasts a long time in groundwater.

- Chloroform doesn't appear to build up in great amounts in plants and animals.

How Might I Be Exposed to Chloroform?

- drinking water or beverages made using water containing chloroform

- breathing indoor or outdoor air containing it, especially in the workplace

- eating food that contains it

- skin contact with chloroform or water that contains it, such as in swimming pools

How Can Chloroform Affect My Health?

Animal testing is sometimes necessary to find out how toxic substances might harm people or to treat those who have been exposed. Laws today protect the welfare of research animals and scientists must follow strict guidelines. Breathing about 900 parts of chloroform per million parts air (900 ppm) for a short time can cause dizziness, fatigue, and headache. Breathing air, eating food, or drinking water containing high levels of chloroform for long periods of time may damage your liver and kidneys. Large amounts of chloroform can cause sores when chloroform touches your skin.

It isn't known whether chloroform causes reproductive effects or birth defects in people.

Animal studies have shown that miscarriages occurred in rats and mice that breathed air containing 30–300 ppm chloroform during pregnancy and also in rats that ate chloroform during pregnancy. Offspring of rats and mice that breathed chloroform during pregnancy had birth defects. Abnormal sperm were found in mice that breathed air containing 400 ppm chloroform for a few days.

How Likely Is Chloroform to Cause Cancer?

The Department of Health and Human Services (DHHS) has determined that chloroform may reasonably be anticipated to be a carcinogen.

Rats and mice that ate food or drank water with chloroform developed cancer of the liver and kidneys.

Is there a medical test to show whether I've been exposed to chloroform?

Although the amounts of chloroform in the air that you exhale and in blood, urine, and body tissues can be measured, there is no reliable test to determine how much chloroform you have been exposed to or whether you will experience any harmful effects.

The measurement of chloroform in body fluids and tissues may help to determine if you have come into contact with large amounts of chloroform, but these tests are useful for only a short time after you are exposed. Chloroform in your body might also indicate that you have come into contact with other chemicals.

Has the federal government made recommendations to protect human health? The EPA drinking water limit for total trihalomethanes, a class of chemicals that includes chloroform, is 100 micrograms per liter of water (100 μg/L). The EPA requires that spills or accidental releases of 10 pounds or more of chloroform into the environment be reported to the EPA.

The Occupational Safety and Health Administration (OSHA) has set the maximum allowable concentration of chloroform in workroom air during an 8-hour workday in a 40-hour workweek at 50 ppm.

Where Can I Get More Information?

The Agency for Toxic Substances and Disease Registry (ATSDR) can tell you where to find occupational and environmental health clinics. Their specialists can recognize, evaluate, and treat illnesses resulting from exposure to hazardous substances. You can also contact your community or state health or environmental quality department if you have any more questions or concerns. [See the resources section of this sourcebook for ATSDR contact information.]

References

ATSDR. 1997. "Toxicological profile for chloroform." Atlanta, GA: U.S. Department of Health and Human Services, Public Health Service.

Chapter 35

Burning Issues about Flammable Liquid Storage

When it comes to preventing flammable liquid fires, following Occupational Safety and Health Administration (OSHA) standards is just not sufficient.

Flammable liquids fires are much more volatile than fires fueled by ordinary combustibles such as wood, paper, and cloth. Flammable vapors can ignite with explosive force and the resulting fire gives off more than twice as much heat as ordinary combustibles—about 16,000 to 24,000 Btu/lb for flammable liquids versus 8,000 to 10,000 Btu/lb for ordinary materials.

The rate of temperature rise is greater and burning liquids produce billowing clouds of thick, black and acrid smoke. Flammable liquid fires also spread rapidly when spilled material flows into low-lying areas, dozens or even hundreds of feet away.

Because of these hazards, special precautions are required when storing, handling and using flammable liquids. Don't be lulled into a false sense of security, believing that everything will be OK if you comply with OSHA standards. OSHA's flammable liquids standard, 29 CFR 1910.106, is based on the 1969 edition of the "National Fire Protection Association's Flammable and Combustible Liquids Code" (NFPA 30). NFPA 30 has been revised eight times since adoption by OSHA in 1972, with the most recent edition published in 1996.

John F. Rekus, *Occupational Hazards*, November 1997, Vol. 59, N. 11, pp. 27–31, Copyright 1999 Penton Media Inc. Reprinted with permission.

Origin and History of NFPA 30

NFPA 30 was originally published in 1913 as the "Suggested Ordinance for the Storage, Handling and Use of Flammable Liquids." Over the last 80 years, it has been revised regularly to reflect changes dictated both by fire loss experience and advances in technology.

In 1984, the chapter on automotive and marine service stations evolved into NFPA 30A, the "Automotive and Marine Service Station Code."

In 1987, four separate chapters—"Industrial Plants," "Bulk Plants and 'Terminals," "Process Plants," and "Refineries, Chemical Plants, and Distilleries" were distilled into a single chapter entitled "Operations."

In 1990, a new section was added on hazardous materials storage lockers and more detailed guidance was provided on ventilating enclosed process areas. All references to flammable aerosols were also removed because these materials were now addressed by NFPA 30B, "Manufacture and Storage of Aerosol Products."

In 1993, a complete rewrite of the "Container and Portable Tank Storage" chapter clarified storage requirements, especially for mercantile occupancies. Changes were also made to the provisions for tank diking and the spill control requirements for certain secondary containment-type tanks.

In 1996, new fire protection design criteria were established for flammable liquid storage areas. The "Operations" chapter was also revised, making it easier to use with OSHA's chemical process safety standard.

In the wake of these monumental changes, the OSHA standard remains immutably frozen in time, reflecting information that is now almost 30 years out of date. The differences are so significant that OSHA 7(c)(1) consultants would be doing their clients a disservice if they advised them to follow 29 Code of Federal Regulations (CFR) 1910.106 when designing new storage rooms. This advice would result in implementing needless provisions such as self-closing fire doors, while at the same time neglecting important considerations such as deflagration venting that could keep the building from blowing up.

As a practical matter, people who are seriously interested in flammable liquid safety should throw their OSHA standards in the trash and get a copy of the 1996 edition of NFPA 30. Or better yet, get a copy of the NPFA 30 Code Handbook, which in addition to providing the full text of the code, also contains technical guidance, commentary and important interpretations of code requirements.

Flash Point

A fire will not occur until a flammable liquid is heated above a certain temperature called the flash point. Put more scientifically, flash point is the lowest temperature at which a liquid gives off enough vapor to cause a momentary flame in the presence of an ignition source.

Flash point can be used as a relative index of the hazard posed by a flammable liquid. In general, the lower the flash point, the greater the hazard. If the liquid's temperature is below the flash point, it simply will not give off enough vapor to burn.

For example, the flash point of one of my favorite compounds, ethyl alcohol, is 55° F. If we put a lighted match into an ice-cold glass of Scotch or brandy, the match would go out. However, when the glass warms up to a little over 55° F, the vapors formed at the mouth would ignite if the match is brought close to the edge.

Boiling Point

The boiling point is the temperature at which the vapor pressure of a liquid exceeds atmospheric pressure. Since atmospheric pressure can no longer keep the substance in the liquid state, bubbles begin to form and the material converts into a vapor.

Boiling point provides a relative index of a liquid's volatility because low-boiling liquids have higher vapor pressures than high-boiling liquids at the same temperature. Low boiling liquids are more hazardous because they evaporate more quickly.

Liquid Classes

Flash point and boiling point are important to know because they are used as the basis for identifying liquids that present a similar degree of hazard. Those with flash points less than 100° F are referred to as "flammable liquids," while those with flash points greater than, or equal to 100° F, are called "combustible liquids."

Flammable and combustible liquids can be further divided into classes. Class I-A flammable liquids are those with flash points less that 73° F, and boiling points less than 100° F. Ethyl ether, pentane and ethylene oxide are examples of Class I-A materials.

Class I-B flammable liquids include materials like acetone, cyclohexane and gasoline that have flash points less than 73° F and boiling points at or above 100° F. Class I-C flammable liquids are solvents like butyl alcohol, turpentine and xylene with flash points between 73° F and 100° F.

Class II combustible liquids are those with a flash point above 100° F but below 140° F. Kerosene, diesel fuel and No. 2 heating oil are familiar examples. Class III-A combustible liquids have a flash point between 140° F and 200° F and include acetophenone, diethyl benzene and isopherone. Class III-B are those with a flash point greater than 200° F and include many natural oils like castor oil, olive oil and peanut oil.

Incidental Use

As a general rule, the amount of flammable liquid used outside of an "approved" cabinet or storage room should be as small as is practical. However, NFPA 30 allows the sum of the following quantities to be located in the general plant area:

- 25 gallons of Class I-A liquid in containers

- 120 gallons of Class I-B, I-C, II or III-A liquids in containers

- two portable 660-gallon tanks of class I-B, II-C, II or III-A

- twenty 660-gallon portable tanks of Class III-B

Alternatively, one day's supply, whatever that quantity happens to be, is also permitted.

Although OSHA allows the same quantities, ambiguity in the standard's wording has led some compliance officers to incorrectly believe that quantity cannot exceed any one of the limits listed above, not the aggregate. Although this misunderstanding was addressed in OSHA Standards Notice STD 1-5.14, some compliance officers are unaware of the correct interpretation and continue to cite and fine employers for a condition that is not actually a violation.

Storage Cabinet Construction

Flammable liquids cabinets are designed to protect their contents for up to 10 minutes in a fire. This is the estimated time that a room is likely to be seriously burning. For a cabinet to provide this kind of protection, it must meet the following requirements:

- at least 18 gauge steel with riveted or welded joints

- double-wall construction with inch and a half air gap between the walls for insulation

- have a 2-inch raised door sill to contain spills
- be equipped with a door lock that catches at the top, bottom, and middle to prevent buckling in a fire

Ordinary office supply cabinets do not provide this protection and are not approved for storage of flammable liquids; however, wooden cabinets are, if built to the following specifications:

- constructed of exterior grade plywood at least 1-inch thick and of a type that will not delaminate under fire conditions
- have rabbeted joints that are fastened in two directions with wood screws
- if there is more than one door, there must be at least a 1-inch rabbeted overlap
- there must be a raised sill or pan capable of holding at least 2 inches of spilled liquid

This last provision was not incorporated into 29 CFR 1910.106 due to an inadvertent omission in the 1969 version of NFPA 30 that OSHA adopted. Although the mistake was corrected in revisions to NFPA 30, it persists to this day in the OSHA standard.

Storage Cabinet Quantity

Not more than 60 gallons of a Class I or II liquid or 120 gallons of a Class III-A liquid may be stored in a single cabinet, and not more than three cabinets are permitted in the same fire area unless they are separated by 100 feet.

Table 35.1. Fire Protection Rating for Fire Doors

Fire resistance rating of wall [in hours]	Fire protection rating of Door [in hours]
1	3/4
2	1 1/2
4	3

Note: One fire door is required on each side of interior openings for attached warehouses.

A fire area is a portion of a building separated from other areas by a one-hour fire-rated wall. Openings such as doorways, duct openings and pass-through counters must also be protected by an assembly having at least a one-hour fire resistance rating.

Storage Rooms

Since only three cabinets can be kept in one fire area, large quantities of flammable liquids must be kept in a specially designed flammable liquid storage room.

Storage areas are classified as "inside rooms", "cutoff rooms," or attached buildings. Inside storage rooms are fully enclosed within a building and have no exterior structural walls. Cut-off rooms, on the other hand, have one or two walls in common with the building exterior. The number of common walls depends on whether the room construction incorporates a building side wall or a corner. Attached buildings have three exterior walls and share only one wall with the main structure.

Storage Room Requirements

Because of the severe risk posed by bulk flammable liquids, storage rooms must conform to very rigorous requirements:

Fire resistant. Storage areas must meet the fire resistance ratings.

Opening protection. Openings in interior walls and exterior fire-rated walls must be provided with normally closed, fire-rated doors as specified in Table 35.1. The doors may be kept open during material handling operations if they are provided with listed closures which are designed to operate automatically in a fire emergency.

Deflagration venting. Deflagration venting—often improperly referred to as "explosion venting"—must be incorporated into an exterior wall or roof of rooms where Class I-A, I-B or unstable liquids are dispensed, or where Class I-A or unstable liquids are stored in containers larger than one gallon. Exceptions are made for inside storage rooms, and for dispensing Class I-B liquids from containers smaller than 60 gallons.

Spill containment. It is important to understand that NFPA 30's spill containment provisions are not based on environmental concerns, but rather on preventing spills from migrating to other areas of a building where they could be ignited. Exemptions are provided for small quantities, water miscible liquids, those with a specific gravity greater than water, Class III-B liquids and those that are highly viscous. Consequently, local environmental ordinances should be consulted because they may be more restrictive.

Electrical wiring. Electrical wiring in rooms where Class I liquids are stored must conform to requirements for a Class I Division 2 hazardous location; however, general-purpose wiring is acceptable if only Class II or III liquids are stored. Where Class I liquids are dispensed, or where Class II or III liquids are dispensed at temperatures above their flash points, all wiring within 3 feet of dispensing nozzles must conform to Class I Division 1 requirements.

Ventilation. Either mechanical or natural ventilation may be employed if the room is used solely for storage. However, if flammable liquids are dispensed, mechanical ventilation must be provided at a rate of at least 1 cubic foot per minute (CFM) per square foot of floor area, with a minimum of 150 CFM. The ventilation system must also be provided with an air-flow interlock which activates an audible alarm in the event of a ventilation failure.

Dispensing. Dispensing of Class I, or Class II and III at temperatures above their flash points, is not permitted in cut-off rooms, attached buildings, or liquid warehouses larger than 1,000 square feet unless the dispensing area is cut off from the storage area and conforms to the other requirements described above.

Quantity limitations. The maximum quantity of a liquid that can be stored is determined by a variety of tables that consider factors such as: the class of liquid, container type and size, storage rack configuration, the characteristics of the fire protection system and whether material is stored in the basement, ground level or upper floors of a building .

Fixed Fire Protection

Perhaps the most significant change in the 1996 edition of NFPA 30 is that there are new fixed fire protection design criteria for storage areas which were developed from data obtained from full-scale fire tests. The tests examined the major variables that influence a fire's severity and growth rate as well as the ability of fixed fire-suppression systems to control or extinguish a flammable liquid fire.

The fire test data were used to develop a set of tables that govern the acceptable storage methods for flammable liquids in containers. These methods are based on the following factors:

- the specific type of sprinkler system
- the container type and size
- the liquid class
- the storage array
- the maximum allowable storage height
- the maximum ceiling height

Fully charged portable fire extinguishers must be provided outside of flammable liquid storage areas and employees who are required to use them must be trained in their use.

At least one 40:B extinguisher must be located outside of the room, but within 10 feet of the door leading into it. Alternatively, at least one 80:B extinguisher may be located within 50 feet of the storage area.

Extinguishers must be visually inspected monthly and receive annual maintenance checks. The visual inspection should verify that they are in place, fully charged, and free of defects such as inoperable gauges, missing safety pins, cracked discharge hoses and broken nozzles. The person who performs the inspection should initial and date the inspection tag accompanying the extinguishers. The annual maintenance is usually performed by an extinguisher maintenance contractor and includes a comprehensive visual check and a hydrostatic pressure test.

Summary

Because of the severe fire hazard posed by flammable and combustible liquids, special precautions are required for their storage, handling and use. The OSHA flammable liquids standard, which is almost 30 years out of date, is not a reliable source for current storage room design criteria. Instead, the 1996 edition of NFPA's "Flammable and Combustible Liquids Code" should be consulted.

— by John Rekus

Contributing editor John Rekus is an independent consultant and author of the National Safety Council's "Complete Confined Spaces Handbook." With more than 20 years of OSHA compliance experience, Rekus specializes in conducting OSHA compliance surveys and providing safety training for workers and managers. He resides near Baltimore and may be reached at (410) 583-7954.

Chapter 36

Electric and Magnetic Fields (EMFs) in the Workplace

Everyone in our modern society is exposed to the electric and magnetic fields (EMFs) that surround all electric devices. Recently, scientific studies have raised questions about the possible health effects of EMFs. This chapter answers frequently asked questions about EMFs in the workplace. You can use this information to help identify EMF sources at work and to take simple steps for reducing exposures. However, you cannot use this information to judge the safety of your exposures, since the scientific evidence does not yet show whether EMF exposures are hazardous.

What Are EMFs?

EMFs are invisible lines of force created whenever electricity is generated or used. EMFs are produced by power lines, electric wiring, and electric equipment and appliances. The frequency of EMFs is measured in hertz (Hz, or cycles per second). People are exposed to both electric and magnetic fields, but scientists are most concerned about magnetic fields. This fact sheet deals only with magnetic fields that have frequencies near 60 Hz, the frequency of electric power in North America.

National Institute of Occupational Safety and Health, DHHS (NIOSH) Pub. No. 96-129, 1996.

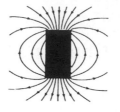

Figure 36.1. Static magnetic field around a bar magnet.

What Do We Know about Workplace Exposures to EMFs?

Workers may be exposed to high magnetic fields if they work near electrical systems that use large amounts of electric power (for example, large electric motors, generators, or the power supply or electric cables of a building). High magnetic fields are also found near power saws, drills, copy machines, electric pencil sharpeners, and other small electric appliances. The strength of the magnetic field depends on equipment design and current flow, not on equipment size, complexity, or voltage. Though some electric equipment produces EMFs of other frequencies, most health research has considered only frequencies near 60 Hz.

What Are Some Typical EMF Exposures on the Job?

The EMF exposures for many jobs have not been measured, but the following table shows average exposures to magnetic fields for typical workers who use electric equipment. Exposures during a work shift vary with the strength of the magnetic field, the worker's distance from the EMF source, and the time the worker spends in the field. For comparison, the table also lists worker exposures off the job.

Do EMFs Cause Cancer or Other Health Effects?

Studies have shown that some workers exposed to high magnetic fields have increased cancer rates, but such associations do not necessarily show that EMF exposures cause cancer (any more than the springtime association of robins and daffodils shows that one causes the other). Scientists have looked carefully at all the EMF evidence,

Table 36.1. Average magnetic field exposures for various types of workers (in milligauss—one thousandth of a gauss = 1 milligauss).

Type of Worker	Average Daily Exposures	
	Median	Range
Workers on the Job:		
Clerical workers without computers	0.5	0.2–2.0
Clerical workers with computers	1.2	0.5–4.5
Machinists	1.9	0.6–27.6
Electric line workers	2.5	0.5–34.8
Electricians	5.4	0.8–34.0
Welders	8.2	1.7–96.0
Workers off the Job (home, travel, etc.)	0.9	0.3–3.7

but they disagree about the health effects of EMFs except to say that better information is needed.

What Do Studies Show about the Health Effects of EMFs in Workers?

Many studies report small increases in the rate of leukemia or brain cancer in groups of people living or working in high magnetic fields. Other studies have found no such increases. The most important data come from six recent studies of workers wearing EMF monitors to measure magnetic fields. All but one study found significantly higher cancer rates for men with average workday exposures above 4 milligauss. However, the results of these studies disagree in important ways, such as the type of cancer associated with EMF exposures. So scientists cannot be sure whether the increased risks are caused by EMFs or by other factors. A few preliminary studies have also associated workplace EMFs with breast cancer, and one study has reported a possible link between occupational EMF exposure and Alzheimer s disease.

The data from all of these studies are too limited for scientists to draw conclusions. However, a national research effort is under way, and more study results are expected in a few years.

Have Limits Been Set for Worker Exposures to EMFs?

Because of the scientific uncertainty, no Federal limits for worker exposures to EMFs have been recommended or established in the United States. Two private organizations have developed guidelines to protect workers from the known effects of extremely high exposures (that is, those more than 1,000 times the exposures typically found in occupational environments). However, these guidelines do not address the possible health effects of the low EMF exposures usually found on the job.

Should Workers and Employers Try to Reduce Exposures to EMFs?

The National Institute for Occupational Safety and Health (NIOSH) and other government agencies do not consider EMFs a proven health hazard. Because some studies have associated high magnetic field exposures with increased cancer risks, the government will continue studying EMFs. While research continues, concerned workers and employers might consider the following simple, inexpensive measures for reducing EMF exposures:

- Inform workers and employers about possible hazards of magnetic fields.

- Increase the worker's distance from the EMF source. Since magnetic fields often drop off dramatically within about 3 feet of the source, workers can stand back from electrical equipment, and workstations can be moved out of the three-foot range of stronger EMF sources.

- Use low-EMF designs wherever possible (for the layout of office power supplies, for example).

- Reduce EMF exposure times. No action should be taken to reduce EMF exposure if it increases the risk of a known safety or health hazard, such as electrocution.

What Is NIOSH Doing about EMF Exposures?

NIOSH has been evaluating the possible health effects of EMFs since 1991. NIOSH scientists have measured the fields in workplaces where employees are concerned about their EMF exposures; they are also studying the biological effects of EMFs. In addition, NIOSH scientists work cooperatively with researchers in universities and other Federal agencies to share their study results. These cooperative efforts have increased recently under the National EMF Research and Public Information Dissemination (RAPID) program.

How to Find Out More about EMFs in the Workplace

To provide more details, a 68-page booklet "Questions and Answers: EMF in the Workplace" (Publication Number DOE/GO-10095-218, DE95013123) has been published by NIOSH together with the Department of Energy and the National Institute for Environmental Health Sciences. See the resources section of this sourcebook for NIOSH contact information.

Chapter 37

Cancer and the Workplace

Introduction

Although occupationally related cancers make up only a small fraction of all cancers, many environmental carcinogens have first been discovered in occupational settings. The estimate typically found in the scientific literature is that about two to eight percent of all human cancers are of occupational origin. However, by averaging the unexposed population in with the exposed, such estimates tend to obscure the heavy toll that occupational cancer can take on specific populations of exposed workers. Among persons actually exposed to carcinogens at work, risk estimates are much higher. For instance, Morabia et al. have put the attributable risk for lung cancer at 9.2 percent for men employed in occupations characterized by exposure to established carcinogens. For bladder cancer, the population attributable risk from occupational exposures may exceed one case in five for men and one in ten for women.

Indeed, despite the relatively small "contribution" that occupational cancer makes to the total cancer burden, recognition and concern for cancers related to workplace exposures have been central themes in control of environmental carcinogens. There are several good reasons for this. One is the unique nature of the workplace, which serves as a focal point in which large numbers of people may be exposed to high concentrations of chemicals or other hazardous situations. Another is that the very nature of work creates a cohort for the kinds of epidemiologic studies that can help establish a cause-effect relationship between an environmental exposure and cancer. It is because of the exposures to large doses and the opportunities to implement effective procedures for risk assessment and control in the workplace that the study of occupational cancer plays so important a role in the control of cancer in general.

Finally, perhaps the most important reason to identify occupational carcinogens and to elucidate their role in cancer causation is that occupational cancers are, for the most part, entirely preventable through appropriate engineering, personnel practices, and strict governmental protective legislation.

The ultimate goal of collecting, evaluating, and disseminating data on carcinogenicity of occupational exposures is to develop strategies for prevention of disease. The most efficient strategy relies on primary prevention, that is, identification and elimination of sources of exposure. Secondary prevention through screening of asymptomatic illness plays a lesser role, but may still be valuable in specific workplaces. Recent advances in molecular biology have led to identification of tests that can identify workers exposed to various carcinogens. Such tests, however. are at present extremely expensive, and their predictive value is no greater than that of traditional industrial hygiene workplace evaluations. Occupational screening may have its greatest usefulness as a tool for educating workers to potential hazards in the workplace.

Identifying Human Carcinogens

Despite the fact that more than six million chemicals have already been identified and registered with the Chemical Abstracts Service and more than 50,000 are estimated to be regularly used in commerce, probably fewer than 1,000 chemicals or exposure situations have been scrutinized as to their potential for cancer causation. Even so, the literature on evaluation of cancer risks for even this small fraction of known exposures is massive and not altogether consistent for many specific substances. Estimation of actual cancer risks to humans requires careful sitting and evaluation of large quantities of data from many different studies. Since the early 1970s, an extensive effort has been made to systematize the available data on cancer risks. A comprehensive methodology for assessment of human cancer risks has been developed by the International Agency for Research on Cancer (IARC) that draws on data from a variety of disciplines.

The IARC methods, which are widely regarded as definitive, rely on the judgment of internationally recognized experts. Groups of scientists with expertise in various disciplines are convened to discuss and summarize the literature on individual carcinogens, groups of related carcinogens, or in some cases entire industries. These critical evaluations are ultimately presented as monographs, each of which contains a critical evaluation of the carcinogenicity of one or more target exposures. The evaluations take into account many different types of information, including data from epidemiology, experimental studies on rodents and other laboratory animals, in vitro studies where appropriate, and other relevant data including toxicity, metabolism, genotoxicity, and metabolic studies.

According to the IARC, "Each monograph consists of a brief description of the chemical and physical properties of the agent; methods for its analysis; a description of the methods and volumes of production and use; data on occurrence and human exposure; summaries of case reports and epidemiologic studies of cancer in humans; summaries of experimental carcinogenicity tests; a brief description of other relevant biologic data, such as toxicity and genetic effects, that may indicate its possible mechanism of action; and an evaluation of its carcinogenicity." Because the IARC periodically revises its evaluations to reflect accumulation of new data and evolution of methods of assessment, the information in these monographs is generally current.

Categories of Carcinogenicity to Humans

The IARC classifies the evidence for carcinogenicity of specific exposures into four categories: sufficient, limited, or inadequate evidence of carcinogenicity, or evidence suggesting lack of carcinogenicity. Sufficient evidence of carcinogenicity implies that a causal relationship has been established between exposure to the agent, mixture, or exposure circumstance and human cancer and that chance, bias, and confounding have been ruled out with reasonable confidence.

Limited evidence of carcinogenicity, implies that a positive association has been observed between exposure to the agent, mixture, or exposure circumstance and cancer for which a causal interpretation is considered to be credible, but chance, bias, or confounding cannot be ruled out with reasonable confidence.

Inadequate evidence of carcinogenicity means that the available studies are of insufficient quality, consistency, or statistical power to permit a conclusion regarding the presence or absence of a causal association or that no data on cancer in humans are available.

Evidence suggesting lack of carcinogenicity means that there are several adequate studies covering the full range of exposure levels that human beings are known to encounter that are mutually consistent in not showing a positive association between exposure to the agent and the studied cancer at any observed level of exposure.

Criteria for Evaluating Carcinogenicity Based on Total Evidence

A set of criteria analogous to those for assessing risk in human studies is used to classify cancer risk even when definitive human data are not available. This process takes into account information from carcinogenesis bioassays and other experimental studies of animals along with toxicity and other biologic data. The expert committee deliberations take into account epidemiologic, animal, and other types of data, including in vitro and metabolic studies where appropriate, from which an overall assessment of carcinogenicity to humans is synthesized within a scheme that consists of four broad groups. To date, 61 volumes of IARC Monographs have been published, and 782 agents or exposure circumstances have been classified.

The distribution of these 782 agents or exposure circumstances within the carcinogenicity groupings is shown in Table 37.1. Group 2, likely carcinogens, is subdivided into Group 2A, probably carcinogenic to humans, and Group 2B, possibly carcinogenic to humans. These

Table 37.1 International Agency for Research on Cancer Assessments of Chemical Carcinogenicity

Category	Carcinogenicity	Number of Agents or Exposure Situations [1972-1995]
Group 1:	Carcinogenic to humans	66
Group 2A:	Probably carcinogenic to humans	51
Group 2B:	Possibly carcinogenic to humans	210
Group 3:	Data insufficient to decide carcinogenicity	454
Group 4:	Probably not carcinogenic to humans	1
Total Evaluated		782

categorizations take explicit note of the relevance of animal studies to human cancer risk and are most often used to classify substances for which human data may be limited or inadequate but where animal data are deemed sufficient and mechanistically relevant to humans (Group 2A) or less than sufficient but strongly supportive of existing human data (Group 2B).

The seemingly large number of agents denoted as carcinogenic or probably carcinogenic (Groups 1 and 2A, N=117) is a reflection of the selection process for inclusion in the monographs. Agents are generally evaluated only when substantial data bases already exist. These data bases, in turn, have usually evolved over a period of years in response to concerns of industry, workers, or the public.

Some Examples of Exposures and Controls in Health-Care

The history of occupational cancer identification and control has been recounted by many authors. The potential for work-related cancers has been recognized at least since the work of Ramazzini in the sixteenth century, and in fact our modern understanding of the influence of environmental factors on human cancer is due in large measure to occupational studies, ironically many of them drawn from the exposures of people in the health-care professions. Examination of the known and probable occupational carcinogens and exposure situations reveals a number that are found in health-care situations and for which work practices are still inadequate to protect health-care personnel with potential exposures.

X-rays provide a good case study. Much of the knowledge about the dangers of the industrial use of x-rays is based on the "lamentable history" of the pioneers in the medical field, according to occupational medicine pioneer Donald Hunter. The first death recognized to be the result of the action of x-rays occurred in 1914 to the Italian radiologist, Emilio Tiraboschi. By 1922 at least one hundred radiologists had died from malignant diseases arising from their occupation. Much of the natural course of radiation poisoning was elucidated by following the progression of disease among these early victims. It is estimated that many hundreds of people have died as a result of occupational exposures to medical x-rays.

The recognition of the potential deadliness of exposure to x-rays led to the relatively early establishment of national and international regulatory bodies, such as the International Commission on Radiological Protection, which was formed in 1928. Important safety concepts, such as maximum permissible dose, appropriate design and control of x-ray equipment, and basic principles for the elimination of unnecessary exposures, were developed over the years, along with systems of administrative control for registration and surveillance of people occupationally exposed to radiation.

In many ways the control of exposure to x-rays is a paradigm for the basic principles for prevention of occupational cancer. The primary means of prevention is to reduce exposure to x-rays. This is facilitated by providing equipment designed to be as safe as possible and by testing and maintaining the equipment on a specified schedule. Exposure is also minimized through the use of appropriate shielding. Other preventive measures include administrative procedures to control potential exposures and rigorous programs of registration and surveillance (medical record keeping and exposure monitoring by radiation badges). All personnel who work with x-rays must receive training, and some job categories require specific licensure. A regulatory structure provides guidance and specifies the minimum legal requirements.

Other Exposures

While studies of occupational cancers focus by definition on potential carcinogenic exposures in the workplace, workers can be exposed to cancer-causing or cancer-preventing substances or conditions outside of the workplace. Cigarette smoking is the most-recognized non-occupational carcinogenic exposure, and it is well recognized that information on smoking habits should be collected when feasible. Unfortunately, this is sometimes impossible, especially in studies where exposure data are reconstructed from past employment and medical records or from death certificates.

Less well understood is the possible influence of diet and nutrition on occupational cancer. Fruits and vegetables have been associated with reduced lung cancer risk in many studies, even after adjustment for smoking. In a large-scale, prospective study in Japan, Hirayama found independent (additive) effects for employment as a "material metal worker" and cigarette smoking on the risk of death from lung cancer. The study also found an independent protective effect for regular consumption of green-yellow vegetables. Nevertheless, few occupational studies have actually taken nutrition into account as a possible etiologic factor, and the negative association between consumption of fruits and vegetables with cigarette smoking makes it difficult to generalize such findings to occupational settings.

Evaluating Occupational Exposures in a Clinical Setting

In this era of increased public awareness and concern about occupational and environmental health hazards, clinicians should be alert to the possibility that cancers may have occupational origins. This concern is appropriate if only because it may lead to reduction of the harmful exposure for the patient and his or her coworkers. As we have noted previously, it is especially important to keep the patient fully informed of any findings relating his or her illness to the workplace, as there may be many other workers who can benefit from this knowledge. Also, while physicians should take every opportunity to counsel their patients who smoke to give up the habit, the possibility that smoking may exacerbate cancer risk simply increases the importance of this step.

While there has been dramatic growth in the number of professionals with formal training in occupational and environmental health and parallel growth in the resources available to clinicians for diagnosing occupational diseases, most clinicians require assistance when faced with determining whether a particular cancer can be linked to an occupational or environmental origin.

A work or exposure history is an essential component for diagnosis of an occupational cancer. The Agency for Toxic Substances and Disease Registry has developed a form for taking a patient's exposure history. The form is designed for quick scanning of important details. The form comprises three components: a survey of possible exposures to physical and chemical agents, a work history of every job held over the working lifetime, and an environmental history of hobbies and conditions in the home environment that could be associated with the cancer.

In general, it is not necessary to understand the jargon of a particular trade to take an adequate exposure history. According to the Agency for Toxic Substances and Disease Registry, persistent questioning by the clinician can clarify the tasks involved in most jobs and can reveal possible exposures.

It may be, however, that further technical information is required. This can usually be obtained from the employer or a local government or university resource. The American College of Occupational and Environmental Medicine can provide a list of board-certified occupational physicians, and the Association of Occupational and Environmental Clinics is a network of clinics affiliated with medical schools throughout the United States. The National Institute for Occupational Safety and Health has established Education Resource Centers that can also provide information as well as formal training opportunities. Often the local Poison Control Center can provide specific information about the toxicity and health effects of hazardous exposures involved in poisonings. This may be of use in attempting to evaluate the more chronic effects generally associated with long-term environmental exposures. Finally, systematic and extensive information is now available in electronic format on the toxicology of thousands of chemicals used in the occupational environment. Many are available on CD-ROM. The National Library of Medicine in Bethesda, Maryland, and the Agency for Toxic Substances and Disease Registry in Atlanta, Georgia, are two important resources for obtaining such information. The resources section of this sourcebook lists addresses and telephone numbers for these resources:

- The American College of Occupational and Environmental Medicine
- The Association of Occupational and Environmental Clinics
- The National Institute for Occupational Safety and Health
- The American Association of Poison Control Centers
- The Agency for Toxic Substances and Disease Registry
- The National Library of Medicine

Part Eight

Reproductive and Pregnancy Issues

Chapter 38

The Effects of Workplace Hazards on Female Reproductive Health

Introduction

Many factors can affect a woman's reproductive health and her ability to produce healthy children. We know that the health of an unborn child can suffer if a woman fails to eat right, smokes, or drinks alcohol during pregnancy. However, we know very little about the cause of most reproductive health problems such as infertility, miscarriage, and birth defects. We do know that some workplace hazards can affect a woman's reproductive health, her ability to become pregnant, or the health of her unborn children. This chapter answers the following questions:

- What are reproductive hazards for female workers?

- How does the female reproductive system work?

- What reproductive problems might be caused by workplace exposures?

- How are workers and their babies exposed?

- How are families exposed?

- How can exposures be prevented?

National Institute of Occupational Safety and Health Centers for Disease Control and Prevention (OSHA DHHS), Pub. No. 99-104, February 1999.

423

What Are Reproductive Hazards for Female Workers?

Substances or agents that affect the reproductive health of women or men or the ability of couples to have healthy children are called reproductive hazards. Radiation, some chemicals, certain drugs (legal and illegal), cigarettes, some viruses, and alcohol are examples of reproductive hazards. This chapter focuses on reproductive hazards in the workplace that affect women and their ability to have healthy children.

The harmful effects of a few agents found in the workplace have been known for many years. For example, more than 100 years ago, lead was discovered to cause miscarriages, stillbirths, and infertility in female pottery workers. Rubella (German measles) was recognized as a major cause of birth defects in the 1940s. However, the causes of most reproductive health problems are still not known. Many of these problems—infertility, miscarriage, low birth weight—are fairly common occurrences and affect working and non-working women.

A reproductive hazard could cause one or more health effects, depending on when the woman is exposed. For example, exposure to harmful substances during the first 3 months of pregnancy might cause a birth defect or a miscarriage. During the last 6 months of pregnancy, exposure to reproductive hazards could slow the growth of the fetus, affect the development of its brain, or cause premature labor. Reproductive hazards may not affect every worker or every pregnancy.

Table 38.1 lists chemical and physical reproductive hazards for women in the workplace. The list is not complete and is constantly being revised. Therefore, do not assume that a substance is safe if it is missing from the list.

Table 38.2 lists viruses and other disease-causing (infectious) agents that are found in some workplaces and that have harmful reproductive effects in pregnant women.

Workers with immunity through vaccinations or earlier exposures are not generally at risk from diseases such as hepatitis B, human parvovirus B19, German measles, or chicken pox. But pregnant workers without prior immunity should avoid contact with infected children or adults.

Workers should also use good hygienic practices such as frequent handwashing to prevent the spread of infectious diseases among workers in elementary schools, nursery schools, and daycare centers. In addition, they should use universal precautions—such as glove wearing and safe disposal of needles—to protect against disease-causing agents found in blood.

424

How Does the Female Reproductive System Work?

To understand how reproductive hazards can affect a woman's reproductive health and her ability to have healthy children, it is helpful to understand how the female reproductive system works.

The main reproductive tissues in women are the ovaries, uterus, and fallopian tubes. The functions of these tissues are largely controlled by hormones produced by the brain and the pituitary gland. Hormones are chemicals that are formed in the body and circulate in

Table 38.1. Chemical and Physical Agents That Are Reproductive Hazards for Women in the Workplace

Agent	Observed Effects	Potentially Exposed Workers
Cancer treatment drugs (e.g., methotrexate)	Infertility, miscarriage, birth defects, low birth weight	Health care workers, pharmacists
Certain ethylene glycol ethers such as 2-ethoxyethanol (2EE) and 2-methoxyethanol (2ME)	Miscarriages	Electronic and semi-conductor workers
Carbon disulfide (CS2)	Menstrual cycle changes	Viscose rayon workers
Lead	Infertility, miscarriage, low birth weight, developmental disorders	Battery makers, solderers, welders, radiator repairers, bridge re-painters, firing range workers, home remodelers
Ionizing radiation (e.g., X-rays and gamma rays)	Infertility, miscarriage, birth defects, low birth weight, developmental disorders, childhood cancers	Health care workers, dental personnel, atomic workers
Strenuous physical labor (e.g., prolonged standing, heavy lifting)	Miscarriage late in pregnancy, premature delivery	Many types of workers

the blood. These hormones regulate the menstrual cycle, pregnancy, and the production of breast milk. Estrogen and progesterone—the sex hormones—are produced by the ovaries. These hormones are responsible for sexual development and for preparing the uterine wall to hold and nourish a fertilized egg every month. These sex hormones also contribute to the basic health of the heart, bones, liver, and many other tissues. Finally, during pregnancy the placenta produces a hormone (human chorionic gonadotropin, or hCG) that signals the body to support the pregnancy.

Table 38.2. Disease-Causing Agents That Are Reproductive Hazards for Women in the Workplace

Agent	Observed effects	Potentially exposed workers	Preventive measures
Cytomegalo-virus (CMV)	Birth defects, low birth weight, developmental disorders	Health care workers, workers in contact with infants and children	Good hygienic practices such as handwashing
Hepatitis B virus	Low birth weight	Health care workers	Vaccination
Human immuno-deficiency virus (HIV)	Low birth weight, childhood cancer	Health care workers	Practice universal precautions
Human parvovirus B19	Miscarriage	Health care workers, workers in contact with infants and children	Good hygienic practices such as handwashing
Rubella (German measles)	Birth defects, low birth weight	Health care workers, workers in contact with infants and children	Vaccination before pregnancy if no prior immunity
Toxoplasmosis	Miscarriage, birth defects, developmental disorders	Animal care workers, veterinarians	Good hygiene practices such as handwashing
Varicella zoster virus (chicken pox)	Birth defects, low birth weight	Health care workers, workers in contact with infants and children	Vaccination before pregnancy if no prior immunity

A woman is born with all of the eggs that she will ever have. Therefore, if her eggs are damaged or destroyed, she will not be able to replace them. At puberty, a woman begins to have menstrual cycles, which enable her to release an egg each month from one of her ovaries. Each cycle begins with a few days of menstrual flow. When each new cycle begins, a new egg starts to grow. After 2 to 3 weeks, a mature egg (ovum) is released from the ovary into the fallopian tubes, where it might be fertilized by one of the many sperm that may surround it. If the egg is not fertilized, it will die and leave the body about 2 weeks later in the woman's menstrual flow. Then the process begins again with a new menstrual cycle.

If the egg is fertilized, the complex process of reproduction continues. The fertilized egg travels for about a week down the fallopian tube to reach the uterus, where it attaches to the wall. A specialized tissue called the placenta forms between the uterus and the newly developing fetus. The placenta transfers oxygen and nutrients from the mother to the fetus. During the first 3 months of pregnancy (first trimester), the major fetal organs are formed. During the remainder of the pregnancy, these organs mature and the fetus grows rapidly.

What Reproductive Hazards Might Be Caused by Workplace Exposures?

Only a few substances (some viruses, chemicals, and drugs) are known to cause reproductive health problems. Scientists are just beginning to discover how workplace exposures might cause reproductive

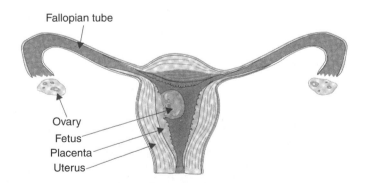

Figure 38.1. Female Reproductive Organs

problems. The following problems may be caused by workplace exposures:

- menstrual cycle effects
- infertility and subfertility
- miscarriage and stillbirths
- birth defects
- low birth weight and premature birth
- developmental disorders
- childhood cancer

Each problem is discussed in more detail in the following sections.

Menstrual Cycle Effects

High levels of physical or emotional stress or exposure to chemicals such as carbon disulfide may disrupt the balance between the brain, pituitary, and ovaries. This disruption can result in an imbalance of estrogen and progesterone, and lead to changes in menstrual cycle length, regularity, and ovulation. Because these sex hormones have effects throughout a woman's body, severe or long-lasting hormone imbalances may affect a woman's overall health.

Infertility and Subfertility

About 10% to 15% of all couples are unable to conceive a child after 1 year of trying to become pregnant. Many factors can affect fertility, and these factors can affect one or both partners. Damage to the woman's eggs or the man's sperm, or a change in the hormones needed to regulate the normal menstrual cycle are just a few things that can cause problems with fertility.

Miscarriage and Stillbirths

About 1 in every 6 pregnancies ends in a miscarriage—the unplanned termination of a pregnancy. Miscarriages can occur very early in pregnancy, even before the woman knows she is pregnant. Miscarriages and stillbirths occur for many reasons, such as the following:

- The egg or sperm may be damaged so that the egg cannot be fertilized or cannot survive after fertilization.

- A problem may exist in the hormone system needed to maintain the pregnancy.

- The fetus may not have developed normally.

- Physical problems may exist with the uterus or cervix.

What causes most of these problems is still unknown.

Birth Defects

A birth defect is a physical abnormality present at birth, though it may not be detected until later. About 2% to 3% of babies are born with a major birth defect. In most cases, the cause of the birth defect is unknown. The first 3 months of the pregnancy is a very sensitive time of development because the internal organs and limbs are formed during this period. Many women are not aware that they are pregnant during much of this critical period.

Low Birth Weight and Premature Birth

About 7% of babies born in the United States are born underweight or prematurely. Poor maternal nutrition, smoking, and alcohol use during pregnancy are believed to be responsible for most of these cases. Although better medical care has helped many under-weight or premature babies to develop and grow normally, they are more likely than other babies to become ill or even die during their first year of life.

Developmental Disorders

Sometimes the brain of the fetus does not develop normally, which leads to developmental delays or learning disabilities later in life. About 10% of children in the United States have some form of developmental disability. Such problems are often not noticeable at birth. They can be difficult to measure, may be temporary or permanent, and range from mild to severe. Developmental problems may appear as hyperactivity, short attention span, reduced learning ability, or (in severe cases) mental retardation.

Childhood Cancer

Ionizing radiation has caused cancer in some children whose mothers were exposed during pregnancy. The current practice of minimizing the use of X-rays on pregnant women, the use of newer equipment that reduces the risk of exposure, and the use of protective shields have all helped to decrease the likelihood of harmful radiation exposure to fetuses.

How Are Workers and Their Babies Exposed?

Harmful substances can enter a woman's body through

- breathing in (inhalation)
- contact with the skin
- swallowing (ingestion)

Pregnant workers and those planning to become pregnant should be especially concerned about exposure to reproductive hazards. Some chemicals (such as alcohol) can circulate in the mother's blood, pass through the placenta, and reach the developing fetus. Other hazardous agents can affect the overall health of the woman and reduce the delivery of nutrients to the fetus. Radiation can pass directly through the mother's body to harm her eggs or the fetus. Some drugs and chemicals can also pass through a mother's body into the nursing baby through the breast milk. However, breast feeding has many positive effects. Thus, a woman who may be exposed to reproductive hazards on the job should consult with her doctor or other health care provider before deciding whether or not to breast feed.

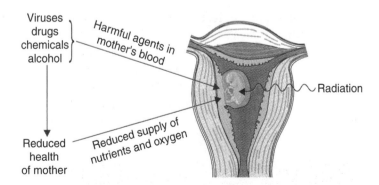

Figure 38.2. *The Effect of Reproductive Hazards on Pregnancy*

Reproductive hazards do not affect every woman or every pregnancy. Whether a woman or her baby is harmed depends on how much of the hazard they are exposed to, when they are exposed, how long they are exposed, and how they are exposed.

How Are Families Exposed?

Workplace substances that affect female workers and their pregnancies can also harm their families. Without knowing it, workers can bring home harmful substances that can affect the health of other family members—both adults and children. For example, lead brought home from the workplace on a worker's skin, hair, clothes, shoes, tool box, or car can cause lead poisoning in family members, especially young children.

How Can Exposures Be Prevented?

Employers are responsible for training and protecting their workers. Employees are responsible for learning about the hazards in their workplace, using personal protective equipment, and following proper work practices. Since little is known about reproductive hazards in the workplace, workers should also take the following steps to ensure their own safety:

- Store chemicals in sealed containers when they are not in use.

- Wash hands after contact with hazardous substances and before eating, drinking, or smoking.

- Avoid skin contact with chemicals.

- If chemicals contact the skin, follow the directions for washing in the material safety data sheet (MSDS). Employers are required to have copies of MSDSs for all hazardous materials used in their workplaces and to provide them to workers upon request.

- Review all MSDSs to become familiar with any reproductive hazards used in your workplace. If you are concerned about reproductive hazards in the workplace, consult your doctor or health care provider.

- Participate in all safety and health education, training, and monitoring programs offered by your employer.

- Learn about proper work practices and engineering controls (such as improved ventilation).

- Use personal protective equipment (gloves, respirators, and personal protective clothing) to reduce exposures to workplace hazards.

- Follow your employer's safety and health work practices and procedures to prevent exposures to reproductive hazards.

Prevent home contamination with the following steps:

- Change out of contaminated clothing and wash with soap and water before going home.

- Store street clothes in a separate area of the workplace to prevent contamination.

- Wash work clothing separately from other laundry (at work if possible).

- Avoid bringing contaminated clothing or other objects home. If work clothes must be brought home, transport them in a sealed plastic bag.

Chapter 39

The Effects of Workplace Hazards on Male Reproductive Health

Introduction

Many factors can contribute to producing healthy children. It is well known that the health of an unborn child can suffer if a woman fails to eat right, smokes, or drinks alcohol during pregnancy. It is not well known, however, that a man's exposure to substances in the workplace can affect his ability to have healthy children.

This chapter provides general information about reproductive hazards, an explanation of how substances in the workplace can cause reproductive problems in men, and suggestions for preventing exposure to reproductive hazards.

What Are Reproductive Hazards?

Substances that affect the ability to have healthy children are called reproductive hazards. Radiation, many chemicals, drugs (legal and illegal), cigarettes, and heat are examples of reproductive hazards.

What Reproductive Hazards Exist in the Workplace?

A number of workplace substances such as lead and radiation have been identified as reproductive hazards for men (see Table 39.1).

National Institute of Occupational Safety and Health, Centers for Disease Control and Prevention (OSHA DHHS), Pub. No. 96-132, January 23, 1997.

However, there is no complete list of reproductive hazards in the workplace. Scientists are just beginning to understand how these hazards affect the male reproductive system. Although more than 1,000 workplace chemicals have been shown to have reproductive effects on animals, most have not been studied in humans. In addition, most of the 4 million other chemical mixtures in commercial use remain untested.

Although studies have found that workplace exposures affect the reproductive system in some men, these effects do not necessarily occur in every worker. Whether individuals are affected depends on how much of the hazard they are exposed to, how long they are exposed, how they are exposed, and other personal factors.

How Are Workers Exposed?

Harmful substances can enter the body by inhalation, contact with the skin, or ingestion (if workers do not properly wash their hands before eating, drinking, or smoking).

Can a Worker Expose His Family to These Hazards?

Workplace substances that affect male workers may also indirectly cause harm to their families. Certain substances unintentionally brought home by a worker may affect a woman's reproductive system or the health of an unborn child. For example, lead brought home from the workplace on a worker's skin, hair, clothes, shoes, tool box, or car can cause severe lead poisoning among family members and can cause neurobehavioral and growth effects in a fetus.

The Male Reproductive System

To understand how reproductive hazards affect a man's ability to have healthy children, it is important to understand how the male reproductive system works.

The testicles have two important functions:

- They produce the hormone testosterone, which produces the deep male voice, beard, and sex drive.

- They produce sperm.

After the sperm are made (in about 72 days), they are stored in the epididymis, the outer structure of the testicles. The sperm remain in the epididymis for about 15 to 25 days. While there, they mature and develop the ability to swim. If the sperm are not ejaculated, they eventually die and are absorbed by the body.

When a man ejaculates, the mature sperm cells move through the vas deferens (the tube cut in a vasectomy) and past the seminal vesicles and prostate gland. The seminal vesicles and the prostate

Table 39.1. Male Reproductive Hazards

	Observed Effects			
Type of Exposure	Lowered Number of Sperm	Abnormal Sperm Shape	Altered Sperm Transfer	Altered Hormones/ Sexual Performance
Lead	x	x	x	x
Dibromochloropropane	x			
Carbaryl (Sevin)		x		
Toluenediamine and dinitrotoluene	x			
Ethylene dibromide	x	x	x	
Plastic production (styrene and acetone)		x		
Ethylene glycol monoethyl ether	x			
Welding		x	x	
Perchloroethylene			x	
Mercury vapor				x
Heat	x		x	
Military radar	x			
Kepone			x	
Bromine vapor	x	x	x	
Radiation	x	x	x	x
Carbon disulfide				x
2,4-Dichlorophenoxy acetic acid (2,4-D)		x	x	

provide most of the liquid in semen. The semen is deposited in the vagina and the sperm must then swim through the cervix into the uterus and up into the fallopian tubes. If an egg is present, it is fertilized in the fallopian tubes. The fertilized egg then moves down to the uterus, where it attaches to the wall and continues to grow. If no egg is present, the sperm may live within the uterus for up to 2 days.

How Do Reproductive Hazards Affect the Male Reproductive System?

Number of Sperm

Some reproductive hazards can stop or slow the actual production of sperm. This means that there will be fewer sperm present to fertilize an egg; if no sperm are produced, the man is sterile. If the hazard prevents sperm from being made, sterility is permanent.

Sperm Shape

Reproductive hazards may cause the shape of sperm cells to be different. These sperm often have trouble swimming or lack the ability to fertilize the egg.

Sperm Transfer

Hazardous chemicals may collect in the epididymis, seminal vesicles, or prostate. These chemicals may kill the sperm, change the way in which they swim, or attach to the sperm and be carried to the egg or the unborn child.

Sexual Performance

Changes in amounts of hormones can affect sexual performance. Some chemicals, like alcohol, may also affect the ability to achieve erections, whereas others may affect the sex drive. Several drugs (both legal and illegal) have effects on sexual performance, but little is known about the effects of workplace hazards.

Sperm Chromosomes

Reproductive hazards can affect the chromosomes found in sperm. The sperm and egg each contribute 23 chromosomes at fertilization. The DNA stored in these chromosomes determines what we will look like and how our bodies will function. Radiation or chemicals may cause changes or breaks in the DNA. If the sperm's DNA is damaged, it may not be able to fertilize an egg; or if it does fertilize an egg, it may affect the development of the fetus. Some cancer treatment drugs are known to cause such damage. However, little is known about the effects of workplace hazards on sperm chromosomes.

Pregnancy

If a damaged sperm does fertilize an egg, the egg might not develop properly, causing a miscarriage or a possible health problem in the baby. If a reproductive hazard is carried in the semen, the fetus might be exposed within the uterus, possibly leading to problems with the pregnancy or with the health of the baby after it is born.

How Can Workers Be Protected from Reproductive Hazards?

Employers have a responsibility to protect their workers. However, because so little is known about reproductive hazards, workers should also take the following steps to ensure their own safety:

- Store chemicals in sealed containers when they are not in use.

- Wash hands before eating, drinking, or smoking.

- Avoid skin contact with chemicals.

- If chemicals contact the skin, follow directions for washing provided in the material safety data sheet (MSDS). Employers are required to provide an MSDS for all hazardous materials used in the workplace.

- Become familiar with the potential reproductive hazards used in your workplace.

- To prevent home contamination:
  - Change out of contaminated clothing and wash with soap and water before going home.
  - Store street clothes in a separate area of the workplace to prevent contamination.
  - Wash work clothing separately from other laundry (at work if possible).
  - Avoid bringing contaminated clothing or other objects home.

- Participate in all safety and health education, training, and monitoring programs offered by your employer.

- Learn about proper work practices, engineering controls, and personal protective equipment (i.e., gloves, respirators, and personal protective clothing) that can be used to reduce exposures to hazardous substances.

- Follow the safety and health work practices and procedures implemented by your employer to prevent exposures to reproductive hazards in the workplace.

Part Nine

Personal Protective Equipment Issues

Chapter 40

Protect Yourself with Personal Protective Equipment

Hard hats, goggles, face shields, earplugs, steel-toed shoes, respirators. What do all these items have in common? They are all various forms of personal protective equipment.

Yet, data from the Bureau of Labor Statistics show:

- Hard hats were worn by only 16% of those workers who sustained head injuries, although two-fifths [40%] were required to wear them for certain tasks at specific locations.[1]

- Only 1% of approximately 770 workers suffering face injuries were wearing face protection.[2]

- Only 23% of the workers with foot injuries wore safety shoes or boots.[3]

- About 40% of the workers with eye injuries wore eye protective equipment.[4]

A majority of these workers were injured while performing their normal jobs at regular worksites.

Occupational Safety and Health Administration (OSHA) standards require employers to furnish and require employees to use suitable

---

Occupational Safety and Health Administration (OSHA), U.S. Department of Labor (DOL), Fact Sheet No. 92-08, http://www.osha-slc.gov/OshDoc/Fact_data/FSNO92-08.html, January 1992. Despite the age of this document, readers seeking understanding of personal protective equipment will still find the information useful.

protective equipment where there is a "reasonable probability" that injury can be prevented by such equipment. The standards also set provisions for specific equipment.

While use of personal protective equipment is important, it is only a supplementary form of protection, necessary where all hazards have not been controlled through other means such as engineering controls. Engineering controls are especially important in hearing and respiratory protection which have specific standards calling for employers to take all feasible steps to control the hazards.

Head Protection

Cuts or bruises to the scalp and forehead occurred in 85% of the cases, concussions in 26%. Over a third of the cases resulted from falling objects striking the head.[5]

Protective hats for head protection against impact blows must be able to withstand penetration and absorb the shock of a blow. In some cases hats should also protect against electric shock. Recognized standards for hats have been established by the American National Standards Institute (ANSI).

Foot and Leg Protection

Sixty-six percent of injured workers were wearing safety shoes, protective footwear, heavy-duty shoes, or boots; and 33%, regular street shoes. Of those wearing safety shoes, 85% were injured because the object hit an unprotected part of the shoe or boot.[6]

For protection against falling or rolling objects, sharp objects, molten metal, hot surfaces and wet, slippery surfaces workers should use appropriate footguards, safety shoes, or boots and leggings. Safety shoes should be sturdy and have an impact-resistant toe. Shoes must meet ANSI standards.

Eye and Face Protection

Injured workers surveyed indicated that eye and face protection was not normally used or practiced in their work areas or it was not required for the type of work performed at the time of the accident.

Almost one-third of face injuries were caused by metal objects, most often blunt and weighing one pound or more. Accidents resulted in cuts, lacerations, or punctures in 48% of the total, and fractures (including broken or lost teeth) in 27%.[7]

442

Protection should be based on kind and degree of hazard present and should:

1. be reasonably comfortable,
2. fit properly,
3. be durable,
4. be cleanable,
5. be sanitary, and
6. be in good condition.

Ear Protection

Exposure to high noise levels can cause irreversible hearing loss or impairment. It can also create physical and psychological stress.

Preformed or molded ear plugs should be individually fitted by a professional. Waxed cotton, foam or fiberglass wool earplugs are self-forming. Disposable earplugs should be used once and thrown away; non-disposable ones should be cleaned after each use for proper maintenance.

OSHA has promulgated a final rule on requirements for a hearing conservation program. Information on the program is available from the closest OSHA office.

Arm and Hand Protection

Burns, cuts, electrical shock, amputation and absorption of chemicals are examples of hazards associated with arm and hand injuries. A wide assortment of gloves, hand pads, sleeves, and wristlets for protection from these hazards is available.

The devices should be selected to fit the specific task. Rubber is considered the best material for insulating gloves and sleeves and must conform to ANSI standards.

Torso Protection

Many hazards can threaten the torso: heat, splashes from hot metals and liquids, impacts, cuts, acids, and radiation. A variety of protective clothing is available: vests, jackets, aprons, coveralls, and full body suits.

Fire retardant wool and specially treated cotton clothing items are comfortable, and they adapt well to a variety of workplace temperatures. Other types of protection include leather, rubberized fabrics, and disposable suits.

Respirator Protection

Information on the requirements for respirators to control of occupational diseases caused by breathing air contaminated with harmful dusts, fogs, fumes, mists, gases, smokes, sprays, and vapors is available in 29 CFR 1910.134. Proper selection of respirators should be made according to the guidance of ANSI Practices for Respiratory Protection.

Remember!!!

Using personal protective equipment requires hazard awareness and training on the part of the user. Employees must be aware that the equipment alone does not eliminate the hazard. If the equipment fails, exposure will occur.

References

1. U.S. Department of Labor, Bureau of Labor Statistics, "Accidents Involving Head Injuries, Report 605," (Washington, D.C., Government Printing Office, July 1980) p. 1.

2. U.S. Department of Labor, Bureau of Labor Statistics, "Accidents Involving Face Injuries, Report 604," (Washington, D.C., GPO, May 1980) p. 10, Table 10.

3. U.S. Department of Labor, Bureau of Labor Statistics, "Accidents Involving Foot Injuries, Report 626," (Washington, D.C., GPO, January 1981) p. 13, Table 11.

4. U.S. Department of Labor, Bureau of Labor Statistics, "Accidents Involving Eye Injuries, Report 597," (Washington, D.C., GPO, April 1980) p. 12, Table 9.

5. U.S. Department of Labor, Bureau of Labor Statistics, "Accidents Involving Head Injuries, Report 605," (Washington, D.C., GPO, July 1980) p. 7, Table 6.

6. U.S. Department of Labor, Bureau of Labor Statistics, "Accidents Involving Foot Injuries, Report 626," (Washington, D.C., GPO, January 1981) p. 13, Table 11, and p. 1.

7. U.S. Department of Labor, Bureau of Labor Statistics, "Accidents Involving Face Injuries, Report 604," (Washington, D.C., May 1980) p. 4, Table 3, and p. 2, Table 2.

Chapter 41

Protective Clothing and Ergonomics

A good safety program is a three-legged stool: without strong engineering controls, administrative controls, and personal protective equipment acting in concert, the program could not function. Indeed, personal protective equipment, including those that promote ergonomics, are the last line of defense against disabling injuries.

Prudent selection and use are critical to gaining optimal value from three of the most common ergonomic products in use: back supports, knee and elbow pads, and anti-vibration gloves.

Back Belts

The popularity of back supports is undaunted by conflicting scientific studies about their value and the disapprobation of the National Institute for Occupational Safety and Health (NIOSH) and the Occupational Safety and Health Administration (OSHA). Even without formal support from management, employees have embraced backbelts for both work and non-work use.

Kent Wilson, CIE, an ergonomist with Ergodyne Corp., warns that "companies that look at a back support as the one and only cure [for low back injuries] are really misleading themselves. It is a tool like any other, and one of the many tools that make up the ergonomic environment." Phil Welch, vice president of sales at Valeo Corp., advises making the supports part of a package with training on proper lifting techniques.

"Ergonomics," *Occupational Hazards*, January 1999, Vol. 61, I. 1, pp. 53–56, copyright 1999 Penton Media Inc. Reprinted with permission.

Back supports serve two functions: they stabilize the spine by acting as external ligaments and actively remind the wearer to use proper lifting techniques. As such, they are most appropriate for those who lift and carry as part of their job function and those who are on their feet all day, since fatigue produces poor posture.

Finding the appropriate back belt is dictated by the nature of the work and the preference of the user. Models range from six to ten inches in width, and from simple foam belts to elastic models with suspenders to elastic leather belts with stays.

Comfort, says Wilson, is critical to the belts' acceptance and proper use by the work force. "Avoid at all costs back belts advertised as one-size-fits-all. It doesn't. You have waists ranging from 20 inches to 65 inches; you need multiple sizes, as with any piece of clothing." The width of the belt is a matter of personal preference, based on comfort. Narrower belts, for example, would be less likely to cut into the flesh of obese workers than the standard-width belts. All belts should have stays for support and some kind of rubber track or gripping mechanism that holds the belt firmly against the wearer's clothing to prevent it from riding up during bending. The belt should have a two-stage closure that allows the wearer to tighten the belt prior to lifting and loosen it for other activities.

"A good fit means the belt should allow freedom of movement, and should not be so tight that it cuts off circulation," advises Lisa Ieyer, president of Valeo Corp. She notes that belts come with written instructions, and that the distributor should be trained to assist with any questions you have about proper wearing of the belts.

For proper fit, Wilson suggests:

- Put on the belt, leaving a few fingers' width between the front panel and the body.

- The front panel should align with the wearer's navel or fall just below it, and the panel sections should overlap by four to six inches.

- Tighten the belt by pulling the elastic side panels toward the front and attaching them to the front panel. Never pull the side bands to their fullest extent. When properly fitted, the belt should conform to the body, offer stability, and hold up to normal use.

- Overweight workers should wear the belt just below the belly, still using the navel as a guide.

- Females should wear a back belt at or below their navels, not under the bustline.

446

When Should You Replace a Backbelt?

It depends on the belt, the amount of use, and whether it rubs up against surfaces when in use. Ieyer notes that leather backbelts can stand up to years of use, and that rigid belts hold up through repeated washings. "Elastic belts have a life-span of about six months to one year," she says. "The elastic tends to stretch out from wearing." Before investing in a belt, examine the closures, the materials and the construction to avoid belt failure during use and to avoid early and frequent replacement.

Anti-Vibration Gloves

One of the most dangerous ergonomic risk factors is vibration, which, paired with extreme cold, awkward postures or prolonged exposure, leads quickly to severe injury and, in some cases, to tissue death.

Tools with vibration frequencies of 250 Hz or less are far more dangerous than those with higher frequencies. Wilson strongly recommends checking the American National Standards Institute/International Standards Organization (ANSI/ISO) close-response guidelines for hand/arm vibrations when you buy or specify vibrating tools. Knowing the close-response rating is critical in selecting the most appropriate hand protection for the workers using the tools.

"Often, people think that if they wear gloves, their hands are protected, not realizing that tools vibrate at a variety of rates of frequency," Wilson says. "You may have 'antivibration' gloves that don't protect your hands at all. In the United States, nothing keeps manufacturers from marketing gloves as 'antivibration,' even if they aren't." His advice: Match the close-response rating for the tool with the glove manufacturer's specifications.

Further, Valeo's vice president of sales, Phil Welch, warns that there is a difference between anti-impact and anti-vibration gloves. "If you work on something where you have to hit it hard with your hand to install it (as on an assembly line), you need an impact-resistant glove. If you're using air- or electrical-powered equipment all day, such as a drill, and your hands are exposed to vibration, you need the anti-vibration gloves."

There is some debate about whether fingerless gloves constitute adequate anti-vibration protection. Wilson contends, "Your fingers are still exposed to the source of the vibration (the tool)." In applications in which digital dexterity is important, however, some users prefer fingerless gloves.

What Are Hallmarks of Good Anti-Vibration Gloves?

- Fit matters: uncomfortable gloves won't be used or, if used, may cause the tool to slip or may force users to employ excessive force or awkward postures to grip the tool. Wrist closures can ensure a good fit.

- Gloves should allow the user to grip the tool securely, without undue pressure or force. Pads should not inhibit grip.

- Glove pads (of polymer or similar substance) should damp vibration at a wide spectrum of frequencies. (Check it against the ANSI/ISO close-response guidelines for the tool being used.)

- The quality of the leather in the gloves is directly related to their durability, as well as to their cost.

- Exterior palm and finger surfaces should have gripping material to prevent the tool from slipping.

- Watch exposure time. Prolonged hand/arm vibration, even when workers are gloved, is dangerous.

- Work in neutral postures.

- Gloves should keep out cold air and exhaust from the tools and should resist environmental moisture. Glove liners can keep hands warm and dry without impairing grip.

- Never wrap tools. Wraps are no substitute for proper gloves, and may, in fact, increase the transmission of vibration into the hand by requiring more pressure to grip the tool securely.

What should you do if your employees bring in their own personal protective equipment? Wilson advises, "An ergonomist or safety person should analyze the tools and PPE on site from both PPE and engineering perspectives. People who bring in their own PPE may be telling you there is a problem that has to be addressed. You may want to control the PPE that is brought in—and offer training, as well."

Knee and Elbow Protection

Knee and elbow protection isn't for everyone—just those whose work involves contact between these exposed hinge joints and hard surfaces or who could use additional support and comfort for these areas.

Don't confuse pads with supports. Pads are used to protect and cushion joints during use. Baggage handlers, landscapers, construction workers, and carpet installers use them regularly.

Comfort and application should dictate the pads selected, Wilson advises, noting that the first priority should be given to designing out the situations that occasion the use of knee and elbow pads (such as using carpet stretchers, rather than kickers, to fit carpeting into place). Workers whose tasks require pivoting on the knees should look for pads with ball caps; those who want to avoid marring surfaces need no-mar pads. Some pads have straps to hold them up; others slip into pockets sewn into clothing or attach with hook-and-loop fasteners.

When selecting knee and elbow pads, try them on before buying. Look for the following:

- Do they stabilize the patella (kneecap) so it does not push to one side?

- If you have knee problems, do the pads conform to your knees?

- Does the pad compress when you kneel? Wilson warns that if the pad bottoms out during trials, it will fail during intensive use.

- How thick is the padding? Thin padding wears out quickly, and protection will be compromised.

- Is the padding firm or soft?

Similarly, forearm pads should be selected along the same lines, the goal being to prevent repeated shocks to the limbs when pressure is applied over the long term.

Unlike pads, the purpose of knee and elbow supports is to provide support, comfort and warmth, rather than protection. "There are different levels of support," Ieyer says.

For those who require firm support, the types of braces worn by athletes would be appropriate, but for those whose aims are comfort and warmth with limited support, Ieyer recommends looking for supports made from Neoprene (for breathability) and lined with terrycloth to keep the skin warm and dry.

Chapter 42

Protective Clothing and Chemical Hazards

In environments in which fire, chemicals and traffic are constant perils for workers, protective clothing provides a barrier to injury and death. Because the array of garments and fabrics from which workers can select protection is dizzying, specifiers and buyers must rely on standards and solid advice to guide them through the maze of choices.

As with all protective equipment, the first step must be a hazards assessment and a consultation for the applicable materials safety data sheets (MSDS). There is a small catch, however. Occupational Safety and Health Administration (OSHA) 1910.132 (Personal Protective Equipment for General Industry) covers a broad spectrum of protective equipment. It requires that employers perform a hazards assessment and select appropriate equipment for the hazard, but Philip Mann, technical services manager at Kappler Protective Apparel and Fabrics, asks, "What does 'appropriate' mean? For protective equipment other than suits, there is additional guidance, but there's really nothing for skin protection, although there is a performance standard [from the Industrial Safety Equipment Association (ISEA)] being worked on that will be comparable to the CE (European Conformity) standard in Europe. But there is no guarantee that OSHA will adopt ISEA's standard."

In addition to defining the level and type of protection needed, the hazards assessment offers another benefit. "If you don't [perform a hazards assessment], you run the risk of overprotecting, as well as underprotecting [the worker]," Mann says. "People who wear these suits are stressed. Anyone who wears one has a specific job he has to accomplish. Nobody wears a protective suit as a fashion statement. In some cases, the suit will get in the person's way, and he cannot do his job. The point is to give him adequate protection without undue stress."

Once potential hazards and the appropriate protection (both in terms of level and intensity of hazard exposure) have been identified, the next step is to find garments that are comfortable to the wearer and that fit. "Comfort is the key factor in choice of apparel and compliance with correct wearing procedures," says Monie Bardoul, marketing manager for Kimberly-Clark. "If the suit is so uncomfortable that you cut the fabric in order to stay cool, you're compromising protection. In a study we did of protective apparel, 92 percent of the specifiers agreed that comfort drives compliance."

"In protective clothing, barrier and comfort are compromise," says Mann. "Products that are comfortable offer the least protection, and the opposite also is true. The people who buy and specify these garments are not the ones who wear them, and users may be reluctant to wear a garment if it's uncomfortable, even if they know they are up against a hazard. That's particularly true if protection was not necessarily required previously. There's no question that user education is critical to the acceptance of protective clothing."

"Actual fit of the garment is very important in making sure the level of protection is maintained as wearers increase their work," Bardoul concurs. "People typically buy one or two sizes larger than the typical American Standards Institute (ANSI)-sized garments to make sure they don't rip out." An alternative is to look for garments that have a flexible design to accommodate workers' movements without the disadvantages of an oversized garment. A good fit is less a function of height than weight, since weight varies among persons of the same height, and height eventually levels off. Elastic cuffs, gussets and design elements (such as storm flaps) can modify a garment's fit. In a confined space environment, however, wearers require a suit that conforms to the body (to prevent snags and tears), but that also accommodates breathing apparatus.

In addition to protection and fit, Mann ranks function as a top criterion in suit selection. "Function is not just contingent upon sizing, but upon the variety of styles of garments. You can get a coverall in a lot of different styles that offer variety and comfort." He also counts the seaming—how well the garment is put together—as an important factor in garment selection, since specific types of seams are most effective with specific types of fabrics. Four types generally are available: sewn seams (usually used with Tyvek), bound (reinforced) seams, taped seams (which offer protection from liquids and gases) and ultrasonically or RF-welded seams (less expensive and effective than taped seams, though sturdy).

Bodywear for protection from chemical hazards should be selected primarily for its ability to protect users against both the chemicals (i.e., flammable, acids, caustics) and the form of chemical exposure (i.e., liquid, gas, solid, spray); the work environment; whether high visibility is desirable; length of exposure; and type of air supply. Specifiers should be certain the valve on the suit matches the connection on the air supply hose.

How important is appearance? Workers who feel they look good in their protective clothing are more likely to wear it. Where possible, offering choices in clothing styles gives workers autonomy and encourages use. Educating them in proper donning/wearing/dolling practices and the capabilities and limitations of the garments reinforces the importance of wearing them.

Specifiers should be aware of two new ANSI/ISEA protective clothing standards on the horizon: Chemical Protective Clothing and High-visibility Reflective Safety Apparel.

Christine Fargo, technical projects coordinator, industrial Safety Equipment Association, notes that the Chemical Protective Standard is intended to fill the gaps in OSHA 29 CFR 1910.132 standard for personal protective equipment. "This standard will help delineate the types of hazards and the appropriate chemical protective clothing to help users comply with the OSHA requirement and afford appropriate protection to their employees."

The standard is based on a type/class system, in which users can select types of garments defined by naturally anticipated chemical exposures, and classes of performance that each type of garment provides, based on certain chemical exposures. The criteria are based on European test standards recognized regionally or globally, as well as testing methods from the American Society for Testing Materials (ASTM) and others. Fargo cautions that this standard is for general industry use only, and that it does not cover protective clothing used against biological, radiological or thermal hazards, nor does it include any clothing covered by the National Fire Protection Association's (NFPA) clothing standard.

Once the chemical hazard has been identified according to OSHA guidelines, users will look up the type of specific garment configuration appropriate to the hazard. Looking at the classes of garment within that type, the user refers to the MSDS to determine the nature of the hazard, then, using a matrix within the standard, selects the personal protective equipment appropriate to his needs. Appendices document testing methods and applications, written in an easy-to-understand and use format.

Later this year, says Fargo, ISEA will meet with marketers of various types of personal protective clothing to integrate them. For example, when earmuffs (hearing protection) are worn with a hard hat, which standard takes precedence? Are individual components compromised by compiling the two products? Where does the liability fall? "The market is driving this project, and the manufacturers agree that it's a good idea," Fargo says. An exploratory integrated products group meeting is due later this year.

Reflective Clothing

For road crews, construction workers and safety forces, bad weather, dusk and dawn light, and speeding vehicles create a potentially deadly work environment. Transportation and construction industry groups, utility companies, safety forces and governmental agencies—particularly state and regional bodies—are enthusiastic supporters of the proposed High-visibility Protective Safety Apparel standard, Fargo says.

"While reflective clothing is available, the materials in these garments are not reflective enough or the reflective areas on them are not large enough for drivers to see the wearers in enough time to react to avoid the hazard," she says. "I can see this [being applied] in recreational clothing, for those who run at dusk or ushers at concerts, where the wearers need to be seen." She explains that, in environments in which visibility is limited, traffic cones, barriers or striping may be below drivers' line of vision, and the reflective materials and their performance in stationary objects are different from those needed to see mobile workers. "You need to be able to anticipate the movement of an object in order to have sufficient time to react to it," Fargo explains.

Using the relevant European standard as a resource, the U.S. counterpart will provide minimum design and performance bases for garments that cover the torso, but not caps, gloves or footwear.

Four Levels of Chemical Protective Clothing

Level A. Required where the potential for exposure to skin, respiratory and eye hazards is greatest. Includes respiratory protection with positive pressure, full-facepiece self contained breathing apparatus (SCBA) or positive-pressure supplied air respirator with escape SCBA; totally encapsulated chemical- and vapor-protective suits; inner and outer chemical-resistant gloves; and disposable protective suits, gloves, and boots.

Level B. Offers the highest level of respiratory protection, but a lesser level of skin protection. Includes respiratory protection with positive pressure, full-facepiece SCBA or positive-pressure supplied air respirator with escape SCBA; inner and outer chemical-resistant gloves; faceshield; hooded chemical-resistant clothing; coveralls; chemical-resistant boots.

Level C. Required where concentration and type of airborne substances are known and the criteria for using air-purifying respirators has been met. May include full-face air-purifying respirators; inner and outer chemical-resistant gloves; hard hat; escape mask; disposable chemical-resistant outer boots.

Level D. Sufficient where no contaminants are present or work operations precludes splashes, immersion or the potential for unexpected inhalation or contact with hazardous chemicals. May include gloves, coveralls, safety glasses, faceshield, and chemical-resistant steel-toe shoes or boots.

Protective Clothing: Making the Right Choices

1. Determine the risks of the situation:

   - Type and nature of hazards (chemical, biological, thermal, physical, other)

   - Likelihood of events that expose people to these hazards (toxicity may be of less concern than the potential for flash fire, for example).

   - Possible consequences of exposure to the hazards (again, toxicity may be less hazardous than the perils of flash fire).

455

2. When deciding whether to choose reusable or disposable protective clothing, find out:

    - How easy or difficult it is to decontaminate the clothing.

    - The likelihood of damage to the clothing during use. (Working in construction rubble is more likely to rip suits than cleaning up contaminated soil.)

    - The costs for using the clothing, taking into account the costs and materials associated with storage, testing, repair and disposal. (The best approach is to determine the cost of CPC per use.)

3. Obtain chemical resistance data on all parts of the ensemble—the fabric seams, visors, gloves, zippers, boots, etc.

4. Make sure the suits fit your wearers. Sizes are not consistent from manufacturer to manufacturer, and a suit too large or too small introduces safety risks. This is an area ripe for end-user standards, especially with sizing for women and minority populations.

5. Decide how much of the body needs protection. For whole-body ensemble protection against a very toxic chemical, it makes sense to use a high-performance fabric. Using a high-performance fabric in an apron does not because the wearer will be exposed to the chemical on all unprotected skin or mucous membranes anyway. Make sure, however, that the clothing selected provides the necessary liquid or vapor-tight protection for the affected portion of the body.

6. If gloves are involved, consider what dexterity will be needed, available sizing, and what tasks need to be done. This is another area where end-user performance standards would be helpful, Stull said.

Chapter 43

Heat and Cold Protection

Chapter Contents

457

Section 43.1

Protecting Workers in Hot Environments

Occupational Safety and Health Administration (OSHA), U.S. Department of Labor (DOL), Fact Sheet 95-16, http://www.osha-slc.gov/OshDoc/Fact_data/ FSNO95-16.html, January 1995.

Introduction

Many workers spend some part of their working day in a hot environment. Workers in foundries, laundries, construction projects, and bakeries—to name a few industries—often face hot conditions which pose special hazards to safety and health.

Heat Stress Causes Body Reactions

Four environmental factors affect the amount of stress a worker faces in a hot work area: temperature, humidity, radiant heat (such as from the sun or a furnace) and air velocity. Perhaps most important to the level of stress an individual faces are personal characteristics such as age, weight, fitness, medical condition, and acclimatization to the heat.

The body reacts to high external temperature by circulating blood to the skin which increases skin temperature and allows the body to give off its excess heat through the skin. However, if the muscles are being used for physical labor, less blood is available to flow to the skin and release the heat.

Sweating is another means the body uses to maintain a stable internal body temperature in the face of heat. However, sweating is effective only if the humidity level is low enough to permit evaporation and if the fluids and salts lost are adequately replaced.

Of course there are many steps a person might choose to take to reduce the risk of heat stress, such as moving to a cooler place, reducing the work pace or load, or removing or loosening some clothing.

But if the body cannot dispose of excess heat, it will store it. When this happens, the body's core temperature rises and the heart rate increases. As the body continues to store heat, the individual begins to lose concentration and has difficulty focusing on a task, may become irritable or sick and often loses the desire to drink. The next stage is most often fainting, and death is possible if the person is not removed from the heat stress.

Heat Disorders

Heat stroke, the most serious health problem for workers in hot environments, is caused by the failure of the body's internal mechanism to regulate its core temperature. Sweating stops and the body can no longer rid itself of excess heat. Signs include:

1. mental confusion, delirium, loss of consciousness, convulsions or coma

2. a body temperature of 106° F or higher

3. hot dry skin which may be red, mottled, or bluish

Victims of heat stroke will die unless treated promptly. While awaiting medical help, the victim must be removed to a cool area and his or her clothing soaked with cool water. He or she should be fanned vigorously to increase cooling. Prompt first aid can prevent permanent injury to the brain and other vital organs.

Heat exhaustion results from loss of fluid through sweating when a worker has failed to drink enough fluids or take in enough salt, or both. The worker with heat exhaustion still sweats but experiences extreme weakness or fatigue, giddiness, nausea, or headache. The skin is clammy and moist, the complexion pale or flushed, and the body temperature normal or slightly higher. Treatment is usually simple: the victim should rest in a cool place and drink an electrolyte solution (a beverage used by athletes to quickly restore potassium, calcium, and magnesium salts). Severe cases involving victims who vomit or lose consciousness may require longer treatment under medical supervision.

Heat cramps, painful spasms of the muscles, are caused when workers drink large quantities of water but fail to replace their bodies' salt loss. Tired muscles—those used for performing the work—are usually the ones most susceptible to cramps. Cramps may occur during or after working hours and may be relieved by taking liquids

459

by mouth or saline solutions intravenously for quicker relief, if medically determined to be required.

Fainting (heat syncope) may be a problem for the worker unacclimatized to a hot environment who simply stands still in the heat. Victims usually recover quickly after a brief period of lying down. Moving around, rather than standing still, will usually reduce the possibility of fainting.

Heat rash, also known as prickly heat, may occur in hot and humid environments where sweat is not easily removed from the surface of the skin by evaporation. When extensive or complicated by infection, heat rash can be so uncomfortable that it inhibits sleep and impedes a worker's performance or even results in temporary total disability. It can be prevented by resting in a cool place and allowing the skin to dry.

Preventing Heat Stress

Most heat-related health problems can be prevented or the risk of developing them reduced. Following a few basic precautions should lessen heat stress.

1. A variety of engineering controls including general ventilation and spot cooling by local exhaust ventilation at points of high heat production may be helpful. Shielding is required as protection from radiant heat sources. Evaporative cooling and mechanical refrigeration are other ways to reduce heat. Cooling fans can also reduce heat in hot conditions. Eliminating steam leaks will also help. Equipment modifications, the use of power tools to reduce manual labor and personal cooling devices or protective clothing are other ways to reduce the hazards of heat exposure for workers.

2. Work practices such as providing plenty of drinking water—as much as a quart per worker per hour—at the workplace can help reduce the risk of heat disorders. Training first aid workers to recognize and treat heat stress disorders and making the names of trained staff known to all workers is essential. Employers should also consider an individual worker's physical condition when determining his or her fitness for working in hot environments. Older workers, obese workers and personnel on some types of medication are at greater risk.

3. Alternating work and rest periods with longer rest periods in a cool area can help workers avoid heat stress. If possible, heavy work should be scheduled during the cooler parts of the day and appropriate protective clothing provided. Supervisors should be trained to detect early signs of heat stress and should permit workers to interrupt their work if they are extremely uncomfortable.

4. Acclimatization to the heat through short exposures followed by longer periods of work in the hot environment can reduce heat stress. New employees and workers returning from an absence of two weeks or more should have a 5-day period of acclimatization. This period should begin with 50 percent of the normal workload and time exposure the first day, and gradually building up to 100 percent on the fifth day.

5. Employee education is vital so that workers are aware of the need to replace fluids and salt lost through sweat and can recognize dehydration, exhaustion, fainting, heat cramps, salt deficiency, heat exhaustion, and heat stroke as heat disorders. Workers should also be informed of the importance of daily weighing before and after work to avoid dehydration.

Section 43.2

Protecting Workers in Cold Environments

Occupational Safety and Health Administration (OSHA),
U.S. Department of Labor (DOL), Fact Sheet 98-55,
http://www.osha-slc.gov/OshDoc/Fact_data/FSNO98-55.html,
December 22, 1998.

Introduction

As the weather becomes "frightful" during winter months, workers who must brave the outdoor conditions face the occupational hazard of exposure to the cold. Prolonged exposure to freezing temperatures can result in health problems as serious as trench foot, frostbite, and hypothermia. Workers in such industries as construction, commercial fishing and agriculture need to be especially mindful of the weather, its effects on the body, proper prevention techniques, and treatment of cold-related disorders.

The Cold Environment

An individual gains body heat from food and muscular activity and loses it through convection, conduction, radiation and sweating to maintain a constant body temperature. When body temperature drops even a few degrees below its normal temperature of 98.6° F (37° C), the blood vessels constrict, decreasing peripheral blood flow to reduce heat loss from the surface of the skin. Shivering generates heat by increasing the body's metabolic rate.

The four environmental conditions that cause cold-related stress are low temperatures, high/cool winds, dampness, and cold water. Wind chill, a combination of temperature and velocity, is a crucial factor to evaluate when working outside. For example, when the actual air temperature of the wind is 40°F (4° C) and its velocity is 35 miles per hour (mph), the exposed skin receives conditions equivalent to the still-air temperature being 11° F (-11° C)! A dangerous situation of rapid heat loss may arise for any individual exposed to high winds and cold temperatures.

Major Risk Factors for Cold-Related Stresses

- Wearing inadequate or wet clothing increases the effects of cold on the body.

- Taking certain drugs or medications such as alcohol, nicotine, caffeine, and medication that inhibits the body's response to the cold or impairs judgment.

- Having a cold or certain diseases, such as diabetes, heart, vascular, and thyroid problems, may make a person more susceptible to the winter elements.

- Being a male increases a person's risk to cold-related stresses. Sad, but true, men experience far greater death rates due to cold exposure than women, perhaps due to inherent risk-taking activities, body-fat composition or other physiological differences.

- Becoming exhausted or immobilized, especially due to injury or entrapment, may speed up the effects of cold weather.

- Aging—the elderly are more vulnerable to the effects of harsh winter weather.

Harmful Effects of Cold

Trench Foot

Trench foot is caused by long, continuous exposure to a wet, cold environment, or actual immersion in water. Commercial fishermen, who experience these types of cold, wet environments daily, need to be especially cautious.

Symptoms

Symptoms include a tingling and/or itching sensation, burning, pain, and swelling, sometimes forming blisters in more extreme cases.

Treatment

Move individuals with trench foot to a warm, dry area, where the affected tissue can be treated with careful washing and drying, re-warming and slight elevation. Seek medical assistance as soon as possible.

Frostbite

Frostbite occurs when the skin tissue actually freezes, causing ice crystals to form between cells and draw water from them, which leads to cellular dehydration. Although this typically occurs at temperatures below 30° F (-1° C), wind chill effects can cause frostbite at above-freezing temperatures.

Symptoms

Initial effects of frostbite include uncomfortable sensations of coldness; tingling, stinging or aching feeling of the exposed area followed by numbness. Ears, fingers, toes, cheeks, and noses are primarily affected. Frost-bitten areas appear white and cold to the touch. The appearance of frostbite varies depending on whether re-warming has occurred.

Deeper frostbite involves freezing of deeper tissues (muscles, tendons, etc.) causing exposed areas to become numb, painless, hard to the touch.

Treatment

If you suspect frostbite, you should seek medical assistance immediately. Any existing hypothermia should be treated first (See hypothermia below). Frostbitten parts should be covered with dry, sterile gauze or soft, clean cloth bandages. Do not massage frostbitten tissue because this sometimes causes greater injury. Severe cases may require hospitalization and even amputation of affected tissue. Take measures to prevent further cold injury. If formal medical treatment will be delayed, consult with a licensed health care professional for training on re-warming techniques.

General Hypothermia

General Hypothermia occurs when body temperature falls to a level where normal muscular and cerebral functions are impaired. While hypothermia is generally associated with freezing temperatures, it may occur in any climate where a person's body temperature falls below normal. For instance, hypothermia is common among the elderly who live in cold houses.

Symptoms

The first symptoms of hypothermia, shivering, an inability to do complex motor functions, lethargy, and mild confusion, occur as the core body temperature decreases to around 95° F (35° C).

As body temperature continues to fall, hypothermia becomes more severe. The individual falls into a state of dazed consciousness, failing to complete even simple motor functions. The victim's speech becomes slurred and his or her behavior may become irrational.

The most severe state of hypothermia occurs when body temperature falls below 90° F (32° C). As a result, the body moves into a state of hibernation, slowing the heart rate, blood flow, and breathing. Unconsciousness and full heart failure can occur in the severely hypothermic state.

Treatment

Treatment of hypothermia involves conserving the victim's remaining body heat and providing additional heat sources. Specific measures will vary depending upon the severity and setting (field or hospital). Handle hypothermic people very carefully because of the increased irritability of the cold heart. Seek medical assistance for persons suspected of being moderately or severely hypothermic.

If the person is unresponsive and not shivering, assume he or she is suffering from severe hypothermia. Reduction of heat loss can be accomplished by various means: obtaining shelter, removal of wet clothing, adding layers of dry clothing, blankets, or using a pre-warmed sleeping bag.

For mildly hypothermic cases or those more severe cases where medical treatment will be significantly delayed, external re-warming techniques may be applied. This includes body-to-body contact (e.g., placing the person in a pre-warmed sleeping bag with a person of normal body temperature), chemical heat packs, or insulated hot water bottles. Good areas to place these packs are the armpits, neck, chest, and groin. It is best to have the person lying down when applying external re-warming. You also may give mildly hypothermic people warm fluids orally, but avoid beverages containing alcohol or caffeine.

Preventing Cold-Related Disorders

Personal protective clothing. Perhaps the most important step in fighting the elements is providing adequate layers of insulation from them. Wear at least three layers of clothing:

- an outer layer to break the wind and allow some ventilation (like Gore-Tex® or nylon)

- a middle layer of wool or synthetic fabric (Qualofil or Pile) to absorb sweat and retain insulation in a damp environment. Down is a useful lightweight insulator; however, it is ineffective once it becomes wet.

- an inner layer of cotton or synthetic weave to allow ventilation.

Pay special attention to protecting feet, hands, face and head. Up to 40 percent of body heat can be lost when the head is exposed. Footgear should be insulated to protect against cold and dampness. Keep a change of clothing available in case work garments become wet.

Engineering controls in the workplace, through a variety of practices, help reduce the risk of cold-related injuries.

- Use an on-site source of heat, such as air jets, radiant heaters, or contact warm plates.

- Shield work areas from drafty or windy conditions.

- Provide a heated shelter for employees who experience prolonged exposure to equivalent wind-chill temperatures of 20° F (-6° C) or less.

- Use thermal insulating material on equipment handles when temperatures drop below 30° F (-1° C).

Safe work practices, such as changes in work schedules and practices, are necessary to combat the effects of exceedingly cold weather.

- Allow a period of adjustment to the cold before embarking on a full work schedule.

- Always permit employees to set their own pace and take extra work breaks when needed.

- Reduce, as much as possible, the number of activities performed outdoors. When employees must brave the cold, select the warmest hours of the day and minimize activities that reduce circulation.

- Ensure that employees remain hydrated.

- Establish a buddy system for working outdoors.

- Educate employees to the symptoms of cold-related stresses— heavy shivering, uncomfortable coldness, severe fatigue, drowsiness, or euphoria.

The quiet symptoms of potentially deadly cold-related ailments often go undetected until the victim's health is endangered. Knowing the facts on cold exposure and following a few simple guidelines can ensure that this season is a safe and healthy one.

Section 43.3

Heat and Cold Protection

Excerpted from *Occupational Hazards,* January 1999, Vol. 61, I. 1, pp. 64–65, copyright 1999 Penton Media Inc. Reprinted with permission.

Whether it is the raw blast of frigid ocean air on a drilling platform or the intense heat of a steel plant, workers are exposed to a wide variety of temperature extremes, both indoors and outside. Too much heat or cold can have debilitating, even deadly, consequences for workers.

In hot environments, it is important to ensure that clothing keeps workers cool and prevents dehydration. Experts suggest clothing that is light in color and fabric and fits loosely to allow sweat to evaporate. Natural woven fabrics assist in the evaporation of sweat. Wide-brimmed attachments on helmets or hard hats can be effective in deflecting direct sunlight away from the head.

Where employees arc exposed to high levels of radiant heat, reflective clothing, including jackets, pants, full body suits, tinted faceshields and hoods and gloves block the heat from being absorbed by the skin.

In situations where engineering controls, such as air conditioning or fans, or administrative controls cannot be introduced, cooling vests can provide additional comfort for workers.

Studies by the U.S. Navy have shown that crewmen using cooling vests can safely work in hot environments for twice as long as those without them. The workers wearing the vests showed no thermal strain, the studies found.

Passive cooling vests generally involve water-based or liquid chemical solutions packaged in sealed sectional plastic strips that can move with a worker. Once frozen, the packs are inserted into insulated vests.

Frozen strips and gel packs may last from two to eight hours before they have to be replaced.

Active cooling devices most commonly circulate cool water through a garment with tubes running through it. The tubes carry chilled water through the vest and re-circulate water warmed by the body to an ice water reservoir, where it is re-cooled. Another version pushes compressed air through vortex tubes that separate hot air from cold air, ensuring that the cold air is spread over the body.

In cold conditions, when the body cannot generate enough heat to stay warm, the blood vessels in the extremities constrict, directing more blood to the internal organs. Hands and feet become cold as a result. As a person becomes colder, the body starts to shiver in an attempt to generate heat via muscle contraction. Employees and supervisors should be alert to signs of frostbite and hypothermia. "A loss of feeling and a white or pale appearance in fingers, toes, nose or ear lobes are symptoms of frostbite," explains Allstate Insurance Co. "Uncontrollable shivering, slow speech, memory lapses, frequent stumbling, drowsiness and exhaustion are symptoms of hypothermia."

Most experts recommend that workers dress in multiple layers of clothing to protect against the cold. The Ohio Industrial Commission's Division of Safety & Hygiene notes that layers of clothing permit "adjustment to changing circumstances during the exposure—a decrease in wind or sun, or an increase in workload..." Such layering might consist, the agency notes, of "thermal or woolen underwear, an insulating layer that holds in body heat, outer garments that repel wind and water, head and ear coverings, warm boots and wool-lined mittens or gloves."

Chapter 44

Construction Site Fire and General Safety

As the individual responsible for your company's fire protection program, you arrive for the construction project design meeting on time, daily planner in hand, and await the engineering staff and other members of the plant's administration.

While the project engineer starts to drone on about funding, contractors, safety and all the other aspects of a major building project, your eyes become fixed on the "artist's rendition" of the project hanging at the front of the room. It's a four-story process building, 80-by-200 feet.

When the project engineer mentions "fire protection features," you snap out of your reverie. As you pay closer attention to the specifics, you realize that this will be a 2-year project from the time they start to grade the area until the first process gets rolling.

Though these projects are done all of the time inside and outside of industrial properties, that doesn't diminish their impact on your operations. Construction adds truck traffic and personnel, as well as new demands for parking, security and the like. You'll need to keep access roads clear for normal and emergency traffic. Each manager or sub-manager must do his or her part to ensure that the building will get built with a minimum amount of disruption.

What follows is a breakdown of areas to consider regarding fire and general safety during construction on an industrial site.

Excerpted from Ronald E. Kanterman, *Occupational Hazards*, January 1995, Vol. 57, N. 1, pp. 95–98. Copyright 1999 Penton Media Inc. Reprinted with permission.

Safety Orientation

All contract personnel entering the site should be required to go through a safety orientation. Some companies show a short video about the site's policies and procedures, then give out a pamphlet and follow it with a short 10-question test based on the film and the booklet. This not only reinforces your policies, but helps you document the training and gives you the clout you may need down the road in the event a person flagrantly violates procedures and is asked to leave the site. Any method by which you can inform the contract worker that there are rules and these rules must be followed is fine, as long as it's cost effective, quick and easy.

Remember that there must be a firm foundation of fire safety and general safety on the site for all permanent employees before you can preach to the contractors. You must show credibility to the outside people in order for your mandates to be taken seriously. Tell them what is expected of all personnel on the site, no matter who they are paid by. The site's safety policy for permanent employees and the safety policy for contract employees should compliment each other.

General Safety Guidelines

Consider establishing the following programs/systems to promote and project general safety on the site.

Contractor violations program. While this may sound harsh at first, such a program puts contract personnel on notice that they will be monitored for fire and safety infractions. Lay out the ground rules that serious infractions may cause that person or firm to be removed from the site and possibly from bidding on future jobs for the company. The project engineer, safety staff, security or other site departments may be involved in this monitoring program.

Self-audit system. Under this program, the contractor appoints a safety director to oversee the job. The safety director is responsible for holding safety meetings, reporting accidents and near-misses and acting as a liaison with the safety, security and site emergency services departments. This person will also be the point of contact for the Occupational Safety and Health Administration (OSHA) or other outside agencies who inspect the construction site. (Upon entering the gate to your facility, these agencies should be escorted by a representative of the company at all times even if they are there only in connection with the construction project.)

Hazardous Work and Permit Systems

These systems include the following:

Hot work and burning. Hot work is a major source of accidents on a construction site. All hot work should be done through a permit system, whether administered by the site safety department, the fire brigade or the project engineers themselves. Never depend on contract workers to precisely follow your hot work procedures; many of the other sites where they work do not have such regulations. These operations must be monitored through inspection. Key things to look for are: properly rated, charged and certified fire extinguishers; clearance around the site to combustibles (35 feet recommended); clearance to flammable or combustible liquids (50 feet recommended); and a fire watch whose sole duty is to monitor the safety of the job and have the capability to summon help and use portable fire extinguishing equipment. Also, ensure that compressed gas cylinders are properly secured and standing upright when being used or stored.

Confined spaces. Yes, OSHA standard 1910.146 is upon us and yes, contract personnel are required to comply with it as we are. Ensure that there is an entry permit system in place, all precautions are taken and all required entry equipment is on hand. You may consider requiring: an additional attendant at the entry to act as a runner to summon help; that all entrants be trained on self-contained breathing apparatus; that a blower be used on all entries to help maintain a hazard-free atmosphere (be aware that vapors or fumes can still pass through the space with a blower on); and that there is a communications system between the attendant and the entrant. It is also recommended that your site emergency services or municipal rescue service be notified prior to making an entry.

Lock out/tag out. You should already have this type of procedure in place. Contractors should use their own locks when locking out utilities to ensure the safety of those working in the area. Inform them that they are not to remove another person's lock in order to activate a valve, switch or other device.

Line breaking permit system. This is another recommended permit system that can prevent serious injury. Any time a line has to be opened that contains hazardous material such as a petroleum pipeline or is normally under pressure such as steam or fire water, this permit should be obtained. The permit tells workers that someone

471

signed off either that the pressure has been relieved on the line or that it has be drained and flushed.

Flammables and Combustibles

Flammable and combustible materials—diesel or gasoline to refill vehicles, epoxies and coatings for floors and walls, glues for joining plastic pipe, and gasses for hot work, to name a few—are usually found in fairly large quantities on a construction site. Anywhere there is storage, use or dispensing of these materials, a properly rated, charged and sealed fire extinguisher should be on hand. Limit portable storage cans containing flammable liquids to 5 gallons maximum and use only approved safety cans. Also, limit inside storage to no more than 25 gallons unless the cans are kept in an approved storage cabinet. Outside, store flammables at least 20 feet from the building. It's good practice to have the workers remove all flammable liquids from the roof (if being used for a special roofing operation) at the end of the day so responding emergency services find no surprises during a fire.

Of course, ignition sources should be avoided or eliminated by guarding against sparks, nearby steam lines, smoking materials and heaters.

A word on portable heaters. Make sure that you insist on heaters that bear the label of a nationally recognized testing laboratory. Heaters are not an exception to the Hot Work permit rules and procedures. Ensure that you have the proper clearances and take all other required hot work precautions for heaters, since they will be fired by some form of combustible liquid or gas.

Housekeeping/Trash/Dumpsters™

All scrap and trash should be removed from the building on a daily basis. Don't allow it to block egress from the building during the day. Ensure that oil-soaked rags and other similar types of debris are placed in metal cans with self-closing lids.

Dumpsters™ should be provided by contractors to handle their trash loads without having to use "company" trash receptacles. Dumpsters™ containing combustibles should be kept a minimum of 25 feet from any building, trailer, substation or overhead pipe rack or power line. If the contractor is using a trash chute from the upper stories to the Dumpster™, the chute should be removed from the Dumpster™ at the end of the day. Otherwise, the chute will act as a chimney or flue if a fire should break out in the Dumpster™, and will

472

help to transmit the fire into the building at a rapid pace. There are hundreds of documented cases where Dumpster™ fires have become building fires, not only during construction but in existing buildings as well.

Fire Prevention and Protection

Access and egress. Movement in and out of the construction area as well as the building itself must not be impaired so that workers can evacuate if necessary and to give easy access to incoming emergency services. All buildings must be accessible from all sides for emergency vehicles to gain access. A good rule of thumb is a 20-foot fire aisle with at least 14 feet of overhead clearance.

Fire protection systems and equipment. In buildings under renovation, the existing sprinkler and stand-pipe systems should remain active until all interior demolition has taken place. If the fire protection system is being replaced, the new system should be completed and activated prior to occupancy of the area. If the old system is to remain, the system should stay in service as reconstruction begins and progresses. However, activation of the sprinkler system should be handled as a priority in all cases.

Fire extinguishers should be strategically placed (about every 4,000 square feet) throughout open floor areas and clearly marked for easy location identification.

The use of site fire protection equipment such as hydrants should be cleared through the site's fire protection manager, brigade chief or other responsible person who is monitoring fire protection at the site. This equipment (hydrants, hose houses, wheeled extinguishers, etc.) should not be blocked or its use impeded in any way. In the event that a tie-in needs to be made to the fire water loop or main system, a permit should be obtained and the proper shutdown arranged for this work. Except in the event of an emergency, use of any site fire protection equipment should be considered a safety violation.

Hazardous Materials. There are a few additional precautions to consider regarding hazardous materials. If the project needs to store liquids, gasses, solvents, etc. in bulk (over 30 gallons), permission should be secured through the responsible site person or department so special arrangements can be made to accommodate this request.

The bulk storage should be at least 50 feet from any building and no more than a working day's supply of these materials should be brought into the building. If the materials to be used may cause harmful vapors or nuisance odors, the project should be required to adequately ventilate the work area using exhaust fans or similar devices.

Any modifications to existing gas piping systems should be performed with the supply shut, locked and tagged and the piping properly purged. Tar kettles for roofing should be kept on the ground and at least 25 feet from the building with the proper fire extinguisher (minimum rating of 20B) within a 25-foot travel distance of the kettle.

Tar kettles should have a self-closing lid, should be attended to when in operation, and never be permitted on the roof of any building.

Pre-Planning Your Construction Site

Fire prevention pre-planning is as imperative with a construction site as with any occupied building. If your first line of defense against fire is the local municipal fire department, invite them in periodically to look around and get familiar with the construction area. If you have a fire brigade or industrial fire department on site, they need to get out and pre-plan this site as well. Consider the following items or questions when you pre-plan:

- Is there access in and around the site? What are the traffic patterns?

- Where are hydrants and fire protection system control valves, etc. located?

- What are the access patterns within the building itself. Are there stairs? Are there shafts?

- What types of hazardous materials are in use? Where are they located? How are they used? Are the MSDSs available if needed?

- Is there an evacuation and emergency plan for the construction site personnel? Is there an accountability mechanism?

- Are fire protection systems activated? Where are the fire department connections located? Can fire protection be fed through the fire department connection?

- Are the names and phone numbers of company engineers, contractors and off-hours emergency contacts readily available?

- What materials were used in construction? Is there a truss roof? What types of floors are present? Are there fire walls, fire-resistant separations and protected penetrations in the structure?

It is imperative that you periodically update your pre-plan as construction sites change very rapidly. This is only your first installment. When the building is completed, a full pre-plan must be made for emergency response to the building once occupied.

Inspections and Compliance

There are many laws and standards governing construction sites, but home rule wins every time. It takes vigilance and persistence to oversee large construction projects. The effort you put into prevention will always pay off.

I offer you a simple but effective Construction Site Checklist. Take it, use it, modify it, create your own, but act. Taking a proactive approach to construction site safety will protect your company from liability and save you lots of time-consuming, unnecessary paperwork! More importantly, you may save lives or prevent serious injury.

—by Ronald E. Kanterman

Ronald E. Kanterman is the chief of emergency services for Merck and Co. and is based in Rahway, N.J. He has a B.S. in Fire Science and an M.S. in Fire Protection Management, both from John Jay College of Criminal Justice in New York City. He is an adjunct professor of Fire Science at Middlesex County College in Edison, N.J., and a former deputy chief inspector, Bureau of Fire Prevention, New York City Fire Department.

Part Ten

Child Labor, Workplace Violence, and Job Stress Issues

Chapter 45

Child Labor: Still with Us after All These Years

Child labor. The grim words conjure up visions of Charles Dickens and of soot-laden workhouses in Victorian London[1,2] or, closer to home, pictures of little children in the early 1900s sorting coal in the mines of Pennsylvania and West Virginia.[3] This is the image most Americans have of child labor in this country. It is accompanied by the belief that the practice was evil but that it existed long ago and the problem has been remedied.

Most Americans today believe that exploitative child labor is a problem mainly of the developing world and that if it exists at all in the United States it is an isolated phenomenon found only at the far fringes of society, affecting highly marginalized groups such as migrant farmworker children, the children of deaf Mexicans in New York City who sold trinkets on the subways, or workers from Thailand imprisoned in a factory in California. Unfortunately, this view is far from accurate.

Child labor—in both its legal and illegal forms—is widespread in the United States and needs to be reexamined. Modern child labor has positive as well as negative aspects. On the plus side, legal work such as baby-sitting, grocery bagging, lawn work, and odd jobs can

Philip J. Landrigan; Jane B. McCammon, "Child Labor: Still with Us after All These Years," *Public Health Reports*, Nov–Dec 1997, Vol. 112 N. 6 pg. 466-474, Copyright 1997 by U.S. Department of Health and Human Services. Readers interested in understanding the historical development of the issues presented in this chapter will find in-depth information in the sources listed at the end of this chapter.

encourage the development of discipline, teach a child or teen the meaning of money, and provide valuable role models. But on the negative side, exploitative and illegal child labor is as ugly now as it was a hundred years ago. You just need to know where to look.

I first became aware of the problem of child labor a few years ago when Ernest Drucker, MD, of the Albert Einstein School of Medicine told me the horrifying tale of two adolescent boys in New York City who, within approximately six months, had both suffered high amputations of their arms while working in the same butcher shop. In each instance, the boy was cutting heavy sides of beef on an unguarded power-driven bandsaw. Each slipped on the blood-wet floor and fell into the moving saw. Other examples of illegal child labor include the child doing industrial piecework at home in the evening and then falling asleep the next day at school; the teenager delivering pizzas becoming involved in a car crash while driving illegally and trying to deliver food within a 30-minute deadline; and the four-year-old working under her mother's skirts in a garment factory passing along the fabric so that the piecework can go faster.

Child labor is found in every region of the nation and in every sector of society.[4] According to data from the U. S. Department of Labor, more than four million children younger than 18 years of age worked in paid employment outside the home in 1993.[5] Illegal child labor, defined as working under age, for long hours, at less than minimum wage, or on dangerous and prohibited machinery, is also wide-spread, and has recently stabilized after increasing through the 1980s into the 1990s. Detected violations of child labor law in the United States have more than doubled in the past decade.[6-8]

Data collected in 1993 highlight the following child labor facts:[9]

- Forty-two percent of 16- and 17-year-olds reported in 1993 that they had been employed at some time during the previous year.

- Sixteen- and seventeen-year-olds reported working an average of 24 hours per week for 25 weeks of the year.

- By high school graduation, 80% of adolescents in the United States have worked.

- The most common jobs for children and adolescents are in restaurants, grocery stores, farms, nursing homes, and factories.

- Low-income teens are more likely than their higher-income peers to be employed in high risk jobs such as in agriculture, manufacturing, and construction.

Work has been documented to account for 64,000 annual emergency room visits by children and adolescents.[10] From these reports we estimate that the actual numbers of child and adolescent workers injured each year in the United States is 200,000. Approximately 70 of those injuries result in deaths.[10]

Work is clearly an increasingly important part of the life of American children. Some recent case histories from the files of the Massachusetts Department of Public Health and the Colorado Department of Public Health and Environment show us why we should be paying more attention to this growing segment of the working population.

Death of a seventeen-year-old exposed to perchloroethylene. On February 3, 1994, a 17-year-old child laborer in Colorado began work at 4:00 P.M. in a plastic products manufacturing plant. His assigned task was to clean the insides of metal molds used to form plastic containers. He performed this task by soaking perchloroethylene solvent into a cloth rag. He then used the wet rag to wipe the interior surface of the mold. The mold in which he was working was a 40-gallon container that was 191/2 inches in diameter and 32 inches deep.

In the moments before he was overcome and asphyxiated, the boy had propped the mold so that the open side faced up and had then leaned into the mold to clean the bottom. His body was found at the bottom of the mold at midnight when a co-worker arrived on the scene.

The autopsy report listed the cause of death as consistent with asphyxiation due to exposure to toxic vapors. A postmortem toxicologic screen of his blood showed a perchloroethylene concentration of 23.24 mg per liter. This level is far above the biological exposure index established by the American Conference of Governmental Industrial Hygienists for perchloroethylene in blood of 1 mg per liter.

The reconstruction of events indicated that the depth of the mold was greater than the boys arm length. Thus, to reach the bottom of the mold, he had to bend deeply over the rim and place his head inside the mold. The space was not ventilated. There was no designated standby person. The worker was not wearing a respirator. And, finally, it was not legal for this 17-year-old boy to be working alone at night.

Electrocution of Colorado farmworkers. Aluminum irrigation pipes are generally 30 feet in length. The pipes are connected to a pump located in the center of the area to be irrigated. High voltage lines (7200 or 7620 volts), suspended 20 feet above the ground on poles, supply power to the pump.

Every year, several agricultural workers in arid climate zones are electrocuted when they contact overhead high voltage lines with aluminum irrigation pipes that they are lifting. Between 1982 and 1989, 34 such deaths were reported to state health departments in the western United States, according to the Colorado Department of Health and Environment.[11]

In May 1990 in Colorado, three teenage migrant farmworkers were attempting to move a 30-foot section of aluminum irrigation pipe. A 15-year-old was kneeling on the ground and anchoring one end of the pipe while the other two lifted the pipe. The pipe made contact with the 7200-volt power line, and the 15-year-old worker was fatally electrocuted. The other two child laborers sustained serious electrical burns to their hands and feet.

Electrocution of a fifteen-year-old carwash worker. In September 1995, a 15-year-old boy working at an automated full service carwash in Colorado was instructed to remove a defective motor from the carwash machine. This motor operated spinning brushes and was powered by 460 volts of electricity. It appears that the manager disconnected the wires supplying power to the motor but that power to the circuit was not de-energized. Then, while the teenager was following instructions to remove the motor, the car-wash equipment was re-energized and an electrical short circuit occurred. The 15-year-old was electrocuted.

Deaths of newspaper carriers in Massachusetts. During a six-month period, two Massachusetts news carriers, employed by different newspapers, were killed by motor vehicles while delivering their papers from bicycles. Neither child was wearing a helmet. Although safety materials were handed out during orientations, neither employer had a comprehensive safety program for their carriers. One employer offered a reflective vest and armband, but, according to several of the carriers families, this equipment was not provided consistently.

Federal child labor law does not apply to news carriers because they are considered to be independent contractors. News carriers in Massachusetts, unlike other working minors, are not required to obtain work permits before they begin employment. Instead, all that is necessary is a written statement of permission from a parent or guardian. Moreover, only one of the two employers required parental permission and actively involved parents in the childs employment.

The first victim was a 14-year-old boy who had delivered newspapers for approximately 15 months. He would pick up newspapers from a distribution vehicle at a drop-off point less than one block from a busy suburban street. The boy crossed the street each day on his bicycle to pick up his papers.

On the day of his death, the boy was en route to the drop-off point and was about to cross the street on his bicycle when he was hit by a van. He was wearing a stadium jacket with a large thick hood that may have blocked his peripheral vision. Apparently the side mirror of the van struck the child on the back of the neck. The impact threw him from the bike. The boy suffered two head injuries, one from the impact of the mirror, the other from his fall to the ground. He died of severe brain trauma.

The second victim was a 12-year-old girl who had delivered newspapers for approximately six months. Her route consisted of 29 customers on two streets. The girl had just made a delivery and was coming out of a customers driveway on her bicycle when she was struck by a jeep. She was wearing a reflective vest and a white jacket but no helmet. The driveway was steep and was lined with a row of five tall pine trees that obstructed the view from the street. The girl died from blunt head trauma one hour after being hit.

Why Has Child Labor Increased in the Last 15 Years?

A reconvergence of economic and social factors similar to those that produced the major increases in child labor at the beginning of the Industrial Revolution has produced the last two decades' increase in prevalence of child labor.[4]

Increased child poverty. More American children live below the poverty line today than 20 years ago. For those American children who live in poverty, financial need constitutes a compelling reason to seek employment.

- *Massive immigration.* More immigration into the United States has occurred in the decades of the 1980s and 1990s than in any period in this century except the decade between 1900 and 1910. Illegal immigrants, particularly children without parents, are highly vulnerable to exploitation in the workplace.[8] The recent surge of immigration has led to the reemergence of illegal immigrant sweatshops in large cities such as New York, Chicago, and Los Angeles.[6-8]

- *Growing frequency of student workers.*[9] Student workers are a phenomenon unique to North America. These children and adolescents, employed after school, on weekends, and during vacation are employed in all industrial sectors, but especially in the fast-food and service industries.

483

- *Relaxation in enforcement of Federal child labor law*. Since 1980, there has been lax enforcement of the Federal law, including relaxation of the provisions limiting the maximum permissible hours of work and the prohibitions against use of dangerous machinery. Repeal of the ban on industrial homework, which was created 40 years ago to protect working women and children from exploitation in piecework industries, has further undermined the historic intent of child labor law. There are now fewer than 1000 Federal labor inspectors for 113 million workers.

Illegal employment of children occurs today in all industrial sectors in the United States. Sweatshop conditions are increasingly common.[6-8] A sweatshop is defined as any establishment that routinely and repeatedly violates wage, hour, and child labor laws as well as the laws protecting occupational safety and health. Traditionally, these shops have been considered fringe establishments, such as those in the garment and meat-packing industries. Increasingly, however, restaurants and grocery stores, not typically considered sweatshops, are also meeting the definition.

Health and safety conditions in sweatshops are often very poor.[12] Fire hazards may be created by blocked exit doors, accumulations of combustible materials, and inadequate ventilation; electrocution hazards result form overloaded electrical connections, work stations located close to exposed wires, and bare fuseboxes. The most recent data on the large number of fire code violations being discovered by the inspectors of the Garment Industry Task Force of the New York State Department of Labor suggest that sweatshop workers, including children, are at very high risk of dying in a fire if these conditions are not corrected.[13]

Hazards of Child Labor

The hazards of child labor fall into two categories:

a. threats to education and development

b. risks of injury and of illness due to toxic exposure

Educational and Developmental Risks

One of the principal hazards of child labor is interference with school performance. Employed children risk having too little time for homework and being overtired on school days; teachers of children in areas where pre-holiday employment is common or industrial homework is escalating have reported declines in the academic performance of previously adequate students. These children are described as falling asleep at their desks, and they are unable to learn.[12] Even if they maintain their academic standing, working children are able to participate less than their peers in after-school activities and sports. Child labor also interferes with play, which is very important for normal development throughout childhood, and relaxation and freedom from fatigue are necessary for children to grow and learn. Also, being in the workplace can increase the exposure of adolescents to drugs and alcohol.[14,15]

Health Risks

Injuries

The leading cause of death in children older than one year, injuries account for 45% of all deaths of 5- to 14-year-old children in the United States. According to the most recent data available from 1989, approximately 10,000 children die from injuries each year,[16] and injuries are the leading cause of potential years of life lost in this country.[17]

Injuries associated with child labor appear to pose a significant public health problem.[18] Data reported by the Centers for Disease Control and Prevention indicate that in 1993 child and adolescent workers in the United States sustained an estimated 21,620 injuries involving lost work days.[18] The Bureau of Labor Statistics of the U.S. Department of Labor reports that each year between 1992 and 1995 an average of 180 work-related traumatic deaths occurred among working children and adolescents.[19] The largest number of deaths were among young farmworkers. Workers in jobs in which they interacted with the public, such as retail sales clerks, also had high numbers of work-related fatalities; homicide accounted for over 70% of deaths in these occupations.[18] Data from 1992 to 1995 collected by the National Electronic Injury Surveillance System indicate that 18- and 19-year old workers had the highest injury rates in the entire U.S. workforce, followed closely by 16- and 17-year old workers.[19]

Illustrating the importance of the workplace as a source of injury for children and adolescents, a recent review of adolescent visits to emergency rooms in Massachusetts found that of injuries that occurred in a known location, work accounted for 13.3% of all emergency visits for 14- to 17-year-olds and for 26.2% of visits among 17-year-olds.[20] The proportion of injuries related to work exceeded the proportion related to sports. Important data tabulating injuries to working children have been reported through injury surveillance programs in Texas,[21] Connecticut,[22] Saskatchewan,[23] and North Carolina.[24]

The fast food industry is among the fastest growing and largest sectors employing youth in the United States today. Lacerations and burns are common hazards in fast food establishments. There is also a risk of electrocution, although this may have been reduced by changes mandated subsequent to the death by electrocution in 1987 of a teenage worker in a hamburger restaurant; the source was a power outlet on a wet floor in an improperly grounded building.[25]

The delivery of pizzas and other hot food items has proven to be extremely hazardous to working children. The rash promise made by one national pizza company that all pizzas would be delivered within 30 minutes of the time of placing an order has been shown to encourage reckless driving by young, often inexperienced motor vehicle operators.[26] A total of 20 fatalities within a single year among children working in pizza delivery and the people in the vehicle with which they collided were documented to be associated with the ill-conceived delivery policies of this firm.[26] Commercial driving is illegal under the age of 18 years.

In the years 1980 to 1987, workers compensation awards were made to 10,047 children under 18 years old in New York State for work-related injuries; 44% of these resulted in some degree of permanent disability. There were also 35 deaths.[27] These injuries and deaths occurred in a wide range of industries.

Risk of Illness Due to Toxic Exposure

Little information is available on the incidence or severity of illness caused in children by toxic occupational exposures. However, we do know that children are particularly sensitive to toxic substances and that they experience a variety of toxic exposures at work. These include formaldehyde and dyes in the garment industry, solvents in paint shops, organophosphate and other pesticides in agricultural as well as in lawn care jobs, asbestos in building abatement, and benzene in pumping unleaded gasoline. Given the wide occurrence of these exposures, it seems plausible that some still undefined portion of adolescent asthma cases might be related to occupational exposures to dusts or formaldehyde or that some cases of leukemia in children and adolescents may be the consequence of occupational exposure to benzene in unleaded gasoline. Noise exposure in adolescence may begin the sequence of destructive events in the auditory system that lead to noise-induced hearing loss in adult life.[28]

486

Agricultural Hazards

Rural children are employed extensively in agriculture, both on family farms and commercially. The hazards to health associated with agricultural work include lacerations, amputations, and crush injuries from farm machinery, blunt trauma from large animals; motor vehicle accidents involving farm vehicles on public roads; risk of suffocation in grain elevators and silos; and exposure to pesticides. Small physical size and inexperience may superimpose additional risk for young workers.

Although the number of children working in agriculture is not as large as in other sectors, the potential hazards (especially those involving machinery and large animals) coupled with the historical lack of regulation of agriculture combine to create an important problem, particularly in rural states. Agriculture has come to surpass mining as the most dangerous occupation.[29] Perhaps for this reason, much of the scanty literature available on work-related injury and illness in children focuses on agriculture.[29-32]

Prevention Strategies

Prevention of injury and illness in working children requires a variety of strategies:

Enforcement

Relaxation in the enforcement of Federal regulations protecting child workers along with a decrease in the number of inspectors and, consequently, a decrease in the number of inspections have contributed to the last decades resurgence of child labor abuses in the United States. Strong enforcement of existing legislation and regulations is necessary to protect the health and safety of working children and to support legitimate employers whose businesses are financially endangered by those who hire children under illegal working conditions.

Education

Working children and their parents, employers, and school authorities as well as physicians and other health care providers need to be educated about the hazards associated with child labor and about the relevant legal proscriptions. Education of child workers should attempt to temper their enthusiasm and lack of fear of workplace hazards. School authorities exercising their responsibilities under the work permit system and health care providers performing physical examinations of job applicants under age 18 have a unique opportunity to ensure that minors are not working in prohibited occupations or other unprescribed yet hazardous situations. Health care providers, particularly emergency room staff, need to remember that work can be a cause of injury and illness in childhood. The importance of an occupational history cannot be overemphasized. Finally, the business community must be educated on the hazards of child labor and reminded of its responsibilities under the law.

Surveillance

One of the major impediments to defining and resolving the problem of child labor in the United States is the lack of up-to-date descriptive data on the size and demographic characteristics of the population of working children. Data on the incidence of work-related injuries and illnesses in children are limited and fragmented due to a lack of both numerator and denominator data. Federal and state governments need to develop mechanisms for collecting these data more efficiently and for accessing other datasets that are potentially useful but currently only minimally available, such as information on work permits issued by local school boards. These data need to be published and publicized. Departments of health and labor at both the state and Federal levels need to work together and exchange data. Furthermore, Federal and state agencies should institute active surveillance of occupational injuries and illnesses in minors, using workers compensation claims, hospital visits, and other sources to identify sentinel health events for follow-up and preventive intervention. Active surveillance and epidemiological studies of work-related injury and illness in minors also will permit targeting of enforcement. They will facilitate evaluation of the effectiveness of current laws and may suggest possible modifications, such as additions to the list of proscribed occupations.

National Institute for Occupational Safety and Health Recommendations on Adolescent Labor

The following are a series of specific recommendations on adolescent labor development by the National Institute for Occupational Safety and Health (NIOSH):[25]

Employers

NIOSH recommends that employers take the following steps to protect adolescent workers:

- Know and comply with child labor laws and occupational safety and health regulations that apply to your business. Post these regulations for workers to read.

- Assess and eliminate the potential for injury or illness associated with tasks required of adolescents.

- Provide training to ensure that adolescents recognize hazards and are competent in safe work practices.

- Routinely verify that the adolescents are required to operate to ensure that it is both legal and safe for use by adolescents.

- Ensure that adolescents are appropriately supervised to prevent injuries and hazardous exposures.

- Involve supervisors and experienced workers in developing an injury and illness prevention program and in identifying and solving safety and health problems.

Parents

Parents should take the following steps to protect adolescent workers:

- Take an active role in the employment decision of your children.

- Discuss the types of work involved and the training and supervision provided by the employer.

Educators

Educators should take the following steps to protest adolescent workers:

- If you are responsible for signing work permits, know the state and Federal child labor laws.

- Talk to students about safety health hazards in the workplace and students rights and responsibilities as workers.

- Ensure that school-based work experience programs (such as vocational education programs and School-to-Work programs) provide students with work experience in safe and healthful environments free of recognized hazards.

- Ensure that school-based work experience programs incorporate information about workers legal rights and responsibilities and occupational safety and health into high school and junior high curricula to prepare students for the world of work.

Children and Adolescents

Adolescent workers should take the following steps to protect themselves:

- Be aware that you have the right to work in a safe and healthful work environment free of recognized hazards and that you have the right to refuse unsafe work tasks and conditions.

- Know that you have the right to file complaints with the U.S. Department of Labor when you feel your rights have been violated or your safety has been jeopardized.

- Remember that adolescent workers are entitled to workers compensation in the state labor departments.

- Participate in any training programs offered by your employer, or request training if none is offered.

- Recognize the potential for injury at work and seek information about safe work practices from employers and state labor departments.

- Follow safe work practices.

—by Philip J. Landrigan

Dr. Landrigan is a Professor of Pediatrics and Chair of the Department of Community Medicine at the Mount Sinai School of Medicine, New York, NY. Ms. McCammon is the Manager, Occupational Epidemiology, Colorado Department of Public Health and Environment, on detail from the National Institute for Occupational Safety and Health. Address correspondence to Dr. Landrigan, Dept. of Community Medicine, Mount Sinai School of Medicine, One Gustave L. Levy Place, New York NY 10029-6574; tel. 212-241-4805; fax 212-996-0407; e-mail: plandrigan@smtplink.mssm.edu

References

1. Hunter D. *The diseases of occupations. 5th ed.* London: English University Press; 1974.

2. Trollope F. *The life and adventures of Michael Armstrong, the factory boy.* London: Colburn; 1840.

3. Zinn H. *A People's History of the United States*. New York: Harper; 1980. p. 43–4.

4. Pollack SH, Landrigan PJ, Mallino DL. "Child labor in 1990: prevalence and health hazards." *Annu Rev Public Health* 1990;11:359–75.

5. Bureau of Labor Statistics (US). "Employment and earnings." Vol. 41, No. 1. Washington: Department of Labor; 1994 Jan.

6. General Accounting Office (US). "Sweatshops and child labor violations: a growing problem in the United States." Washington: GAO; 1989.

7. General Accounting Office (US). "Sweatshops in the U.S.— opinions on their extent and possible enforcement actions." Washington: GAO; 1988. Report No.: GAO/HRD 88-130BR.

8. "Child labor and sweatshops." *Congressional Q* 1996;6: 721–44.

9. "Children's Safety Network. Protecting working teens—a public health resource guide." Newton (MA): Education Development Center; 1995.

10. Landrigan PJ, Belville R. "The dangers of illegal child labor." *Amer J Dis Child* 1993;147:1029–1030.

11. Colorado Department of Health and Environment. Hazard Alert; 1993 Spring.

12. Postol T. "Public health and working children in twentieth century America: an historical overview." *J Public Health Policy* 1993;14:348–54.

13. New York State Department of Labor. "Transcript of hearings on child labor law (Albany, Buffalo, Manhattan, Hauppauge and Syracuse)." Albany: The Department; 1988.

14. Cohen S. "Social and personality development in childhood." New York. Macmillan; 1976. p. 163–86.

15. Greenberger E, Steinberg L. *When teenagers work: the psychological and social costs of adolescent employment*. New York. Basic Books; 1986. p. 13.

16. Waller A-E, Baker SP, Szocka A. "Childhood injury deaths: national analysis and geographical variations." *Am J Public Health* 1989;79:310–5.

17. "Years of potential life lost before age 65—United States, 1987." *Morb Mortal Wkly Rep* 1989;38:27–9.

18. "Work-related injuries associated with child labor—United States, 1993." *Morb Mortal Wkly Rep* 1996;45:464–8.

19. Derstine B. "Job-related fatalities involving youths, 1992–95." Compensation and Working Conditions 1996;40–2.

20. Brooks DR, Davis LK, Gallagher SS. "Work-related injuries among Massachusetts children: a study based on emergency department data." *Amer J Industr Med* 1993;24:313–24.

21. Cooper SP, Rothstein MA. "Health hazards among working children in Texas." *Southern Med J* 1995;88:550–4.

22. Banco L, Lapidus G, Braddock M. "Work-related injury among Connecticut minors." *Pediatrics* 1992;89:957–60.

23. Glor ED. "Survey of comprehensive accident and injury experience of high school students in Saskatchewan." *Canad J Public Health* 1989;80:435–40.

24. Dunn KA, Runyan CW. "Deaths at work among children and adolescents." *Amer J Dis Child* 1993;147:1044–7.

25. National Institute for Occupational Safety and Health (US). "Request for assistance in preventing deaths and injuries of adolescent workers." Cincinnati: NIOSH; 1995. DHHS Pub. No. 95-125.

26. Butterfield, BD. "Injured, then abandoned." *Boston Globe*. 1990 Aug 5; Sect. A1.

27. Belville R, Pollack SH, Godbold JH, Landrigan PJ. "Occupational injuries among working adolescents in New York State." *JAMA* 1993;269:2754–9.

28. Broste SK, Hinsen DA, Strand RL, Steuland DT. "Hearing loss among high school farm students." *Am J Public Health* 1989;79:619–22.

29. Swanson JA, Sachs MI, Dahlgren KA, Tinguely SJ. "Accidental farm injuries in children." *Am J Dis Child* 1987;141: 1276–9.

30. Cogbill TH, Busch HM, Stiers GR. "Farm accidents in children." *Pediatrics* 1988;76:562–6.

31. "Fatalities associated with improper hitching to farm tractors—New York, 1991–1995." *Morb Mortal Wkly Rep* 1996;45:307–11.

32. Rivara FP. "Fatal and nonfatal farm injuries to children and adolescents in the United States." *Pediatrics* 1985;76: 567–73.

Chapter 46

Workplace Violence

Workplace Violence—Introduction

Workplace violence has emerged as an important safety and health issue in today's workplace. It's most extreme form, homicide, is the second leading cause of fatal occupational injury in the United States. Nearly 1,000 workers are murdered, and 1.5 million are assaulted in the workplace each year. According to the Bureau of Labor Statistics (BLS) Census of Fatal Occupational Injuries (CFOI), there were 709 workplace homicides in 1998, accounting for 12% of the total 6,026 fatal work injuries in the United States.[1-2] Environmental conditions associated with workplace assaults have been identified and control strategies implemented in a number of work settings. The Occupational Safety and Health Administration (OSHA) has developed guidelines and recommendations to reduce worker exposures to this hazard but is not initiating rulemaking at this time.

Non-Fatal Assaults

According to the Department of Justice's National Crime Victimization Survey (NCVS), assaults and threats of violence against Americans at work number almost 2 million a year. The most common type

This chapter includes text from "Workplace Violence," Occupational Safety and Health Administration, http://www.osha.gov/oshinfo/priorities/violence.html, revised August 18, 1999, and Rebecca A. Speer, "Can Workplace Violence be prevented?" *Occupational Hazards*, August 1998, Vol. 60, N. 8, pp. 26–30, copyright 1999 Penton Media Inc. Reprinted with permission.

of workplace violent crime was simple assault with an average of 1.5 million a year. There were 396,000 aggravated assaults, 51,000 rapes and sexual assaults, 84,000 robberies, and 1,000 homicides.

Again, according to the NCVS, retail sales workers were the most numerous victims, with 330,000 being attacked each year. They were followed by police, with an average of 234,200 officers victimized. The risk rate for various occupations was as follows: (per 1,000)

- 306 Police officers
- 218 Private security guards
- 184 Taxi drivers
- 117 Prison guards
- 91 Bartenders
- 80 Mental health professionals
- 79 Gas station attendants
- 68 Convenience, liquor store clerks
- 63 Mental health custodial workers
- 57 Junior high/middle school teachers
- 45 Bus drivers
- 41 Special education teachers
- 29 High school teachers
- 16 Elementary school teachers
- 3 College teachers

Homicide

Workplace homicides fell to their lowest level in the past six years in 1997, but continued as the second leading cause of job-related deaths. Robbery continued to be the primary motive of job-related homicide, accounting for 85% of the deaths. Disputes among coworkers and with customers and clients accounted for about one-tenth of the total.[3]

Sales workers experienced the highest number of workplace homicides—an average of 327 each year from 1993 to 1996. Annually, 74 taxi drivers and chauffeurs were murdered while working or on duty. About 70 law enforcement officers were killed in the line of duty each year.[4] Although it does not have the highest number of homicides, the taxicab industry has the highest risk at 41.4 per 100,000 persons. Job-related homicides in retail trade account for almost half of all workplace homicides.[5]

Risk Factors

Factors which may increase a worker's risk for workplace assault, as identified by the National Institute for Occupational Safety and Health (NIOSH), are:[6]

- contact with the public
- exchange of money
- delivery of passengers, goods, or services
- having a mobile workplace such as a taxicab or police cruiser
- working with unstable or volatile persons in health care, social services, or criminal justice settings
- working alone or in small numbers
- working late at night or during early morning hours
- working in high-crime areas
- guarding valuable property or possessions
- working in community-based settings

OSHA's Commitment

OSHA does not have a specific standard for workplace violence. However, under the Occupational Safety and Health Act of 1970 (the OSH Act, or the Act), the extent of an employer's obligation to address workplace violence is governed by the General Duty Clause.

> Section 5(a)(1) of the OSH Act, or P.L. 91-596 (the "General Duty Clause") provides that: "Each employer shall furnish to each of his employees employment and a place of employment which are free from recognized hazards that are causing or are likely to cause death or serious physical harm to his employees." 29 U.S.C. 654(a)(1)

It is, therefore, OSHA's commitment to encourage employers to develop workplace violence prevention programs.

Prevention Programs

The Occupational Safety and Health Administration's (OSHA's) response to the problem of workplace violence in certain industries has been the production of OSHA's guidelines and recommendations to those industries for implementing workplace violence prevention programs. The guidelines and recommendations are based on OSHA's Safety and Health Program Management Guidelines and contain four basic elements:

- *Management commitment and employee involvement*. May include simply clear goals for worker security in smaller sites or a written program for larger organizations.

- *Worksite analysis*. Involves identifying high-risk situations through employee surveys, workplace walkthroughs, and reviews of injury/illness data.

- *Hazard prevention and control*. Calls for designing engineering, administrative, and work practice controls to prevent or limit violent incidents.

- *Training and education*. Ensures that employees know about potential security hazards and ways to protect themselves and their co-workers.

Engineering controls remove the hazard from the workplace or create a barrier between the worker and the hazard. Administrative and work practice controls affect the way jobs or tasks are performed.

Some Recommended Engineering and Administrative Controls

- physical barriers such as bullet-resistant enclosures, pass-through windows, or deep service counters

- alarm systems, panic buttons

- convex mirrors, elevated vantage points, clear visibility of service and cash register areas

- bright and effective lighting

- adequate staffing

- arrange furniture to prevent entrapment

- cash-handling controls, use of drop safes

- height markers on exit doors

- emergency procedures to use in case of robbery

- training in identifying hazardous situations and appropriate responses in emergencies

- video surveillance equipment and closed circuit TV

- establish liaison with local police

Post-Incident Response and Evaluation

Post-incident response and evaluation are essential to an effective violence prevention program. All workplace violence programs should provide treatment for victimized employees and employees who may be traumatized by witnessing a workplace violence incident. Several types of assistance can be incorporated into the post-incident response including:

- trauma-crisis counseling

- critical incident stress debriefing

- employee assistance programs to assist victims

Can Workplace Violence Be Prevented?

Workplace Violence Is Multicide: Mass Murder

It's the most prevalent form of mass murder, and what managers don't know about it will hurt them, warns Deborah Schurman-Kauflin. An FBI-trained profiler who specializes in serial and mass murderers and whose 15-year study on the subject forms the core of her doctoral dissertation, she is president of the Cincinnati-based Violent Crimes Institute. Schurman-Kauflin has plenty to say about who commits workplace violence, all of it chilling.

"These people do not explode out of the blue. They have had problems all their lives," she says. "They typically are under psychiatric care when they act, but they are not raving maniacs. They have a skewed perception of the world. There is a very thin line between those who act and those who do not. Each of us is capable of doing this (workplace violence) under the right circumstances."

The Violent Employee

The violent employee frequently is (but is not necessarily) a white male, fascinated with weapons, who has been fired or who is on disability or medical leave. He may have been held back at work as uncooperative and intolerant of change. He sees himself as special or unique, and delineates the world around him into "us" and "them." He perceives himself as a martyr, blaming others for his problems.

His violent act is in revenge for being "personally wronged." He does not have a history of criminal behavior. "He has the same mind set as one who does, but he has not acted out—yet," says Schurman-Kauflin.

He spends a considerable amount of time planning his retribution in detail, and acts in a controlled rage. He locks onto a target—someone whom he feels has wronged him unjustly and to whom he is uniquely tied—and acts, undeterred, until the target is destroyed. His target is seen as an object, not a person. Further, because everyone between him and that target also is perceived as an obstacle, he does not hesitate to kill or wound them.

If you think the employee who turns violent is easy to spot among your hires, think again. "These people can—and do—fit right in," Schurman-Kauflin says. "They fit in long enough and get by long enough to surprise us with their violence."

But the violent act should not surprise anyone, she warns. The employee often voices a threat to a coworker (not necessarily a close associate) in advance, and not in a joking manner. Employees should take all threats seriously and report them to the supervisor, says Schurman-Kauflin, and they should remind employees not to joke about workplace violence, since all such comments will be seen as potential threats.

"Bear in mind that you cannot talk the person making the threat out of it; you cannot change his mind," she cautions. "You can only report the threat."

What Can Companies and Managers Do to Prevent Workplace Violence?

Look for a cluster of things, Schurman-Kauflin advises, including:

- resentful, frustrated employees who blame others
- threats against individuals or the company
- individuals who have been let go, laid off, or placed on leave
- those who have been affected by reassignment or budget cuts

The problem, according to Schurman-Kauflin, has its seeds in the home and in society at large.

"We as a society set ourselves up for violence," she says. "Think about it. Can you name two serial killers? Can you name two of their victims? The fact that you can name the killers and not their victims tells you how we really look at violence: we glorify it."

Mass layoffs dehumanize people in the same way that the violent employee objectivizes his target. Schurman-Kauflin notes that many decision-makers look only at budget or profit numbers, not at individuals' contributions to the company. (Can your decision-maker name the people who were laid off and their job titles and departments?)

Parents and Schools

She holds accountable parents who don't take care of their children, who withhold affection from them and who fail to nurture them. Parental abandonment—emotional or de facto—is a huge influence on those who commit multicide, as mass murderers have an unmet need for attention. They characteristically cannot form attachments with other people, often describe themselves as "cold", and have a history of hurting animals and smaller children (whom they see only as objects) and of destroying property. They see themselves as already dead, and their rampages often end in suicide, either by their own hand or by the police.

Finally, Schurman-Kauflin suggests that the educational system in the United States fails to prepare people for coping with modern life. Skill deficiencies make layoffs easy and employment transitions difficult. Many individuals who turn violent feel those effects acutely because they cannot adapt to workplace changes.

A More Humanizing Workplace

"Creating a more humanizing workplace is important," she says. "If you are going to let people go, tell them, person-to-person. Give each individual an explanation. It is harder to discard a person than an object. If you see your employees as people, they are less likely to objectify you."

—by Rebecca A. Speer

Rebecca A. Speer is a San Francisco employment lawyer and recognized expert who speaks nationally concerning the steps organizations can take to prevent and manage violence. A strong advocate of workplace violence prevention, Ms. Speer provides comprehensive services and training to help organizations effectively address this critical problem. She is Chair of the Model Work Plan Subcommittee of the Santa Clara County (Calif.) Workplace Violence Committee and Chair of the Workplace Violence Committee of the National Association of Women Lawyers. She can be contacted at (415) 283-4888. Deborah

Schurman-Kauflin can be contacted at The Violent Crimes Institute at P.O. Box 54358, Cincinnati, Ohio 45254-0358.

References

1. Bureau of Labor Statistics (1999). National Census of Fatal Occupational Injuries, 1998.

2. Warchol, Greg (1998). Workplace Violence, 1992–96. National Crime Victimization Survey. (Report No. NCJ-168634).

3. Bureau of Labor Statistics (1998). National Census of Fatal Occupational Injuries, 1997.

4. Bureau of Labor Statistics. National Census of Fatal Occupational Injuries, 1993–1996.

5. NIOSH Facts Sheet. Violence in the Workplace, 1997.

6. NIOSH Current Intelligence Bulletin 57. Violence in the Workplace: Risk Factors and Prevention Strategies, 1996.

7. Washington State Department of Labor and Industries (1990). Late Night Retail Workers Crime Protection. WAC 296-24-102, 296-24-10203.

8. New Jersey Department of Labor. Guidelines on Measures and Safeguards in Dealing with Violent or Aggressive Behavior in Public Sector Health Care Facilities. New Jersey Department of Labor, Public Employees Occupational Safety and Health Program.

9. Simonowitz, Joyce A. (1993). Guidelines for Security and Safety of Health Care and Community Service Workers. California Department of Industrial Relations. Division of Occupational Safety and Health, Medical Unit.

10. CAL/OSHA (1995). CAL/OSHA Guidelines for Workplace Security. California Department of Industrial Relations, Division of Occupational Safety and Health. Revised March 30, 1995.

11. CAL/OSHA (1995). Model Injury and Illness Prevention Program for Workplace Security. California Department of Industrial Relations, Division of Occupational Safety and Health. March 30, 1995.

Chapter 47

Guidelines for Preventing Workplace Violence for Workers

There are four main components to any effective safety and health program that also apply to preventing workplace violence:

1. management commitment and employee involvement

2. worksite analysis

3. hazard prevention and control

4. safety and health training

Management Commitment and Employee Involvement

Management commitment and employee involvement are complementary and essential elements of an effective safety and health program. To ensure an effective program, management and front-line employees must work together, perhaps through a team or committee approach. If employers opt for this strategy, they must be careful to comply with the applicable provisions of the National Labor Relations Act.. Management commitment, including the endorsement and visible involvement of top management, provides the motivation and resources to deal effectively with workplace violence, and should include the following:

Excerpted from "Guidelines for Preventing Workplace Violence for Health Care and Social Service Workers," Occupational Safety and Health Administration, OSHA 3148, http://www.osha-slc.gov/SLTC/workplaceviolence/guideline.html, 1998.

- Demonstrated organizational concern for employee emotional and physical safety and health.

- Equal commitment to worker safety and health and client safety.

- Assigned responsibility for the various aspects of the workplace violence prevention program to ensure that all managers, supervisors, and employees understand their obligations.

- Appropriate allocation of authority and resources to all responsible parties.

- A system of accountability for involved managers, supervisors, and employees.

- A comprehensive program of medical and psychological counseling and debriefing for employees experiencing or witnessing assaults and other violent incidents.

- Commitment to support and implement appropriate recommendations from safety and health committees.

Employee involvement and feedback enable workers to develop and express their own commitment to safety and health and provide useful information to design, implement, and evaluate the program. Employee involvement should include the following:

- Understanding and complying with the workplace violence prevention program and other safety and security measures.

- Participation in an employee complaint or suggestion procedure covering safety and security concerns.

- Prompt and accurate reporting of violent incidents.

- Participation on safety and health committees or teams that receive reports of violent incidents or security problems, make facility inspections, and respond with recommendations for corrective strategies.

- Taking part in a continuing education program that covers techniques to recognize escalating agitation, assaultive behavior, or criminal intent, and discusses appropriate responses.

Written Program

A written program for job safety and security, incorporated into the organization's overall safety and health program, offers an effective approach for larger organizations. In smaller establishments, the program need not be written or heavily documented to be satisfactory. What is needed are clear goals and objectives to prevent workplace violence suitable for the size and complexity of the workplace operation and adaptable to specific situations in each establishment.

The prevention program and startup date must be communicated to all employees. At a minimum, workplace violence prevention programs should do the following:

- Create and disseminate a clear policy of zero-tolerance for workplace violence, verbal and nonverbal threats, and related actions. Managers, supervisors, co-workers, clients, customers and visitors must be advised of this policy.

- Ensure that no reprisals are taken against an employee who reports or experiences workplace violence.

- Encourage employees to promptly report incidents and to suggest ways to reduce or eliminate risks. Require records of incidents to assess risk and to measure progress.

- Outline a comprehensive plan for maintaining security in the workplace. This plan should include establishing a liaison with law enforcement representatives and others who can help identify ways to prevent and mitigate workplace violence.

- Assign responsibility and authority for the program to individuals or teams with appropriate training and skills. The written plan should ensure that there are adequate resources available for this effort and that the team or responsible individuals develop expertise on workplace violence prevention.

- Affirm management commitment to a worker-supportive environment that places as much importance on employee safety and health as on serving the client or customer.

- Set up a company briefing as part of the initial effort to address such issues as preserving safety, supporting affected employees, and facilitating recovery.

Worksite Analysis

Worksite analysis involves a step-by-step, common-sense look at the workplace to find existing or potential hazards for workplace violence. This entails reviewing specific procedures or operations that contribute to hazards and specific locales where hazards may develop.

A "Threat Assessment Team," "Patient Assault Team," similar task force, or coordinator may assess the vulnerability to workplace violence and determine the appropriate preventive actions to be taken. Implementing the workplace violence prevention program then may be assigned to this group. The team should include representatives from senior management, operations, employee assistance, security, occupational safety and health, legal, and human resources staff.

The team or coordinator can review injury and illness records and workers' compensation claims to identify patterns of assaults that could be prevented by workplace adaptation, procedural changes, or employee training. As the team or coordinator identifies appropriate controls, these should be instituted.

The recommended program for worksite analysis includes, but is not limited to, analyzing and tracking records, monitoring trends and analyzing incidents, screening surveys, and analyzing workplace security.

Records Analysis and Tracking

This activity should include reviewing medical, safety, workers' compensation and insurance records—including the Occupational Safety and Health Administration (OSHA) 200 log, if required—to pinpoint instances of workplace violence. Scan unit logs and employee and police reports of incidents or near-incidents of assaultive behavior to identify and analyze trends in assaults relative to particular departments, units, job titles, unit activities, work stations, and/or time of day. Tabulate these data to target the frequency and severity of incidents to establish a baseline for measuring improvement.

Monitoring Trends and Analyzing Incidents

Contacting similar local businesses, trade associations, and community and civic groups is one way to learn about their experiences with workplace violence and to help identify trends. Use several years of data, if possible, to trace trends of injuries and incidents of actual or potential workplace violence.

Screening Surveys

One important screening tool is to give employees a questionnaire or survey to get their ideas on the potential for violent incidents and to identify or confirm the need for improved security measures. Detailed baseline screening surveys can help pinpoint tasks that put employees at risk. Periodic surveys—conducted at least annually or whenever operations change or incidents of workplace violence occur—help identify new or previously unnoticed risk factors and deficiencies or failures in work practices, procedures, or controls. Also, the surveys help assess the effects of changes in the work processes. The periodic review process should also include feedback and follow-up.

Independent reviewers, such as safety and health professionals, law enforcement or security specialists, insurance safety auditors, and other qualified persons may offer advice to strengthen programs. These experts also can provide fresh perspectives to improve a violence prevention program.

Workplace Security Analysis

The team or coordinator should periodically inspect the workplace and evaluate employee tasks to identify hazards, conditions, operations, and situations that could lead to violence.

To find areas requiring further evaluation, the team or coordinator should do the following:

- Analyze incidents, including the characteristics of assailants and victims, an account of what happened before and during the incident, and the relevant details of the situation and its outcome. When possible, obtain police reports and recommendations.

- Identify jobs or locations with the greatest risk of violence as well as processes and procedures that put employees at risk of assault, including how often and when.

- Note high-risk factors such as types of clients or customers (e.g., psychiatric conditions or people disoriented by drugs, alcohol, or stress); physical risk factors of the building; isolated locations/job activities; lighting problems; lack of phones and other communication devices, areas of easy, unsecured access; and areas with previous security problems.

- Evaluate the effectiveness of existing security measures, including engineering control measures. Determine if risk factors have been reduced or eliminated, and take appropriate action.

Hazard Prevention and Control

After hazards of violence are identified through the systematic worksite analysis, the next step is to design measures through engineering or administrative and work practices to prevent or control

507

these hazards. If violence does occur, post-incidence response can be an important tool in preventing future incidents.

Engineering Controls and Workplace Adaptation

Engineering controls, for example, remove the hazard from the workplace or create a barrier between the worker and the hazard. There are several measures that can effectively prevent or control workplace hazards, such as those actions presented in the following paragraphs. The selection of any measure, of course, should be based upon the hazards identified in the workplace security analysis of each facility.

- Assess any plans for new construction or physical changes to the facility or workplace to eliminate or reduce security hazards.

- Install and regularly maintain alarm systems and other security devices, panic buttons, hand-held alarms or noise devices, cellular phones, and private channel radios where risk is apparent or may be anticipated, and arrange for a reliable response system when an alarm is triggered.

- Provide metal detectors—installed or hand-held, where appropriate—to identify guns, knives, or other weapons, according to the recommendations of security consultants.

- Use a closed-circuit video recording for high-risk areas on a 24-hour basis. Public safety is a greater concern than privacy in these situations.

- Place curved mirrors at hallway intersections or concealed areas.

- Enclose nurses' stations, and install deep service counters or bullet-resistant, shatter-proof glass in reception areas, triage, admitting, or client service rooms.

- Provide employee "safe rooms" for use during emergencies.

- Establish "time-out" or seclusion areas with high ceilings without grids for patients acting out and establish separate rooms for criminal patients.

- Provide client or customer waiting rooms designed to maximize comfort and minimize stress.

- Ensure that counseling or patient care rooms have two exits.

- Limit access to staff counseling rooms and treatment rooms controlled by using locked doors.

- Arrange furniture to prevent entrapment of staff. In interview rooms or crisis treatment areas, furniture should be minimal, lightweight, without sharp corners or edges, and/or affixed to the floor. Limit the number of pictures, vases, ashtrays, or other items that can be used as weapons.

- Provide lockable and secure bathrooms for staff members separate from customer, client, and visitor facilities.

- Lock all unused doors to limit access, in accordance with local fire codes.

- Install bright, effective lighting indoors and outdoors.

- Replace burned-out lights, broken windows, and locks.

- Keep automobiles, if used in the field, well-maintained. Always lock automobiles.

Administrative and Work Practice Controls

Administrative and work practice controls affect the way jobs or tasks are performed. The following examples illustrate how changes in work practices and administrative procedures can help prevent violent incidents.

- State clearly to customers, clients, and employees that violence is not permitted or tolerated.

- Establish liaison with local police and state prosecutors. Report all incidents of violence. Provide police with physical layouts of facilities to expedite investigations.

- Require employees to report all assaults or threats to a supervisor or manager (e.g., can be confidential interview). Keep log books and reports of such incidents to help in determining any necessary actions to prevent further occurrences.

- Advise and assist employees, if needed, of company procedures for requesting police assistance or filing charges when assaulted.

- Provide management support during emergencies. Respond promptly to all complaints.

- Set up a trained response team to respond to emergencies.

- Use properly trained security officers, when necessary, to deal with aggressive behavior. Follow written security procedures.

- Ensure adequate and properly trained staff for restraining customers or clients.

- Provide sensitive and timely information to persons waiting in line or in waiting rooms. Adopt measures to decrease waiting time.

- Ensure adequate and qualified staff coverage at all times. Times of greatest risk occur during patient transfers, emergency responses, meal times, and at night. Locales with the greatest risk include admission units and crisis or acute care units.

- Institute a sign-in procedure with passes for visitors.

- Review and revise visitor check systems, when necessary. Limit information given to outsiders on hospitalized victims of violence.

- Supervise the movement of psychiatric clients and patients throughout medical facilities.

- Control access to facilities other than waiting rooms, particularly drug storage or pharmacy areas.

- Prohibit employees from working alone in emergency areas or walk-in clinics, particularly at night or when assistance is unavailable.

- Employees should never enter seclusion rooms alone.

- Establish policies and procedures for secured areas and emergency evacuations.

- Treat and/or interview aggressive or agitated clients and customers in relatively open areas that still maintain privacy and confidentiality (e.g., rooms with removable partitions).

- Use case management conferences with co-workers and supervisors to discuss ways to effectively treat potentially violent customers.

- Prepare contingency plans to treat clients and customers who are "acting out" or making verbal or physical attacks or threats. Consider using certified employee assistance professionals (CEAPs), in-house social service, or occupational health service staff to help diffuse customer or client anger.

- Make sure that nurses and/or physicians are not alone when performing intimate physical examinations of patients.

- Discourage employees (especially in health care and social service settings) from wearing jewelry to help prevent possible strangulation in confrontational situations. Community workers should carry only required identification and money.

- Periodically survey the facility to remove tools or possessions left by visitors or maintenance staff which could be used inappropriately by customers or patients.

- Provide staff with identification badges, preferably without last names, to readily verify employment.

- Discourage employees from carrying keys, pens, or other items that could be used as weapons.

- Provide staff members with security escorts to parking areas in evening or late hours. Parking areas should be highly visible, well-lighted, and safely accessible to the building.

- Use the "buddy system," especially when personal safety may be threatened. Encourage home health care providers, social service workers, and others to avoid threatening situations. Staff should exercise extra care in elevators, stairwells and unfamiliar residences.

- Immediately leave premises if there is a hazardous situation; or request police escort if needed.

- Develop policies and procedures covering home health care providers, such as contracts on how visits will be conducted, the presence of others in the home during the visits, and the refusal to provide services in a clearly hazardous situation.

- Establish a daily work plan for field staff to keep a designated contact person informed about workers' whereabouts throughout the workday. If an employee does not report in, the contact person should follow-up.

- Conduct a comprehensive post-incident evaluation, including psychological as well as medical treatment, for employees who have been subjected to abusive behavior.

Post-Incident Response

Post-incident response and evaluation are essential to an effective violence prevention program. All workplace violence programs should provide comprehensive treatment for victimized employees and employees who may be traumatized by witnessing a workplace violence incident. Injured staff should receive prompt treatment and psychological evaluation whenever an assault takes place, regardless of severity. Transportation of the injured to medical care should be provided if care is not available on-site.

Victims of workplace violence suffer a variety of consequences in addition to their actual physical injuries. These include short and long-term psychological trauma, fear of returning to work, changes in relationships with co-workers and family, feelings of incompetence, guilt, powerlessness, and fear of criticism by supervisors or managers.

Consequently, a strong follow-up program for these employees will not only help them to deal with these problems but also to help prepare them to confront or prevent future incidents of violence (Flannery, 1991, 1993; 1995).

There are several types of assistance that can be incorporated into the post-incident response. For example, trauma-crisis counseling, critical incident stress debriefing, or employee assistance programs may be provided to assist victims. Certified employee assistance professionals, psychologists, psychiatrists, clinical nurse specialists, or social workers could provide this counseling, or the employer can refer staff victims to an outside specialist. In addition, an employee counseling service, peer counseling, or support groups may be established.

In any case, counselors must be well trained and have a good understanding of the issues and consequences of assaults and other aggressive, violent behavior. Appropriate and promptly rendered post-incident debriefings and counseling reduce acute psychological trauma and general stress levels among victims and witnesses. In addition, such counseling educates staff about workplace violence and positively influences workplace and organizational cultural norms to reduce trauma associated with future incidents.

Training and Education

Training and education ensure that all staff are aware of potential security hazards and how to protect themselves and their co-workers through established policies and procedures.

All Employees

Every employee should understand the concept of "Universal Precautions for Violence," i.e., that violence should be expected but can be avoided or mitigated through preparation. Staff should be instructed to limit physical interventions in workplace altercations whenever possible, unless there are adequate numbers of staff or emergency response teams and security personnel available. Frequent training also can improve the likelihood of avoiding assault (Carrnel and Hunter, 1990).

Employees who may face safety and security hazards should receive formal instruction on the specific hazards associated with the unit or job and facility. This includes information on the types of injuries or problems identified in the facility and the methods to control the specific hazards.

The training program should involve all employees, including supervisors and managers. New and reassigned employees should receive an initial orientation prior to being assigned their job duties. Visiting staff, such as physicians, should receive the same training as permanent staff. Qualified trainers should instruct at the comprehension level appropriate for the staff. Effective training programs should involve role playing, simulations, and drills.

Topics may include Management of Assaultive Behavior Professional Assault Response Training; police assault avoidance programs, or personal safety training such as awareness, avoidance, and how to prevent assaults. A combination of training maybe used depending on the severity of the risk.

Required training should be provided to employees annually. In large institutions, refresher programs may be needed more frequently (monthly or quarterly) to effectively reach and inform all employees. The training should cover topics such as the following:

- The workplace violence prevention policy.

- Risk factors that cause or contribute to assaults.

- Early recognition of escalating behavior or recognition of warning signs or situations that may lead to assaults.

- Ways of preventing or diffusing volatile situations or aggressive behavior, and managing anger.

- Information on multicultural diversity to develop sensitivity to racial and ethnic issues and differences.

- A standard response action plan for violent situations, including availability of assistance, response to alarm systems, and communication procedures.

- How to deal with hostile persons other than customers and clients, such as relatives and visitors.

- Progressive behavior control methods and safe methods of restraint application or escape.

- The location and operation of safety devices such as alarms systems, along with the required maintenance schedules and procedures.

- Ways to protect oneself and coworkers, including use of the "buddy system."

- Policies and procedures for reporting and record-keeping.

- Policies and procedures for obtaining medical care, counseling, workers' compensation, or legal assistance after a violent episode or injury.

Supervisors, Managers, and Security Personnel

Supervisors and managers should ensure that employees are not placed in assignments that compromise safety and should encourage employees to report incidents. Employees and supervisors should be trained to behave compassionately towards coworkers when an incident occurs.

They should learn how to reduce security hazards and ensure that employees receive appropriate training. Following training, supervisors and managers should be able to recognize a potentially hazardous situation and to make any necessary changes in the physical plant, patient care treatment program, and staffing policy and procedures to reduce or eliminate the hazards.

Security personnel need specific training from the hospital or clinic, including the psychological components of handling aggressive and abusive clients, types of disorders, and ways to handle aggression and defuse hostile situations.

The training program should also include an evaluation. The content, methods, and frequency of training should be reviewed and evaluated annually by the team or coordinator responsible for implementation. Program evaluation may involve supervisor and/or employee interviews, testing and observing, and/or reviewing reports of behavior of individuals in threatening situations.

Record-Keeping and Evaluation of the Program

Record-keeping and evaluation of the violence prevention program are necessary to determine overall effectiveness and identify any deficiencies or changes that should be made.

Record-Keeping

Record-keeping is essential to the success of a workplace violence prevention program. Good records help employers determine the severity of the problem, evaluate methods of hazard control, and identify training needs. Records can be especially useful to large organizations and for members of a business group or trade association who "pool" data. Records of injuries, illnesses, accidents, assaults, hazards, corrective actions, patient histories, and training, among others, can help identify problems and solutions for an effective program.

The following records are important:

- OSHA Log of Injury and Illness (OSHA 200). OSHA regulations require entry on the Injury and Illness Log of any injury that requires more than first aid, is a lost-time injury, requires modified duty, or causes loss of consciousness (this applies only to establishments required to keep OSHA logs). Injuries caused by assaults, which are otherwise recordable, also must be entered on the log. A fatality or catastrophe that results in the hospitalization of 3 or more employees must be reported to OSHA within 8 hours. This includes those resulting from workplace violence and applies to all establishments.

- Medical reports of work injury and supervisors' reports for each recorded assault should be kept. These records should describe the type of assault (i.e., unprovoked sudden attack or client-to-client altercation), who was assaulted; and all other circumstances of the incident. The records should include a description of the environment or location, potential or actual cost, lost time, and the nature of injuries sustained.

- Incidents of abuse, verbal attacks or aggressive behavior which may be threatening to the worker but do not result in injury— such as pushing or shouting and acts of aggression towards other clients—should be recorded, perhaps as part of an assaultive incident report. These reports should be evaluated routinely by the affected department.

- In health-care or social service settings, information on patients with a history of past violence, drug abuse, or criminal activity should be recorded on the patient's chart. All staff who care for a potentially aggressive, abusive, or violent client should be aware of their background and history. Admission of violent clients should be logged to help determine potential risks.

- Minutes of safety meetings, records of hazard analyses, and corrective actions recommended and taken should be documented.

- Records of all training programs, attendees, and qualifications of trainers should be maintained.

Evaluation

As part of their overall program, employers should evaluate their safety and security measures. Top management should review the program regularly, and with each incident, to evaluate program success. Responsible parties (managers, supervisors, and employees) should collectively reevaluate policies and procedures on a regular basis. Deficiencies should be identified and corrective action taken.

An evaluation program should involve the following:

- Establishing a uniform violence reporting system and regular review of reports.

- Reviewing reports and minutes from staff meetings on safety and security issues.

- Analyzing trends and rates in illness/injury or fatalities caused by violence relative to initial or "baseline" rates.

- Measuring improvement based on lowering the frequency and severity of workplace violence.

- Keeping up-to-date records of administrative and work practice changes to prevent workplace violence to evaluate their effectiveness.

- Surveying employees before and after making job or worksite changes or installing security measures or new systems to determine their effectiveness.

- Keeping abreast of new strategies available to deal with violence as these develop.

- Surveying employees who experience hostile situations about the medical treatment they received initially and, again, several weeks afterward, and then several months later.

- Complying with OSHA and state requirements for recording and reporting deaths, injuries, and illnesses.

- Requesting periodic law-enforcement or outside-consultant reviews of the worksite for recommendations on improving employee safety.

Management should share workplace violence prevention program evaluation reports with all employees. Any changes in the program should be discussed at regular meetings of the safety committee, union representatives, or other employee groups.

Sources of Assistance

Employers who would like assistance in implementing an appropriate workplace violence prevention program can turn to the OSHA Consultation service provided in their state. Primarily targeted at smaller companies, the consultation service is provided at no charge to the employer and is independent of OSHA'S enforcement activity.

OSHA'S efforts to assist employers combat workplace violence are complemented by those of the National Institute of Occupational Safety and Health (NIOSH) and public safety officials, trade associations, unions, insurers, human resource, and employee assistance professionals as well as other interested groups. Employers and employees may contact these groups for additional advice and information. See the Resources section of this sourcebook for contact information.

References

California State Department of Industrial Relations. (1995). "CAL/ OSHA Guidelines for Workplace Security. Division of Occupational Safety and Health," San Francisco, CA.

Fox, S.; Freeman, C.; Barr, B. et al. (1994). "Identifying Reported Cases of Workplace Violence in Federal Agencies," Unpublished Report, Washington DC.

Goodman, R.; Jenkins, L; and Mercy, J. (1994). "Workplace-Related Homicide Among Health Care Workers in the United States, 1980 through 1990." *JAMA* 272(21): 1686–1688.

Liss, G. (1993). "Examination of Workers' Compensation Claims Among Nurses in Ontario for Injuries Due to Violence." Health and Safety Studies Unit, Ontario Ministry of Labour.

Novello, A. (1992). "A Medical Response to Violence." *JAMA* 267:3007.

Oregon State Department of Consumer and Business Services. (1994). "Violence in the Workplace, Oregon, 1988 to 1992-A Special Study of Worker's Compensation Claims Caused by Violent Acts." Information Management Division, Salem, OR.

Simonowitz, J. (1993). "Guidelines for Security and Safety of Health Care and Community Service Workers." Division of Occupational Safety and Health. Department of Industrial Relations, San Francisco, CA.

State of Washington, Department of Labor and Industries. (1993). "Study of Assaults on Staff in Washington State Psychiatric Hospitals."

(1995). "Violence in Washington Workplaces," 1992.

Toscano, Guy; and Weber, William. (1995). "Violence in the Workplace." Bureau of Labor Statistics. Washington, DC. Table 11.

U.S. Department of Labor, Bureau of Labor Statistics. (1995). "Census of Fatal Occupational Injuries, 1994." *News Bulletin* 95-288.

Chapter 48

Helping Employees Deal with Grief and Trauma in the Workplace

Introduction

Many of us are ill-prepared to handle the traumatic events discussed in this chapter—suicides, assaults, threats, natural disasters, etc. And yet these events can and do occur in our workplaces. They are events for which preparation helps, and this chapter tells us how to prepare.

In addition to using this chapter for preparation purposes, it is an invaluable guide to follow should a traumatic event occur at your workplace. It will give you practical ideas on what to say to your employees and approaches to take to facilitate recovery.

When Tragedy Strikes at Work

Imagine that you, as a manager, are busy with your many daily responsibilities, when tragedy strikes:

- You hear a commotion down the hall, respond, and discover that an employee has swallowed a lethal dose of drugs in the presence of his co-workers.

- An irate individual storms into your section's work area and shoots an employee while you and other employees look on, shocked and helpless to intervene.

From "A Manager's Handbook: Handling Traumatic Events," United States Office of Personnel Management, Office of Workforce Relations, Pub. No. OWR-15, December 1996.

- A dazed-looking employee walks into the work area, bruised and disheveled, collapses at her desk, and reports that she was attacked while conducting a routine business call.

Initially, your responses will probably be almost automatic. You will notify the proper authorities and take whatever steps are necessary to preserve life and safety. After the paramedics and the investigators leave, the hard questions begin for you as a manager:

- How do you help your employees recover from this event, so their personal well-being and professional effectiveness will not suffer long-term effects as a result of trauma?

- How do you get your staff moving again after employees have suffered from injury, bereavement, or emotional trauma?

As you would expect, there are no easy answers, and each situation presents its own set of challenges. However, there are some general guidelines to help you in most situations:

Stay firmly in charge. Let all employees know that you are concerned and doing all you can to help them. You represent the organization to your employees, and your caring presence can mean a great deal in helping them feel supported. You don't have to say anything profound; just be there, do your best to manage, and let your employees know you are concerned about them. Be visible to your subordinates, and take time to ask them how they are doing. Try to keep investigations and other official business from pulling you out of your work area for long periods of time.

Ask for support from higher management. Relief from deadlines and practical help such as a temporary employee to lighten your burden of administrative work can make it easier for you to focus on helping your employees and your organization return to normal functioning.

Don't "keep a stiff upper lip" or advise anybody else to do so. Let people know, in whatever way is natural for you, that you are feeling fear, grief, shock, anger, or whatever your natural reaction to the situation may be. This shows your employees you care about them. Since you also can function rationally in spite of your strong feelings, they know that they can do likewise.

Share information with your employees as soon as you have it available. Don't be afraid to say, "I don't know." Particularly in the first few hours after a tragedy, information will be scarce and much in demand. If you can be an advocate in obtaining it, you will show your employees you care and help lessen anxiety.

Ask for support from your Employee Assistance Program (EAP). The EAP is available to offer professional counseling to those who wish it, and to provide debriefings to groups affected by trauma. Encourage your employees to take advantage of the EAP as a way of preserving health, not as a sign of sickness.

Encourage employees to talk about their painful experiences. This is hard to do, but eases healing as people express their painful thoughts and feelings in a safe environment, and come to realize that their reactions are normal and shared by others. You may want to have a mental health professional come in to facilitate a special meeting for this purpose. Or your group may prefer to discuss the situation among themselves. Don't be afraid to participate, and to set a positive example by discussing your own feelings openly. Your example says more than your words.

Build on the strengths of the group. Encourage employees to take care of one another through such simple measures as listening to those in distress, offering practical help, visiting the hospitalized, or going with an employee on the first visit to a feared site. The more you have done to build a cohesive work group, and to foster self-confidence in your employees, the better your staff can help one another in a crisis.

Build on your work group's prior planning. If you have talked together about how you, as a group, would handle a hypothetical crisis, it will help prepare all employees, mentally and practically, to deal with a real one. Knowing employees' strengths and experience, having an established plan for communication in emergencies, and being familiar with EAP procedures can help you "hit the ground running" when a crisis actually strikes.

Be aware of the healing value of work. Getting back to the daily routine can be a comforting experience, and most people can work productively while still dealing with grief and trauma. However, the process of getting a staff back to work is one which must be approached with great care and sensitivity. In particular, if anyone has died or been seriously injured, the process must be handled in a way that shows appropriate respect for them.

This gives you a general model for management in a traumatic situation. Later sections will deal more specifically with different types of traumas and the specific managerial challenges they present.

How to Listen to Someone Who Is Hurting

Whenever people face bereavement, injury, or other kinds of trauma, they need to talk about it in order to heal. To talk, they need willing listeners. Unfortunately, many of us shrink from listening to people in pain. We may feel like we have enough troubles of our own, or be afraid of making matters worse by saying the wrong thing.

Sometimes we excuse ourselves by assuming that listening to people who are hurting is strictly a matter for professionals such as psychotherapists or members of the clergy. It is true that professional people can help in special ways, and provide the suffering individual with insights that most of us aren't able to offer. However, their assistance, although valuable, is no substitute for the caring interest of supervisors, co-workers, friends, and others from the person's normal daily life.

It is natural to feel reluctant or even afraid of facing another person's painful feelings. But it is important not to let this fear prevent us from doing what we can to help someone who is suffering.

Though each situation is unique, some guidelines can help make the process easier:

- The most important thing to do is simply to be there and listen and show you care.

- Find a private setting where you won't be overheard or interrupted. Arrange things so that there are no large objects, such as a desk, between you and the person.

- Keep your comments brief and simple so that you don't get the person off track.

- Ask questions which show your interest and encourage the person to keep talking, for example:

> "What happened next?"
> "What was that like?"

- Give verbal and non-verbal messages of caring and support. Facial expressions and body posture go a long way toward showing your interest. Don't hesitate to interject your own feelings as appropriate, for example:

> *"How terrible."*
> *"I'm so sorry."*

- Let people know that it's OK to cry. Some people are embarrassed if they cry in front of others. Handing over a box of tissues in a matter-of-fact way can help show that tears are normal and appropriate. It's also OK if you get a bit teary yourself.

- Don't be distressed by differences in the way people respond. One person may react very calmly, while another expresses strong feelings. One person may have an immediate emotional response; another may be "numb" at first and respond emotionally later. Emotions are rarely simple; people who are suffering loss often feel anger along with grief. Unless you see signs of actual danger, simply accept the feelings as that person's natural response at the moment. If a person is usually rational and sensible, those qualities will return once their painful feelings are expressed.

- Don't offer unsolicited advice. People usually will ask for advice later if they need it; initially it just gets in the way of talking things out.

- Don't turn the conversation into a forum for your own experiences. If you have had a similar experience, you may want to mention that briefly when the moment seems right. But do not say, "I know exactly how you feel," because everybody is different.

- It's natural to worry about saying the "wrong thing." The following is a brief but helpful list of three other things not to say to someone who is suffering. DO NOT SAY:

anything critical of the person.

> *"You shouldn't take it so hard."*
> *"You're overreacting."*

anything which tries to minimize the person's pain.

> *"It could be a lot worse."*
> *"You're young; you'll get over it."*

anything which asks the person to disguise or reject his/her feelings.

"You have to pull yourself together."
"You need to be strong for your children's sake."

These are helpful guidelines, but the most important thing is to be there and listen in a caring way. People will understand if you say something awkward in a difficult situation.

Once you have finished talking, it may be appropriate to offer simple forms of help. Check about basic things like eating and sleeping. Sharing a meal may help the person find an appetite. Giving a ride to someone too upset to drive may mean a lot. Ask what else you can do to be of assistance.

After you have talked to someone who is hurting, you may feel as if you have absorbed some of that person's pain. Take care of yourself by talking to a friend, taking a walk, or doing whatever helps restore your own spirits. Congratulate yourself on having had the courage to help someone in need when it wasn't easy.

Recovering from the Death of a Co-Worker

The death of a co-worker is a painful experience under any circumstances, and all the more difficult if it is unexpected. Recovery of individuals and of your workgroup itself depends to a great extent on the effectiveness of the grief leadership provided by you—the group's manager. Effective grief leadership guides members of the work group as they mourn and memorialize the dead, help their families, and return to effective performance of their duties. The following guidelines have proved helpful:

Provide a private area were co-workers can mourn without public scrutiny. Initially, close friends and associates will feel shock and intense grief. If the loss is to be resolved, it is essential for all affected employees to spend time talking about the deceased person, sharing memories, and discussing the loss. This "grief work," which is essential for recovery, is intensely painful when done alone, but much less so when it can be shared with friends. Providing a private area where co-workers can talk together and shed tears without public scrutiny will ease this process.

Share information. Employees will feel a particularly strong need for information at this time. Managers can show their concern by making a concerned effort to get that information, and share it in a timely manner. Until you get the information, simply admitting honestly that you don't know is more comforting to employees than not being told anything.

Contact employees who are temporarily away from the office. Ordinarily, people in a small work group are aware of friendship patterns, and will take steps to ensure that those in particular need of comfort are given support. However, problems may occur if co-workers are on leave or travel. The manager and group members may need to reach out to those temporarily away from the office to make sure they don't get left out of the grieving process.

Serve as a role model. Managers need to serve as role models for appropriate grieving. If you show that you are actively grieving, but still able to function effectively, other employees will realize that they can also be sad without losing their ability to perform their duties rationally. You should avoid hiding your own feelings, as this often leads employees to misperceive you as not caring.

Consider offering a "debriefing." Often, a cohesive work group can go through the grief process without help. However, if members do not know each other well, or for whatever reason have difficulty talking, a professional person may need to come in and facilitate a "debriefing," or meeting in which grief is discussed.

Consider holding a memorial service, especially if co-workers cannot attend the funeral. A memorial service can be very helpful and is often a turning point in restoring a work group to normal productivity. This is not to imply that the deceased is forgotten; rather people find after a point that they can continue to work while grieving. Consider the following points in planning a memorial service:

- The memorial service should honor the deceased and provide an opportunity to say good-bye. Unlike a funeral, a memorial is not a religious service and should be suitable for employees of all faiths. Friends may speak about the qualities they admired in the deceased, the person's contributions to the work and the morale of the group. Poetry or music reminiscent of the deceased might be shared.

- The most common mistake in planning memorials is to plan them at too high a level. Senior officials may want to take charge, to show that they care, and to assure a polished product. This approach usually "backfires," for example, "The managers don't care about Sam; they just want to put on a show for the executives."

- Memorial services are most effective when the closest associates of the deceased are given key roles in planning and carrying them out. Including the "right" people, i.e., the best friends of the deceased, makes the service more comforting for everyone. If the best friends are too upset to speak, they can take non-verbal roles such as handing out programs.

Reach out to family members. Reaching out to the family of the deceased can be comforting for both employees and family members. Attending the funeral service, sending cards, visiting the bereaved family and offering various forms of help are all positive healing activities.

Support informal rituals. Informal rituals in the office can ease healing. A group of friends might join together to clean out the deceased person's desk, or organize a campaign for contributions to an appropriate charity. Sometimes employees may want to leave a particular work station or piece of equipment unused for a time in memory of the deceased. If possible, this wish should be honored.

Get back to the work routine in a way that shows respect for the deceased. Returning to the work routine can facilitate healing if the work group makes an effort to uphold values held by the deceased and strive toward goals that he/she particularly valued, for example, "I want to show the customers I care, because Sam was such a caring person."

Don't treat a new employee like a "replacement" for the employee who died. It is important that new employees not be made to feel like "replacements" for employees who have died. Reorganizing responsibilities and moving furniture can help spare the new employee and others the painful experience of having somebody new at "Sam's desk" doing "Sam's job."

Remind employees about the services of the Employee Assistance Program. Group members should be reminded that normal grieving can produce upsetting response such as sleeplessness, diminished appetite, and intrusive thoughts of the deceased. Ordinarily, these will subside with time, particularly if the individual receives strong group support. However, some individuals may find these reactions especially troubling or long-lasting, and may need to turn to the Employee Assistance Program for professional help in getting over the experience.

Helping an Employee Recover from an Assault

Being assaulted on the job can lead not only to physical injury, but also to emotional distress. Recovery with return to job effectiveness requires not only the assistance of professional experts such as physicians and psychotherapists, but also the enlightened support of supervisors and co-workers.

The role of the immediate supervisor is especially important, because that person most powerfully represents the organization to the employee. The supervisor needs to convey personal concern for the employee as well as the concern of the organization, and a sense of the employee's unique importance to the work group and its mission. The following guidelines have proved helpful in these situations:

If the employee is hospitalized, visit, send cards, and convey other expressions of concern. It is important that the employee not feel abandoned. The nursing staff can advise you of the length and type of interaction most appropriate. If the person is quite ill, a very brief visit and a few words of concern may be enough. As recovery continues, sharing news from the office will help the person continue to feel a part of the organization.

Encourage co-workers to show support. At some point the employee will need to tell the story of the assault, probably more than once, and may find it easier to discuss this with co-workers who are familiar with the work setting and may have had similar experiences. Co-workers can help significantly by listening in a caring way, showing support and avoiding any second guessing of the situation. Being assaulted is not only physically painful; it can make the world feel like a cold, frightening place. Simple expressions of kindness from friends and co-workers—a visit, a card game, a funny book, a favorite magazine—can help the person regain a sense of safety.

Help the employee's family. If the employee has a family, they may need support as well. If the situation has received media attention, the family may need assistance in screening phone calls and mail. Other kinds of help, such as caring for children while a spouse visits the hospital, can go a long way in showing that the work group cares for its members.

Plan the employee's return to work. The supervisor, employee, employee/labor relations specialist, and health care providers need to work together to plan the employee's return to work. Here are some important points to consider:

- There is truth in the old saying about "getting back on the horse that just threw you," and it can be helpful to get back to the crucial place or activity in a timely manner. The sooner the employee can return, the easier it will be to rejoin the group, and the employee will have missed out on less of the current information needed for effective job performance. However, it is important not to expose the employee to too much stress at once. A flexible approach, for example, part-time work, a different assignment at first, or assignment of a co-worker for support, can often help the employee overcome anxiety and recover self-confidence and may allow the employee to return to work sooner than would otherwise be possible.

- The employee's physical needs must be clarified with health care providers, e.g., the supervisor and employee should understand precisely what is meant by phrases such as "light work." If the employee looks different, from wearing a cast or having visible scars, it is helpful to prepare other employees for this in advance. Advance thought needs to be given to any new environmental needs the employee may have, such as wheelchair access or a place to lie down during the day.

- Working out a flexible plan for a recovering employee may take time and energy in take short run, but that effort will be repaid in the long run by retaining in experienced employee as an integral part of the work group.

Offer counseling. Counseling services should be offered through the Employee Assistance Program (EAP), and with the attitude that it is perfectly natural to use such professional resources in the aftermath of a traumatic experience. Supervisors and EAP personnel should work together to make the experience as convenient and non-bureaucratic as possible. However, individual preferences and differences should be respected. Some employees find that they can recover from the effects of the experience with the help of their friends, family, and co-workers. Others may not feel the need for counseling until weeks have passed and they realize that they are not recovering as well as they would like.

Make career counseling and other forms of assistance available if the employee decides to change jobs. Even with excellent support, employees who have been assaulted sometimes feel, "It just isn't worth it," and decide to transfer to a safer occupation. The employee should be encouraged not to make such an important decision in haste, but career counseling and other forms of assistance should be made available. Supervisors and co-workers who have tried to help the employee may need reassurance that their efforts contributed to the individual's recovery, and that the decision is not a rejection of them.

A Final Note: Tips for Coping with Extreme Stress

- Concentrate on caring for yourself.

- Talk about it with other people in the same situation. Compare reactions, reassure yourself that you are not alone in the way you are feeling.

- Talk about it with friends and relatives who care about you. It's normal to need to tell your story over and over.

- Keep your schedule as routine as possible, and don't overdo it.

- Allow time for hobbies, relaxing activities, being with friends, even if you don't quite feel like it.

- Participate in whatever physical fitness activities you normally enjoy.

- Utilize whatever spiritual resources are part of your normal lifestyle.

- Beware of any temptation to turn to alcohol, tobacco, caffeine, and sweet foods. They may make you feel better momentarily, but can cause more problems in the long run. Concentrate instead on a healthy diet.

- If you can, postpone major life decisions until you have had a chance to get yourself back onto a more even keel.

- Don't hesitate to accept help from friends, co-workers, and others. If you can, offer help to others affected by the event.

- Sometimes good self-care and talking with friends are not enough. You may want to seek professional counseling through your Employee Assistance Program (EAP). This does not mean you are "sick," but rather that a counselor may be able to help you get your recovery process on track.

—by Mary Tyler, Ph.D

This chapter was written by Mary Tyler, Ph.D., of the office of Personnel Management's (OPM) Employee Health Services Policy Center, who is a preeminent expert in the field of workplace violence and trauma. She is well recognized in the United States and Europe for her research on trauma in the workplace, and has provided technical assistance to many organizations. The information in this chapter reflects Dr. Tyler's extensive experience in helping Federal managers cope with traumatic situations. In addition, some sections rely on research studies conducted by Dr. Tyler with Colonel Robert K. Gifford, Ph.D., U.S. Army, for the Walter Reed Army Institute of Research.

Chapter 49

Job Stress

Introduction

The nature of work is changing at whirlwind speed. Perhaps now more than ever before, job stress poses a threat to the health of workers and, in turn, to the health of organizations. This chapter highlights knowledge about the causes of stress at work, and outlines steps that can be taken to prevent job stress.

Stress in Today's Workplace

The longer he waited, the more David worried. For weeks he had been plagued by aching muscles, loss of appetite, restless sleep, and a complete sense of exhaustion. At first he tried to ignore these problems, but eventually he became so short-tempered and irritable that his wife insisted he get a checkup. Now, sitting in the doctor's office and wondering what the verdict would be, he didn't even notice when Theresa took the seat beside him. They had been good friends when she worked in the front office at the plant, but he hadn't seen her since she left three years ago to take a job as a customer service representative. Her gentle poke in the ribs brought him around, and within minutes they were talking and gossiping as if she had never left.

Excerpted from National Institute for Occupational Safety and Health, Pub. No. 99-101, http://www.cdc.gov/niosh/stresswk.html, February 1999. Mention of any company name or product does not constitute endorsement by the National Institute for Occupational Safety and Health.

"You got out just in time," he told her. "Since the reorganization, nobody feels safe. It used to be that as long as you did your work, you had a job. That's not for sure anymore. They expect the same production rates even though two guys are now doing the work of three. We're so backed up I'm working twelve-hour shifts six days a week. I swear I hear those machines humming in my sleep. Guys are calling in sick just to get a break. Morale is so bad they're talking about bringing in some consultants to figure out a better way to get the job done."

"Well, I really miss you guys," she said. "I'm afraid I jumped from the frying pan into the fire. In my new job, the computer routes the calls and they never stop. I even have to schedule my bathroom breaks. All I hear the whole day are complaints from unhappy customers. I try to be helpful and sympathetic, but I can't promise anything without getting my boss's approval. Most of the time I'm caught between what the customer wants and company policy. I'm not sure who I'm supposed to keep happy. The other reps are so uptight and tense they don't even talk to one another. We all go to our own little cubicles and stay there until quitting time. To make matters worse, my mother's health is deteriorating. If only I could use some of my sick time to look after her. No wonder I'm in here with migraine headaches and high blood pressure. A lot of the reps are seeing the employee assistance counselor and taking stress management classes, which seems to help. But sooner or later, someone will have to make some changes in the way the place is run."

Scope of Stress in the American Workplace

David's and Theresa's stories are unfortunate but not unusual. Job stress has become a common and costly problem in the American workplace, leaving few workers untouched. For example, studies report the following:

- One-fourth of employees view their jobs as the number one stressor in their lives. (*Northwestern National Life*)

- Three-fourths of employees believe the worker has more on-the-job stress than a generation ago. (*Princeton Survey Research Associates*)

- Problems at work are more strongly associated with health complaints than are any other life stressor—more so than even financial problems or family problems. (*St. Paul Fire and Marine Insurance Co.*)

Fortunately, research on job stress has greatly expanded in recent years. But in spite of this attention, confusion remains about the causes, effects, and prevention of job stress. This chapter summarizes what is known about job stress and what can be done about it.

What Is Job Stress?

Job stress can be defined as the harmful physical and emotional responses that occur when the requirements of the job do not match the capabilities, resources, or needs of the worker. Job stress can lead to poor health and even injury.

The concept of job stress is often confused with challenge, but these concepts are not the same. Challenge energizes us psychologically and physically, and it motivates us to learn new skills and master our jobs. When a challenge is met, we feel relaxed and satisfied. Thus, challenge is an important ingredient for healthy and productive work. The importance of challenge in our work lives is probably what people are referring to when they say "a little bit of stress is good for you."

But for David and Theresa, the situation is different—the challenge has turned into job demands that cannot be met, relaxation has turned to exhaustion, and a sense of satisfaction has turned into feelings of stress. In short, the stage is set for illness, injury, and job failure.

What Are the Causes of Job Stress?

Nearly everyone agrees that job stress results from the interaction of the worker and the conditions of work. Views differ, however, on the importance of **worker characteristics** versus **working conditions** as the primary cause of job stress. These differing viewpoints are important because they suggest different ways to prevent stress at work.

According to one school of thought, differences in individual characteristics such as personality and coping style are most important in predicting whether certain job conditions will result in stress—in other words, what is stressful for one person may not be a problem for someone else. This viewpoint leads to prevention strategies that focus on workers and ways to help them cope with demanding job conditions.

Although the importance of individual differences cannot be ignored, scientific evidence suggests that certain working conditions are stressful to most people. The excessive workload demands and conflicting expectations described in David's and Theresa's stories are good examples. Such evidence argues for a greater emphasis on working conditions as the key source of job stress, and for job redesign as a primary prevention strategy.

The National Institute of Occupational Safety and Health (NIOSH) Approach to Job Stress

On the basis of experience and research, NIOSH favors the view that working conditions play a primary role in causing job stress. However, the role of individual factors is not ignored. According to the NIOSH view, exposure to stressful working conditions (called job stressors) can have a direct influence on worker safety and health. But individual and other situational factors can intervene to strengthen or weaken this influence. Theresa's need to care for her ill mother is an increasingly common example of an individual or situational factor that may intensify the effects of stressful working conditions. Examples of individual and situational factors that can help to reduce the effects of stressful working conditions include the following:

- balance between work and family or personal life
- a support network of friends and coworkers
- a relaxed and positive outlook

Job Conditions That May Lead to Stress

The Design of Tasks. Heavy workload, infrequent rest breaks, long work hours and shiftwork; hectic and routine tasks that have little inherent meaning, do not utilize workers' skills, and provide little sense of control.

Example: David works to the point of exhaustion. Theresa is tied to the computer, allowing little room for flexibility, self-initiative, or rest.

Management Style. Lack of participation by workers in decision-making, poor communication in the organization, lack of family-friendly policies.

Example: Theresa needs to get the boss's approval for everything, and the company is insensitive to her family needs.

Interpersonal Relationships. Poor social environment and lack of support or help from coworkers and supervisors.

Example: Theresa's physical isolation reduces her opportunities to interact with other workers or receive help from them.

Work Roles. Conflicting or uncertain job expectations, too much responsibility, too many "hats to wear."

Example: Theresa is often caught in a difficult situation trying to satisfy both the customer's needs and the company's expectations.

Career Concerns. Job insecurity and lack of opportunity for growth, advancement, or promotion; rapid changes for which workers are unprepared.

Example: Since the reorganization at David's plant, everyone is worried about their future with the company and what will happen next.

Environmental Conditions. Unpleasant or dangerous physical conditions such as crowding, noise, air pollution, or ergonomic problems.

Example: David is exposed to constant noise at work.

Job Stress and Health

Stress sets off an alarm in the brain, which responds by preparing the body for defensive action. The nervous system is aroused and hormones are released to sharpen the senses, quicken the pulse, deepen respiration, and tense the muscles. This response (sometimes called the fight or flight response) is important because it helps us defend against threatening situations. The response is preprogrammed biologically. Everyone responds in much the same way, regardless of whether the stressful situation is at work or home.

Short-lived or infrequent episodes of stress pose little risk. But when stressful situations go unresolved, the body is kept in a constant state of activation, which increases the rate of wear and tear to biological systems. Ultimately, fatigue or damage results, and the ability of the body to repair and defend itself can become seriously compromised. As a result, the risk of injury or disease escalates.

In the past 20 years, many studies have looked at the relationship between job stress and a variety of ailments. Mood and sleep disturbances, upset stomach and headache, and disturbed relationships with family and friends are examples of stress-related problems that are quick to develop and are commonly seen in these studies. These early signs of job stress are usually easy to recognize. But the effects of job stress on chronic diseases are more difficult to see because chronic diseases take a long time to develop and can be influenced by many factors other than stress. Nonetheless, evidence is rapidly accumulating to suggest that stress plays an important role in several types of chronic health problems—especially cardiovascular disease, musculoskeletal disorders, and psychological disorders.

Job Stress and Health: What the Research Tells Us

- *Cardiovascular Disease*: Many studies suggest that psychologically demanding jobs that allow employees little control over the work process increase the risk of cardiovascular disease.

- *Musculoskeletal Disorders*: On the basis of research by NIOSH and many other organizations, it is widely believed that job stress increases the risk for development of back and upper-extremity musculoskeletal disorders.

- *Psychological Disorders*: Several studies suggest that differences in rates of mental health problems (such as depression and burnout) for various occupations are due partly to differences in job stress levels. (Economic and lifestyle differences between occupations may also contribute to some of these problems.)

- *Workplace Injury*: Although more study is needed, there is a growing concern that stressful working conditions interfere with safe work practices and set the stage for injuries at work.

- *Suicide, Cancer, Ulcers, and Impaired Immune Function*: Some studies suggest a relationship between stressful working conditions and these health problems. However, more research is needed before firm conclusions can be drawn (*Encyclopedia of Occupational Safety and Health*).

Stress, Health, and Productivity

Some employers assume that stressful working conditions are a necessary evil—that companies must turn up the pressure on workers and set aside health concerns to remain productive and profitable in today's economy. But research findings challenge this belief. Studies show that stressful working conditions are actually associated with increased absenteeism, tardiness, and intentions by workers to quit their jobs—all of which have a negative effect on the bottom line.

Recent studies of so-called healthy organizations suggest that policies benefiting worker health also benefit the bottom line. A healthy organization is defined as one that has low rates of illness, injury, and disability in its workforce and is also competitive in the marketplace. NIOSH research has identified organizational characteristics associated with both healthy, low-stress work and high levels of productivity. Examples of these characteristics include the following:

- recognition of employees for good work performance
- opportunities for career development
- an organizational culture that values the individual worker
- management actions that are consistent with organizational values

What Can Be Done about Job Stress?

The examples of Theresa and David illustrate two different approaches for dealing with stress at work.

Stress Management. Theresa's company is providing stress management training and an employee assistance program (EAP) to improve the ability of workers to cope with difficult work situations. Nearly one-half of large companies in the United States provide some type of stress management training for their workforces. Stress management programs teach workers about the nature and sources of stress, the effects of stress on health, and personal skills to reduce stress—for example, time management or relaxation exercises. (EAPs provide individual counseling for employees with both work and personal problems.) Stress management training may rapidly reduce stress symptoms such as anxiety and sleep disturbances; it also has the advantage of being inexpensive and easy to implement. However, stress management programs have two major disadvantages:

- The beneficial effects on stress symptoms are often short-lived.
- They often ignore important root causes of stress because they focus on the worker and not the environment.

Organizational Change. In contrast to stress management training and EAP programs, David's company is trying to reduce job stress by bringing in a consultant to recommend ways to improve working conditions. This approach is the most direct way to reduce stress at work. It involves the identification of stressful aspects of work (e.g., excessive workload, conflicting expectations) and the design of strategies to reduce or eliminate the identified stressors. The advantage of this approach is that it deals directly with the root causes of stress at work. However, managers are sometimes uncomfortable with this approach because it can involve changes in work routines or production schedules, or changes in the organizational structure.

As a general rule, actions to reduce job stress should give top priority to organizational change to improve working conditions. But even the most conscientious efforts to improve working conditions are unlikely to eliminate stress completely for all workers. For this reason, a combination of organizational change and stress management is often the most useful approach for preventing stress at work.

Preventing Job Stress—Getting Started

No standardized approaches or simple "how to" manuals exist for developing a stress prevention program. Program design and appropriate solutions will be influenced by several factors—the size and complexity of the organization, available resources, and especially the unique types of stress problems faced by the organization. In David's company, for example, the main problem is work overload. Theresa, on the other hand, is bothered by difficult interactions with the public and an inflexible work schedule.

Although it is not possible to give a universal prescription for preventing stress at work, it is possible to offer guidelines on the process of stress prevention in organizations. In all situations, the process for stress prevention programs involves three distinct steps:

- problem identification
- intervention
- evaluation

These steps are outlined in the next section. For this process to succeed, organizations need to be adequately prepared. At a minimum, preparation for a stress prevention program should include the following:

- building general awareness about job stress (causes, costs, and control)

- securing top management commitment and support for the program

- incorporating employee input and involvement in all phases of the program

- establishing the technical capacity to conduct the program (e.g., specialized training for in-house staff or use of job stress consultants)

Bringing workers or workers and managers together in a committee or problem-solving group may be an especially useful approach for developing a stress prevention program. Research has shown these participatory efforts to be effective in dealing with ergonomic problems in the workplace, partly because they capitalize on workers' firsthand knowledge of hazards encountered in their jobs.

However, when forming such working groups, care must be taken to be sure that they are in compliance with current labor laws. The National Labor Relations Act may limit the form and structure of employee involvement in worker-management teams or groups. Employers should seek legal assistance if they are unsure of their responsibilities or obligations under the National Labor Relations Act.

Steps Toward Prevention

Low morale, health and job complaints, and employee turnover often provide the first signs of job stress. But sometimes there are no clues, especially if employees are fearful of losing their jobs. Lack of obvious or widespread signs is not a good reason to dismiss concerns about job stress or minimize the importance of a prevention program.

Step 1—Identify the Problem.

The best method to explore the scope and source of a suspected stress problem in an organization depends partly on the size of the organization and the available resources. Group discussions among managers, labor representatives, and employees can provide rich sources of information. Such discussions may be all that is needed to track down and remedy stress problems in a small company. In a larger organization, such discussions can be used to help design formal surveys for gathering input about stressful job conditions from large numbers of employees.

Regardless of the method used to collect data, information should be obtained about employee perceptions of their job conditions and perceived levels of stress, health, and satisfaction. The list of job conditions that may lead to stress and the warning signs and effects of stress provide good starting points for deciding what information to collect.

Objective measures such as absenteeism, illness and turnover rates, or performance problems can also be examined to gauge the presence and scope of job stress. However, these measures are only rough indicators of job stress—at best.

Data from discussions, surveys, and other sources should be summarized and analyzed to answer questions about the location of a stress problem and job conditions that may be responsible—for example, are problems present throughout the organization or confined to single departments or specific jobs?

Survey design, data analysis, and other aspects of a stress prevention program may require the help of experts from a local university or consulting firm. However, overall authority for the prevention program should remain in the organization.

Summary

- Hold group discussions with employees.
- Design an employee survey.
- Measure employee perceptions of job conditions, stress, health, and satisfaction.
- Collect objective data.
- Analyze data to identify problem locations and stressful job conditions.

Step 2—Design and Implement Interventions

Once the sources of stress at work have been identified and the scope of the problem is understood, the stage is set for design and implementation of an intervention strategy. In small organizations, the informal discussions that helped identify stress problems may also produce fruitful ideas for prevention. In large organizations, a more formal process may be needed. Frequently, a team is asked to develop recommendations based on analysis of data from Step 1 and consultation with outside experts.

Certain problems, such as a hostile work environment, may be pervasive in the organization and require company-wide interventions. Other problems such as excessive workload may exist only in some departments and thus require more narrow solutions such as redesign of the way a job is performed. Still other problems may be specific to certain employees and resistant to any kind of organizational change, calling instead for stress management or employee assistance interventions. Some interventions might be implemented rapidly (e.g., improved communication, stress management training), but others may require additional time to put into place (e.g., redesign of a manufacturing process).

Before any intervention occurs, employees should be informed about actions that will be taken and when they will occur. A kick-off event, such as an all-hands meeting, is often useful for this purpose.

Summary

- Target source of stress for change.
- Propose and prioritize intervention strategies.
- Communicate planned interventions to employees.
- Implement interventions.

Step 3—Evaluate the Interventions

Evaluation is an essential step in the intervention process. Evaluation is necessary to determine whether the intervention is producing desired effects and whether changes in direction are needed.

Time frames for evaluating interventions should be established. Interventions involving organizational change should receive both short- and long-term scrutiny. Short-term evaluations might be done quarterly to provide an early indication of program effectiveness or possible need for redirection. Many interventions produce initial effects that do not persist. Long-term evaluations are often conducted annually and are necessary to determine whether interventions produce lasting effects.

Evaluations should focus on the same types of information collected during the problem identification phase of the intervention, including information from employees about working conditions, levels of perceived stress, health problems, and satisfaction. Employee perceptions are usually the most sensitive measure of stressful working conditions and often provide the first indication of intervention effectiveness. Adding objective measures such as absenteeism and health care costs may also be useful. However, the effects of job stress interventions on such measures tend to be less clear-cut and can take a long time to appear.

The job stress prevention process does not end with evaluation. Rather, job stress prevention should be seen as a continuous process that uses evaluation data to refine or redirect the intervention strategy.

Summary

- Conduct both short- and long-term evaluations.

- Measure employee perceptions of job conditions, stress, health, and satisfaction.

- Include objective measures.

- Refine the intervention strategy and return to Step 1.

References

Elisburg D [1995]. Workplace stress: legal developments, economic pressures, and violence. In: Burton JF, ed. 1995 *1995 Workers' Compensation Year Book*. Horsham, PA: LRP Publications, pp. I-217–I-222.

Sauter SL, Murphy LR, Hurrell JJ, Jr. [1990]. Prevention of work-related psychological disorders. *American Psychologist* 45(10):1146–1158.

BLS [1996]. Bureau of Labor Statistics Homepage [http://stats.bls.gov/]. Tabular data, 1992–96: Number and percentage distribution of nonfatal occupational injuries and illnesses involving days away from work, by nature of injury or illness and number of days away from work. Date accessed: 1998.

Sauter S, Hurrell J, Murphy L, Levi L [1997]. Psychosocial and organizational factors. In: Stellman J, ed. *Encyclopedia of Occupational Health and Safety*. Vol. 1. Geneva, Switzerland: International Labor Office, pp. 34.1–34.77.

Bond JT, Galinsky E, Swanberg JE [1998]. The 1997 national study of the changing workforce. New York, NY: Families and Work Institute.

Jones JW, Barge BN, Steffy BD, Fay LM, Kuntz LK, Wuebker LJ [1988]. Stress and medical malpractice: organizational risk assessment and intervention. *Journal of Applied Psychology* 73(4):727–735.

Goetzel RZ, Anderson DR, Whitmer RW, Ozminkowski RJ, Dunn RL, Wasserman J, Health Enhancement Research Organization (HERO) Research Committee [1998]. The relationship between modifiable health risks and health care expenditures: an analysis of the multi-employer HERO health risk and cost database. *Journal of Occupational and Environmental Medicine* 40(10).

Northwestern National Life Insurance Company [1991]. Employee burnout: America's newest epidemic. Minneapolis, MN: Northwestern National Life Insurance Company.

Northwestern National Life Insurance Company [1992]. Employee burnout: causes and cures. Minneapolis, MN: Northwestern National Life Insurance Company.

Princeton Survey Research Associates [1997]. Labor day survey: state of workers. Princeton, NJ: Princeton Survey Research Associates.

St. Paul Fire and Marine Insurance Company [1992]. American workers under pressure technical report. St. Paul, MN: St. Paul Fire and Marine Insurance Company.

Barsade S, Wiesenfeld B, The Marlin Company [1997]. Attitudes in the American workplace III. New Haven, CT: Yale University School of Management.

Chapter 50

Shiftwork and Sleepiness

Shiftwork experts often are asked what is the best or worst work schedule. There is no simple answer to this question because there is no ideal schedule that fits every situation. Both good and bad points can be found in most work schedules. Here we suggest ways to examine work schedules to identify their advantages and disadvantages.

Types of Work Schedules

There are hundreds of different shiftwork schedules. However, it is difficult to accurately count the many shiftwork schedules being used. No thorough records are kept by the federal government, trade organizations, or labor unions. Different schedules might be used by the same occupation, the same industry, or even the same workplace.

The most common shift schedule probably is five days on a single shift followed by two days off. If this is a rotating shift schedule, the worker will change to a new shift after the days off. Depending on the job, it is even possible to work 7, 10, or 14 days in a row. Off-shore

Excerpted from "Plain Language about Shiftwork," Department of Health and Human Services (DHHS), Centers for Disease Control and Prevention (CDC), National Institute for Occupational Safety and Health (NIOSH), DHHS (NIOSH) Pub. No. 97-145, 1997. Mention of company names or products does not constitute endorsement by the National Institute for Occupational Safety and Health (NIOSH), Centers for Disease Control and Prevention (CDC).

oil rig workers, for example, might work two weeks out on the rig followed by two weeks off at home.

Since so many different schedules exist, researchers have thought of ways to measure different features of the schedules. These features are used to study how work schedules might affect safety, health, or productivity.

Work Schedule Features

We already have mentioned the time of the shift and whether shifts are permanent (fixed) or rotating. It also is important to consider:

- how long a shift might be
- how many shifts are worked before a rest day
- how many rest days are on weekends
- whether there is overtime
- how much rest is taken between shifts
- how much rest is taken during the shift
- whether the work schedule is regular and predictable

As we will explain, all of these features can affect the amount of stress and fatigue a person feels because of the work schedule. If people experience too much stress and fatigue, then they might not do their jobs safely and efficiently. Or they might develop health problems. Here are some particulars about the different shift features.

Time of Shift. Twenty-four hour operations usually are divided into two or three shifts. Start- and end-times depend on the length of the shift. Day shift (also called morning or first shift) starts around 5 to 8 a.m. and ends around 2 to 6 p.m. Evening shift (also called afternoon or second shift) starts around 2 to 6 p.m. and ends around 10 p.m. to 2 a.m. Night shift (also called third, "graveyard," or "mid" shift) starts around 10 p.m. to 2 a.m. and ends around 5 to 8 a.m.

Why is the time of shift important? Because people who work in the late night or early morning hours often feel sleepy and fatigued during their shift. This happens because their body rhythm (also called a circadian rhythm) tells them to be asleep at those times. Night workers also must sleep during the day, when their circadian rhythm tells them to be awake. Because of this, day sleep is short and feels "light" or unsatisfying. Often, night workers don't get enough sleep during the day to combat nighttime fatigue and sleepiness. Also, day workers sometimes must wake up very early to go to work. This might cause them to cut off their sleep, which makes them feel tired during the day.

Shift times also determine when a worker can see family and friends. Many social events take place in the evening, which means they might be missed by evening or night workers. Parents who work the evening shift might not see their children during the week because they are at work when the kids return from school. If this happens too often, it can be stressful.

Permanent versus Rotating Schedules. We might think that permanent night workers adapt or get used to their work times. Usually, the longer somebody does something, the easier it becomes. With experience, many night workers figure out tricks or personal methods to fight off some of the nighttime fatigue. However, research tells us that most permanent night workers never really get used to the schedule. That is, there are many nights when they still feel tired and sleepy. Fatigue occurs because most night workers go back to a day schedule on their days off. This is not surprising because family and friends are active during the day. Also, many errands and chores (like getting the car fixed) must be done during the day. Because most night workers often return to a day schedule, they never completely allow their sleep and body rhythms to adapt to being awake at night. They also sleep less during the day, so they don't recover from fatigue. This fatigue can carry over from day to day. Over several days, fatigue can accumulate to unsafe levels.

People working rotating schedules face a similar situation. Because the shift times are always changing, they can never completely adapt to a set work schedule. Rotating schedules are often used because they are considered fairer to all workers. Everybody in the workforce takes their turn at both the popular and unpopular shifts. Rotating shiftworkers are always trying to get used to changing work times. This is not easy, which is why rotating shiftworkers have more complaints than other workers about physical health and psychological stress. Research has shown that rotating shifts have special features that might affect a person's ability to get used to the schedule. These features are explained below.

Speed and Direction of Rotation. Adapting to rotating shifts can be affected by the speed of rotation and the direction of rotation. Speed of rotation means the number of consecutive day, evening, or night shifts before a shift change occurs. Direction of rotation means the order of shift change: A forward rotation is in the clockwise direction, from day to evening to night shift. A backward rotation is in the counterclockwise direction, from day to night to evening shift.

Different rotation speeds also affect a worker's ability to get used to change of shift times. We have already talked about the same situation under permanent versus rotating shifts. Longer rotations (for example, three to four weeks of working the same hours) are supposed to allow workers more time to get used to night shifts. However, workers usually return to a day schedule on their days off. A fast rotation (every two days, for example) allows no time to get used to night work. Some researchers prefer the fast rotation, because the worker quickly gets through the tough shifts and then has a couple of days off. Very fast rotations are used in Europe more than in America.

Direction of rotation can affect the ability of circadian (daily body) rhythms to adapt to the change in work times. Sleep, for example, is a circadian rhythm because each person sleeps for part of every day. Some researchers suggest that a forward, or clockwise, rotation is better for helping a worker adjust to new sleep times. This suggestion was made because it is easier to go to bed later and wake up later than earlier. Our body rhythms make us feel more awake and alert in the early evening. This makes it harder to fall asleep earlier. Backward rotations work against the body rhythm by forcing the worker to go to sleep earlier and earlier.

Although we don't have hard and fast numbers, it seems that backward rotation schedules are used frequently in the United States. It is not completely clear why. It is partly because of custom (we always did it this way) and partly because workers like the "long change." In the long change, workers pick up an extra day off when going to evening shifts after night shifts. This happens because evening shift starts late in the day, which leaves most of that day free for non-work activities.

Work-Rest Ratios (or How Much Work Before a Rest). The more a person works, the less time he or she will have for rest. People who work an 8-hour shift will have 16 hours left in a day to do everything else, and also to get some rest. People who work a 12-hour shift have only 12 hours to do everything else and to rest. In a situation like this, the extra work hours mean more tiredness and less time for rest. This is a two-edged sword. For example, many times a worker's home responsibilities, such as taking care of children, cannot change from day to day. So, if workers do overtime or a 12-hour shift, they still must take care of home duties. Since these duties take the same amount of time every day, workers may sacrifice rest and sleep after a long workday. This example shows us how important the length of shift can be in terms of stress and fatigue.

When looking at work versus rest, we also must consider how many breaks are taken during the shift and the length of breaks. Depending on the type of work and length of the day, several short breaks might be better than a few long breaks. Short breaks might be better particularly for jobs requiring heavy physical labor.

How tired a worker is also depends partly on how many days in a row he or she works. Fatigue builds up over several workdays, as well as over a single workday. This happens especially when a person gets less sleep between workdays than on rest days. As we mentioned earlier, a worker might not get enough sleep between long workdays because of home responsibilities. So, if a person works several days in a row, for example, six or seven, a good deal of sleep might be lost. Then the worker feels quite tired during the last one or two shifts.

How Regular or Predictable? Most jobs have a very regular, set schedule. A worker usually knows the schedule ahead of time. Even if the shift times change, a worker will know several days before-hand. This makes it easy to schedule other non-work activities, such as making sure somebody is at home when the children get there. Other jobs are not so regular or predictable. For example, health-care workers might respond to emergencies that keep them on the job much longer than expected. Or, they might be on call for such emergencies. At a factory, a breakdown or a last-minute call for a product might keep workers at the plant working overtime. Railroad workers sometimes work off a "call board." This means they can be assigned to a train at the last minute to move a "just-in-time" order of goods.

If workers cannot predict their schedules, it is difficult to get adequate rest. Maybe they just get to sleep when they are called back to work, or maybe they have just worked a long shift when an emergency happens. So, they stay at work a few more hours. Maybe they are on call and never get deep, satisfying sleep because they are always listening for the phone. Some people call this "sleeping with one eye open."

Health and Safety Effects of Shiftwork

Because of shiftworkers, our society is kept moving 24 hours a day. To the worker, shiftwork might mean extra pay or more free hours during the daytime. We also mentioned that shiftwork schedules are demanding and likely to produce stress and fatigue. Here we summarize ways that shiftwork might affect safety, health, or ability to do the job. Some of these things happen very soon after starting shiftwork. We talk about these under Immediate Effects. Health changes take a longer time to appear. We talk about health under Long-Term Health Effects.

Immediate Effects

Sleep

Soon after starting shiftwork, people notice changes in their sleep. Night workers usually get the least amount of sleep. Evening shift-workers get the most sleep, and day shiftworkers get a medium amount of sleep. Night workers are forced to sleep during the day, when their circadian rhythm makes them feel more awake. Day sleep is usually shorter than night sleep—sometimes two or three hours shorter. Day sleep also is lighter than night sleep. Day sleepers often say they don't sleep as deeply as they do at night. Because their sleep is lighter, they are easily awakened by sounds. This makes sleeping difficult. Since there is more activity during the day, there are more sounds to wake up the sleeping shiftworker. Both permanent night workers and rotating shiftworkers sleep worse when working nights. However, rotating shiftworkers sleep the least of all.

Sleep loss makes it much easier to fall asleep at inappropriate times. This affects a worker's ability to perform safely and efficiently. Sleepiness can affect performance both on and off the job. Driving to and from work is a major concern. Sleepiness affects our ability to concentrate or pay attention, and driving requires us to pay attention at all times. So, if a person is sleepy, it is easier to have an accident. Several jobs, such as operating dangerous machinery, also require us to pay attention at all times. So sleepiness can be risky in many different occupations. This risk is not simply a matter of falling completely asleep. After sleep loss, it is possible to have very brief periods of sleep that last only a few seconds. Most people may not even realize these short sleeps are happening. During those few seconds of sleep, they are not paying attention at all. If something dangerous happens at those times, the worker or somebody else could get seriously hurt.

Circadian Rhythm, Performance, and Safety

The circadian rhythm is a major body rhythm with regular ups and downs in the 24-hour day. Many systems in the body are very active at certain times of day, and not active at all at other times of day.

Usually the most activity happens in late afternoon or early evening. For example, the body's ability to produce energy from food (metabolism) is highest in the afternoon to evening. The least activity usually happens in the middle of the night when most people are asleep. This is one reason people feel most active and alert around 4 to 6 o'clock in the afternoon, and sleepiest at 4 to 6 o'clock in the morning.

There also are personal differences in circadian rhythms. Some people are morning types or "larks." Morning people feel most active and alert early in the day. They usually go to bed early in the evening. Other people are evening types or "owls." Evening people feel most active in late afternoon or evening, and like to stay up late into the night. Fishermen who are out on the water before dawn usually are morning types. Musicians who perform in the evening usually are evening types. Most people, however, are somewhere in-between the strict morning and evening types.

The internal circadian rhythm affects how alert people feel. This affects their ability to perform. People perform best when alertness and internal body activity is high, and worst when alertness and activity are low. In the normal day-work, night-sleep situation, people work when the circadian rhythm is high and sleep when it is low. On average, this schedule is best for performance, which means it also is best for safety. When workers perform poorly, they are more likely to make errors that could lead to accidents or injuries.

When working the night shift, a person is at work when his or her circadian rhythm is low and asleep when it is high. Such a schedule means that a person is trying to stay alert when the circadian rhythm is low. On average, this is not the best time of day for performance. This low-point affects physical activity and the ability to concentrate. If a worker also has lost sleep, fatigue could combine with the circadian low-point to double the effect on one's ability to perform. Poor performance could affect both productivity and safety. Studies of errors and accidents at different times of day show an increased risk at night when the circadian rhythm is low and sleep has been lost.

Interference with Social and Family Life

Most social and family events happen during the evening or on weekends. Because shiftworkers are on the job in the evening or on weekends, or because they sleep during the day, they often miss out on social or family activities. When shiftworkers are asked about problems with their work schedule, they usually say that the number one problem is missing family and friends. Most shiftworkers agree that sleep also is a problem, but sometimes they would rather lose a little sleep just to see other people, especially their spouse or children.

The amount of time shiftworkers spend with family and friends depends on their schedule. It also depends on their social and leisure activities and how flexible these activities are. Shiftwork interferes little with activities that are not on a strict time schedule. Gardening, woodworking, or fixing cars are these kinds of activities. Shiftwork does interfere with activities that are strictly scheduled, such as clubs or team sports. Shiftworkers often miss these activities because of work. Child care or visits to the children's school also can be a problem because of the work schedule.

A shiftwork schedule affects not only the worker but also the rest of the family. For example, children at play must be quiet during the day because the shiftworker is asleep.

Long-Term Health Effects

In the long run, it is possible for a demanding work schedule to affect a person's health. However, studying health problems in workers is difficult. If possible, workers will change jobs if they think the work is making them ill. A shiftworker might change to a day job for that reason. This is called the "healthy worker" or the "survivor" effect. Workers who stay on the job are those who can "take it." Because sick workers leave the job, it is much harder to show a relationship between job factors and poor health. Therefore, researchers have only fairly healthy shiftworkers to study.

With that in mind, it is not clear whether or not one's work schedule is the actual cause of health problems. But, workers who quit doing shiftwork often point to health problems as a major reason for quitting. Plus, a stressful schedule can combine with other factors to hurt a person's health. If a person has other major stresses in life, such as a bad marriage or a loved one with a chronic illness, a demanding work schedule certainly won't help the situation. If a worker has poor health habits, such as using too much alcohol or tobacco, it will be more difficult to resist the stress of the work schedule. A demanding schedule also might aggravate an existing health problem.

Digestive Problems

Some research has suggested that shiftworkers have more upset stomachs, constipation, and stomach ulcers than day workers. Other research has not backed up this suggestion. But, there is always the problem of having only healthy workers to study. Digestive problems could be more common in shiftworkers because digestion follows a circadian rhythm. Usually people eat at regular times during the day. They also eliminate waste at regular times during the day. Shiftwork can interfere with regular eating and digestive patterns by changing work and sleep times frequently. So, it is not surprising that this could lead to nausea and other stomach problems. However, digestive problems also could be caused by lack of nutritious food. For example, sometimes on night shift only junk food from vending machines is available.

Heart Disease

Heart problems also have been noted more often among shiftworkers than day workers. For example, Swedish researchers studied paper mill workers in a small town for several years. This study is especially meaningful, because the paper mill was the only employer in town. This made it difficult for the employees to stop working shifts. Most of them had done shiftwork for most of their lives. Researchers found that the longer people worked shifts, the more likely they were to develop heart disease. However, the way in which the work schedule affects the heart is not at all clear. Work schedule stress might cause heart disease, but it is more likely a combination of stress, diet, smoking and drinking habits, other life stresses, and family history of heart disease.

It is difficult to say exactly how the work schedule fits in with all the other factors producing heart disease. Earlier we talked about several different work schedule features that could cause stress and fatigue. Right now we can only guess about which combination of those features has the most impact on a person's health. Constantly shifting from a day to a night schedule may be one of the stressful factors. But long work hours, high workloads, and irregular schedules also can play a role.

Coping Strategies for the Individual

Getting Enough Good Sleep

Take responsibility for getting enough sleep to feel rested and restored. For some people this happens without doing anything special. However, most shiftworkers need to become more aware of what to do to get satisfying sleep and when to do it.

When to Sleep after Night Shift

This depends on the individual. Try different times and see what works best for you. As you experiment with different sleep times, keep a written record of when you go to sleep, when you wake up, and how rested you feel. This will help you identify which sleep schedule works best for you.

Some workers like to sleep in one longer period, but many workers need two shorter sleep periods to get enough sleep after the night shift. It is a good idea to go to bed as early as possible after the night shift in order to maximize sleep. A second sleep also could be taken in the afternoon to get ready for night shift. Try taking advantage of the natural tendency to be sleepy in mid-afternoon. You might get your most satisfying sleep at that time.

Does Rest Equal Sleep?

Just resting without sleep is not enough. The brain has to have sleep, or you will be sleepy later in the day or during night shift. However, rest without sleep still is valuable for body and muscle recovery. Schedule at least seven hours in bed, even if you don't sleep the whole time.

What Is the Minimum Amount of Sleep?

The vast majority of workers need at least six hours of sleep but most need more than this. Most people do not feel refreshed and at their best with just six hours. Staying with your own preferred amount of sleep is best in the long run. You might find that you need less as you become more experienced with shiftwork.

Switching Back to Days

When switching back to days after the night shift, it is best to get most of your sleep the following night. Sleep just a couple of hours shortly after night shift to shake off sleepiness. Then stay awake all day and go to sleep at your regular bedtime at night.

Napping

Shiftworkers frequently nap, especially when working night shift. Added to your regular sleep, a short afternoon or evening nap will help fight sleepiness during the night. However, napping is not long enough to replace regular sleep. If you nap, allow enough time for drowsiness to wear off before starting work. If you have time to nap at work during your break, don't make the nap too short. A nap of 15 minutes or less might actually make you more sleepy. Twenty to 30 minutes should be the minimum for a nap during a work break. Again, allow enough time for drowsiness to wear off before doing hazardous work. And don't use work-break naps to replace your sleep at home. Naps work best when they are extra sleep time. They don't work as well when you are trying to make up for lost sleep.

Protect Sleep

Block Out Noise

Switch off the phone and disconnect the doorbell. Use ear plugs. Ask the family to use headphones for the stereo or TV. Set strict times for noisy activity, such as vacuuming, clothes washing, or children playing. Don't allow these activities during your sleep times. Locate your bedroom in the quietest place. If possible, get away from outside noise and also away from the kitchen or bathroom. Soundproof the bedroom with insulation and heavy curtains. Put signs out to say you are sleeping. Tell friends and neighbors when not to call.

Keep a Regular Sleep Routine

Make the bedroom as dark as possible. Always sleep in the bedroom. Follow your regular bedtime routine every time you go to sleep. For example, wash up and brush your teeth so you feel comfortable. This can serve as a signal to your body that it is time to sleep. Don't use the bed for anything except what it is intended for. For example, don't read, eat, watch TV, write bills, or argue with your spouse in bed. Make sure you have a comfortable bed that won't disturb your sleep.

Avoid Heavy Foods and Alcohol before Sleep

Heavy, greasy foods are anti-sleep because of stomach upsets. If you must eat, a light snack won't disturb your sleep. Alcohol might make you feel sleepy, but it will wake you up too quickly after falling asleep. Don't drink alcohol in the hour or two before sleep.

Exercise

In general, keeping physically fit helps resist stress and illness. Regular exercise also keeps a person from becoming tired too quickly.

A big question for the shiftworker is when to exercise. The timing of exercise is important, so that it does not make a person too tired to work. Exercise also should not interfere with sleep. If a worker does physical labor, too much exercise before work might make work too tiring. Twenty minutes of aerobic exercise before work (for example, a brisk walk, bike ride, jog, or swim) is enough to help any worker wake up and get going and also keep the heart in shape. Try to avoid exercise in the three hours before sleep. Exercise tends to activate the body or wake it up. This might make it difficult to fall asleep.

The timing of exercise also might help a person rotate from one shift to another. Since brisk exercising activates the body to produce energy, it also might help the body rhythm shift to the new work time. Try exercise before going on shift. Early morning exercise is good for day shift, afternoon exercise is good for evening shift, and early evening exercise is good for night shift. Don't overdo it or you will be too exhausted to work.

Relaxation Techniques

Being able to wind down and take it easy is just as important as being able to wake up and get going. Give yourself time to relax and get rid of work-time stresses. This will make home life and sleep easier. Find out what is best for you personally to help you relax best. It could be just sitting down and closing your eyes for a while. Or it could be meditating, praying, reading, taking a bath, or watching TV.

The following simple exercise may help you start your quiet relaxation time. Try lying down on the carpet or bed, or sitting in an easy chair. One by one, slowly tense each muscle group in your body, then slowly let them relax. Do this for your arms, legs, stomach, neck, and face muscles. Breath deeply during this exercise and go slowly. Try to feel all the muscle tension draining away from your body. This is a simple way to let go of all the stresses of the day and to slow down.

Diet

TV and the newspapers have highlighted diets recommending certain foods to help people wake up and other foods to help them relax. Right now we cannot recommend either diet for the shiftworker. There have not been enough scientific tests to decide whether either diet really helps a person wake up or relax. In some cases the two diets recommend the same kinds of foods to do opposite things: one diet recommends eating protein to wake up, while the other diet recommends eating protein to relax or become sleepy. This conflict makes it even more difficult to decide whether either diet really works. There simply are not enough studies of people using these diets to be able to recommend them.

We can recommend sticking to a diet that, along with exercise, helps a person stay physically fit. This means avoiding fatty and sugary foods, which make a person gain too much weight. Heavy or fatty meals should be avoided especially in the middle of the night because they are the most difficult to digest at that time. Eating lighter meals in the middle of the night helps reduce stomach upsets.

Bright Light

Recent research tells us that bright light can affect our circadian rhythm. As we mentioned already, the circadian rhythm normally makes us feel most active and alert in the late afternoon, and most tired and sleepy in the middle of the night. Lately, we have learned that the high-point and the low-point of the circadian rhythm can be changed by exposure to bright light. By bright light we mean as much sunlight as on a bright summer day. Bright light affects melatonin, which is a chemical naturally produced by the brain. More melatonin makes us feel sleepier. Melatonin usually is produced during the early part of nighttime sleep. Bright light in the evening will reduce melatonin, or make it appear later in the night.

In laboratory research, people exposed to a few hours of bright light in the morning felt alert earlier in the day. They also felt sleepier earlier in the night. People exposed to bright light late in the afternoon felt most alert in late evening. Their low-point in alertness during the night also was delayed.

Some researchers have suggested that exposure to bright light could control the alertness of shiftworkers. The well-timed exposure of a worker to bright light could quickly increase alertness at night. After exposure to more bright light, they then could quickly switch back to being alert during the day. Right now, we see this as a promising idea that needs more work to be practical. Unlike use of drugs, it appears that there are no bad side effects from controlling bright light exposure. Still, workers have to be careful about using bright light, so that they will be alert at the right time. For bright light to work, a worker also must stay in low light or in darkness during some times of day. In other words, if you get too much bright light at the wrong time, this might change the circadian rhythm in the wrong direction. If this happens, you won't be alert at the times you really need to be.

To sum up, we think it is possible to use bright light to change peak alertness to different times of the day. But right now, it takes an expert to work out the right light-dark schedule to fit a particular work schedule. If workers are exposed to bright light and low light at the wrong times, they might end up moving their circadian rhythm in the wrong direction. Using this strategy requires a lot of careful effort from the worker. This might make it too impractical for some shift-workers.

Caffeine, Alcohol, and Other Drugs

Just like many people in our society, some shiftworkers drink caffeinated beverages as a pick-me-up before or during work. They also might drink alcoholic beverages to relax or to be social. Other types of drugs, such as amphetamines and sleeping pills, also have been used to help people wake up or relax and go to sleep. Here we discuss these substances and whether we can recommend them at this time.

Caffeine

Caffeine is a mild stimulant that helps a person feel more alert and perhaps perform better. Caffeine is the most widely used drug in the world. It is a natural ingredient in coffee and tea (iced tea too!), and it is added to many soft drinks (for example, most colas, some root beers, Dr. Pepper, and Mountain Dew). Caffeinated beverages are a common part of our everyday diet and are easily available.

Because of this, caffeine is used more than any other drug to maintain alertness and performance, or to help fight off sleepiness. Research backs up our everyday experience. There are many studies that show caffeine does help maintain alertness and performance. Research also tells us that caffeine is a fairly safe drug if used in small doses. By a small dose, we mean one to three cups of coffee or tea, or one to three soft drinks per day.

In small doses, caffeine is the only drug we can recommend as an aid for the shiftworker. If you drink caffeinated beverages, do so before the shift or early in the shift. Try to avoid caffeine late in the shift, especially late in the night shift. Too much caffeine, or caffeine late in the shift, makes it difficult to fall asleep after the shift. If you do get to sleep, caffeine makes sleep lighter and less satisfying. So don't drink too much and don't drink late in the shift.

If you now are drinking a lot of caffeine (say five to six cups of coffee every day), we recommend that you cut down. Cutting down may make relaxation easier and might improve sleep. Reduce caffeine use gradually over several days. Cut down only by one-half cup or one cup every couple of days. Cutting down too fast could produce headaches, nervousness, and bad moods or irritable feelings.

Amphetamines, Diet Pills, "Uppers"

These types of drugs are very strong stimulants that increase alertness and can eliminate sleep all together. Unfortunately, they are too strong and cannot be recommended. Most of these drugs are either illegal or can be obtained only by prescription. It is too easy to become addicted to these drugs. A worker might end up using them every day just to get going. Also, over the long run a person has to take more and more of these drugs just to make them continue to work. This increases the possibility of becoming addicted. Frequent use produces extreme nervousness and mood changes, and performance actually becomes worse.

Alcohol

One or two alcoholic drinks per day, taken with food, is OK for relaxation and to be social. By one drink, we mean eight to twelve ounces of beer, four to six ounces of wine, or one ounce of hard liquor. However, we recommend avoiding alcohol during work time, even during meal breaks. Also, we do not recommend using alcohol to help sleep. Alcohol can make a person sleepy, so falling asleep is easy. But, alcohol actually disturbs sleep. After drinking alcohol, a person wakes up more frequently and sleeps more lightly. Alcohol can also reduce sleep so a person doesn't sleep as long as they want or need to. Avoid alcohol for one to two hours before sleep, especially if you have to go to work after sleeping.

Sleeping Pills

These drugs can be divided into prescription and non-prescription (over-the-counter) types. Non-prescription sleeping pills usually contain the same drug used in allergy and sinus medicines. Non-prescription drugs sometimes make a person drowsy and help them fall asleep. However, most are fairly long acting, which means that the user can still feel drowsy after waking up. If used often (e.g., more than once or twice per week), non-prescription pills usually stop working and fail to make a person drowsy.

Prescription sleeping pills work pretty well to help a person fall asleep and stay asleep, even during the daytime. However, we cannot recommend regular use (e.g., more than once or twice per week) because there is no research on shiftworkers and long-term use of sleeping pills. It probably is not a good idea for shiftworkers to use sleeping pills every time they want to sleep during the day. For some people, it is too easy to become dependent on sleeping pills. They might end up using them every time they have to sleep. When this happens, they become nervous or irritable if they run out of pills. Also, some long-acting sleeping pills produce too much drowsiness after waking from sleep. This is less of a problem with the newer, short-acting sleeping pills. However, before considering prescription drugs, we recommend trying the other techniques for improving sleep. If all else fails and there still are problems with sleep, the worker should discuss taking prescription sleeping pills with his or her doctor.

Melatonin

As we mentioned already, melatonin is produced naturally by the brain at certain times of the day. The timing of the brain's melatonin production can be controlled by bright light. Melatonin also can be taken as a drug. Taken this way, melatonin makes a person feel sleepy. So it might help improve daytime sleep for the shiftworker.

Melatonin often is sold in health food stores and can be bought without a prescription. However, we cannot recommend melatonin for regular use by the shiftworker until more research is conducted. We need to find out how much melatonin should be taken. We need to learn the best time to take melatonin for a particular work shift. We also need to know if taking too much can damage your health. If taken too often, melatonin could create unknown problems. Also, the different brands of melatonin sold in stores might have different strengths or potency. So, we don't know whether taking one amount of one brand works as well as taking the same amount of another brand. Right now, we will have to take a wait-and-see attitude about melatonin until more research is done.

Part Nine

Additional Help and Information

Chapter 51

Glossary

abrasion: Rubbed-away or scraped off the surface covering the body (e.g., of skin or mucous membrane).

absorption: The process of taking in, as when a sponge takes up water. Chemicals can be absorbed through the skin into the bloodstream and then transported to other organs. Chemicals can also be absorbed into the bloodstream after breathing or swallowing.

ACGIH: American Conference of Governmental Industrial Hygienists, which develops and publishes recommended occupational exposure limits for hundreds of chemical substances and physical agents.

This chapter includes definitions excerpted from "Glossary," Clearinghouse for Training, Education and Development, Office of Training and Human Resource Development website, U.S. Department of Energy, http://cted.inel.gov/cted/or/osgloss.pdf; "Glossary of Terms [general]," Agency for Toxic Substances and Disease Registry (ATSDR) http://www.atsdr.cdc.gov/glossary.html#General; "Glossary of Terms," Occupational Safety and Health Administration (OSHA), Office of Training and Education, U.S. Department of Labor (DOL), Construction Safety and Health Outreach Program, http://www.osha-slc.gov/doc/outreachtraining/htmlfiles/hazglos.html; "Glossary of Respiratory Terms," National Institute for Occupational Safety and Health (NIOSH), http://www.osha-slc.gov/SLTC/respiratory_advisor/oshafiles/glossary.html; and "Fitting the Job to the Worker, An Ergonomics Program Guideline—Glossary," Washington Industrial Safety and Health Act (WISHA), http://www.lni.wa.gov/wisha/ergo/veg/vegglsry.htm.

acid: Chemical compound that dissociates hydrogen ions when dissolved in water. The resulting acid solutions taste sour, turn litmus paper or solution red, and neutralize bases.

action level: Term used by OSHA and the National Institute for Occupational Safety and Health to express the level of toxicant that requires medical surveillance, usually one-half the permissible exposure level.

acute: Occurring over a short time, usually a few minutes or hours. An acute exposure can result in short-term or long-term health effects. An acute effect happens a short time (up to 1 year) after exposure.

administrative controls: Methods of controlling employee exposures by job rotation, work assignment, or time periods away from the hazard.

adsorption: The condensation of gases, liquids, or dissolved substances on the surfaces of solids.

AIHA: American Industrial Hygiene Association.

air-purifying respirator: Respirator that uses filters or sorbents to remove harmful substances from the air.

air-supplied respirator: Respirator that provides a supply of breathable air from a clean source outside the contaminated work area.

ambient: Surrounding. For example, ambient air is usually outdoor air (as opposed to indoor air).

anemia: Low numbers of red blood cells or hemoglobin.

ANSI: The American National Standards Institute is a voluntary membership organization (run with private funding) that develops consensus standards nationally for a wide variety of devices and procedures.

asbestosis: Chronic lung disease with signs and symptoms resulting from permanent changes in the lung tissue due to inhalation of fine airborne fibers of asbestos.

asphyxiant: A vapor or gas which can cause unconsciousness or death by suffocation (lack of oxygen). Asphyxiation is one of the principal potential hazards of working in confined spaces.

atopic: An individual with a propensity to develop allergies.

audible range: Frequency range over which normal ears hear: approximately 20 hertz (Hz) through 20,000 Hz.

base: A compound that reacts with an acid to form a salt. It is another term for alkali.

benign: Not malignant. A benign tumor is one which does not metastasize or invade tissue. Benign tumors may still be lethal, due to pressure on vital organs.

biohazard: A combination of the words biological hazard. Organisms or products of organisms that present a risk to humans.

bloodborne pathogen: Pathogenic microorganisms that are present in human blood and cause disease in humans. These include, but are not limited to, hepatitis B (HBV) and human immunodeficiency virus (HIV).

boiling point: Temperature at which a liquid starts to boil, or the temperature at which the vapor pressure of a liquid equals atmospheric pressure.

carcinogen: Any substance that may produce cancer.

case study: The medical or epidemiologic evaluation of a single person or a small number of individuals to determine descriptive information about their health status or potential for exposure through interview or biomedical testing.

CFR (Code of Federal Regulations): Includes the rules that are promulgated under U.S. law, published in the Federal Register, and actually in force at the end of a calendar year.

chronic: Occurring over a long period of time (more than 1 year).

combustible liquid: Combustible liquids are those having a flash point at or above 37.8° C (100° F).

controls: In general, measures including devices to regulate a machine, apparatus, system, or action within prescribed limits or standards of safety and operational effectiveness.

corrosive: A substance that causes visible destruction or permanent changes in human skin tissue at the site of contact.

cutaneous: Pertaining to or affecting the skin.

density: The mass per unit volume of a substance. For example, lead is much more dense than aluminum.

dermal: Referring to the skin. Dermal absorption means absorption through the skin.

dermatitis: Inflammation of the skin from any cause.

DOL: U.S. Department of Labor. OSHA and MSHA are part of the DOL.

dyspnea: Shortness of breath, difficult or labored breathing.

endothermic: Characterized by or formed with absorption of heat.

engineering controls: a method of controlling worker exposure to risk factors by redesigning equipment, tools, and work stations. Engineering controls are part of hazard prevention and control.

EPA: U.S. Environmental Protection Agency.

ergonomics: Multidisciplinary activity dealing with the interactions between man and his total working environment plus stresses related to such environmental elements as atmosphere, heat, light, and sound, as well as all tools and equipment in the workplace.

fatigue: A condition that results when the body cannot provide enough energy for the muscles to perform a task..

Federal Register: Publication of U.S. government documents officially promulgated under the law, documents whose validity depends upon such publication. It is published on each day following a government working day. It is, in effect, the daily supplement to the Code of Federal Regulations.

filter or air-purifying element: A component used in respirators to remove solid or liquid aerosols from the inspired air.

filtering facepiece: A particulate respirator with a filter as an integral part of the facepiece or with the entire facepiece composed of the filtering medium.

fit test: Means the use of a protocol to qualitatively or quantitatively evaluate the fit of a respirator on an individual.

flash point: The minimum temperature at which a liquid gives off vapor within a test vessel in sufficient concentration to form an ignitable mixture with air near the surface of the liquid. Two tests are used—open cup and closed cup.

fume: Airborne particulate formed by the evaporation of solid materials, e.g. metal fume emitted during welding. Usually less than one micron in diameter.

gram (g): A metric unit of weight. One ounce equals 28.4 grams.

ground: Conductor that provides an electrical path for the flow of current into the earth.

hand-arm vibration: vibration (generally from a hand tool) that goes through the hand, then travels through the rest of the body.

hazard: Condition or changing set of circumstances that presents a potential for injury, illness, or property damage.

heat cramps: Painful muscle spasms as a result of exposure to excess heat.

heat exhaustion: Condition usually caused by loss of body water due to exposure to excess heat. Symptoms include headaches, tiredness, nausea, and sometimes fainting.

heat stroke: Condition resulting from excessive exposure to intense heat, characterized by high fever, collapse, and sometimes convulsions or coma.

hepatitis: Inflammation of the liver resulting from a virus or toxic origin.

hood: (1) Enclosure, part of a local exhaust ventilation system; (2) a device that completely covers the head, neck, and portions of the shoulders.

IDLH: Immediately dangerous to life or health.

inert gas: Gas that does not normally combine chemically with the base metal or filler metal.

ingestion: Taking in by the mouth.

inhalation: Breathing of a substance in the form of a gas, vapor, fume, mist, or dust.

insoluble: Incapable of being dissolved in a liquid.

lethal: Capable of causing death.

loose-fitting facepiece: A respiratory inlet covering that is designed to form a partial seal with the face.

malignant: As applied to a tumor. Cancerous and capable of undergoing metastasis, or invasion of surrounding tissue.

manometer: Instrument for measuring pressure of gases or vapors by changing the level of a fluid in a tube. It consists essentially of a U-tube partially filled with a liquid and constructed so that the amount of displacement of the liquid indicates the pressure

microgram: One millionth of a gram.

micron (micrometer, m): A unit of length equal to one millionth of a meter, approximately 1/25,000 of an inch.

milligram (mg): A unit of weight in the metric system. One thousand milligrams equals one gram.

milligrams per cubic meter (mg/m3): Unit used to measure air concentrations of dusts, gases, mists, and fumes.

mists: Suspended liquid droplets generated by condensation from the gaseous to the liquid state or by breaking up a liquid into a dispersed state, such as by splashing, foaming, or atomizing. Mist is formed when a finely divided liquid is suspended in air.

morbidity: Illness or disease. Morbidity rate is the number of illnesses or cases of disease in a population.

MSDS: Material Safety Data Sheet.

MSHA: Mine Safety and Health Administration, U.S. Department of Labor.

mucous membranes: Lining of the hollow organs of the body, notably the nose, mouth, stomach, intestines, bronchial tubes, and urinary tract.

musculoskeletal system: the soft tissue and bones in the body. The parts of the musculoskeletal system are bones, muscles, tendons, ligaments, cartilage, nerves, and blood vessels.

mutagen: Any substance that causes changes in the genetic structure in a living cell and can be passed on to subsequent generations of the animal or human.

neutral posture: Comfortable working posture that reduces the risk of musculoskeletal disorders. The joints are naturally aligned with elbows at the side of the body and wrists straight.

NFPA: The National Fire Protection Association is a voluntary membership organization whose aim is to promote and improve fire protection and prevention. The NFPA publishes 16 volumes of codes known as the National Fire Codes.

NIOSH: The National Institute for Occupational Safety and Health is a federal agency. It conducts research on health and safety concerns, tests and certifies respirators, and trains occupational health and safety professionals.

OSHA: U.S. Occupational Safety and Health Administration, U.S. Department of Labor.

particulate matter: A suspension of fine solid or liquid particles in air, such as dust, fog, fume, mist, smoke or sprays. Particulate matter suspended in air is commonly known as an aerosol.

pathogen: Capable of producing disease.

PEL Permissible exposure limit. An exposure limit that is published and enforced by OSHA as a legal standard.

personal protective equipment: Gloves, kneepads and other equipment that may help reduce hazards until other controls can be implemented, or to supplement existing controls.

pneumoconiosis: Disease of the lungs resulting from the inhalation of various kinds of dusts and other particles, e.g., asbestosis, siderosis, silicosis.

qualitative fit test (QLFT): A pass/fail fit test to assess the adequacy of respirator fit that relies on the individual's response to the test agent.

quantitative fit test (QNFT): An assessment of the adequacy of respirator fit by numerically measuring the amount of leakage into the respirator.

radiation: Emission and propagation of energy and/or particles in the form of waves through space or through a material medium.

respirable size particulates: Particulates in the size range that permits them to penetrate deep into the lungs upon inhalation.

respirator: Protective device to protect the wearer from inhaling contaminated air.

route of entry: The path by which chemicals can enter the body. There are three main routes of entry. inhalation, ingestion, and skin absorption.

SCBA: Self-contained breathing apparatus. An atmosphere-supplying respirator for which the breathing air source is designed to be carried by the user.

silicosis: Chronic lung disease, due to the inhalation of silica dust.

sorbent: (1) A material that a removes toxic gases and vapors from air inhaled through a canister or cartridge. (2) Material used to collect gases and vapors during air-sampling.

supplied-air respirator (SAR) or airline respirator: An atmosphere-supplying respirator for which the source of breathing air is not designed to be carried by the user.

systemic: Spread throughout the body, affecting all body systems and organs, not localized in one spot or area.

time-weighted average (TWA): Refers to concentrations of airborne toxic materials that have been weighted for a certain time duration, usually eight hours.

toxicity: A relative property of a chemical agent and refers to a harmful effect on some biologic mechanism and the conditions under which this effect occurs.

trauma: Injury, wound, or shock brought about by an outside force.

ultraviolet: Those wavelengths of the electromagnetic spectrum that are shorter than those of visible light and longer than X-rays.

vapor: The gaseous form of a substance that is normally in the solid or liquid state (at room temperature and pressure).

viscosity: The property of a fluid that resists internal flow by releasing counteracting forces.

worksite analysis: A safety and health review that addresses work-related musculoskeletal disorders. It is a structured way of identifying jobs and workstations that may contain musculoskeletal hazards, the risk factors that pose the hazards, and the causes of the risk factors.

Chapter 52

References

This chapter lists book titles, brochures, pamphlets, and articles that contain useful information on many of the topics in this sourcebook. For easy reference, the topics are organized in the same format as the chapters of the sourcebook itself. Email, website, and other contact information is included when available.

Workplace Health and Safety Basics

How to Make Your Job Healthier, New Jersey Department of Health and Senior Services, 4th Printing, December 1996, adapted by Eileen Senn, M.S., C.I.H. from "How To Make Your Job Safer," by Tim Morse, State of Connecticut Workers' Compensation Commission.

OSHA: New Ways of Working, an undated pamphlet from the Occupational Safety and Health Administration (OSHA), U.S. Department of Labor (DOL).

Lung Issues

"Asthma, Causes and Triggers," from the Mayohealth website: http://www.mayohealth.org/mayo/9602/htm/asthma2.htm, © 2000 Mayo Foundation for Medical Education and Research.

"Common Indoor Air Pollutants—Asbestos," Environmental Protection Agency, http://www.epa.gov/iaq/asbestos.html, February 1999.

"Making Your Workplace Smoke-Free—A Decision Makers Guide," an undated booklet from the Centers for Disease Control and Prevention (CDC), Office on Smoking and Health, http://www.cdc.gov/tobacco/etsguide.htm.

"Working Safely with Silica—If It's Silica, It's Not Just Dust," an undated booklet produced by the National Institute for Occupational Safety and Health (NIOSH), U.S. Department of Labor (DOL).

Skin and Issues

[1991]. "FDA Medical Alert: Allergic Reactions to Latex-Containing Medical Devices," Rockville, MD: Food and Drug Administration, MDA 91-1.

Cassidy J [1994]. "Latex Glove Allergy Warning," *Nursing Times* 90(32):5.

Charous BL [1994]. "The Puzzle of Latex Allergy: Some Answers, Still More Questions (Editorial)," *Ann Allergy,* 73(10):277–281.

Kelly KJ, Kurup VP, Reijula KR, Fink JN [1994]. "The Diagnosis of Natural Rubber Latex Allergy," *J Allergy Clin Immunol,* 93(5):813–816.

Slater JE [1994]. "Latex Allergy." *J Allergy Clin Immunol,* 94(2, Part 1):139–149.

Sussman GL [1992]. "Latex Allergy: Its Importance in Clinical Practice," *Allergy Proc,* 13(2):67–69.

Noise and Hearing Issues

OSHA's Field Instruction Reference Manual (FIRM), which you can find on the OSHA CD-ROM or on OSHA's web page, http://www.osha.gov.

Berg, Stacie Zoe, "Sound Advice—Protect Your Ears in Noisy Work Environments," *Safeworker,* National Safety Council, http://www.nsc.org/pubs/sw.htm, February 2000.

"Criteria for a Recommended Standard—Occupational Noise Exposure," National Institute for Occupational Safety and Health (NIOSH), Centers for Disease Control and Prevention (CDC), Pub. No. 98-126, http://www.cdc.gov/niosh/98-126.html, June 1998.

Work-Related Musculoskeletal Disorders

Bongers PM, de Winter CR, Kompier MA, Hildebranndt VH [1993]. "Psychosocial Factors at Work and Musculoskeletal Disease." *Scand J Work Environ Health*;19:297–312.

Gerr F, Letz R, Landrigan PJ [1991]. "Upper-Extremity Musculoskeletal Disorders of Occupational Origin," *Ann Rev Publ Health*;12:543–66.

Kuorinka I, Forcier L, eds. *Work Related Musculoskeletal Disorders (WMSDs): A Reference Book for Prevention,* London: Taylor and Francis, 1995.

Hagberg M. [1994]. "Neck and Shoulder Disorders." In: Rosenstock L, Cullen MR, eds. *Textbook of Occupational And Environmental Medicine,* Philadelphia, PA: W B Saunders, 356–64.

Infectious Disease Issues

"Bloodborne Pathogens Exposure Control Plan," Department of the Army Headquarters, Walter Reed Army Medical Center, Washington, DC, WRAMC Regulation No. 4615, http://www.wramc.amedd.army.mil/departments/PM/ep/bloodpath.htm, April 1999.

"Goals for Working Safely With Mycobacterium Tuberculosis in Clinical, Public Health, and Research Laboratories," Centers for Disease Control and Prevention (CDC), http://siri.org/library/tb.txt, 1997.

"Viral Hepatitis Homepage," Centers for Disease Control and Prevention (CDC), National Center for Infectious Diseases (NCID), http://www.cdc.gov/ncidod/diseases/hepatitis/index.htm, last modified February 25, 2000.

Toxins, Electro-Magnetic Fields, and Hazardous Chemicals in the Workplace

"Questions and Answers: EMF in the Workplace," National Institute for Occupational Safety and Health (NIOSH), Department of Energy (DOE), and the National Institute for Environmental Health Sciences, Pub. No. DOE/GO-10095-218, DE95013123, http://www.niehs.nih.gov/emfrapid/html/Q&A-Workplace.html, September 1996.

"Recognition and Management of Pesticide Poisonings," Fifth Edition 1998, Environmental Protection Agency (EPA), 735/R-98/00, http://www.epa.gov/oppfead1/safety/healthcare/handbook/handbook.htm. Hard copies are available by contacting the Office of Pesticide Programs: Phone: (703) 305-7666, Fax: (703) 308-2962.

"Recommended Classification of Pesticides by Hazard, and Guidelines to Classification, 1998–1999," World Health Organization (WHO), Doc. No. WHO/PCS/98.21. Available on request from: Division of Environmental Health, World Health Organization, 1211 Geneva 27, Switzerland.

Reproductive and Pregnancy Issues

"Working During Your Pregnancy," The American College of Obstetricians and Gynecologists. For a copy, contact the organization at 409 12th St. SW, Washington, DC 20024-2188, (202) 638-5577.

Child Labor, Workplace Violence, and Job Stress Issues

Folkard, S. and Monk, T.H. (editors), *Hours of Work: Temporal Factors in Work-Scheduling*, John Wiley and Sons, New York 1985.

Lamberg, L. *Bodyrhythms: Chronobiology and Peak Performance*, William Morrow and Company, New York 1994.

Monk, T.H. *How to Make Shift Work Safe and Productive*, American Society of Safety Engineers, Des Plaines, Illinois, 1988.

"Violence in the Workplace (Current Intelligence Bulletin 57)," National Institute for Occupational Safety and Health (NIOSH), Division of Safety Research, Centers for Disease Control and Prevention (CDC), Department of Health and Human Services (DHHS), DHHS (NIOSH), Pub. No. 96-100, http://www.cdc.gov/niosh/violcont.html, July 1996.

Wedderburn, A. *Guidelines for Shiftworkers*, European Foundation for the Improvement of Living and Working Conditions, Dublin, Ireland, 1991.

"Work Safe This Summer—Employer's Guide To Teen Worker Safety," U.S. Department of Labor (DOL), http://www.dol.gov/dol/esa/public/summer/employer.htm.

"Working in Hot Environments," National Institute for Occupational Safety and Health (NIOSH), available free, 4676 Columbia Parkway, Cincinnati, Ohio 45226; telephone (513) 533-8287.

Chapter 53

Resources

This chapter lists contact information for some of the government agencies, professional organizations, websites, and publications involved in workplace health and safety. Information is listed alphabetically according to the name of the organization.

Agency for Toxic Substances and Disease Registry (ATSDR)
U.S. Department of Health and Human Services
Public Health Service
1600 Clifton Road NE, Mailstop E-29
Atlanta, GA 30333
Phone: (404) 639-6300
Fax: (404) 639-6315
Toll Free: 1-888-422-8737
Website: http://www.atsdr.cdc.gov

ATSDR can tell you where to find occupational and environmental health clinics. Their specialists can recognize, evaluate, and treat illnesses resulting from exposure to hazardous substances. You can also contact your community or state health or environmental quality department if you have any more questions or concerns.

The resources listed in this section were compiled from a wide variety of sources deemed accurate. Contact information was updated and verified in April 2000. Inclusion does not constitute endorsement.

The American Association of Poison Control Centers
3201 New Mexico Avenue, Suite 310
Washington, DC 20016
Phone: (202) 362-7217
E-Mail: aapcc@poison.org
Website: http://www.aapcc.org

The American Association of Poison Control Centers is a clearinghouse for Regional Poison Control Centers. Regional centers can be found in the blue pages of the telephone directory. Most operate under the aegis of the local department of health.

The American College of Occupational and Environmental Medicine
1114 N. Arlington Heights Road
Arlington Heights, IL 60004
Phone: (847) 818-1800
Fax: (847) 818-9266
E-Mail:
Website: http://www.acoem.org

The official publication of The American College of Occupational and Environmental Medicine is the *Journal of Occupational and Environmental Medicine*.

American National Standards Institute (ANSI)
11 West 42nd Street
New York, NY 10036
Phone: (212) 642-4900
Fax: (212) 398-0023
Website: http://www.ansi.org

American Society of Heating, Refrigerating and Air-Conditioning Engineers (ASHRAE)
1791 Tullie Circle, NE
Atlanta, GA 30329
Toll Free: (800) 527-4723
Phone: (404) 636-8400
Fax: (404) 321-5478
Website: http://www.ashrae.org

American Health Consultants
3525 Piedmont Rd
Building 6, Suite 400
Atlanta, GA 30305
Phone: (404) 262-7436, (800) 688-2421
Fax: (800) 284-3291
E-Mail: customerservice@ahcpub.com
Website: http://www.ahcpub.com

The Association of Occupational and Environmental Clinics
1010 Vermont Avenue, NW, Suite 513
Washington, DC 20005
Phone: (202) 347-4976
Fax: (202) 347-4950
E-Mail: aoec@aoec.org
Website: http://www.aoec.org

Building Owners and Managers Association International
1201 New York Avenue, NW
Washington, DC 20005
Phone: (202) 408-2662
Fax: (202) 371-0181
Website: http://www.boma.org

Bureau of Labor Statistics (BLS)
Division of Information Services
2 Massachusetts Avenue, NE
Room 2860
Washington, DC 20212
Phone: (202) 691-5200
Fax: (202) 691-7890
Website: http://www.bls.gov

The Canadian Center for Occupational Health and Safety (CCOHS)
250 Main Street East
Hamilton ON L8N 1H6 Canada
Toll Free: (800) 668-4284
Phone: (905) 572-2981
Fax: (905) 572-2206
E-Mail: custservf@ccohs.ca
Website: http://www.ccohs.ca

Canadian National Occupational Safety and Health Website

Website: http://www.canoshweb.org

Centers for Disease Control and Prevention (CDC)

National Prevention Information Network
P.O. Box 6003
Rockville, MD 20849-6003
Phone: (800) 458-5231
TTY: (800) 243-7012
Fax: (888) 282-7681
E-Mail: pubs@cdcpin.org
Website: http://www.cdcnpin.org

CTD (Cumulative Trauma Disorders) News On-line

Website: http://www.ctdnews.com

Environmental Protection Agency (EPA)

1200 Pennsylvania Avenue, NW
Washington, DC 20460
Website: http://www.epa.gov

EPA Many EPA documents can be viewed on-line and printed using EPA's National Environmental Publications Internet Site (NEPIS), a database of over 7,000 documents. NOTE: NEPIS contains both current documents and archival material which is no longer available in hard-copy format. NEPIS can be found on the web at: http://www.epa.gov/cincl

ErgoWeb

PO Box 1089
93 West Main Street
Midway, Utah 84049
Toll Free: (888) 374-6972
Phone: (435) 654-4284
Fax: (435) 654-5433
E-Mail: inquire@ergoweb.com
Website: http://ergoweb.com

Human Factors and Ergonomics Society
PO Box 1369
Santa Monica, CA 90406-1369
Phone: (310) 394-1811
Fax: (310) 394-2410
Email: hfes@compuserve.com
Website: http://hfes.org

Indoor Air Quality Information Clearinghouse (IAQ INFO)
PO Box 37133
Washington DC 20013-7133
Phone: (703) 356-4020 or (800) 438-4318
Fax: (703) 356-5386
E-mail: iaqinfo@aol.com
Website: http://www.epa.gov/iaq/iaqinfo.html

The Indoor Air Quality Information Clearinghouse is sponsored by the U.S. EPA

Integrated Risk Information System (IRIS)
Phone: (513) 569-7254
Fax: (513) 569-7159
E-Mail: RIH.IRIS@epamail.epa.gov
Website: http://www.epa.gov/iris

Mine Safety and Health Administration (MSHA)
Health Division (Coal)
Phone: (703) 235-1358
Health Division (Metal and Nonmetal)
Phone: (703) 235-8307
Website: http://www.msha.gov

In the mining industry, for compliance assistance, technical support, educational materials, or for information about an inspection, contact the nearest MSHA district office.

Coal Mining

District 1	District 2	District 3
Wilkes-Barre, PA	Hunker, PA	Morgantown, WV
(570) 826-6321	(724) 925-5150	(304) 291-4277

District 4	District 5	District 6
Mt. Hope, WV	Norton, VA	Pikeville, KY
(304) 877-3900	(540) 679-0230	(606) 432-0943

District 7	District 8	District 9
Barbourville, KY	Vincennes, IN	Denver, CO
(606) 546-5123	(812) 882-7617	(303) 231-5458

District 10	District 11
Madisonville, KY	Birmingham, AL
(502) 821-4180	(205) 290-7300

Metal and Non-Metal Mining

Northeast District	Southeast District	North Central District
Cranberry Twp, PA	Birmingham, AL	Duluth, MN
(724) 772-2333	(205) 290-7294	(218) 720-5448

South Central District	Rocky Mountain	Western District
Dallas, TX	District	Vacaville, CA
(214) 767-8401	Denver, CO	(707) 447-9844
	(303) 231-5465	

The National Ag Safety Database (NASD)

Website: http://www.cdc.gov/niosh/nasd/nasdhome.html

NASD is a database of materials devoted to increased safety, health, and injury prevention in agriculture.

National Institute for Occupational Safety and Health (NIOSH)

U.S. Department of Health and Human Services
4676 Columbia Parkway
Cincinnati, Ohio 45226
Phone: (202)523-8151, (800) 35-NIOSH, (800) 356-4674
Fax: (513) 533-8573
Website: http://www.cdc.gov/niosh/homepage.html

New York Committee for Occupational Safety and Health (NYCOSH)
275 Seventh Avenue
New York, NY 10001
Phone: (212) 627-3900
E-Mail: nycosh@nycosh.org
Website: http://www.nycosh.org

Occupational Hazards Magazine On-line
Website: http://www.occupationalhazards.com

Occupational Safety and Health Administration (OSHA)
U.S. Department of Labor
Room N3647
200 Constitution Avenue, NW
Washington, DC 20210
Phone: (202) 693-1999
Toll Free: (800) 321-6742
Website: http://www.osha.gov

For free help in establishing or improving your safety and health program, small businesses can contact the OSHA Consultation Program in their state (visit http://www.osha.gov/oshdir/consult.html):

Alabama (205) 348-3033
Alaska (907) 269-4957
Arizona (602) 542-5795
Arkansas (501) 682-4522
California (415) 703-5270
Colorado (970) 491-6151
Connecticut (860) 566-4550
Delaware (302) 761-8219
District of Columbia
   (202) 576-6339
Florida (850) 922-8955
Georgia (404) 894-2643
Guam 011 (671) 475-0136
Hawaii (808) 586-9100
Idaho (208) 385-3283
Illinois (312) 814-2337
Indiana (317) 232-2688
Iowa (515) 965-7162

Kansas (785) 296-7476
Kentucky (502) 564-6895
Louisiana (225) 342-9601
Maine (207) 624-6460
Maryland (410) 880-4970
Massachusetts (617) 727-3982
Michigan (517) 332-6823
Minnesota (651) 297-2392
Mississippi (601) 987-3981
Missouri (573) 751-3403
Montana (406) 444-6418
Nebraska (402) 471-4717
Nevada (702) 486-9140
New Hampshire (603) 271-2024
New Jersey (609) 292-3923
New Mexico (505) 827-4230
New York (518) 457-2238
North Carolina (919) 807-2905

North Dakota (701) 328-5188
Ohio (614) 644-2246
Oklahoma (405) 528-1500
Oregon (503) 378-3272
Pennsylvania (724) 357-2396
Puerto Rico (787) 754-2171
Rhode Island (401) 222-2438
South Carolina (803) 734-9614
South Dakota (605) 688-4101
Tennessee (615) 741-7036

Texas (512) 804-4640
Utah (801) 530-6901
Vermont (802) 828-2765
Virginia (804) 786-6359
Virgin Islands (340) 772-1315
Washington (360) 902-5638
West Virginia (304) 558-7890
Wisconsin (608) 266-8579,
  (262) 532-3040
Wyoming (307) 777-7786

For compliance assistance or technical support in construction, maritime, and general industries, contact the nearest OSHA Regional Office. States and territories marked with an "*" operate their own OSHA-approved job safety and health programs (Connecticut and New York plans cover public employees only). States with approved programs must have a standard that is identical to, or at least as effective as, the federal standard.

Region I
(CT,* MA, ME, NH, RI, VT*)
JKF Federal Building
Room E-340
Boston, MA 02203
Phone: (617) 565-9860

Region II
(NJ, NY,* PR,* VI*)
201 Varick Street
Room 670
New York, NY 10014
Phone: (212) 337-2378

Region III
(DC, DE, MD,* PA, VA,* WV)
The Curtis Center, Suite 740 W.
170 S. Independence Mall West
Philadelphia, PA 19104-3309
Phone: (215) 861-4900

Region IV
(AL, FL, GA, KY,* MS, NC, SC,*
TN*)
61 Forsyth Street, SW
Atlanta, GA 30303
Phone: (404) 562-2300

Region V
(IL, IN,* MI,* MN,* OH, WI)
230 South Dearborn Street
Room 3244
Chicago, IL 60604
Phone: (312) 353-2220

Region VI
(AR, LA, NM,* OK, TX)
525 Griffin Street
Room 602
Dallas, TX 75202
Phone: (214) 767-4731

Region VII
(IA,* KS, MO, NE)
City Center Square
1100 Main Street
Suite 800
Kansas City, MO 64105
Phone: (816) 426-5861

Region VIII
(CO, MT, ND, SD, UT,* WY*)
1999 Broadway, Suite 1690
Denver, CO 80202-5716
Phone: (303) 844-1600

Region IX
(American Samoa, AZ,* CA,* Guam,
HI,* NV,* Trust Territories of the
Pacific)
71 Stevenson Street, Room 420
San Francisco, CA 94105
Phone: (415) 975-4310

Region X
(AK,* ID, OR,* WA*)
1111 Third Avenue, Suite 715
Seattle, WA 98101-3212
Phone: (206) 553-5930

The National Library of Medicine
8600 Rockville Pike
Bethesda, MD 20894
Website: http://medlineplus.gov
Phone: (888) 346-3656

The National Library of Medicine is connected to a vast network of on-line data resources, including Medline, PDQ, and Toxnet. Many physicians and researchers may already have access to these resources through their institutional libraries, which should be consulted first.

Prevent Blindness America
500 East Remington Road
Schaumburg, IL 60173
(847) 843-2020, (800) 331-2020 (toll-free)
Website: http://www.preventblindness.org

Prevent Blindness America is an excellent source of training materials for preventing eye injuries. Prevent Blindness America offers information, referral services, safety literature and videos on eye health and safety, and the Wise Owl Personal Protective Equipment (PPE) safety program.

United States Office of Personnel Management
Office of Workforce Relations, Theodore Roosevelt Building
1900 E St. NW
Washington, DC 20415
Website: http://www.usajobs.opm.gov

The United States Department of Labor (DOL)
Office of Public Affairs
200 Constitution Ave., NW
Room S-1032
Washington, DC 20210
(202) 693-4650
Website: http://www.dol.gov

White Lung Association
PO Box 1483
Baltimore, MD 21203-1483
Phone: (410) 243-5864
Website: http://www.whitelung.org

The White Lung Association alerts asbestos victims of their legal rights and makes referrals to lawyers and physicians. The Association will maintain exposure data for victims or potential victims.

Index

Index

Page numbers followed by 'n' indicate a footnote. Page numbers in *italics* indicate a table or illustration.

A

abdominal belts *see* back belts
abrasion, defined 563
absorption, defined 563
acetone 399, 435
acetophenone 400
ACGIH *see* American Conference of Governmental Industrial Hygienists
"Achieving Safe Sight 24 Hours a Day" 176n
acid, defined 564
ACOEM *see* American College of Occupational and Environmental Medicine
ACS *see* American Cancer Society
actinolite 57
action level, defined 564
active ingredient, described 355–56
active noise control systems 205–6
acupuncture, occupational injury 256
acute, defined 564
ADA *see* American Dental Association

administrative controls
　defined 564
　respiratory protection 130
　workplace violence 498–99, 509–11
adolescents
　child labor 479–93
　occupational hazards 4
adsorption, defined 564
Advanstar Communications, Inc., chemical burns 170n
AFSCME *see* American Federation of State, County and Municipal Employees
age factor
　cold environments 463
　hearing loss 13
　musculoskeletal disorders risk 254
Agency for Toxic Substances and Disease Registry (ATSDR)
　cancer and the workplace 419, 420
　chloroform 393n, 395
　contact information 577
　"Lead" fact sheet 341n
airline respirators, defined 570
airline workers 99–100
air pollution
　formaldehyde 383
　lung cancer 97
air-purifying element *see* filter

589

E

Health Reference Series
COMPLETE CATALOG

AIDS Sourcebook, 1st Edition

Basic Information about AIDS and HIV Infection, Featuring Historical and Statistical Data, Current Research, Prevention, and Other Special Topics of Interest for Persons Living with AIDS

Along with Source Listings for Further Assistance

Edited by Karen Bellenir and Peter D. Dresser. 831 pages. 1995. 0-7808-0031-1. $78.

"One strength of this book is its practical emphasis. The intended audience is the lay reader . . . useful as an educational tool for health care providers who work with AIDS patients. Recommended for public libraries as well as hospital or academic libraries that collect consumer materials."
— *Bulletin of the Medical Library Association, Jan '96*

"This is the most comprehensive volume of its kind on an important medical topic. Highly recommended for all libraries." — *Reference Book Review, '96*

"Very useful reference for all libraries."
— *Choice, Association of College and Research Libraries, Oct '95*

"There is a wealth of information here that can provide much educational assistance. It is a must book for all libraries and should be on the desk of each and every congressional leader. Highly recommended."
— *AIDS Book Review Journal, Aug '95*

"Recommended for most collections."
— *Library Journal, Jul '95*

◼

AIDS Sourcebook, 2nd Edition

Basic Consumer Health Information about Acquired Immune Deficiency Syndrome (AIDS) and Human Immunodeficiency Virus (HIV) Infection, Featuring Updated Statistical Data, Reports on Recent Research and Prevention Initiatives, and Other Special Topics of Interest for Persons Living with AIDS, Including New Antiretroviral Treatment Options, Strategies for Combating Opportunistic Infections, Information about Clinical Trials, and More

Along with a Glossary of Important Terms and Resource Listings for Further Help and Information

Edited by Karen Bellenir. 751 pages. 1999. 0-7808-0225-X. $78.

"Highly recommended."
— *American Reference Books Annual, 2000*

"Excellent sourcebook. This continues to be a highly recommended book. There is no other book that provides as much information as this book provides."
— *AIDS Book Review Journal, Dec-Jan 2000*

"Recommended reference source."
— *Booklist, American Library Association, Dec '99*

"A solid text for college-level health libraries."
— *The Bookwatch, Aug '99*

Cited in *Reference Sources for Small and Medium-Sized Libraries, American Library Association, 1999*

◼

Alcoholism Sourcebook

Basic Consumer Health Information about the Physical and Mental Consequences of Alcohol Abuse, Including Liver Disease, Pancreatitis, Wernicke-Korsakoff Syndrome (Alcoholic Dementia), Fetal Alcohol Syndrome, Heart Disease, Kidney Disorders, Gastrointestinal Problems, and Immune System Compromise and Featuring Facts about Addiction, Detoxification, Alcohol Withdrawal, Recovery, and the Maintenance of Sobriety

Along with a Glossary and Directories of Resources for Further Help and Information

Edited by Karen Bellenir. 635 pages. 2000. 0-7808-0325-6. $78.

SEE ALSO Drug Abuse Sourcebook, Substance Abuse Sourcebook

◼

Allergies Sourcebook

Basic Information about Major Forms and Mechanisms of Common Allergic Reactions, Sensitivities, and Intolerances, Including Anaphylaxis, Asthma, Hives and Other Dermatologic Symptoms, Rhinitis, and Sinusitis

Along with Their Usual Triggers Like Animal Fur, Chemicals, Drugs, Dust, Foods, Insects, Latex, Pollen, and Poison Ivy, Oak, and Sumac; Plus Information on Prevention, Identification, and Treatment

Edited by Allan R. Cook. 611 pages. 1997. 0-7808-0036-2. $78.

◼

Alternative Medicine Sourcebook

Basic Consumer Health Information about Alternatives to Conventional Medicine, Including Acupressure, Acupuncture, Aromatherapy, Ayurveda, Bioelectromagnetics, Environmental Medicine, Essence Therapy, Food and Nutrition Therapy, Herbal Therapy, Homeopathy, Imaging, Massage, Naturopathy, Reflexology, Relaxation and Meditation, Sound Therapy, Vitamin and Mineral Therapy, and Yoga, and More

Edited by Allan R. Cook. 737 pages. 1999. 0-7808-0200-4. $78.

"Recommended reference source."
— *Booklist, American Library Association, Feb '00*

"A great addition to the reference collection of every type of library."
—*American Reference Books Annual, 2000*

■

Alzheimer's, Stroke & 29 Other Neurological Disorders Sourcebook, 1st Edition

Basic Information for the Layperson on 31 Diseases or Disorders Affecting the Brain and Nervous System, First Describing the Illness, Then Listing Symptoms, Diagnostic Methods, and Treatment Options, and Including Statistics on Incidences and Causes

Edited by Frank E. Bair. 579 pages. 1993. 1-55888-748-2. $78.

"Nontechnical reference book that provides reader-friendly information."
— *Family Caregiver Alliance Update, Winter '96*

"Should be included in any library's patient education section." — *American Reference Books Annual, 1994*

"Written in an approachable and accessible style. Recommended for patient education and consumer health collections in health science center and public libraries." — *Academic Library Book Review, Dec '93*

"It is very handy to have information on more than thirty neurological disorders under one cover, and there is no recent source like it." — *Reference Quarterly, American Library Association, Fall '93*

SEE ALSO *Brain Disorders Sourcebook*

■

Alzheimer's Disease Sourcebook, 2nd Edition

Basic Consumer Health Information about Alzheimer's Disease, Related Disorders, and Other Dementias, Including Multi-Infarct Dementia, AIDS-Related Dementia, Alcoholic Dementia, Huntington's Disease, Delirium, and Confusional States

Along with Reports Detailing Current Research Efforts in Prevention and Treatment, Long-Term Care Issues, and Listings of Sources for Additional Help and Information

Edited by Karen Bellenir. 524 pages. 1999. 0-7808-0223-3. $78.

"Provides a wealth of useful information not otherwise available in one place. This resource is recommended for all types of libraries."
—*American Reference Books Annual, 2000*

"Recommended reference source."
—*Booklist, American Library Association, Oct '99*

Arthritis Sourcebook

Basic Consumer Health Information about Specific Forms of Arthritis and Related Disorders, Including Rheumatoid Arthritis, Osteoarthritis, Gout, Polymyalgia Rheumatica, Psoriatic Arthritis, Spondyloarthropathies, Juvenile Rheumatoid Arthritis, and Juvenile Ankylosing Spondylitis

Along with Information about Medical, Surgical, and Alternative Treatment Options, and Including Strategies for Coping with Pain, Fatigue, and Stress

Edited by Allan R. Cook. 550 pages. 1998. 0-7808-0201-2. $78.

". . . accessible to the layperson."
—*Reference and Research Book News, Feb '99*

■

Asthma Sourcebook

Basic Consumer Health Information about Asthma, Including Symptoms, Traditional and Nontraditional Remedies, Treatment Advances, Quality-of-Life Aids, Medical Research Updates, and the Role of Allergies, Exercise, Age, the Environment, and Genetics in the Development of Asthma

Along with Statistical Data, a Glossary, and Directories of Support Groups, and Other Resources for Further Information

Edited by Annemarie S. Muth. 650 pages. 2000. 0-7808-0381-7. $78.

■

Back & Neck Disorders Sourcebook

Basic Information about Disorders and Injuries of the Spinal Cord and Vertebrae, Including Facts on Chiropractic Treatment, Surgical Interventions, Paralysis, and Rehabilitation

Along with Advice for Preventing Back Trouble

Edited by Karen Bellenir. 548 pages. 1997. 0-7808-0202-0. $78.

"The strength of this work is its basic, easy-to-read format. Recommended."
— *Reference and User Services Quarterly, American Library Association, Winter '97*

■

Blood & Circulatory Disorders Sourcebook

Basic Information about Blood and Its Components, Anemias, Leukemias, Bleeding Disorders, and Circulatory Disorders, Including Aplastic Anemia, Thalassemia, Sickle-Cell Disease, Hemochromatosis, Hemophilia, Von Willebrand Disease, and Vascular Diseases

Along with a Special Section on Blood Transfusions and Blood Supply Safety, a Glossary, and Source Listings for Further Help and Information

Edited by Karen Bellenir and Linda M. Shin. 554 pages. 1998. 0-7808-0203-9. $78.

Brain Disorders Sourcebook

Basic Consumer Health Information about Strokes, Epilepsy, Amyotrophic Lateral Sclerosis (ALS/Lou Gehrig's Disease), Parkinson's Disease, Brain Tumors, Cerebral Palsy, Headache, Tourette Syndrome, and More

Along with Statistical Data, Treatment and Rehabilitation Options, Coping Strategies, Reports on Current Research Initiatives, a Glossary, and Resource Listings for Additional Help and Information

Edited by Karen Bellenir. 481 pages. 1999. 0-7808-0229-2. $78.

SEE ALSO Alzheimer's, Stroke & 29 Other Neurological Disorders Sourcebook, 1st Edition

Breast Cancer Sourcebook

Basic Consumer Health Information about Breast Cancer, Including Diagnostic Methods, Treatment Options, Alternative Therapies, Help and Self-Help Information, Related Health Concerns, Statistical and Demographic Data, and Facts for Men with Breast Cancer

Along with Reports on Current Research Initiatives, a Glossary of Related Medical Terms, and a Directory of Sources for Further Help and Information

Edited by Edward J. Prucha. 600 pages. 2000. 0-7808-0244-6. $78.

SEE ALSO Cancer Sourcebook for Women, 1st and 2nd Editions, Women's Health Concerns Sourcebook

Burns Sourcebook

Basic Consumer Health Information about Various Types of Burns and Scalds, Including Flame, Heat, Cold, Electrical, Chemical, and Sun Burns

Along with Information on Short-Term and Long-Term Treatments, Tissue Reconstruction, Plastic Surgery, Prevention Suggestions, and First Aid

Edited by Allan R. Cook. 604 pages. 1999. 0-7808-0204-7. $78.

SEE ALSO Skin Disorders Sourcebook

Cancer Sourcebook, 1st Edition

Basic Information on Cancer Types, Symptoms, Diagnostic Methods, and Treatments, Including Statistics on Cancer Occurrences Worldwide and the Risks Associated with Known Carcinogens and Activities

Edited by Frank E. Bair. 932 pages. 1990. 1-55888-888-8. $78.

Cited in *Reference Sources for Small and Medium-Sized Libraries, American Library Association, 1999*

New Cancer Sourcebook, 2nd Edition

Basic Information about Major Forms and Stages of Cancer, Featuring Facts about Primary and Secondary Tumors of the Respiratory, Nervous, Lymphatic, Circulatory, Skeletal, and Gastrointestinal Systems, and Specific Organs; Statistical and Demographic Data; Treatment Options; and Strategies for Coping

Edited by Allan R. Cook. 1,313 pages. 1996. 0-7808-0041-9. $78.

"The amount of factual and useful information is extensive. The writing is very clear, geared to general readers. Recommended for all levels."
—Choice, Association of College and Research Libraries, Jan '97

Cancer Sourcebook, 3rd Edition

Basic Consumer Health Information about Major Forms and Stages of Cancer, Featuring Facts about Primary and Secondary Tumors of the Respiratory, Nervous, Lymphatic, Circulatory, Skeletal, and Gastrointestinal Systems, and Specific Organs

Along with Statistical and Demographic Data, Treatment Options, Strategies for Coping, a Glossary, and a Directory of Sources for Additional Help and Information

Edited by Edward J. Prucha. 1,069 pages. 2000. 0-7808-0227-6. $78.

Cancer Sourcebook for Women, 1st Edition

Basic Information about Specific Forms of Cancer That Affect Women, Featuring Facts about Breast Cancer, Cervical Cancer, Ovarian Cancer, Cancer of the Uterus and Uterine Sarcoma, Cancer of the Vagina, and Cancer of the Vulva; Statistical and Demographic Data; Treatments, Self-Help Management Suggestions, and Current Research Initiatives

Edited by Allan R. Cook and Peter D. Dresser. 524 pages. 1996. 0-7808-0076-1. $78.

". . . written in easily understandable, non-technical language. Recommended for public libraries or hospital and academic libraries that collect patient education or consumer health materials."
— Medical Reference Services Quarterly, Spring '97

"Would be of value in a consumer health library. . . . written with the health care consumer in mind. Medical jargon is at a minimum, and medical terms are explained in clear, understandable sentences."
— Bulletin of the Medical Library Association, Oct '96

"The availability under one cover of all these pertinent publications, grouped under cohesive headings, makes this certainly a most useful sourcebook."
— Choice, Association of College and Research Libraries, Jun '96

"Presents a comprehensive knowledge base for general readers. Men and women both benefit from the gold mine of information nestled between the two covers of this book. Recommended."
—Academic Library Book Review, Summer '96

"This timely book is highly recommended for consumer health and patient education collections in all libraries." — Library Journal, Apr '96

SEE ALSO Breast Cancer Sourcebook, Women's Health Concerns Sourcebook

Cancer Sourcebook for Women, 2nd Edition

Basic Consumer Health Information about Specific Forms of Cancer That Affect Women, Including Cervical Cancer, Ovarian Cancer, Endometrial Cancer, Uterine Sarcoma, Vaginal Cancer, Vulvar Cancer, and Gestational Trophoblastic Tumor; and Featuring Statistical Information, Facts about Tests and Treatments, a Glossary of Cancer Terms, and an Extensive List of Additional Resources

Edited by Edward J. Prucha. 600 pages. 2000. 0-7808-0226-8. $78.

SEE ALSO Breast Cancer Sourcebook, Women's Health Concerns Sourcebook

Cardiovascular Diseases & Disorders Sourcebook, 1st Edition

Basic Information about Cardiovascular Diseases and Disorders, Featuring Facts about the Cardiovascular System, Demographic and Statistical Data, Descriptions of Pharmacological and Surgical Interventions, Lifestyle Modifications, and a Special Section Focusing on Heart Disorders in Children

Edited by Karen Bellenir and Peter D. Dresser. 683 pages. 1995. 0-7808-0032-X. $78.

". . . comprehensive format provides an extensive overview on this subject."
—Choice, Association of College and Research Libraries, Jun '96

". . . an easily understood, complete, up-to-date resource. This well executed public health tool will make valuable information available to those that need it most, patients and their families. The typeface, sturdy non-reflective paper, and library binding add a feel of quality found wanting in other publications. Highly recommended for academic and general libraries. "
—Academic Library Book Review, Summer '96

SEE ALSO Healthy Heart Sourcebook for Women, Heart Diseases & Disorders Sourcebook, 2nd Edition

Communication Disorders Sourcebook

Basic Information about Deafness and Hearing Loss, Speech and Language Disorders, Voice Disorders, Balance and Vestibular Disorders, and Disorders of Smell, Taste, and Touch

Edited by Linda M. Ross. 533 pages. 1996. 0-7808-0077-X. $78.

"This is skillfully edited and is a welcome resource for the layperson. It should be found in every public and medical library." — Booklist Health Sciences Supplement, American Library Association, Oct '97

Congenital Disorders Sourcebook

Basic Information about Disorders Acquired during Gestation, Including Spina Bifida, Hydrocephalus, Cerebral Palsy, Heart Defects, Craniofacial Abnormalities, Fetal Alcohol Syndrome, and More

Along with Current Treatment Options and Statistical Data

Edited by Karen Bellenir. 607 pages. 1997. 0-7808-0205-5. $78.

"Recommended reference source."
—Booklist, American Library Association, Oct '97

SEE ALSO Pregnancy & Birth Sourcebook

Consumer Issues in Health Care Sourcebook

Basic Information about Health Care Fundamentals and Related Consumer Issues, Including Exams and Screening Tests, Physician Specialties, Choosing a Doctor, Using Prescription and Over-the-Counter Medications Safely, Avoiding Health Scams, Managing Common Health Risks in the Home, Care Options for Chronically or Terminally Ill Patients, and a List of Resources for Obtaining Help and Further Information

Edited by Karen Bellenir. 618 pages. 1998. 0-7808-0221-7. $78.

"Both public and academic libraries will want to have a copy in their collection for readers who are interested in self-education on health issues."
—American Reference Books Annual, 2000

"The editor has researched the literature from government agencies and others, saving readers the time and effort of having to do the research themselves. Recommended for public libraries."
—Reference and User Services Quarterly, American Library Association, Spring '99

"Recommended reference source."
—Booklist, American Library Association, Dec '98

Contagious & Non-Contagious Infectious Diseases Sourcebook

Basic Information about Contagious Diseases like Measles, Polio, Hepatitis B, and Infectious Mononucleosis, and Non-Contagious Infectious Diseases like Tetanus and Toxic Shock Syndrome, and Diseases Occurring as Secondary Infections Such as Shingles and Reye Syndrome

Along with Vaccination, Prevention, and Treatment Information, and a Section Describing Emerging Infectious Disease Threats

Edited by Karen Bellenir and Peter D. Dresser. 566 pages. 1996. 0-7808-0075-3. $78.

Death & Dying Sourcebook

Basic Consumer Health Information for the Layperson about End-of-Life Care and Related Ethical and Legal Issues, Including Chief Causes of Death, Autopsies, Pain Management for the Terminally Ill, Life Support Systems, Insurance, Euthanasia, Assisted Suicide, Hospice Programs, Living Wills, Funeral Planning, Counseling, Mourning, Organ Donation, and Physician Training

Along with Statistical Data, a Glossary, and Listings of Sources for Further Help and Information

Edited by Annemarie S. Muth. 641 pages. 1999. 0-7808-0230-6. $78.

"This book is a definite must for all those involved in end-of-life care." *—Doody's Review Service, 2000*

Diabetes Sourcebook, 1st Edition

Basic Information about Insulin-Dependent and Noninsulin-Dependent Diabetes Mellitus, Gestational Diabetes, and Diabetic Complications, Symptoms, Treatment, and Research Results, Including Statistics on Prevalence, Morbidity, and Mortality

Along with Source Listings for Further Help and Information

Edited by Karen Bellenir and Peter D. Dresser. 827 pages. 1994. 1-55888-751-2. $78.

". . . very informative and understandable for the layperson without being simplistic. It provides a comprehensive overview for laypersons who want a general understanding of the disease or who want to focus on various aspects of the disease."
—Bulletin of the Medical Library Association, Jan '96

Diabetes Sourcebook, 2nd Edition

Basic Consumer Health Information about Type 1 Diabetes (Insulin-Dependent or Juvenile-Onset Diabetes), Type 2 (Noninsulin-Dependent or Adult-Onset Diabetes), Gestational Diabetes, and Related Disorders, Including Diabetes Prevalence Data, Management Issues, the Role of Diet and Exercise in Controlling Diabetes, Insulin and Other Diabetes Medicines, and Complications of Diabetes Such as Eye Diseases, Periodontal Disease, Amputation, and End-Stage Renal Disease

Along with Reports on Current Research Initiatives, a Glossary, and Resource Listings for Further Help and Information

Edited by Karen Bellenir. 688 pages. 1998. 0-7808-0224-1. $78.

"This comprehensive book is an excellent addition for high school, academic, medical, and public libraries. This volume is highly recommended."
—American Reference Books Annual, 2000

"An invaluable reference." *—Library Journal, May '00*

Selected as one of the 250 "Best Health Sciences Books of 1999." —*Doody's Rating Service, Mar-Apr 2000*

"Recommended reference source."
—*Booklist, American Library Association, Feb '99*

". . . provides reliable mainstream medical information . . . belongs on the shelves of any library with a consumer health collection." —*E-Streams, Sep '99*

"Provides useful information for the general public."
—*Healthlines, University of Michigan Health Management Research Center, Sep/Oct '99*

■

Diet & Nutrition Sourcebook, 1st Edition

Basic Information about Nutrition, Including the Dietary Guidelines for Americans, the Food Guide Pyramid, and Their Applications in Daily Diet, Nutritional Advice for Specific Age Groups, Current Nutritional Issues and Controversies, the New Food Label and How to Use It to Promote Healthy Eating, and Recent Developments in Nutritional Research

Edited by Dan R. Harris. 662 pages. 1996. 0-7808-0084-2. $78.

"Useful reference as a food and nutrition sourcebook for the general consumer." —*Booklist Health Sciences Supplement, American Library Association, Oct '97*

"Recommended for public libraries and medical libraries that receive general information requests on nutrition. It is readable and will appeal to those interested in learning more about healthy dietary practices."
—*Medical Reference Services Quarterly, Fall '97*

"An abundance of medical and social statistics is translated into readable information geared toward the general reader." —*Bookwatch, Mar '97*

"With dozens of questionable diet books on the market, it is so refreshing to find a reliable and factual reference book. Recommended to aspiring professionals, librarians, and others seeking and giving reliable dietary advice. An excellent compilation." —*Choice, Association of College and Research Libraries, Feb '97*

SEE ALSO *Digestive Diseases & Disorders Sourcebook, Gastrointestinal Diseases & Disorders Sourcebook*

■

Diet & Nutrition Sourcebook, 2nd Edition

Basic Consumer Health Information about Dietary Guidelines, Recommended Daily Intake Values, Vitamins, Minerals, Fiber, Fat, Weight Control, Dietary Supplements, and Food Additives

Along with Special Sections on Nutrition Needs throughout Life and Nutrition for People with Such Specific Medical Concerns as Allergies, High Blood Cholesterol, Hypertension, Diabetes, Celiac Disease, Seizure Disorders, Phenylketonuria (PKU), Cancer, and Eating Disorders, and Including Reports on Current Nutrition Research and Source Listings for Additional Help and Information

Edited by Karen Bellenir. 650 pages. 1999. 0-7808-0228-4. $78.

"This reference document should be in any public library, but it would be a very good guide for beginning students in the health sciences. If the other books in this publisher's series are as good as this, they should all be in the health sciences collections."
—*American Reference Books Annual, 2000*

"Recommended reference source."
—*Booklist, American Library Association, Dec '99*

SEE ALSO *Digestive Diseases & Disorders Sourcebook, Gastrointestinal Diseases & Disorders Sourcebook*

■

Digestive Diseases & Disorders Sourcebook

Basic Consumer Health Information about Diseases and Disorders that Impact the Upper and Lower Digestive System, Including Celiac Disease, Constipation, Crohn's Disease, Cyclic Vomiting Syndrome, Diarrhea, Diverticulosis and Diverticulitis, Gallstones, Heartburn, Hemorrhoids, Hernias, Indigestion (Dyspepsia), Irritable Bowel Syndrome, Lactose Intolerance, Ulcers, and More

Along with Information about Medications and Other Treatments, Tips for Maintaining a Healthy Digestive Tract, a Glossary, and Directory of Digestive Diseases Organizations

Edited by Karen Bellenir. 335 pages. 1999. 0-7808-0327-2. $48.

"Recommended reference source."
—*Booklist, American Library Association, May '00*

SEE ALSO *Diet & Nutrition Sourcebook, 1st and 2nd Editions, Gastrointestinal Diseases & Disorders Sourcebook*

■

Disabilities Sourcebook

Basic Consumer Health Information about Physical and Psychiatric Disabilities, Including Descriptions of Major Causes of Disability, Assistive and Adaptive Aids, Workplace Issues, and Accessibility Concerns

Along with Information about the Americans with Disabilities Act, a Glossary, and Resources for Additional Help and Information

Edited by Dawn D. Matthews. 616 pages. 2000. 0-7808-0389-2. $78.

"Recommended reference source."
—*Booklist, American Library Association, Jul '00*

"An involving, invaluable handbook."
—*The Bookwatch, May '00*

Domestic Violence & Child Abuse Sourcebook

Basic Consumer Health Information about Spousal/Partner, Child, Sibling, Parent, and Elder Abuse, Covering Physical, Emotional, and Sexual Abuse, Teen Dating Violence, and Stalking; Includes Information about Hotlines, Safe Houses, Safety Plans, and Other Resources for Support and Assistance, Community Initiatives, and Reports on Current Directions in Research and Treatment

Along with a Glossary, Sources for Further Reading, and Governmental and Non-Governmental Organizations Contact Information

Edited by Helene Henderson. 600 pages. 2000. 0-7808-0235-7. $78.

Drug Abuse Sourcebook

Basic Consumer Health Information about Illicit Substances of Abuse and the Diversion of Prescription Medications, Including Depressants, Hallucinogens, Inhalants, Marijuana, Narcotics, Stimulants, and Anabolic Steroids

Along with Facts about Related Health Risks, Treatment Issues, and Substance Abuse Prevention Programs, a Glossary of Terms, Statistical Data, and Directories of Hotline Services, Self-Help Groups, and Organizations Able to Provide Further Information

Edited by Karen Bellenir. 629 pages. 2000. 0-7808-0242-X. $78.

SEE ALSO *Alcoholism Sourcebook, Substance Abuse Sourcebook*

Ear, Nose & Throat Disorders Sourcebook

Basic Information about Disorders of the Ears, Nose, Sinus Cavities, Pharynx, and Larynx, Including Ear Infections, Tinnitus, Vestibular Disorders, Allergic and Non-Allergic Rhinitis, Sore Throats, Tonsillitis, and Cancers That Affect the Ears, Nose, Sinuses, and Throat

Along with Reports on Current Research Initiatives, a Glossary of Related Medical Terms, and a Directory of Sources for Further Help and Information

Edited by Karen Bellenir and Linda M. Shin. 576 pages. 1998. 0-7808-0206-3. $78.

"Overall, this sourcebook is helpful for the consumer seeking information on ENT issues. It is recommended for public libraries."
—*American Reference Books Annual, 1999*

"Recommended reference source."
—*Booklist, American Library Association, Dec '98*

Endocrine & Metabolic Disorders Sourcebook

Basic Information for the Layperson about Pancreatic and Insulin-Related Disorders Such as Pancreatitis, Diabetes, and Hypoglycemia; Adrenal Gland Disorders Such as Cushing's Syndrome, Addison's Disease, and Congenital Adrenal Hyperplasia; Pituitary Gland Disorders Such as Growth Hormone Deficiency, Acromegaly, and Pituitary Tumors; Thyroid Disorders Such as Hypothyroidism, Graves' Disease, Hashimoto's Disease, and Goiter; Hyperparathyroidism; and Other Diseases and Syndromes of Hormone Imbalance or Metabolic Dysfunction

Along with Reports on Current Research Initiatives

Edited by Linda M. Shin. 574 pages. 1998. 0-7808-0207-1. $78.

"Omnigraphics has produced another needed resource for health information consumers."
—*American Reference Books Annual, 2000*

"Recommended reference source."
—*Booklist, American Library Association, Dec '98*

Environmentally Induced Disorders Sourcebook

Basic Information about Diseases and Syndromes Linked to Exposure to Pollutants and Other Substances in Outdoor and Indoor Environments Such as Lead, Asbestos, Formaldehyde, Mercury, Emissions, Noise, and More

Edited by Allan R. Cook. 620 pages. 1997. 0-7808-0083-4. $78.

"Recommended reference source."
—*Booklist, American Library Association, Sep '98*

"This book will be a useful addition to anyone's library." —*Choice Health Sciences Supplement, Association of College and Research Libraries, May '98*

". . . a good survey of numerous environmentally induced physical disorders . . . a useful addition to anyone's library."
—*Doody's Health Sciences Book Reviews, Jan '98*

". . . provide[s] introductory information from the best authorities around. Since this volume covers topics that potentially affect everyone, it will surely be one of the most frequently consulted volumes in the *Health Reference Series.*" —*Rettig on Reference, Nov '97*

Family Planning Sourcebook

Basic Consumer Health Information about Planning for Pregnancy and Contraception, Including Traditional Methods, Barrier Methods, Permanent Methods, Future Methods, Emergency Contraception, and Birth Control Choices for Women at Each Stage of Life

Along with Statistics, Glossary, and Sources of Additional Information

Edited by Amy Marcaccio Keyzer. 600 pages. 2000. 0-7808-0379-5. $78.

SEE ALSO *Pregnancy & Birth Sourcebook*

Fitness & Exercise Sourcebook

Basic Information on Fitness and Exercise, Including Fitness Activities for Specific Age Groups, Exercise for People with Specific Medical Conditions, How to Begin a Fitness Program in Running, Walking, Swimming, Cycling, and Other Athletic Activities, and Recent Research in Fitness and Exercise

Edited by Dan R. Harris. 663 pages. 1996. 0-7808-0186-5. $78.

"A good resource for general readers."
— *Choice, Association of College and Research Libraries, Nov '97*

"The perennial popularity of the topic . . . make this an appealing selection for public libraries."
— *Rettig on Reference, Jun/Jul '97*

◼

Food & Animal Borne Diseases Sourcebook

Basic Information about Diseases That Can Be Spread to Humans through the Ingestion of Contaminated Food or Water or by Contact with Infected Animals and Insects, Such as Botulism, E. Coli, Hepatitis A, Trichinosis, Lyme Disease, and Rabies

Along with Information Regarding Prevention and Treatment Methods, and Including a Special Section for International Travelers Describing Diseases Such as Cholera, Malaria, Travelers' Diarrhea, and Yellow Fever, and Offering Recommendations for Avoiding Illness

Edited by Karen Bellenir and Peter D. Dresser. 535 pages. 1995. 0-7808-0033-8. $78.

"Targeting general readers and providing them with a single, comprehensive source of information on selected topics, this book continues, with the excellent caliber of its predecessors, to catalog topical information on health matters of general interest. Readable and thorough, this valuable resource is highly recommended for all libraries."
— *Academic Library Book Review, Summer '96*

"A comprehensive collection of authoritative information."   — *Emergency Medical Services, Oct '95*

◼

Food Safety Sourcebook

Basic Consumer Health Information about the Safe Handling of Meat, Poultry, Seafood, Eggs, Fruit Juices, and Other Food Items, and Facts about Pesticides, Drinking Water, Food Safety Overseas, and the Onset, Duration, and Symptoms of Foodborne Illnesses, Including Types of Pathogenic Bacteria, Parasitic Protozoa, Worms, Viruses, and Natural Toxins

Along with the Role of the Consumer, the Food Handler, and the Government in Food Safety; a Glossary, and Resources for Additional Help and Information

Edited by Dawn D. Matthews. 339 pages. 1999. 0-7808-0326-4. $48.

"This book takes the complex issues of food safety and foodborne pathogens and presents them in an easily understood manner. [It does] an excellent job of covering a large and often confusing topic."
— *American Reference Books Annual, 2000*

"Recommended reference source."
— *Booklist, American Library Association, May '00*

◼

Forensic Medicine Sourcebook

Basic Consumer Information for the Layperson about Forensic Medicine, Including Crime Scene Investigation, Evidence Collection and Analysis, Expert Testimony, Computer-Aided Criminal Identification, Digital Imaging in the Courtroom, DNA Profiling, Accident Reconstruction, Autopsies, Ballistics, Drugs and Explosives Detection, Latent Fingerprints, Product Tampering, and Questioned Document Examination

Along with Statistical Data, a Glossary of Forensics Terminology, and Listings of Sources for Further Help and Information

Edited by Annemarie S. Muth. 574 pages. 1999. 0-7808-0232-2. $78.

"There are several items that make this book attractive to consumers who are seeking certain forensic data. . . . This is a useful current source for those seeking general forensic medical answers."
— *American Reference Books Annual, 2000*

"Recommended for public libraries."
— *Reference & User Services Quarterly, American Library Association, Spring 2000*

"Recommended reference source."
— *Booklist, American Library Association, Feb '00*

"A wealth of information, useful statistics, references are up-to-date and extremely complete. This wonderful collection of data will help students who are interested in a career in any type of forensic field. It is a great resource for attorneys who need information about types of expert witnesses needed in a particular case. It also offers useful information for fiction and nonfiction writers whose work involves a crime. A fascinating compilation. All levels."
— *Choice, Association of College and Research Libraries, Jan 2000*

◼

Gastrointestinal Diseases & Disorders Sourcebook

Basic Information about Gastroesophageal Reflux Disease (Heartburn), Ulcers, Diverticulosis, Irritable Bowel Syndrome, Crohn's Disease, Ulcerative Colitis, Diarrhea, Constipation, Lactose Intolerance, Hemorrhoids, Hepatitis, Cirrhosis, and Other Digestive Problems, Featuring Statistics, Descriptions of Symptoms, and Current Treatment Methods of Interest for Persons Living with Upper and Lower Gastrointestinal Maladies

Edited by Linda M. Ross. 413 pages. 1996. 0-7808-0078-8. $78.

618

"... very readable form. The successful editorial work that brought this material together into a useful and understandable reference makes accessible to all readers information that can help them more effectively understand and obtain help for digestive tract problems."
— *Choice, Association of College and Research Libraries, Feb '97*

SEE ALSO Diet & Nutrition Sourcebook, 1st and 2nd Editions, Digestive Diseases & Disorders Sourcebook

■

Genetic Disorders Sourcebook, 1st Edition

Basic Information about Heritable Diseases and Disorders Such as Down Syndrome, PKU, Hemophilia, Von Willebrand Disease, Gaucher Disease, Tay-Sachs Disease, and Sickle-Cell Disease, Along with Information about Genetic Screening, Gene Therapy, Home Care, and Including Source Listings for Further Help and Information on More Than 300 Disorders

Edited by Karen Bellenir. 642 pages. 1996. 0-7808-0034-6. $78.

"Recommended for undergraduate libraries or libraries that serve the public."
— *Science & Technology Libraries, Vol. 18, No. 1, '99*

"Provides essential medical information to both the general public and those diagnosed with a serious or fatal genetic disease or disorder."
— *Choice, Association of College and Research Libraries, Jan '97*

"Geared toward the lay public. It would be well placed in all public libraries and in those hospital and medical libraries in which access to genetic references is limited." — *Doody's Health Sciences Book Review, Oct '96*

■

Genetic Disorders Sourcebook, 2nd Edition

Basic Consumer Health Information about Hereditary Diseases and Disorders, Including Cystic Fibrosis, Down Syndrome, Hemophilia, Huntington's Disease, Sickle Cell Anemia, and More; Facts about Genes, Gene Research and Therapy, Genetic Screening, Ethics of Gene Testing, Genetic Counseling, and Advice on Coping and Caring

Along with a Glossary of Genetic Terminology and a Resource List for Help, Support, and Further Information

Edited by Kathy Massimini. 650 pages. 2000. 0-7808-0241-1. $78.

■

Head Trauma Sourcebook

Basic Information for the Layperson about Open-Head and Closed-Head Injuries, Treatment Advances, Recovery, and Rehabilitation

Along with Reports on Current Research Initiatives

Edited by Karen Bellenir. 414 pages. 1997. 0-7808-0208-X. $78.

Health Insurance Sourcebook

Basic Information about Managed Care Organizations, Traditional Fee-for-Service Insurance, Insurance Portability and Pre-Existing Conditions Clauses, Medicare, Medicaid, Social Security, and Military Health Care

Along with Information about Insurance Fraud

Edited by Wendy Wilcox. 530 pages. 1997. 0-7808-0222-5. $78.

"Particularly useful because it brings much of this information together in one volume. This book will be a handy reference source in the health sciences library, hospital library, college and university library, and medium to large public library."
— *Medical Reference Services Quarterly, Fall '98*

Awarded "Books of the Year Award"
— *American Journal of Nursing, 1997*

"The layout of the book is particularly helpful as it provides easy access to reference material. A most useful addition to the vast amount of information about health insurance. The use of data from U.S. government agencies is most commendable. Useful in a library or learning center for healthcare professional students."
— *Doody's Health Sciences Book Reviews, Nov '97*

■

Health Resources Sourcebook

Basic Consumer Health Information about Sources of Medical Assistance, Featuring an Annotated Directory of Private and Public Consumer Health Organizations and Listings of Other Resources, Including Hospitals, Hospices, and State Medical Associations

Along with Guidelines for Locating and Evaluating Health Information

Edited by Dawn D. Matthews. 500 pages. 2000. 0-7808-0328-0. $78.

■

Healthy Aging Sourcebook

Basic Consumer Health Information about Maintaining Health through the Aging Process, Including Advice on Nutrition, Exercise, and Sleep, Help in Making Decisions about Midlife Issues and Retirement, and Guidance Concerning Practical and Informed Choices in Health Consumerism

Along with Data Concerning the Theories of Aging, Different Experiences in Aging by Minority Groups, and Facts about Aging Now and Aging in the Future; and Featuring a Glossary, a Guide to Consumer Help, Additional Suggested Reading, and Practical Resource Directory

Edited by Jenifer Swanson. 536 pages. 1999. 0-7808-0390-6. $78.

"Recommended reference source."
— *Booklist, American Library Association, Feb '00*

SEE ALSO Physical & Mental Issues in Aging Sourcebook

Healthy Heart Sourcebook for Women

Basic Consumer Health Information about Cardiac Issues Specific to Women, Including Facts about Major Risk Factors and Prevention, Treatment and Control Strategies, and Important Dietary Issues

Along with a Special Section Regarding the Pros and Cons of Hormone Replacement Therapy and Its Impact on Heart Health, and Additional Help, Including Recipes, a Glossary, and a Directory of Resources

Edited by Dawn D. Matthews. 336 pages. 2000. 0-7808-0329-9. $48.

SEE ALSO *Cardiovascular Diseases & Disorders Sourcebook, 1st Edition, Heart Diseases & Disorders Sourcebook, 2nd Edition, Women's Health Concerns Sourcebook*

Heart Diseases & Disorders Sourcebook, 2nd Edition

Basic Consumer Health Information about Heart Attacks, Angina, Rhythm Disorders, Heart Failure, Valve Disease, Congenital Heart Disorders, and More, Including Descriptions of Surgical Procedures and Other Interventions, Medications, Cardiac Rehabilitation, Risk Identification, and Prevention Tips

Along with Statistical Data, Reports on Current Research Initiatives, a Glossary of Cardiovascular Terms, and Resource Directory

Edited by Karen Bellenir. 612 pages. 2000. 0-7808-0238-1. $78.

SEE ALSO *Cardiovascular Diseases & Disorders Sourcebook, 1st Edition, Healthy Heart Sourcebook for Women*

Immune System Disorders Sourcebook

Basic Information about Lupus, Multiple Sclerosis, Guillain-Barré Syndrome, Chronic Granulomatous Disease, and More

Along with Statistical and Demographic Data and Reports on Current Research Initiatives

Edited by Allan R. Cook. 608 pages. 1997. 0-7808-0209-8. $78.

Infant & Toddler Health Sourcebook

Basic Consumer Health Information about the Physical and Mental Development of Newborns, Infants, and Toddlers, Including Neonatal Concerns, Nutrition Recommendations, Immunization Schedules, Common Pediatric Disorders, Assessments and Milestones, Safety Tips, and Advice for Parents and Other Caregivers

Along with a Glossary of Terms and Resource Listings for Additional Help

Edited by Jenifer Swanson. 585 pages. 2000. 0-7808-0246-2. $78.

Kidney & Urinary Tract Diseases & Disorders Sourcebook

Basic Information about Kidney Stones, Urinary Incontinence, Bladder Disease, End Stage Renal Disease, Dialysis, and More

Along with Statistical and Demographic Data and Reports on Current Research Initiatives

Edited by Linda M. Ross. 602 pages. 1997. 0-7808-0079-6. $78.

Learning Disabilities Sourcebook

Basic Information about Disorders Such as Dyslexia, Visual and Auditory Processing Deficits, Attention Deficit/Hyperactivity Disorder, and Autism

Along with Statistical and Demographic Data, Reports on Current Research Initiatives, an Explanation of the Assessment Process, and a Special Section for Adults with Learning Disabilities

Edited by Linda M. Shin. 579 pages. 1998. 0-7808-0210-1. $78.

Named "Oustanding Reference Book of 1999."
— *New York Public Library, Feb 2000*

"An excellent candidate for inclusion in a public library reference section. It's a great source of information. Teachers will also find the book useful. Definitely worth reading."
— *Journal of Adolescent & Adult Literacy, Feb 2000*

"Readable . . . provides a solid base of information regarding successful techniques used with individuals who have learning disabilities, as well as practical suggestions for educators and family members. Clear language, concise descriptions, and pertinent information for contacting multiple resources add to the strength of this book as a useful tool."
— *Choice, Association of College and Research Libraries, Feb '99*

"Recommended reference source."
— *Booklist, American Library Association, Sep '98*

"This is a useful resource for libraries and for those who don't have the time to identify and locate the individual publications."
— *Disability Resources Monthly, Sep '98*

Liver Disorders Sourcebook

Basic Consumer Health Information about the Liver and How It Works; Liver Diseases, Including Cancer, Cirrhosis, Hepatitis, and Toxic and Drug Related Diseases; Tips for Maintaining a Healthy Liver; Laboratory Tests, Radiology Tests, and Facts about Liver Transplantation

Along with a Section on Support Groups, a Glossary, and Resource Listings

Edited by Joyce Brennfleck Shannon. 591 pages. 2000. 0-7808-0383-3. $78.

"Recommended reference source."
—*Booklist, American Library Association, Jun '00*

Medical Tests Sourcebook

Basic Consumer Health Information about Medical Tests, Including Periodic Health Exams, General Screening Tests, Tests You Can Do at Home, Findings of the U.S. Preventive Services Task Force, X-ray and Radiology Tests, Electrical Tests, Tests of Blood and Other Body Fluids and Tissues, Scope Tests, Lung Tests, Genetic Tests, Pregnancy Tests, Newborn Screening Tests, Sexually Transmitted Disease Tests, and Computer Aided Diagnoses

Along with a Section on Paying for Medical Tests, a Glossary, and Resource Listings

Edited by Joyce Brennfleck Shannon. 691 pages. 1999. 0-7808-0243-8. $78.

"A valuable reference guide."
—*American Reference Books Annual, 2000*

"Recommended for hospital and health sciences libraries with consumer health collections."
—*E-Streams, Mar '00*

"This is an overall excellent reference with a wealth of general knowledge that may aid those who are reluctant to get vital tests performed."
—*Today's Librarian, Jan 2000*

Men's Health Concerns Sourcebook

Basic Information about Health Issues That Affect Men, Featuring Facts about the Top Causes of Death in Men, Including Heart Disease, Stroke, Cancers, Prostate Disorders, Chronic Obstructive Pulmonary Disease, Pneumonia and Influenza, Human Immunodeficiency Virus and Acquired Immune Deficiency Syndrome, Diabetes Mellitus, Stress, Suicide, Accidents and Homicides; and Facts about Common Concerns for Men, Including Impotence, Contraception, Circumcision, Sleep Disorders, Snoring, Hair Loss, Diet, Nutrition, Exercise, Kidney and Urological Disorders, and Backaches

Edited by Allan R. Cook. 738 pages. 1998. 0-7808-0212-8. $78.

"This comprehensive resource and the series are highly recommended."
—*American Reference Books Annual, 2000*

"Recommended reference source."
—*Booklist, American Library Association, Dec '98*

Mental Health Disorders Sourcebook, 1st Edition

Basic Information about Schizophrenia, Depression, Bipolar Disorder, Panic Disorder, Obsessive-Compulsive Disorder, Phobias and Other Anxiety Disorders, Paranoia and Other Personality Disorders, Eating Disorders, and Sleep Disorders

Along with Information about Treatment and Therapies

Edited by Karen Bellenir. 548 pages. 1995. 0-7808-0040-0. $78.

"This is an excellent new book . . . written in easy-to-understand language." —*Booklist Health Sciences Supplement, American Library Association, Oct '97*

". . . useful for public and academic libraries and consumer health collections."
—*Medical Reference Services Quarterly, Spring '97*

"The great strengths of the book are its readability and its inclusion of places to find more information. Especially recommended." —*Reference Quarterly, American Library Association, Winter '96*

". . . a good resource for a consumer health library."
—*Bulletin of the Medical Library Association, Oct '96*

"The information is data-based and couched in brief, concise language that avoids jargon. . . . a useful reference source." —*Readings, Sep '96*

"The text is well organized and adequately written for its target audience." —*Choice, Association of College and Research Libraries, Jun '96*

". . . provides information on a wide range of mental disorders, presented in nontechnical language."
—*Exceptional Child Education Resources, Spring '96*

"Recommended for public and academic libraries."
—*Reference Book Review, 1996*

Mental Health Disorders Sourcebook, 2nd Edition

Basic Consumer Health Information about Anxiety Disorders, Depression and Other Mood Disorders, Eating Disorders, Personality Disorders, Schizophrenia, and More, Including Disease Descriptions, Treatment Options, and Reports on Current Research Initiatives

Along with Statistical Data, Tips for Maintaining Mental Health, a Glossary, and Directory of Sources for Additional Help and Information

Edited by Karen Bellenir. 605 pages. 2000. 0-7808-0240-3. $78.

Mental Retardation Sourcebook

Basic Consumer Health Information about Mental Retardation and Its Causes, Including Down Syndrome, Fetal Alcohol Syndrome, Fragile X Syndrome, Genetic Conditions, Injury, and Environmental Sources

Along with Preventive Strategies, Parenting Issues, Educational Implications, Health Care Needs, Employment and Economic Matters, Legal Issues, a Glossary, and a Resource Listing for Additional Help and Information

Edited by Joyce Brennfleck Shannon. 642 pages. 2000. 0-7808-0377-9. $78.

"From preventing retardation to parenting and family challenges, this covers health, social and legal issues and will prove an invaluable overview."
— *Reviewer's Bookwatch, Jul '00*

Obesity Sourcebook

Basic Consumer Health Information about Diseases and Other Problems Associated with Obesity, and Including Facts about Risk Factors, Prevention Issues, and Management Approaches

Along with Statistical and Demographic Data, Information about Special Populations, Research Updates, a Glossary, and Source Listings for Further Help and Information

Edited by Wilma Caldwell and Chad T. Kimball. 400 pages. 2000. 0-7808-0333-7. $48.

Ophthalmic Disorders Sourcebook

Basic Information about Glaucoma, Cataracts, Macular Degeneration, Strabismus, Refractive Disorders, and More

Along with Statistical and Demographic Data and Reports on Current Research Initiatives

Edited by Linda M. Ross. 631 pages. 1996. 0-7808-0081-8. $78.

Oral Health Sourcebook

Basic Information about Diseases and Conditions Affecting Oral Health, Including Cavities, Gum Disease, Dry Mouth, Oral Cancers, Fever Blisters, Canker Sores, Oral Thrush, Bad Breath, Temporomandibular Disorders, and other Craniofacial Syndromes

Along with Statistical Data on the Oral Health of Americans, Oral Hygiene, Emergency First Aid, Information on Treatment Procedures and Methods of Replacing Lost Teeth

Edited by Allan R. Cook. 558 pages. 1997. 0-7808-0082-6. $78.

"Unique source which will fill a gap in dental sources for patients and the lay public. A valuable reference tool even in a library with thousands of books on dentistry. Comprehensive, clear, inexpensive, and easy to read and use. It fills an enormous gap in the health care literature." — *Reference and User Services Quarterly, American Library Association, Summer '98*

"Recommended reference source."
— *Booklist, American Library Association, Dec '97*

Osteoporosis Sourcebook

Basic Consumer Health Information about Primary and Secondary Osteoporosis, Juvenile Osteoporosis, Related Conditions, and Other Such Bone Disorders as Fibrous Dysplasia, Myeloma, Osteogenesis Imperfecta, Osteopetrosis, and Paget's Disease

Along with Information about Risk Factors, Treatments, Traditional and Non-Traditional Pain Management, and Including a Glossary and Resource Directory

Edited by Allan R. Cook. 600 pages. 2000. 0-7808-0239-X. $78.

SEE ALSO Women's Health Concerns Sourcebook

Pain Sourcebook

Basic Information about Specific Forms of Acute and Chronic Pain, Including Headaches, Back Pain, Muscular Pain, Neuralgia, Surgical Pain, and Cancer Pain

Along with Pain Relief Options Such as Analgesics, Narcotics, Nerve Blocks, Transcutaneous Nerve Stimulation, and Alternative Forms of Pain Control, Including Biofeedback, Imaging, Behavior Modification, and Relaxation Techniques

Edited by Allan R. Cook. 667 pages. 1997. 0-7808-0213-6. $78.

"The text is readable, easily understood, and well indexed. This excellent volume belongs in all patient education libraries, consumer health sections of public libraries, and many personal collections."
— *American Reference Books Annual, 1999*

"A beneficial reference." — *Booklist Health Sciences Supplement, American Library Association, Oct '98*

"The information is basic in terms of scholarship and is appropriate for general readers. Written in journalistic style . . . intended for non-professionals. Quite thorough in its coverage of different pain conditions and summarizes the latest clinical information regarding pain treatment."
— *Choice, Association of College and Research Libraries, Jun '98*

"Recommended reference source."
— *Booklist, American Library Association, Mar '98*

Pediatric Cancer Sourcebook

Basic Consumer Health Information about Leukemias, Brain Tumors, Sarcomas, Lymphomas, and Other Cancers in Infants, Children, and Adolescents, Including Descriptions of Cancers, Treatments, and Coping Strategies

Along with Suggestions for Parents, Caregivers, and Concerned Relatives, a Glossary of Cancer Terms, and Resource Listings

Edited by Edward J. Prucha. 587 pages. 1999. 0-7808-0245-4. $78.

"A valuable addition to all libraries specializing in health services and many public libraries."
— *American Reference Books Annual, 2000*

Physical & Mental Issues in Aging Sourcebook

Basic Consumer Health Information on Physical and Mental Disorders Associated with the Aging Process, Including Concerns about Cardiovascular Disease, Pulmonary Disease, Oral Health, Digestive Disorders, Musculoskeletal and Skin Disorders, Metabolic Changes, Sexual and Reproductive Issues, and Changes in Vision, Hearing, and Other Senses

Along with Data about Longevity and Causes of Death, Information on Acute and Chronic Pain, Descriptions of Mental Concerns, a Glossary of Terms, and Resource Listings for Additional Help

Edited by Jenifer Swanson. 660 pages. 1999. 0-7808-0233-0. $78.

SEE ALSO *Healthy Aging Sourcebook*

Plastic Surgery Sourcebook

Basic Consumer Health Information on Cosmetic and Reconstructive Plastic Surgery, Including Statistical Information about Different Surgical Procedures, Things to Consider Prior to Surgery, Plastic Surgery Techniques and Tools, Emotional and Psychological Considerations, and Procedure-Specific Information

Along with a Glossary of Terms and a Listing of Resources for Additional Help and Information

Edited by M. Lisa Weatherford. 400 pages. 2000. 0-7808-0214-4. $48.

Podiatry Sourcebook

Basic Consumer Health Information about Foot Conditions, Diseases, and Injuries, Including Bunions, Corns, Calluses, Athlete's Foot, Plantar Warts, Hammertoes and Clawtoes, Club Foot, Heel Pain, Gout, and More

Along with Facts about Foot Care, Disease Prevention, Foot Safety, Choosing a Foot Care Specialist, a Glossary of Terms, and Resource Listings for Additional Information

Edited by M. Lisa Weatherford. 600 pages. 2000. 0-7808-0215-2. $78.

Pregnancy & Birth Sourcebook

Basic Information about Planning for Pregnancy, Maternal Health, Fetal Growth and Development, Labor and Delivery, Postpartum and Perinatal Care, Pregnancy in Mothers with Special Concerns, and Disorders of Pregnancy, Including Genetic Counseling, Nutrition and Exercise, Obstetrical Tests, Pregnancy Discomfort, Multiple Births, Cesarean Sections, Medical Testing of Newborns, Breastfeeding, Gestational Diabetes, and Ectopic Pregnancy

Edited by Heather E. Aldred. 737 pages. 1997. 0-7808-0216-0. $78.

SEE ALSO *Congenital Disorders Sourcebook, Family Planning Sourcebook*

Public Health Sourcebook

Basic Information about Government Health Agencies, Including National Health Statistics and Trends, Healthy People 2000 Program Goals and Objectives, the Centers for Disease Control and Prevention, the Food and Drug Administration, and the National Institutes of Health

Along with Full Contact Information for Each Agency

Edited by Wendy Wilcox. 698 pages. 1998. 0-7808-0220-9. $78.

Rehabilitation Sourcebook

Basic Consumer Health Information about Rehabilitation for People Recovering from Heart Surgery, Spinal Cord Injury, Stroke, Orthopedic Impairments, Amputation, Pulmonary Impairments, Traumatic Injury, and More, Including Physical Therapy, Occupational Therapy, Speech/ Language Therapy, Massage Therapy, Dance Therapy, Art Therapy, and Recreational Therapy

Along with Information on Assistive and Adaptive Devices, a Glossary, and Resources for Additional Help and Information

Edited by Dawn D. Matthews. 531 pages. 1999. 0-7808-0236-5. $78.

Respiratory Diseases & Disorders Sourcebook

Basic Information about Respiratory Diseases and Disorders, Including Asthma, Cystic Fibrosis, Pneumonia, the Common Cold, Influenza, and Others, Featuring Facts about the Respiratory System, Statistical and Demographic Data, Treatments, Self-Help Management Suggestions, and Current Research Initiatives

Edited by Allan R. Cook and Peter D. Dresser. 771 pages. 1995. 0-7808-0037-0. $78.

"Designed for the layperson and for patients and their families coping with respiratory illness. . . . an extensive array of information on diagnosis, treatment, management, and prevention of respiratory illnesses for the general reader." — *Choice, Association of College and Research Libraries, Jun '96*

"A highly recommended text for all collections. It is a comforting reminder of the power of knowledge that good books carry between their covers." — *Academic Library Book Review, Spring '96*

"A comprehensive collection of authoritative information presented in a nontechnical, humanitarian style for patients, families, and caregivers." — *Association of Operating Room Nurses, Sep/Oct '95*

Sexually Transmitted Diseases Sourcebook

Basic Information about Herpes, Chlamydia, Gonorrhea, Hepatitis, Nongonoccocal Urethritis, Pelvic Inflammatory Disease, Syphilis, AIDS, and More

Along with Current Data on Treatments and Preventions

Edited by Linda M. Ross. 550 pages. 1997. 0-7808-0217-9. $78.

Sexually Transmitted Diseases Sourcebook, 2nd Edition

Basic Consumer Health Information about Sexually Transmitted Diseases, Including Information on the Diagnosis and Treatment of Chlamydia, Gonorrhea, Hepatitis, Herpes, HIV, Mononucleosis, Syphilis, and Others

Along with Information on Prevention, Such as Condom Use, Vaccines, and STD Education; And Featuring a Section on Issues Related to Youth and Adolescents, a Glossary, and Resources for Additional Help and Information

Edited by Dawn D. Matthews. 600 pages. 2000. 0-7808-0249-7. $78.

Skin Disorders Sourcebook

Basic Information about Common Skin and Scalp Conditions Caused by Aging, Allergies, Immune Reactions, Sun Exposure, Infectious Organisms, Parasites, Cosmetics, and Skin Traumas, Including Abrasions, Cuts, and Pressure Sores

Along with Information on Prevention and Treatment

Edited by Allan R. Cook. 647 pages. 1997. 0-7808-0080-X. $78.

". . . comprehensive, easily read reference book." — *Doody's Health Sciences Book Reviews, Oct '97*

SEE ALSO *Burns Sourcebook*

Sleep Disorders Sourcebook

Basic Consumer Health Information about Sleep and Its Disorders, Including Insomnia, Sleepwalking, Sleep Apnea, Restless Leg Syndrome, and Narcolepsy

Along with Data about Shiftwork and Its Effects, Information on the Societal Costs of Sleep Deprivation, Descriptions of Treatment Options, a Glossary of Terms, and Resource Listings for Additional Help

Edited by Jenifer Swanson. 439 pages. 1998. 0-7808-0234-9. $78.

"This text will complement any home or medical library. It is user-friendly and ideal for the adult reader." — *American Reference Books Annual, 2000*

"Recommended reference source." — *Booklist, American Library Association, Feb '99*

"A useful resource that provides accurate, relevant, and accessible information on sleep to the general public. Health care providers who deal with sleep disorders patients may also find it helpful in being prepared to answer some of the questions patients ask." — *Respiratory Care, Jul '99*

Sports Injuries Sourcebook

Basic Consumer Health Information about Common Sports Injuries, Prevention of Injury in Specific Sports, Tips for Training, and Rehabilitation from Injury

Along with Information about Special Concerns for Children, Young Girls in Athletic Training Programs, Senior Athletes, and Women Athletes, and a Directory of Resources for Further Help and Information

Edited by Heather E. Aldred. 624 pages. 1999. 0-7808-0218-7. $78.

"Public libraries and undergraduate academic libraries will find this book useful for its nontechnical language." — *American Reference Books Annual, 2000*

"While this easy-to-read book is recommended for all libraries, it should prove to be especially useful for public, high school, and academic libraries; certainly it should be on the bookshelf of every school gymnasium." — *E-Streams, Mar '00*

624

Substance Abuse Sourcebook

Basic Health-Related Information about the Abuse of Legal and Illegal Substances Such as Alcohol, Tobacco, Prescription Drugs, Marijuana, Cocaine, and Heroin; and Including Facts about Substance Abuse Prevention Strategies, Intervention Methods, Treatment and Recovery Programs, and a Section Addressing the Special Problems Related to Substance Abuse during Pregnancy

Edited by Karen Bellenir. 573 pages. 1996. 0-7808-0038-9. $78.

"A valuable addition to any health reference section. Highly recommended."
— *The Book Report, Mar/Apr '97*

". . . a comprehensive collection of substance abuse information that's both highly readable and compact. Families and caregivers of substance abusers will find the information enlightening and helpful, while teachers, social workers and journalists should benefit from the concise format. Recommended."
— *Drug Abuse Update, Winter '96/'97*

SEE ALSO *Alcoholism Sourcebook, Drug Abuse Sourcebook*

Traveler's Health Sourcebook

Basic Consumer Health Information for Travelers, Including Physical and Medical Preparations, Transportation Health and Safety, Essential Information about Food and Water, Sun Exposure, Insect and Snake Bites, Camping and Wilderness Medicine, and Travel with Physical or Medical Disabilities

Along with International Travel Tips, Vaccination Recommendations, Geographical Health Issues, Disease Risks, a Glossary, and a Listing of Additional Resources

Edited by Joyce Brennfleck Shannon. 613 pages. 2000. 0-7808-0384-1. $78.

Women's Health Concerns Sourcebook

Basic Information about Health Issues That Affect Women, Featuring Facts about Menstruation and Other Gynecological Concerns, Including Endometriosis, Fibroids, Menopause, and Vaginitis; Reproductive Concerns, Including Birth Control, Infertility, and Abortion; and Facts about Additional Physical, Emotional, and Mental Health Concerns Prevalent among Women Such as Osteoporosis, Urinary Tract Disorders, Eating Disorders, and Depression

Along with Tips for Maintaining a Healthy Lifestyle

Edited by Heather E. Aldred. 567 pages. 1997. 0-7808-0219-5. $78.

"Handy compilation. There is an impressive range of diseases, devices, disorders, procedures, and other physical and emotional issues covered . . . well organized, illustrated, and indexed." — *Choice, Association of College and Research Libraries, Jan '98*

SEE ALSO *Breast Cancer Sourcebook, Cancer Sourcebook for Women, 1st and 2nd Editions, Healthy Heart Sourcebook for Women, Osteoporosis Sourcebook*

Workplace Health & Safety Sourcebook

Basic Consumer Health Information about Workplace Health and Safety, Including the Effect of Workplace Hazards on the Lungs, Skin, Heart, Ears, Eyes, Brain, Reproductive Organs, Musculoskeletal System, and Other Organs and Body Parts

Along with Information about Occupational Cancer, Personal Protective Equipment, Toxic and Hazardous Chemicals, Child Labor, Stress, and Workplace Violence

Edited by Chad T. Kimball. 626 pages. 2000. 0-7808-0231-4. $78.

Worldwide Health Sourcebook

Basic Information about Global Health Issues, Including Nutrition, Reproductive Health, Disease Dispersion and Prevention, Emerging Diseases, Health Risks, and the Leading Causes of Death

Along with Global Health Concerns for Children, Women, and the Elderly, Mental Health Issues, Research and Technology Advancements, and Economic, Environmental, and Political Health Implications, a Glossary, and a Resource Listing for Additional Help and Information

Edited by Joyce Brennfleck Shannon. 500 pages. 2000. 0-7808-0330-2. $78.

Health Reference Series Cumulative Index 1999

A Comprehensive Index to the Individual Volumes of the Health Reference Series, Including a Subject Index, Name Index, Organization Index, and Publication Index;

Along with a Master List of Acronyms and Abbreviations

Edited by Edward J. Prucha, Anne Holmes, and Robert Rudnick. 990 pages. 2000. 0-7808-0382-5. $78.